D1623956

NO GUTS NO GLORY

HOW CANADA'S GREATEST CEOS BUILT THEIR EMPIRES

DAVID OLIVE

McGraw-Hill
Ryerson Limited
A Subsidiary of The **McGraw-Hill** Companies

Toronto Montréal Boston Burr Ridge, IL Dubuque, IA Madison, WI New York
San Francisco St. Louis Bangkok Bogotá Caracas Kuala Lumpur Lisbon London
Madrid Mexico City Milan New Delhi Santiago Seoul Singapore Sydney Taipei

McGraw-Hill
Ryerson Limited

A Subsidiary of The McGraw·Hill Companies

ISBN: 0-07-086155-2

1234567890 TRI 01234567890
Printed and bound in Canada.

Canadian Cataloguing in Publication Data
Olive, David, 1957-
    No guts, no glory: How Canada's greatest CEOs built their empires

Includes bibliographical references and index.
ISBN 0-07-086155-2

1. Chief executive officers – Canada – Biography. 2. Corporations – Canada – History – 20th century. I. Title.
HC112.5.A2044   2000   338.7'092'271   C00-932011-3

Publisher: **Joan Homewood**
Editorial Co-ordinator: **Catherine Leek**
Production Co-ordinator: **Susanne Penny**
Editor: **Lynn Schellenberg**
Electronic Page Composition: **Computer Composition of Canada**
Cover Design: **Rebus Creative – Sam Tallo**

For Lynda Sue Bronsten

What is happiness? The feeling that power increases — that resistance is being overcome.

— Friedrich Nietzsche

ACKNOWLEDGEMENTS

The author acknowledges the support of Kenneth Whyte and his fellow editors at *National Post* in granting a leave of absence for the duration of this project, and the assistance of the many public and corporate archivists who were vital to the research. I also wish to thank Joan Homewood and her colleagues at McGraw-Hill Ryerson Ltd., who shepherded the manuscript to completion, and editor Lynn Schellenberg for important contributions to the improvement of the work. I am especially grateful for the encouragement of Lynni Bronsten.

CONTENTS

INTRODUCTION

*"There are geniuses in trade, as well as in war, or the State, or letters;
and the reasons why this or that man is fortunate is not to be told.
It lies in the man; that is all anybody can tell you about it."*
— *Ralph Waldo Emerson, "Character"*

T HIS BOOK examines the lives of highly successful leaders in business, people who helped create the foundation of a dynamic Canadian economy that is blessed with unlimited potential for growth at the dawn of the 21st century.

In an age of corporate caretakers, asset shufflers and slash-and-burn artists, these men have been builders. They symbolize Canada's rapid evolution from an underdeveloped colonial economy into a formidable power in marketing and technological innovation, new-product development, efficient methods of manufacturing and the conquest of daunting export markets. They built world-class firms that are widely emulated at home and abroad.

Each of these leaders has a unique story. Frank Stronach of Magna International and Isadore Sharp of Four Seasons Hotels are self-made men. Galen Weston inherited a business, and Laurent Beaudoin of Bombardier married into one. Max Ward was a classic entrepreneur who built his airline from scratch. Robert Scrivener and John Roth of Nortel Networks have been organization men who radically transformed a venerable firm that was a prisoner of outdated traditions. Paul Reichmann and Andrew Sarlos were revolutionaries in the industries of the so-called Old Economy, while Sharp, Weston and the Nortel CEOs have pioneered in the ascendant service industries and at the frontiers of cyberspace.

Yet most of these CEOs mastered all six of the leadership strategies that give rise to the greatest and most enduring type of success in business: the willingness to set audacious goals, often expressed as a "big idea"; an ability to focus; a willingness to reinvent; a reliance on team-building; a tendency to think globally; and a preparedness to embrace adversity.

Dare to pursue a big idea. "Make no little plans," counselled the 19th-century architect Daniel Burnham. "They have no magic to stir men's blood." Bush pilot Ward dared to create an international charter operation. Paul Reichmann, a con-

1

tractor of one-storey warehouses, set a goal to develop the first high-quality office complex in Canada to be located far from the nearest financial district. Stronach, a humble supplier of auto parts made to specifications provided by the giant automakers, helped smash Detroit's century-old tradition of vertical integration by presuming to take from his giant customers the design responsibility for parts and, eventually, for entire vehicles. Only by setting impossible goals were the leaders in this book able to build enterprises that came to lead their industries, and often to create new industries in the process.

The extraordinary progress of the CEOs described here usually started with a Big Idea.

- Garfield Weston exploited assembly-line methods to create the biggest bakery enterprise on earth.
- Galen Weston used upscale private-label goods to turn the supermarket into a brand.
- Max Ward built a charter airline with the amenities of a first-class scheduled carrier.
- Isadore Sharp became the world's leading operator of luxury lodgings.
- Paul Reichmann commited to huge projects that other developers were afraid to contemplate.
- Frank Stronach supplanted the automakers as the world's best maker of vehicle parts.
- Laurent Beaudoin used R&D prowess to achieve global leadership in mass-transit equipment and civil aviation.
- John Roth's company became the world's top supplier of networks on which the Internet runs.

Focus is essential, for the simple reason that you won't get there if you don't know where you're going. At some point in their development, even the most successful firms lose their sense of direction. They suffer from an affliction that movie director John Sayles has used to describe Japanese films: "They've got a beginning, an end, and six middles." Going against the tide of the conglomerate era of the 20th century, with its fixation on diversity, successful leaders have focused on doing one thing, and doing it better than any competitor. They have grasped the importance of zeroing in on the greatest strengths and competitive advantages of their enterprises, and exploiting those blessings in pursuit of a well-defined objective.

"Clarity of goals" has been the mantra of Galen Weston in reviving a retail chain that was flirting with obsolescence, and in achieving industry dominance by applying all of his managerial and financial assets to the single goal of becoming the most innovative grocer in North America. Isadore Sharp put his firm on the path to unrivalled success in his industry by getting out of the real-estate business, shedding his mid-market hotels and exiting small cities. He then focused like a laser on developing a new type of upscale hotel in business capitals around the globe which put customer service ahead of glitzy architecture. Paul Reichmann's Olympia & York Developments thrived as the undisputed leader in developing prime office space on both sides of the Atlantic, and stumbled after it channelled the resulting abundance of rental income into oil and gas, forest products and other industries not related to property development.

It should be obvious that having a big idea makes it easier to focus on a straightforward objective. Once John Roth had commited Nortel to the era of "convergence" — the melding of traditional modes of electronic communication such as telephony, television and fax transmission with the breakthrough technologies of the Internet — his company was able to concentrate on achieving supremacy as an architect of the World Wide Web. Roth stripped Nortel of the luxury of indulging internal rivalries among products, markets and strategies that compete for limited resources. By choosing to become a formidable player in just one realm, Nortel no longer ran the risk of becoming a bystander in several.

Be prepared to reinvent the company. Reinvention is the key to sustained success. It is also the surest protection from complacency, a corrosive threat to even the most successful institutions. Even companies that have admirably focused on doing just one thing with unequalled excellence have run aground by ignoring the emergence of new products and industries that hold the potential to destroy their franchise. The best leaders create a culture of constant renewal at all levels of the enterprise. They foster a spirit of discovery among front-line employees who are rewarded for identifying novel, improved methods of developing and delivering products and services, and among senior managers who constantly search the horizon for new markets to exploit. The master of reinvention is always asking if there is a better way to serve an existing market. And, for that matter, whether an existing market should continue to be served or be abandoned.

From the time it was founded in the late 1950s, Stronach's Magna International has never stopped reformulating its workplace methods and pioneering new manufacturing technology in order to gain the capabilities required in winning an ever-larger share of business from almost every automaker on the planet. Sharp achieved market leadership by inventing a new niche, perfecting the concept of the small-scale grand hotel for the world's most discriminating business travellers. Beaudoin reinvented his company, not once but twice — first transforming Bombardier from a maker of Ski-Doos to a global leader in mass transit equipment, and then making it a trailblazer in civil aviation. And Weston used upscale private-label merchandise — a novelty in food retailing — to reinvent the supermarket as a retail experience that offered shoppers a sense of excitement and entertainment.

The decision to introduce a new order of things requires the courage to reject a comfortable status quo. "We must reinvent the company, even if it means the new products we launch will cannibalize our existing business," said Roth, who drove a stake through some of the most venerable lines of business at his century-old Nortel Networks as he transformed the firm into one of the world's leading makers of telecommunications gear for the Internet.

Build a team culture. The role of team-building as a key element of outstanding leadership was first highlighted as the era of the sole proprietor, exemplified by the likes of Henry Ford, gave way in the 20th century to the modern corporation that is led by managers who have no significant ownership in the business. Much has been made of that seminal transformation, perhaps the most important commercial development of the 1900s. But the "micromanager" CEO at the modern company who does not own the firm can do as much damage as a sole proprietor who has lost his way. The CEO who refuses to share authority with subordinates for fear of losing his own power is no less a debilitating factor in the life of corporations today than it was in the day of autocratic owner-managers. Meanwhile, the classic entrepreneurial CEO who does exert voting control over his firm often proves to be a superb delegator.

For instance, grocery scion Galen Weston launched his rescue mission at Loblaw by recruiting a team of lieutenants who shared his vision for a new approach to retailing. He then gave them the power to shape and execute that vision, applauding their initiatives even when they failed. In doing so, Weston was mindful of how Loblaw had squandered its market leadership when an earlier dictatorial CEO at Loblaw had rejected input even from his top executives, never mind store managers in the field.

Beaudoin, who inherited control of Bombardier Inc., had been a victim of founder Joseph-Armand Bombardier's second-guessing and his insistence on personally overseeing every aspect of the business. During his own three decades at the helm of his father-in-law's company, Beaudoin was in the habit of scouring the ranks of the best-run companies in each new industry that Bombardier entered for highly talented managers. He then took a back seat to them in implementing the growth strategy he conceived in partnership with a team that shared his passion.

Teamwork also means leading by example. Max Ward helped flight attendants and baggage handlers prepare his planes for takeoff in order to drive home his insistence on high standards of service and attention to detail. By applying the team concept to every level of the Four Seasons organization, from wine stewards and reservations clerks to executives who negotiate leases on new hotel sites, Sharp toiled ceaselessly to create a unique and durable corporate culture. Teamwork also plays a crucial role in succession. At Nortel, John Roth benefited from a mentoring system that nurtured a team of top executives who were each CEO material but did not step on each other's toes. Walter Light, one of Roth's predecessors as CEO at Nortel, was once asked to describe his most important task at the firm. His reply: "Getting a flock of egos to fly in formation."

Most of the leaders described in these pages came to realize that a culture of excellence — in customer satisfaction at Four Seasons, design and manufacturing proficiency at Magna, and R&D at Nortel Networks — would outlive any "cult of personality" that developed around a dynamic CEO. And would carry the enterprise through those difficult times when it was compelled to reinvent itself.

Think globally. Like Sweden, Canada has been required to become an aggressive exporter due to the limited size of its domestic market. Most of the CEOs in this book have achieved mastery in selling world-class goods and services far beyond Canada's borders. But thinking globally is not about planting the flag on distant shores. In the lives of the leaders depicted here, it means using a global yardstick to measure success. It means meeting world standards in both domestic and international operations, and setting new ones. There is no alternative. If a Canadian firm doesn't adopt the best practices of its offshore peers, those companies will threaten to destroy it when they invade the Canadian market. Wal-Mart hastened the demise of Eaton's, which collapsed within a few years of Wal-Mart's invasion of Canada in the mid-1990s. Loblaw is a multinational in food processing but strictly a domestic player in retailing. It thinks globally, however, in searching the world for the best merchandising methods, and adopting and improving them in order to protect a domestic base. Loblaw's own methods are now copied by its offshore peers. Some of them, notably Wal-Mart, go so far as to pay Loblaw for the right to adopt its private-label merchandising formula. "This approach," says Weston, "has put us in a dominant position against local, national and U.S. competitors. A strong domestic operation is the best defense against global competitors."

Seek opportunity in adversity. Adversity is a mainstay of business, where even commonplace goals carry significant risk. The objectives set by CEOs in this book are not commonplace. And the men who set them have shown an extraordinary tolerance for risk. "You don't deserve to be called an entrepreneur unless you've mortgaged your house to the business," says Ted Rogers, the cable TV czar. And risk invites failure — a necessary precondition, the record would seem to indicate, in achieving the highest levels of corporate success. "If at first you don't succeed ... welcome to the club," adds Izzy Asper, founder of CanWest Global Communications. The most talented entrepreneurs thrive on risk and try to be philosophical about failure. More than one tycoon has been known to take inspiration from a desk plaque that reads: BABE RUTH STRUCK OUT 1330 TIMES. All the CEOs in these pages have had to keep their ships afloat during one or more typhoons, when it seemed to their more cautious peers that they had strayed too far from the familiar. In trying to succeed at something never attempted by others, or at which others had failed, each of these leaders let curiosity get the better part of the fear they might have felt about the unknown. They understood, as French novelist André Gide wrote, that "one does not discover new lands without consenting to lose sight of the shore for a very long time."

Nothing reveals character like adversity. Adversity exposes mediocrity. It punishes the panic-stricken and the overly cautious alike. And in rare cases it harnesses those nobler aspects of character to which great institutions owe their existence.

This book does not examine success in the conventional sense. Max Ward and Paul Reichmann ultimately lost the firms they started with. But the audacity of their breathtaking schemes, and the triumphs they achieved as long as they adhered to the leadership strategies that gave rise to their initial success, ensures that their legacy will live on long after them. There is much to be learned from failure. Before he piled up new fortunes in hotels, gold mining and commercial real estate, Peter Munk came to ruin while still in his 30s as a cofounder of Clairtone Sound Corp., an ill-fated maker of state-of-the-art stereo equipment that found its way into the living rooms of Frank Sinatra and Hugh Hefner. Munk was briefly hailed in the 1960s as a rare Canadian exporter of R&D know-how. But from the moment that Clairtone began to flounder, a victim of mismanagement and the growing Japanese dominance of North America's electronics market, Munk was no longer invited to give speeches about his vision for Clairtone or Canada's economic prospects. Yet the lessons Munk gleaned from that debacle were no less instructive to future entrepreneurs than the keys to his initial success. "The speaking invitations stopped coming as soon as the trouble started," Munk recalled a few years after the Clairtone disaster. "That's understandable, I guess. But wouldn't you think I'd have more to tell the Canadian Club now than I did then?"

More often in the stories that follow, the CEOs did not move on to new fields, as Munk did, but were able in moments of danger to seize opportunities to achieve a still higher level of success with their existing business. They recognized in adversity a chance to reinvent their original enterprises. They did not always welcome change, but when it came they embraced rather than feared it. Indeed, without the spur of adversity, their companies might never have gained the summit of global leadership in their industries.

Would Max Ward have created one of the world's most respected airlines had government officials not repeatedly frustrated his modest bid to launch a scheduled air service in the Far North? If the snowmobile market had not collapsed in the 1970s, would Laurent Beaudoin have imagined himself capable of turning Bombardier into the world's top maker of passenger railcars? Would John Roth have dared to commit Nortel Networks to a high-stakes strategy of becoming a global leader in Internet-based telecommunications if his markets for traditional phone equipment had not begun to show signs of a gradual decline? And would Galen Weston have deserted the helm of a thriving retail chain he built in Ireland had he not been challenged to rescue his father's crumbling North American empire?

Character, as it manifests itself in this book, handily trumps genius in every instance. The "geniuses of trade" in these pages are gifted to an unusually abundant degree with the more attractive character traits — curiosity, persistence, resolve. If not quite heroic, such risk-takers nonetheless deserve recognition as agents of social improvement. They have contributed mightily to the acceleration in the standard of living for those millions of people who routinely benefit from their achievements, with little conception of the crises and tests of character that gave rise to them.

No argument is made that the CEOs profiled in these pages typify success in business. In the current era of quickie capitalism, chief executives are not rewarded for patiently building something that is bigger and longer-lasting than themselves. With their pay tied to the gyrating value of stock options, corporate leaders are powerfully tempted to surrender to such impulses as mass layoffs, eradication of the R&D budget, flashy takeovers and grandiose diversification schemes. Invariably dressed up as strategies to "restructure" and "re-engineer" the company, these crude expedients often undermine the strength of the enterprise over the long haul. But then, the long haul — the painstaking effort to lay a foundation for enduring success — is not in vogue.

In 2000, the popular image of business success is the grasping computer geek who becomes an instant multimillionaire while still in his 20s after taking his hot Internet company public just three years after launching it from his college dorm. These drive-by enterprises often make a valuable contribution by introducing a new product or technology to the marketplace. They have also fostered an unhealthy ethic in which companies are regarded as disposable instruments for generating windfall riches, or "shareholder value," in the elegant formulation of stock-market professionals.

In the bestselling *Built to Last: Successful Habits of Visionary Companies*, co-authors Jim Collins and Jerry I. Porras celebrated companies such as General Electric, Hewlett-Packard, IBM and Wal-Mart — "companies of such intrinsic excellence that the world would lose something important if that organization ceased to exist," as Collins put it in 2000, six years after the book first appeared. Today, Collins is dismayed by the fleeting commitment of so-called New Economy entrepreneurs to their enterprises, which they seem eager to abandon for a quick stock-market killing. "Imagine Bill Hewlett and Dave Packard sitting in their garage, sipping lattes, and saying to each other, 'If we do this right, we can sell this thing off and cash out in 12 months.' Or picture Sam Walton collecting a wheelbarrow full of cash from flipping his first store after 18 months, rather than building a company whose annual revenues now exceed $130 billion." At the dawn of the 21st century, Collins complained, "It doesn't matter whether an idea can be built into a profitable business, or a sustainable organization. All that matters is that the idea be flippable: Get in, get out, and get to the next idea before the bubble bursts."

It is possible to exaggerate such fears about a new and soulless entrepreneurialism, of course. The early days of railway promotion, oil, automobiles, Hollywood and personal computing were each characterized by mad striving after vast and immediate profits. From that confusion emerged the durable legacies of William Cornelius Van Horne of the Canadian Pacific Railway, John D. Rockefeller of Standard Oil (which spawned Exxon, Mobil, Amoco, Sohio and Chevron), Walt Disney and Bill Gates. After the gold rush, each new industry in time produced its lonely architects of lasting accomplishments. These men, whom no one would mistake as saintly, methodically set the managerial and technological standards of entire industries while a multitude of speculative contemporaries fell by the wayside, leaving behind a legacy no more relevant to our current understanding of how to run a business than that of the prospectors who rushed into the Klondike in the 1890s.

None of the men chronicled in these pages can be accused of exhibiting a dismissive regard for the riches they piled up. The distinction is that they have seen wealth as a means of perpetuating their enterprises. By constantly reinvesting their profits, these CEOs sought to achieve the power to change the rules of existing industries and to create new ones. None of the CEOs in this book cashed in his chips and walked away from a business he had shaped according to his own peculiar vision.

More than one of these narratives is a study in repeated failure leading to ultimate success, or a parade of triumphs culminating in disaster. The chronic refusal of the greatest achievements in business to conform to the convention of the business-school case study reminds us that trends and epochal phenomena mean nothing until we can put someone's name to them. "Read no history: nothing but biography," said Benjamin Disraeli, "for that is life without theory."

1

GARFIELD AND GALEN WESTON

The world's biggest baker, and the turnaround panache
of a merchant prince who defended his legacy at Loblaws

"We make more money out of men than we ever make out of things."
— *Garfield Weston*

*"I felt that from a retailing standpoint Loblaws was the nucleus of
potentially the finest company in Canada."*
— *Galen Weston*

"YOU KNOW why people come here, don't you?"
Jennifer, a frequent visitor at the Loblaws Forest Hill Market, asks
the question with a tone that suggests the answer is obvious.

Outside, the temperature on this winter evening in midtown Toronto is holding steady at -8 C. Indoors, amid the tropical glade that anchors the supermarket's produce section, Jennifer is tossing an orange in the air, aiming for the cluster of helium balloons tied to an ox cart from which a few hundred oranges spill onto a net carpeting the floor. Nearby, a boy stands with mouth gaping as a clerk places an enormous pineapple on a fruit-coring device. The clerk gives the lever a tremendous yank, and *crunch* — the prickly covering of the sheared fruit goes flying in all directions. This triggers a burst of applause from the balcony café, where a gaggle of amateur chefs is tucking into a snack after their Filo Pastry Workshop.

"They come here," says Jennifer, "because it's cheaper than the movies. And lots more fun."

Loblaws bills its two-year-old Forest Hill emporium as "a street of stores." But there is no street. Instead, shoppers navigate a maze of boutiques whose careful arrangement draws them through every inch of the hangar-sized building. The journey begins at Mövenpick, where visitors rub shoulders with faux-Swiss chefs who prepare entrees and desserts on a flagstone terrace lined with trees. There follows a trapline of snares designed to drain the pockets of the impulse buyer: a Meals to Go deli counter; a natural supplements shop; a pharmacy; a home-furnishings galleria; a banking pavillion; a florist; a dry cleaner; a photo-finishing kiosk; a newsstand that carries *Wine Spectator* and the *International Herald Tribune*; a cellphone store; a shoe-repair stand; a small-business centre with copiers, courier service and Internet terminals; an aromatherapy candle boutique; and a wine store, where modest sampling is encouraged.

The Forest Hill superstore boasts more than 35,000 items — about double the selection of a traditional supermarket. And because this is Loblaws, the most aggressive marketer of private-label goods of any North American grocer, almost every visitor emerges from the store with a handsome array of products that can be found at no other chain. Even more than the one-stop shopping, it's these unique items that build traffic. They stimulate curiosity. What will Loblaw come up with next? The line of 2,000 private-label offerings is constantly changing, with new enticements added every week.

Patrons aren't so much loyal to Loblaws as they are to No Name perogies and tea towels, Club Pack lemon ice tea, Exact contact lens solution, the environmentally correct G.R.E.E.N. line of non-bleached coffee filters and toilet tissue, and the upscale President's Choice line of The Decadent Chocolate Chip Cookies, Memories of Montego Bay Jerk Marinade and Nasi Goreng, a flash-frozen mélange of Indonesian rice and sautéed vegetables.

Industry experts say the Forest Hill store is a foodies' paradise. They're awed by a bounty of exotic culinary treats that surpasses anything ever attempted in a conventional supermarket. But there is more to this store than the mating of a farmers' market and a gourmet food shop. The Loblaw name, after many years of skilful marketing, is associated with a new consumer movement whose aim is to cast the price-gouging makers of national brands out of the supermarket. And the store itself is a highly engineered machine whose seductive vistas of nature's harvest, its theatrical signage and evocative aromas are designed to both soothe and excite the world-weary consumer, and transform the chore of grocery shopping into a poor man's opera. This is the future of food retailing in North America.

Loblaws almost didn't live to see it.

In 2000, the Loblaws Forest Hill Market was one of 1,065 stores operated by Loblaw Cos. Ltd., whose 20 store banners — including Loblaw, Provigo, Zehrs,

Fortinos, No Frills, Valu-mart and Real Canadian Superstore — accounted for a whopping 40 per cent or so of grocery shelf space in Canada. Through bold, ceaseless experimentation, controlling shareholder Galen Weston had taken Loblaw from losses of $4 million a year some three decades earlier to profits of $376 million in 1999. He was one of the biggest employers in Canada, with a combined payroll of 124,000 at Loblaw and its parent, George Weston Ltd., a $20-billion enterprise which operated bakeries and other food-processing firms throughout North America.

Galen Weston had changed the rules of food retailing. Name-brand giants like Nabisco and Coca-Cola no longer dictated prices to supermarket operators. They were forced to upgrade their products and slash prices to counter the private-label threat unleashed by Loblaw. And retailers elsewhere in the world, from Wal-Mart in the U.S. to Coles Myer in Australia, were paying Loblaw for its expertise in marketing, store design and private-label merchandising.

But Weston's role as a pioneer of retail innovations that would lead tradition-bound peers at home and abroad into the 21st century had been incidental to his driving motive. Which was simply to arrest the ruinous decay of his father's North American holdings, and preserve the legacy of a 90-year-old family business.

At the zenith of his career, Garfield Weston, son of a Toronto baker, had been the greatest bakery tycoon in the world. In the 1950s, he held sway over hundreds of companies in Canada, the U.S., Britain, West Germany, South Africa, Australia and New Zealand. But this remarkable industrialist, whose firm was counted alongside Nestlé, Unilever and Procter & Gamble among the world's half-dozen largest food companies, was more skilled at buying firms than managing them.

Garfield Weston, too, had changed the rules. In the 1930s and 1940s, he forced rivals in North America and Britain to follow his example after pioneering in efficient methods of manufacturing, distribution and new-product development. He accumulated a formidable collection of brands, including Sweet Marie chocolate bars, Ryvita biscuits, Neilson and Donlands dairy products, Clover Leaf salmon, Brunswick sardines, McCormick's crackers, McNair spices, MacLaren stuffed olives, Westcane sugar, Nabob coffee, White Swan tissues and Stroehmann and Weston bread.

But Weston eventually lost touch with the market. He once had been an expert at gauging consumers' changing tastes, with a flair for recruiting and motivating skilled lieutenants. But Weston reached a point where he was no longer able to find talent for every outpost of his rapidly expanding operation. He was too busy plotting his next takeover. In a 50-year career of empire building, Weston bought 2,000 companies — or about one every 10 days. He also strayed from his expertise in food, snapping up drugstore chains, slaughterhouses, paper mills and makers of plastics, furniture and linen.

By the early 1970s, the Weston colossus was in steep decline. In his office above the main selling floor at Fortnum & Mason, the London carriage-trade store near Piccadilly Circus that he had bought two decades earlier, Garfield Weston studied the profit-and-loss statements of his North American retail operation with growing dismay. His 1,800 grocery and department stores in Canada and the U.S. Midwest were losing money and market share. Loblaw Cos. Ltd., which ran that sprawling retail network and was the biggest company in the Weston empire, had become so starved for cash that it was in default on its loans. Given Loblaw's miserable condition, there was no question of refinancing it from its own resources. And there were too few unencumbered assets to offer as collateral to any banker willing to extend fresh credit for badly needed store renovations.

Garfield, now entering his eighth decade, lacked the energy to undertake a salvage operation in North America. He asked his son Galen to examine the Loblaw books and offer a prognosis. Galen agreed that the business was a mess. "The big question then," Galen said, "was should this chain be closed up, or should we make the enormous investment in money and time to return it to its former place."

Galen volunteered for the rescue mission. He was only 31, with just a few years' experience in setting up a retail business in Ireland, where competition was scarce. Fewer things, he and Garfield knew, are more difficult to fix than a failing retailer. This is especially true of family-run enterprises, which typically are hobbled by bureaucratic sclerosis and depleted gene pools. And Loblaw, whose stores were concentrated in Ontario, was an also-ran in one of the most fiercely competitive markets in the Western Hemisphere. The Ontario grocery scene was characterized by too many rivals with too many stores, who engaged in mutual destruction with endless price wars.

But Galen regarded Loblaw as the foundation of the Weston fortune, the place where his father and grandfather had first gained a foothold that enabled each, in turn, to revolutionize the food-processing industry. He was certain that the moribund Loblaw "was the nucleus of potentially the finest company in Canada."

In the years ahead, family-run retailers in Canada, the U.S. and Europe would become an endangered species. One by one, venerable firms such as Steinberg, Woodward, Creeds, Birks, Peoples Jewellers and even the mighty Eaton's would succumb to family feuds, managerial ineptitude and a complacency about changing consumer habits.

In 1972, as he packed his bags for Toronto, Galen Weston was advised by more than one friend that he was embarking on a fool's errand. But he hadn't sought a surefire proposition. If Weston wasn't blessed with his father's buccaneering instincts, he did not lack for familial pride. "We've got a pedigree," Galen said, "both the company and the family — a pedigree of performance."

It also had not escaped Galen's notice that Garfield had taken his first step toward success by bailing out *his* father's struggling enterprise.

Boy Staunton made a great deal of money during the Depression because he dealt exclusively in solaces. When a man is down on his luck he seems to consume all he can get of coffee and doughnuts. The sugar in the coffee was Boy's sugar, and the doughnuts were his doughnuts . . . Behind tons of cheap confectionery, sweets, snacks, nibbles, biscuits and simple cooking sugar, and the accompanying oceans of fizzy, sweet water, disguised with chemical versions of every known fruit flavour, stood Boy Staunton, though not many people knew it.
— Robertson Davies, *Fifth Business*

BY THE time he came to write his finest novel in the late 1960s, Robertson Davies had his choice of true stories to draw upon for his depiction of a larger-than-life Canadian entrepreneur who rises from obscurity to take the world by storm. At various points in the narrative, it seems as if the ghosts of Max Aitken (Lord Beaverbrook), Roy Thomson and E. P. Taylor have each whispered in the ear of Davies's scheming tycoon. Yet in his restless pursuit of commercial advantage, and in his anglophilia and Babbittry, the opportunist that Boy Staunton most completely resembles is Garfield Weston.

Yet Staunton is a monster. And Garfield Weston, by contrast, was one of the most popular business figures of the century. He was regarded as a saint by city fathers in North America and Europe where his burgeoning network of Weston bakeries created jobs in the Depression. Even competitors whose factories were driven to the wall by the Canadian's innovations were happy to sell out to him and accept a place on their former rival's payroll. As his biscuits, bread and confections began to proliferate on grocers' shelves, Weston was embraced by shoppers as a champion of low-priced staples. And a generation before Sam Walton opened his first store, Weston was winning the affection of workers with his own cheerleading sessions on the plant floor. More sentimental in his regard for imperialism than the average Briton, he plotted his geographic conquests as if to replicate the British Empire, and was rewarded with a seat in the British House of Commons.

"I deal in bread and dreams," he liked to say. No one dreamed bigger than Weston himself, whose earliest ambition was to become the Henry Ford of the bakery trade.

His own father had taken a step in that direction. George Weston, a child of English immigrants who settled in the Lake Ontario port town of Oswego, New York, seemed less likely than his siblings to achieve renown. One of his brothers was a convicted bigamist, another was a sharpshooter in a circus, and a third was the engineer on a ship that went looking for Dr. Livingston. George, the least eccentric of the brood, did nothing more adventuresome than relocate with his family to Oswego's trading rival, Toronto, where he became a baker's apprentice. The enterprise that evolved into the Loblaws Forest Hill Market began in 1882, when George, then 17, used his meagre savings to acquire a couple of local bread routes. This was at a time when most housewives still baked their own malt, Scotch close-pan and Irish batch loaves. But that would change, Weston figured, with the advent of mechanized baking.

By 1890, Toronto grocers were doing a brisk business in Weston's Home-Made Bread. This "home-made" item was, in fact, cranked out at the astounding rate of 3,200 loaves per day by Weston's new Model Bakery. The plant was hailed at the time of its 1897 opening as a trailblazing advance in hygiene, cost control and high-speed production. By the turn of the century, Weston was Toronto's most successful baker, measuring his progress not in sales or profits but in teams of horses. At his zenith, he had 350 horses to pull his delivery wagons. George Weston also planted the seeds of a dynastic fixation with vertical integration when he merged his bakery with a local flour mill.

Yet even in his most expansive moments, Weston could barely comprehend the fanciful visions of his eldest son, who was born in the family apartment above the Model Bakery. While serving with the Canadian Army Engineers in World War I, Garfield Weston spent every hour of his free time touring European bakeries and biscuit factories. He became obsessed with the futuristic methods of British bakers. In the midst of a global conflict, they somehow were managing to export millions of biscuits to the four corners of the earth. More than once, Weston was lectured by proud factory owners that food processed with state-of-the-art baking and packaging equipment could travel thousands of miles and retain its flavour and freshness many months after popping out of the oven. Weston conceived a grandiose scheme for using imported British equipment in a greatly expanded Toronto bakery to turn out "English-style" biscuits for the Canadian market.

But by now George Weston was in retreat, and had little appetite for his son's ideas. The war had brought supply shortages and rising prices for ingredients. And war's end was followed by a recession — a time, it seemed to Weston père, when people could still find money for bread, but not fancy biscuits. Weston longed to retire, and flirted with selling his Model Bakery. Only after a series of arguments did the founder accede to Garfield's plan, which required the young bakery scion to import not only machinery but British technicians to run it.

English-style biscuits, it turned out, were a necessary solace in hard times. They were an instant success. Garfield celebrated his vindication with a torrent of acquisitions and new-product launches. George Weston did not witness this manic expansion. He died in 1924, a victim of pneumonia that he contracted, legend had it, after choosing to walk for miles through a Toronto blizzard rather than pay for a cab or overnight lodgings. Garfield hastened to ennoble George Weston's legacy. "I'm not going to build a costly monument to my father," he is said to have vowed at the patriarch's gravesite. "I'm going to make his name known around the world."

At the height of the Jazz Age, Garfield moved with lightning speed to build what he would later describe as "a business that would never know completion." The 27-year-old had inherited a clutch of Ontario bakeries with a payroll of fewer than 400 employees. In just six years, he boosted profits more than six-fold, to $167,597, and took his company public, using the proceeds of the stock offering to finance a building blitz in Ontario and the U.S. But Weston's timing was terrible. In the aftermath of the Crash of 1929, the biscuit business — like most industries in the Dirty Thirties — was revealed to be outrageously overbuilt. "It was an awful cropper," Weston later said. "I went almost bankrupt and had a physical breakdown too."

That proved to be a blessing of sorts. While convalescing at a Boston hospital, Weston devoured dozens of inspirational texts, mostly biographies of tycoons and military heroes who had turned disaster to their advantage. It occurred to him that his mistake had been to build factories rather than buy them. He had contributed to the overcapacity, when what he should have done was buy out his weaker rivals. This he proceeded to do, at liquidation prices. In the depths of the Depression, Weston used takeovers to break out of Ontario with a new chain of bakeries strung across Western Canada. And with a war chest of $2 million that he coaxed out of Wall Street investors who had made a killing from short-selling stocks during the market collapse, he mounted an assault on the British industry, as well.

In the early 1930s, the abrupt decline in Britain's finances had brought down the Labour government of prime minister Ramsay MacDonald. The nation's solvency was in doubt. But the baker from the colonies, like Paul Reichmann many years later, took a back seat to no Briton as a John Bull booster. "I am the greatest living exponent of enthusiasm for this country," bellowed the dashing young man from Canada at ribbon-cutting ceremonies for Weston plants throughout Britain, as recounted in *Bread Men*, an account of the family by Charles Davies. "And I want every soul to be sold on the idea of working harder for Britain, just as my salesmen are enthused by me to sell my biscuits."

Ignoring the advice of a consultant's report on the British biscuit trade that he himself had commissioned, Weston took on Britain's Big Seven bakeries with his own network of ailing factories in Edinburgh, London and Belfast. These retrofitted plants were soon the most efficient in the nation, enabling Weston to build and buy still more factories, and to steal market share from larger rivals by underpricing their output. He had no trouble snapping up venerable bakeries from aging proprietors who had lost faith in their country's prospects, or had no heirs and adopted the boyish, dynamic Weston as a surrogate son.

As pioneers of mass production and marketing of food, Weston and his peers at Nestlé, Unilever and A&P were rapidly supplanting Karl Marx's *petite bourgeoisie* of neighbourhood bakers, butchers and shopkeepers. In taking control of the food chain, Weston and his fellow corporate interlopers were accused of predatory practices aimed at wiping out junior capitalists, as a prelude to having consumers at their mercy. Weston was more skilful than rival conglomerateurs in blunting those attacks. He wrapped his company in the flag; of his patriotic motives there seemed little question, as yet another of his 12-passenger trains, loaded with community leaders and bedecked with Union Jacks, made its way out of Paddington Station to the opening of a Weston factory.

Unlike his counterparts at other combines of the day, Weston made himself highly visible at the head of his juggernaut. He took to the stump like a veteran politician. Newspaper publishers, warming to the prospect of a new source of advertising, gave fulsome praise in their coverage of Weston's speeches about his mission to create jobs, boost exports and reduce food prices for the good of Britain. He was equally tireless in spreading this gospel within his firm. The Weston empire was an extension of Garfield's ebullient personality in the same extreme degree that the faceless Nestlé and Unilever heralded instead a new era of the impersonal corporation.

Weston patiently explained to his managers that if they were to boost their production to the point of consuming 50,000 sacks of flour a week instead of 200, why, their flour costs would drop to $4 from $5, an instant profit of $50,000! Slashing the price of bread by as much as 50 per cent required round-the-clock production and three shifts of workers. And that would call for an increased measure of devotion from employees, which compelled Weston to become a shop-floor cheerleader. He was a master of the surprise factory-visits. These were occasions for warm greetings, not remonstrations. Weston "just exuded confidence and success," a factory hand recalled. The company song, later to become a fixture at Thomas Watson's IBM, Tom Bata's shoe factories and Japan's auto-assembly plants, was a conspicuous tactic in the Weston managerial repertoire in the 1930s:

> Forward, yes forward, with main and might,
> Shoulder to shoulder, the goal's in sight.
> For we'll soon be on top of the world all right,
> And that's where we mean to stay.

By the mid-1930s, Weston was one of Europe's biggest bakers, with 5,000 employees at dozens of factories. His attention soon returned to North America, where once again he hit the takeover trail. Nothing could slow him down. Not a duodenal ulcer, not the Depression, not World War II. Frank Riddell, an executive in his North American operation, remembered an auto expedition with

Weston in the U.S. "In Fort Worth we saw a sign: Texas Cookie Co. He just bought it. Another time we went to look at a plant of the Seattle Superior Biscuit Co., and by the time we left, he'd bought it."

Weston was seeking to create a masterpiece of vertical integration. His idea was to bake Weston products with flour and sugar from his own mills, to ship them in cartons furnished by Weston packaging companies which were supplied by Weston paper mills, and distribute the fruits of this labour via Weston-owned wholesalers to a Weston network of grocery stores. In this goal, Garfield Weston succeeded on a grander scale than any rival, and by the 1960s could claim the distinction of holding personal sway over more food-related enterprises than any man on earth.

What he had not done, however, was lay a foundation for lasting success. His son Galen would later credit Garfield with being "one of the first conglomerate operators, ruthless in cleaning up after his own mistakes and others'." But Garfield's empire began to get away from him as it spread from its base in Canada and Britain to the U.S., the European continent, Australasia and South Africa. At its zenith in the 1960s, the Weston colossus owned grocery and department stores on four continents, fish and meat packers, confectioners, fast-food eateries, drugstores and drug factories, makers of plastics, edible oils and animal feed, the Garfields newsstands in Toronto subway stations and Ezra Butler Eddy's decrepit paper mill in Hull, Quebec, a legendary eyesore across the Ottawa River from the Canadian parliament buildings. Some of Weston's core holdings — Loblaw Cos., Britain's Associated British Foods Ltd. (ABF) and Premier Milling Co. Ltd. in Johannesburg — were substantial conglomerates in their own right.

No man could give that scale of enterprise the kind of personal attention to detail that gave rise to Weston's earliest triumphs. And as time went by, Weston seemed less interested in even attempting to do so. The annual meetings of George Weston Ltd., where Garfield led shareholders in hymn sings, became a forum for his outrageous pronouncements on current events. "Believe me," he said, defending South Africa's racist apartheid policies, "every black pickaninny or black mammy can call on the government for solutions to every social problem." He congratulated Richard Nixon on the carpet-bombing of Cambodia, and sided with British xenophobes who were at the point of rioting over their nation's entry into the European Common Market. "It's the beginning of the end of that great organization known as the British Empire," Weston said in 1972. "Now we will have to compete with millions of Frenchmen working in the fields on their knees."

But if he had let himself become out of touch, one of Weston's most winsome traits had been his propensity to recruit promising lieutenants and then defer to them. "Buying companies, then getting someone to run them, that was his strength," said Galen Weston. After putting in a summer stint at the family's Deutscher grocery chain in West Germany with university classmate David

Nichol in tow, Galen could attest to the lack of head-office interference at the far-flung Weston holdings. "Running businesses was not really his bag," said Galen of his father. "He always left his generals completely autonomous."

In that regard, Garfield was in tune with the times. At the dawn of the century, commercial ventures were guided by individuals with a highly vested interest — they owned the business. But in one of the century's most important phenomena, those proprietors gave way to professional managers — individuals who, for the first time, were formally trained at universities in the new calling of business administration. A company that wished to be regarded as a modern enterprise vested enormous responsibility in this new managerial class, which typically had no significant ownership stake in the firm. While Garfield Weston was not about to surrender ownership of his company, he was determined that George Weston Ltd. be regarded as a firm that was run along modern management lines. He was a progressive employer in matters of pay, benefits and working conditions. He made ample use of consultants. He hired, trained and promoted college-educated management prospects and gave them free rein in their fiefdoms. It became a matter of pride with Weston that he wrung profits from personnel, not products. He liked to say, "We make more money out of men than we ever make out of things."

By the late 1960s, however, Weston had come to the slow realization that some of his top generals were unreliable. Like Abraham Lincoln during the U.S. Civil War, he was cursed with field commanders who preferred not to fight or underestimated the skills of the enemy. Sometimes, as in Weston's North American operations, it was both.

North America was overseen by George C. Metcalf, who was no less ambitious a conglomerateur than his boss and was inspired by the same vision of greatness. "The secret of life," Metcalf said, "is to think big, believe big, pray big, act big, hope big — and big results will come."

Riding Canada's postwar boom during 14 years at the helm of George Weston Ltd., Metcalf had pulled off the longest string of takeovers in Canadian history. The primary vehicle for that acquisition drive was Loblaw Groceterias Co. Ltd., founded in 1919 by small-town Ontario grocers Theodore Pringle Loblaw and J. Milton Cork. Loblaw was a thriving chain of 113 grocery stores in Ontario when Garfield Weston first began to accumulate its shares in 1947.

On gaining control of the firm eight years later, Weston turned it into a holding company, Loblaw Cos. Ltd. Headed by Metcalf, a Manchester native and brilliant salesman plucked from chocolate-maker William Neilson Co. Ltd., Loblaw went on a spending spree that had no equal in the North American food industry. Between them, Loblaw and parent George Weston Ltd. gobbled up food processors, wholesalers and retailers from coast to coast in Canada, and National Tea Co., the fourth-largest grocery chain in the U.S. By the mid-1960s, Canada's biggest food company was a $3-billion leviathan whose 225 companies were engaged in every facet of the industry, from fish canneries and sugar and spice makers to restaurant supply companies and one of Canada's biggest packaging firms. "Since 1928," industry analyst Donald Tigert reported in 1976, after a lengthy examination of Garfield's and Metcalf's handiwork, "George Weston Ltd. has probably acquired more companies in more diverse fields than any other company in Canada."

Weston's dominance of the food industry was so nearly complete that it threatened the public interest — or so it seemed to a parliamentary committee in the mid-1960s, which forced the secretive firm to reveal for the first time the extent of its holdings during an inquiry into allegations of price manipulation by a hidden alliance of food processors and grocery chains. It was only at this point that the public and a good many executives in the industry — including a fair number employed by Weston — learned that the nation's most popular brand of ice cream, Neilson's, was owned by the same company that operated the Power supermarkets and Tamblyn drugstores. A decade later, Weston would be targeted yet again, this time by a federal Royal Commission on corporation concentration. The results of that probe were inconclusive. In the U.S., however, the Federal Trade Commission was quite sure Weston was a predator in need of reining-in. It ordered the hyper-acquisitive National Tea, which had grown to 800 stores, to seek prior FTC approval for any further grocery-chain takeovers.

When the OPEC oil crisis raised the curtain on a prolonged era of double-digit inflation, soaring food prices gave all big food companies a villainous cast. But the firm with an identifiable tycoon behind the cash register suffered the wrath of consumer advocates to a greater degree than its competitors. "We say they don't need to go that high," Eugene Whelan, the federal agriculture minister, said of rising food prices. "But Westons or these big companies have got control of the bread manufacturing industry and they can just about damn well do what they please."

What George Weston Ltd. could not do with any consistency, however, was turn a decent profit. It was a victim of imperial overreach, unable to keep track of, much less intelligently direct, its disparate and far-flung enterprises. Few observers had taken seriously the assertion of G. E. (Ted) Creber, a top executive at the firm in the early 1970s, that "profits and sales in our bakery division are hardly large enough to warrant staying in the business, except that we're already in it." Yet Tigert, the industry analyst, had to agree that despite its ostensible might, George Weston Ltd. and its Loblaw arm were chronic underachievers. For the entire duration of its takeover binge, a 20-year period beginning in the early 1950s, George Weston Ltd.'s profit margins in both food processing and grocery stores had registered several notches below the industry average.

But in the absence of an outright crisis on the other side of the Atlantic, Garfield Weston had chosen to ignore the shortcomings at Loblaw. Removing his clone Metcalf would be an act of self-repudiation. And if Weston was in denial, this too was a typical corporate shortcoming of the era. Weston's counterparts at GM, Xerox and Massey-Ferguson, lulled into complacency by decades of hegemony, were oblivious to trends that threatened to destroy them. Fortunately, Weston was pushed into action before all was lost. For by 1971, the unthinkable had happened. Loblaw was facing bankruptcy.

The decline at Loblaw, crown jewel of Weston's North American holdings, had been deceptively gradual. Profits slipped from a healthy $46 million in 1966 to $19 million five years later. Then the huge conglomerate had plunged into the red. Suddenly the entire creaking superstructure of holding companies and pyramiding subsidiaries seemed about to collapse. The rot had been disguised by Metcalf's parade of takeovers, which boosted sales but did nothing to address an ultimately catastrophic erosion in profits at Loblaw's existing operations. "Metcalf believed that as long as sales increased, the auditors would find a way to show a profit," a Toronto stockbroker said.

Now that gambit was played out. Metcalf had piled up some $200 million in debt to finance his acquisition spree. With its profits in free fall, Loblaw would not be able to pay off about $50 million in debentures that were soon to mature, or make dividend payments on the many series of preferred shares that Metcalf had issued to fund his expansion campaign. In 1971, Loblaw was already in default on some of its debt covenants.

In all likelihood, the debt could be restructured. The blue-chip Loblaw could attempt to simply issue more debentures with maturity dates farther out in the future. Failing that, Weston himself could rescue the firm by transferring ownership of Loblaw to ABF, his British conglomerate. A similar ploy had worked years earlier when Weston had arranged to have his North American arm take responsibility for Fine Fare, a U.K. grocery chain that was suffering from start-up pains.

But as he examined the mess, Weston soon grasped that Loblaw did not have a debt crisis. It was more serious than that. The real problem was the disappearing profits. Weston's mistake had been his encouragement of chaotic growth — of placing a great emphasis on buying companies, and almost none on learning how to manage them. That had given rise to unwieldly Weston agglomerations on both sides of the Atlantic. "We just grew like Topsy," Weston later admitted, "acquiring bits and pieces all over the place, especially in North America. We couldn't always do things in an orderly fashion." In abetting Metcalf, Weston had created a crazy-quilt of companies in the New World whose inherent lack of profitability would eventually exhaust the financial resources of Weston's entire empire.

Weston dispatched an emergency task force of consultants to Loblaw. It could find no quick-fix remedies for the company. Loblaw appeared to suffer almost every affliction known to retailing.

As in real-estate development, location is a key determinant of success for the mass-market retailer. Loblaw was endowed with a great many sites, but this was proving to be a mixed blessing. The company suffered from a higher than average number of poor locations, both in Canada and the U.S. In Ontario, home to more than half of its 454 Canadian supermarkets, Loblaw had failed to read demographic trends and follow its customers in their flight from the inner city. Its chief rivals in Central Canada, Dominion Stores Ltd., A&P and Steinberg's Ltd., which operated the Miracle Mart chain, had beaten Loblaw to many of the most lucrative sites in the booming suburbs. Loblaw's U.S. arm, National Tea, was better represented in the ghetto than in middle-class neighbourhoods. And in its rush to expand in the U.S. Midwest, New York State, Pennsylvania and California in the 1960s, National had opted to build small, inefficient stores of 12,000 square feet, while competitors such as Chicago-based Jewel Cos. were making a strategic shift to 22,000 square feet outlets in upscale districts.

Across North America, Loblaw was paying the price for its scattershot approach to store expansion. Outside of Ontario, it had opted for a modest presence in a large number of cities, with the result that it was no better than the third- or fourth-biggest operator in any market. In the U.S., which even by 2000 was still characterized by strong regional chains, National Tea could not match the advertising clout, buying power or extensive store network of the dominant local player in any of the cities where it had a presence. Loblaw was also vulnerable when competing national chains stronger than itself — Dominion in Canada, and A&P in the U.S. — launched price wars in the early 1970s in vain efforts to crush regional barons such as Jewel, Winn-Dixie and Publix in the U.S., and Sobey's and Overwaitea in Canada. And Loblaw was locked into many of its unprofitable locations thanks to complicated leaseback deals that Metcalf had used as a tool for raising cheap funds for expansion.

Many of Loblaw's older stores were in shabby condition, victims of Metcalf's preoccupation with takeovers. And shoppers had only the vaguest idea of what Loblaw stood for. If Dominion was perceived as a leader in fresh produce and meat, and upstarts like Knob Hill Farms were pioneers in bulk-food retailing, Loblaw was an also-ran in every measure of customer satisfaction. It scored poorly on price, selection, quality, service and convenient locations.

The company's internal operations were a similar shambles. There was no marketing strategy to speak of, no proper system for training staff, and no set of cost, profit and market-share goals with which to hold executives accountable for their performance. Naturally enough, many of Loblaw's grocery competitors refused to stock Weston food products. Less understandable was the reluctance of Weston firms to do business with each other. Only 4 per cent of total revenues in the Weston-Loblaw group could be attributed to intercompany sales, an apparent mockery of Garfield's ideal of vertical integration. Worse than that was the internal rivalry. One Weston bakery would duke it out with another, while Loblaw grocery chains operating under different names would compete for the same customers, often within a block of each other. It was not unheard of for one Weston company to sue another, unaware that they shared the same owner.

Overseeing this destructive competition was Metcalf, who in better days had been the first to install air-conditioning in a Canadian supermarket and to display frozen food in open freezers. In the later years of his stewardship, however, Metcalf was a secretive tyrant given to raiding other firms for talent, only to fire those same top managers after a few months with no reason given. "It was an organization largely staffed by people who'd been there a long time, and who were motivated by fear and greed," said Jock McLeod, one of the McKinsey & Co. consultants that Garfield had sent into Loblaw in the late 1960s. "It was a very unpleasant environment."

As the crisis at Loblaw deepened, industry experts began to speculate that Garfield would shed the albatross. But the old man had not reached that point. To abandon Loblaw and retreat to his European redoubt made little sense, given that Weston's grocery chains in Britain, Germany and France were in scarcely better shape than Metcalf's fiefdom. And for all of Weston's global trappings, North America, and Canada in particular, was still the largest source of the empire's revenues. Its economy was expected to grow faster than Europe's. In 1966, after 30 years of British residency, Weston himself had relocated to Toronto, the ancestral home of the family business. His dynastic impulse, undiminished after many years of surrendering authority to professional managers, led him to think that a descendant of George Weston should have a crack at pulling Loblaw out of the flames.

G ARFIELD HAD three sons. Grainger, the eldest, had shown little interest in the business. Weston's fourth child, Garfield Jr., known as Garry, was skilled in the family business but lacked experience in the North American scene. He had studied at Oxford and Harvard, and then spent 14 years running the Weston operation in Australia. Garry had only just been called back to London, and now had his hands full trying to fix the family's European businesses.

That left Galen, the youngest of Garfield's nine children. (None of Garfield's six daughters was active in the family business.) Galen, like Garry, had proved himself overseas, with a thriving retail operation he had built almost from scratch in the Irish Republic. But he was equally at home in North America. Galen had studied at Canada's top business school, the University of Western Ontario in London. He'd worked at Loblaw Groceterias, cleaning out photo pans in the advertising department. Indeed, Galen had worked almost everywhere in the empire, packing gift hampers at Fortnum & Mason and stocking shelves at Deutscher Supermarkt Handels GmbH. His entrepreneurial drive was unmistakable. The youngest Weston had peddled Christmas trees and picked tobacco near

Tillsonburg in southern Ontario to finance his tuition at UWO, which he quit one credit short of a degree in his haste to start a business of his own. "Dozens of young Canadian executives were getting into the retail food business in Europe," said Galen. "I wanted to get in on it."

In 1965 in Ireland, virgin territory for modern retailing methods, Galen, then 24, had started with a single grocery store purchased with an inheritance from his grandmother and built one of the country's largest retail enterprises. He turned that one store into Power, the first supermarket chain in Ireland. He bought a bankrupt department store, renamed it Penney's, and built it into a profitable chain. Galen also acquired and overhauled Brown, Thomas & Co., a venerable high-street retailer in Dublin, and branched into restaurants, shoes, women's apparel and service and supply firms.

That exercise in proving himself outside the ambit of his father's interests gave Galen a taste for cutthroat competition. He was not above dispatching employees to Quinnsworth, a rival retailer he later acquired, to buy its entire supply of loss-leader merchandise. Of necessity, he became an expert in real estate. "You didn't have Cadillac Fairviews in Ireland," he said, "so I had to do my own real estate — looking for locations, building shopping centres and supplying the infrastructure in Ireland that hadn't existed up to that time." And he got a lesson in the dangers of diversification. "After three years in the department store business, I looked over my shoulder and found that the supermarket business was in serious disarray and in deep trouble. So there were a couple of difficult years when I had to restructure all the managements, and finally get us out of trouble."

Most important, Galen had studied up on the crisis at Loblaw. He was strange-ly fascinated by it. Garry, he thought, was stuck with trying to turn a mediocre operation in Europe into a good one. The task of rescuing an abysmal business in North America might actually be easier, and certainly more fun. "The quick and dirty profit opportunities have been exploited over there," Galen would later say of Garry's bailiwick, after it had been subjected to layoffs and asset sales. "That's just what we're starting to do here."

He understood how Loblaw had dug a grave for itself. "I'm part of a family cul-ture where you took one bakery and made it 10 bakeries," Galen said. "You saw an acquisition in the U.S. being turned into five acquisitions." Some worked, some didn't. At Loblaw, he thought, the core business was fundamentally sound. Somewhat naively, perhaps, Galen started out with the idea that a Loblaw turn-around would mostly involve the trimming of dead branches from an otherwise healthy tree. "We had the nucleus of a fine company, but out of 1,800 store loca-tions there were only a couple of hundred very good ones. It was just a question of boiling the business down." Of making what Galen described as "no-brainer" decisions — to fix neglected stores, for instance, which were selling $50,000 worth of merchandise a week and could be doing several multiples of that after a cursory facelift.

There were, Galen assured his father in the fall of 1971, "just so many obvious, great business opportunities at Loblaw. And they would require us to make decisions that didn't take any wits at all."

Turkeys are very dumb birds. In order to get them to eat, farmers put glass pellets into their regular food. The glass is shiny. It attracts them. So they come to eat. That's what President's Choice is to us: It brings shoppers into the store.
— Richard Currie, CEO of Loblaw Cos. in the 1990s

FOOD RETAILING is not a hotbed of innovation.

The essential format of today's food store was determined long ago. The cash-and-carry grocery store was introduced in 1859 in New York City by the Great Atlantic & Pacific Tea Co., better known as A&P. Self-serve was pioneered in 1916 in Memphis, Tennessee, by Clarence Saunders with a store he called Piggly Wiggly. And the first modern supermarket opened in 1930 in Jamaica, Queens. The brainchild of Michael Cullen, a veteran of A&P and Kroger, the first King Kullen sold national brands at a discount, featured meat and dairy sections, and offered free parking. Frank Sobey in Atlantic Canada and Toronto-based Dominion Stores and the partnership of T. P. Loblaw and Milton Cork (both founded in 1919) refined their retailing concepts more or less in tandem with their U.S. peers.

Little changed in subsequent decades. Stores got bigger and moved indoors with the advent of the enclosed mall. In the 1960s, Jack Hooley of Minneapolis and Steve Stavro of Toronto, future owner of the Toronto Maple Leafs and Toronto Raptors, experimented with the first discount food warehouses, named Power Alley and Knob Hill Farms, respectively. (Stavro located his early warehouse stores on rail sidings, where merchandise was unloaded from boxcars and displayed in the homely packing cases in which it had left the factory.) In the 1970s, grocers began to equip their cashiers with electonic scanners to monitor the depletion of inventory. By 2000, that inventory had grown to some 30,000 items in the larger supermarkets, compared with 2,000 in the 1940s.

Grocery executives are schooled in the immutable laws of food merchandizing. They believe, for instance, that visitors want to be greeted by an ambiance of colour and freshness, not a wall of tissue-paper boxes. So 60 per cent of supermarkets put produce at the entrance. The others begin with flowers. Staples such as bread, milk, meat and vegetables are located far from each other, requiring shoppers to take the tourist route through the store. The layout is designed to discourage shortcuts. Jacques Cartier himself would be challenged to find a direct route from the produce section to the checkout.

Grocers know that about 95 per cent of patrons who try a free sample go on to buy. (They don't want to offend the clerk dispensing the freebies.) Products that have been raised from floor to eye level enjoy a boost in sales of 70 per cent and more. "Cereal theory," however, dictates that sugar-laden breakfast foods and other items that have pulling power with children be displayed at ankle level. When tins of soup are arranged alphabetically — a grocery no-no — sales drop exactly 6 per cent. House brands are always placed to the left of the national brand equivalent, because the eye naturally moves from right to left, as if turning to a new page.

In order to slow down buggies, and encourage impulse buys, background music is slowed to a slumbersome adagio of 60 beats per minute (and turned back up to an after-hours allegro of 108 beats to enliven the shelf-stockers). That keeps shoppers blinking their eyes at the groggy rate of just 14 times a minute, compared to the normal 32 times. Typically, two-thirds of the goods with which shoppers leave the store are items they had not planned to buy.

No grocer has ever apologized for those tactics. Profit margins in food retailing are wafer-thin. The supermarket industry is more labour-intensive than most, and is largely unionized. Wage concessions are common, since taking a strike means an immediate and perhaps irrevocable loss of market share. Grocery retailing is a cash business. Both cash and merchandise are easily pilfered, making the industry acutely vulnerable to "shrinkage" — that is, product lost to patrons and employees with sticky fingers. A great deal of the merchandise is perishable. An even greater portion is identical from one competing store to the next, which puts an unhealthy emphasis on price as the chief weapon for achieving or retaining market share. Try as they might, grocers can't kick the habit of mutually destructive price wars.

Retailers try to extract fees from makers of brand-name goods in exchange for putting their product on the shelf. Grocers are especially bold in demanding "allowances," "slotting fees" and so on for the 20,000 new products looking for a space on supermarket shelves each year. But the relationship between retailers and food manufacturers is a tug of war. Shoppers expect to find their favourite, heavily promoted brand-name goods at their local grocery story. Purveyors of national-brand goods know that shoppers will defect from a store if Tide or Chips Ahoy! are chronically out of stock. That limits the ability of grocers to squeeze Procter & Gamble or Nabisco; they can't risk having their supply of a high-volume product cut off.

Those factors conspire to make food retailing one of the least profitable major industries. A well-run grocery operation can expect to earn no more than a couple of pennies on the dollar. And Loblaw was not in that charmed circle when a

31-year-old Galen Weston took over from George Metcalf in the spring of 1972. The consultants that Galen brought in from Garfield's Fine Fare grocery chain in Britain advised him that the Loblaw name was worthless. He should, they told him, abandon the worst locations and put a new name over the door at the remaining stores.

The decay extended far beyond retailing. The bakery divisions of George Weston Ltd. were plagued with duplicated overhead and overlapping product lines. Profits for Clover Leaf, Brunswick and Weston's other fish products were gyrating wildly. And E. B. Eddy had been laid low by a cyclical crash in pulp-and-paper prices. "The company was in bad shape — much more than anyone knew," said Jock McLeod. "Galen kept discovering pieces of companies that they owned, and there was no record of it. It must have taken him two years just to find out what they owned. And when he saw what they had, they were horrified."

"They" were Weston's two new aides-de-camp, Richard J. Currie, 34, and David A. Nichol, 32. Despairing that the grocery trade "did not attract intellectuals, to say the least," Weston had quickly recruited two "really bright people to look at these industries, which are very traditional, and see if we can make a quantam leap."

Currie, a native of Saint John, New Brunswick, was a graduate of the University of Western Ontario (UWO) and a Harvard MBA. He then toiled at the consulting firm of McKinsey and Co. improving profits for food manufacturers and distributors before joining George Weston, shortly before Galen's arrival, to help it design a new sugar refinery. Weston gave him the no-nonsense title "director of profit development" at Loblaw. His job was to help Weston cope with the debt crunch and dead-branch trimming.

Nichol, born in Chatham, Ontario, was the son of a railway station agent. He and Weston first met as freshmen at UWO and became roommates. After UWO, Nichol had peddled bearings from garage to garage across the Canadian prairies before going back to school, graduating second in his class of 200 law students at the University of British Columbia. After earning a master's degree in law at Harvard, he too joined McKinsey, where he and Currie revamped the purchasing department of client H. J. Heinz and Co. in Pittsburgh. Nichol's job at Loblaw was to revitalize its stores in the core Ontario market.

For the next two decades, Loblaw would be run by this triumvirate. The trio was bound by more than collegial ties. Nichol and Weston had been best men at each other's weddings. When Nichol's first marriage failed, Currie had come to his emotional rescue. After Currie's marriage came apart under the strain of his Loblaw duties, it was Nichol who stood by his side at Currie's second wedding. When Weston had tapped his UWO buddy on first arriving for work in Canada, Nichol promptly introduced him to Currie. The three men didn't quite finish each other's sentences, but in the early years of the Loblaw reclamation project they seldom disagreed on major issues. And both Currie and Nichol derived great comfort from Weston's overt self-confidence, which contrasted sharply with Loblaw's battered fortunes. "I don't know what he's afraid of," Nichol would later say of Weston. "I've known him for 30 years, and I haven't found it yet."

For all that, the team wasn't especially cohesive. What made it work was the care Weston took in keeping himself, the patrician heir, Currie, the brilliant financial strategist, and Nichol, the irrepressible marketer, out of each other's hair. And what made the troika remarkable was not only the ability of its members to transcend sharp differences in style in order to embrace each other's ideas, but its openness to suggestions from others.

True, Currie could be impatient with subordinates who had not been schooled in the McKinsey dogma of measuring progress against an ambitious set of financial targets. And it was not unusual for Nichol to explode at a minion who advanced an idea he deemed prosaic. (He was more patient with loopy proposals than conventional ones.) At the same time, all three men were relentless in soliciting ideas. And when they found one deep in the ranks that struck them as a potentially lucrative brainwave, they championed it with such passion and resolve that front-line employees gained a sense of importance. The company's turnover crisis soon abated. It also helped that Weston had moved swiftly to cull deadwood from the management ranks. That dropped the average age of Loblaw store managers from 57 to the mid-30s. And head office soon had a cadre of new management arrivals whose loyalty was to the troika's agenda to reinvent the business.

Loblaw didn't have the option of starting over from scratch, of course. But Weston acted as though it did. Currie and Nichol understood from the outset that Weston was prepared to tear down and rebuild Loblaw until it was no longer recognizable as a family heirloom. Weston played on the vanity of his top two lieutenants, who needed little encouragement to think of themselves as revolutionaries. With their academic background and McKinsey credentials, Currie and Nichol were sophisticates in a plebian trade. Their arrogance and smug denigration of industry traditions made Loblaw something of an alien nation.

But in time, the Loblaw turnaround would also call attention to a laudable aspect of the Canadian character. In the second half of the 20th century, no major economic power was more outward-looking than Canada. The upside of the country's supposed inferiority complex was its unmatched curiosity about innovations taking place elsewhere in the world, spanning every realm of artistic, political and scientific endeavour. That contrasted with insularity on distant shores. In retailing, for instance, Japan clung to its inefficient stores where staff outnumbered patrons. Germany thwarted a planned invasion by France's hypermarchés, determined to protect its mom-and-pop grocery shops. The not-invented-here syndrome was especially prevalent in the U.S., where retailers tended not only to reject foreign ideas but failed to learn from each other. Executives at Woolworth,

Kmart and Sears, Roebuck ridiculed the folksy gimmicks of Sam Walton until his Wal-Mart Stores Inc., founded 1962, had managed in just three decades to eclipse all of them to become the biggest retailer on earth.

Weston had no illusions that any one country held a monopoly on best practices in shopkeeping. He had seen the world, having attended no fewer than 17 schools in Canada, the U.S., England and South Africa before university, thanks to his father's insistence on taking up residence in each new market he conquered. And from the age of 28, when his father had installed him on the boards of his top holding companies, Galen had been studying Weston retail operations on four continents.

In Ireland, Weston had acted as an agent for Marks & Spencer, the British food and clothing retailer. He traded war stories with Lord Marcus Sieff, the M&S chairman. And he became obsessed with the popularity of M&S's St. Michael label, one of the few upscale house brands in the retail world. (But for the hold that St. Michael had on some Canadian shoppers, M&S would not have stuck by its chronically unprofitable Canadian operation for some 20 years before closing it, finally, in 1999.) Weston was also struck by the success of J. Sainsbury, Britain's largest grocer, in nurturing a popular line of house brands at its chain of large-scale supermarkets. He noticed, too, that Safeway Stores Inc., a fast-growing chain based in Oakland, California, had subdivided itself into autonomous profit centres. Now Safeway was outmuscling the venerable A&P on the U.S. West Coast.

Weston was anxious to experiment with such concepts in Canada. But the urgent business at hand was to raise cash. "While our capital was going into expansion in Europe and the U.S.," he said, "our market share in Canada was plunging, and our cash cow in Ontario went dry. My first painful decision was to reverse that policy, sell some businesses, and bring the money back to Canada."

Tapping the resources of the family empire, Galen arranged for various Weston companies to pump $164 million into Loblaw by acquiring some of its assets. In one of the most important transactions, Wittington Realty & Construction Ltd., named for Garfield's estate in England, enabled Loblaw to slip out of its leaseback straitjacket by becoming the new holder of many Loblaw properties and mortgages. That freed Weston and Currie to close 1,200 stores in Canada and the U.S. — although in most cases they hung on to the real estate. It was a deceptive strategy. Competitors assumed that Loblaw was waving a white flag. In reality, it was staunching its losses and raising cash from the sale of inventory. That money would be used in financing the most ambitious store renovation program in history, and an aggressive marketing campaign to draw shoppers into the new stores.

With Safeway as his model, Weston brought order to the Loblaw stable of grocery chains. Power and other lacklustre banners were scrapped. The remaining chains were consolidated into a handful of autonomous divisions arranged along geographic lines. Weston introduced monthly profit-and-loss statements for each store. He told the chains to stop thinking about the banner's overall performance, and focus instead on boosting the market share of each individual store.

Weston then launched his counterattack for regaining the ground lost to Dominion and other rivals. Weston began by confronting Loblaw's reputation as a chronic price follower rather than leader. But his new slogan — "More than the price is right . . . but by gosh the price is right" — was a warning that he was preparing to do battle on more than one front of customer satisfaction. And from the start, Weston was determined to wrap his reborn company in the Maple Leaf. Marketers in Canada tend to recruit fading American stars to peddle the goods: Bea Arthur for Shoppers Drug Mart, Cher for Hudson's Bay Co., Candice Bergen for Sprint Canada. Weston tapped Montreal native William Shatner, a cult hero from his days as *Star Trek*'s Captain Kirk, to saturate the airwaves with a spiel about Loblaw's budding renaissance.

The most dramatic evidence of change at Loblaw, however, was the wrenching overhaul of its Ontario stores by the team of Nichol and graphic designer Don Watt.

The 36-year-old Watt, who hailed from Regina, was an unlikely mastermind for an image makeover. He was colour-blind and had no experience in retailing. After working as an illustrator of children's books and the Bugs Bunny animation director at Warner Bros. in Los Angeles, Watt had approached Dominion Stores with an audacious offer to redesign one of its stores for next to nothing in order to reinvent himself as a corporate designer. Dominion gave him the brush-off. Watt then called on Weston, who was happy to meet him. Loblaw had been canvassing design firms whose proposals ran into the millions of dollars. Weston gave the young designer $30,000 and sent him off to the Toronto intersection of Bayview and Moore Avenues, site of one of Loblaw's shabbiest stores. The outlet was turning in lousy numbers despite its enviable location in an upper-middle-class neighbourhood.

At that time, Loblaw stores were sheathed in the same sickly yellow porcelain tiles that Shell Oil had introduced at its filling stations in the early 1960s. Watt replaced the storefront with a bold, brown wall — a bow to the hip colour of the disco age. Inside, he hung colourful, oversized photos of fresh produce and baked goods above product displays as a guide to shoppers. He created a rustic feel by slapping strips of natural wood over top the cracked mirror tiles that lined the walls. And he conceived a new logo — a stylized L in orange and red in a stream-lined Helvetica typeface — that would still be in use three decades later.

Weston, Currie and Nichol had crisscrossed the U.S., scouting for ideas. Inspired by the emphasis on produce at hot California retailers such as Lucky's and Alpha Beta, Nichol moved the produce section at the Moore-Bayview outlet from its purgatory at the back of the store to the entrance. He stripped the plastic wrap off fruit and vegetables; and introduced kiwi, arugula and other exotic items not seen before in Canadian supermarkets. High-intensity lights were covered with warm-coloured filters to make the food more appealing.

Within a few months of its reopening, the Moore-Bayview store was doing 60 per cent more business than before the retrofit. By that point, Weston had already begun to roll out the redesign to a dozen more stores. Many of these first-generation revamped outlets included a Ziggy's Fantastic Foods in-store deli, a concept developed for Loblaw by a Toronto delicatessen operator named Siegfried Wauro, known locally as Ziggy. The Stuttgart-born master butcher conceived a string of in-store meat counters staffed by women decked out in Alpine garb that were thought to give Loblaw a mildly daring ethnic ambiance.

As the refinements became more elaborate, the store remodelling costs soared to an average $400,000 per outlet. But there was an immediate doubling in sales at overhauled stores, to $135,000 a week. Outlets that once did a mere $65,000 in business per week were generating weekly volume of $340,000 just a year or so after reopening. And Loblaw was clawing its way back into contention in the market-share wars. By 1974, it had recovered from its nadir of 15 per cent a few years earlier to claim some 25 per cent of the huge Ontario market, just shy of Dominion's share.

That rapid progress was misleading, however. It encouraged Weston to believe he was pulling off a miracle turnaround. He was mistaken. The complete comeback in profits he had expected to engineer by 1976 failed to materialize. Instead, 1976 marked Loblaw's worst performance, a loss of $21.7 million. As a result, parent George Weston Ltd. lost $15 million — the first and, to date, only loss in its history. The huge cost of the store renovations had taken its toll, of course. And an anticipated upturn in fishery and forest products failed to materialize.

But hubris, not routine business conditions, were at the root of Loblaw's continuing woes. Weston was not a slash-and-burn artist. He had shown considerable resolve in shrinking the store network. Yet his preference was to grow his way out of trouble. That was a philosophy that would serve him exceptionally well in the long term. But it was all wrong for his family's U.S. retailing business. Weston had overestimated his ability to salvage something from that epic disaster. "It was in the cards that National Tea should be, or could be, disposed of," Weston said. "But I felt we had a tremendous foothold in the U.S. and it must not be lost, almost at any cost."

Barely a year after arriving at Loblaw, Weston and Currie had decamped to National Tea's hometown of Chicago. They rented a house and spent three months crafting a rescue strategy that led to the closing of about half of National Tea's 892 U.S. stores, plus five warehouses and a cattle slaughterhouse. But three years and two presidents later, a leaner National Tea was no better able to cope with industry-wide price wars than its bloated predecessor. Meanwhile, Weston looked over his shoulder and saw that many of George Weston's non-food investments in Canada were sliding toward the abyss.

Conceding defeat in the U.S., Weston pulled National out of its home market of Chicago, as well as from Denver and Davenport, Iowa. Once that decision was made, the retreat was swift — many of the U.S outlets were hastily unloaded at less than book value, leaving only a rump of stores in St. Louis and New Orleans. Back in Canada, Weston sold Somerville Industries, a large packaging concern that also made board games. He closed the money-losing Sayvette department stores. And he dumped G. Tamblyn Ltd. (The drugstore chain would fare scarcely better under its next two owners, Britain's Boots the Chemist and Toronto-based Oshawa Group Ltd., which rechristened it Pharma Plus).

Weston's sudden display of impatience sent a useful message to Loblaw managers. They learned that the young scion's sentimental attachment to his father's legacy had its limits. "We knew it had to be done," said Currie, "because if we didn't do it, the Loblaw companies weren't going to survive. I don't think it's any more courageous than a doctor's decision to amputate a gangrenous arm." A substantial number of non-food holdings, anchored by E. B. Eddy, would survive the great sell-off of the late 1970s. Currie was confident that these operations could be polished to gemstone quality by means of a disciplined, business-school emphasis on strategic planning and rigorous cost control. He was wrong about that. Yet another purge was on the distant horizon. But for now, neither Currie nor Weston could see that Loblaw's success as a grocer would someday require it to abandon everything that didn't relate to food.

By contrast, the future would hold no further major disappointments for Weston in his core Canadian grocery operations. As it entered the 1980s, Loblaw was on the road to sustained and growing success, from which there would be only the slightest deviations. Every obstacle would be overcome as the galaxy of Loblaw grocery banners — including Loblaws itself, No Frills, Zehrs markets, Fortino and the Real Canadian Superstore — gained the upper hand in Ontario, then became a significant factor in Western Canada, and, in the late 1990s, achieved supremacy in the nation's second-largest market, Quebec.

To be sure, Weston had sought only to restore Loblaw to its number-one position in Ontario, dating from the 1950s. Fate took a hand in his larger triumphs. For instance, Weston could not have been more fortunate in his adversaries had he chosen them himself.

Only one new player, Safeway, briefly challenged Loblaw's growing strength in Ontario. Thanks to Weston's strategy of holding onto choice sites, where stores that had temporarily been closed were used as training centres or made available for non-profit food banks, Safeway was obliged to stage its assault on Loblaw's home market from out-of-the-way locations. The effort soon sputtered when

Safeway's U.S. parent succumbed to an ill-advised leveraged buyout, spurring its northern affiliate to retreat to its stronghold in Western Canada.

As for Loblaw's existing rivals in Central Canada, they gradually self-destructed. Steinberg was destroyed by feuding among members of its founding family. Oshawa Group, operator of the Food City, IGA and Price Chopper chains, languished while members of its founding Wolfe family squabbled over succession rites. Provigo, the giant of Quebec grocery retailing, choked on its purchase of the Quebec divisions of Steinberg and Dominion. And the stunning collapse of Dominion itself would have few equals in the annals of Canadian corporate debacles.

It was Dominion, more than any other competitor, that had humbled Loblaw in the 1960s. But by the late 1970s, Dominion had come to resemble the fat and happy Loblaw of Metcalf's regime. Conrad Black, the future press baron, gained control of Dominion with his takeover of its parent, Argus Corp. Ltd., in 1978. He soon became acutely troubled by the management style of Dominion's top managers. Specifically, he was flummoxed by their "refusal to comtemplate anything new [and] their arrogant insistence, as if constant repetition would make it true, that they were the North American continent's greatest food retailers."

The signal achievement of Loblaw's chief nemesis in the early 1980s was to lose market share even as it kept adding new stores. Dominion's many older stores were museum pieces. One of Black's colleagues spotted Galen Weston at a particularly rundown Dominion outlet in north Toronto. Weston, Black recounted in his 1993 memoir, *A Life in Progress*, was "rubbing his hands and excitedly [saying], 'This is a good store!' Good for him, certainly." The annual "shrinkage" at Dominion, Black estimated, was some $30 million to $40 million — no trifling sum, given that Dominion earned only $27 million in its best year. The stealing, Black said, approached "the profligate corruption of looters in a deserted city or even a deserted ship. It would be unfair to blame employees exclusively. They accounted for three-quarters of the theft, but customers took another $10 million. In one quarter, a Protestant minister, a Roman Catholic priest, and a rabbi, each in a different province, were apprehended for shoplifting."

In 1981, Black unloaded Dominion's lacklustre Quebec division. What remained of the chain he regarded as "the beached whale of the industry," whose management was in the hands of "trained reptiles." For all that, though, Black spent four years rebuffing overtures from Richard Currie, Oshawa Group, Steinberg and A&P. He finally consented, in 1985, to an offer from the last of those bidders that he deemed to be sufficiently generous. Had Black parted with Dominion and its still formidable network of stores at an earlier date, Loblaw's progress might yet have been arrested. Instead, Dominion had slipped into a coma by the time Black made his exit. Weston ultimately picked up some of Dominon's stores in Atlantic Canada and a bakery that held a franchise for Wonder Bread.

Galen Weston, shown with wife Hilary (above), turned Loblaw into North America's best-run grocery retailer after rescuing the legacy of his father, Garfield (above right), seen here in the 1950s at the height of his power as the biggest baker in the British Commonwealth. "I deal in bread and dreams," said Garfield, who vowed to build an enterprise that would never know completion. Below, patriarch George Weston's bakery in Toronto in the 1890s, when Galen's grandfather measured success in the number of horses he had in harness.

An early outpost of Theodore Pringle Loblaw's pioneering chain of self-serve grocery stores (above), in west-end Toronto in the 1920s. It had grown to a flourishing network of 113 stores when Garfield Weston first began to acquire its shares in the late 1940s. By the 1990s Loblaw was the most innovative grocer on the continent, leading its peers in product selection and variety of store formats. Visitors at the "street of stores" in Toronto (below) shopped for cellphones, wine, drugs and home mortgages, and signed up for in-store cooking and fitness classes.

Richard Currie (above left), celebrating with Galen Weston at a shareholders meeting in Calgary, plotted the Loblaw campaign of ceaseless store expansion across Canada with Napoleonic precision. David Nichol (below) was the firm's marketing wizard and its public spokesman. "I am a walking Loblaw logo," he said. Nichol's "President's Choice" line of upscale house-brand products gave Loblaw an unassailable competitive edge.

Weston felt he had overpaid for the bakery. But then, as he told an industry seminar where he shared a panel with Black, "Anyone who buys anything from Conrad will be sucking gas."

The death spiral at Dominion should have alerted the industry to the perils of complacency. But as a later wave of consolidation would show, only Loblaw appeared to have been sobered by the demise of its arch-rival.

In pushing his managers to constantly reinvent Loblaw's core retailing business, Weston himself exuded a youthful confidence that all things were possible. And his enthusiasm, backed as it was by one of the world's great family fortunes, was infectious throughout the management ranks at Loblaw.

Weston led still more world tours. His product buyers and store designers visited Tesco, the U.K. chain that would someday knock the family-controlled J. Sainsbury off its perch; Germany's Aldi, a trailblazer in discount food retailing; and Carrefour, the French pioneer in gigantic hypermarchés. Carrefour had been the first supermarket operator to reinvent house-brand goods as "no names." Dubbed "Produit Libre," or "brand free," these items were free of advertising and expensive packaging, which meant they were also free of the usual steep markups. They enabled Carrefour to cast itself in the role of consumer advocate with an extensive line of store-brand products that boasted national-brand quality at low prices.

Some of those concepts did not travel well or had to be extensively reworked for Canada. And even the best of them required patient nurturing. One example was the Loblaw superstores that Currie doted on for more than a decade before they began to pay their way. Another was Nichol's first line of generic house-brand goods, called Exceptional Value. Launched in 1977, it was a resounding flop. Consumers resisted the idea of lugging bulk purchases of detergent and the like out of the store.

Yet Loblaw persisted in experimenting with ideas that often seemed far-fetched. Only in that way was it able to gradually establish a perception of itself as a champion of consumer choice and value. The most dramatic example of the pay-off from that strategy was Loblaw's eventual success with generics, in which it spearheaded an industry revolution that would be felt throughout North America.

Generics had been a staple of grocery retailing for generations. House brands were older than supermarkets, tracing their origins at least as far back as A&P's Quaker Maid line of the 1880s. Nichol's mistake with his first generic line was a lack of daring. In 1978, he was back with a revamped line, called No Name, and this time he broke the rules.

House brands were typically regarded as a necessary evil in the grocery trade. As mass-market retailers, supermarkets were obliged to cater to the low-income segment of their audience. But they did so with obvious reluctance. There was scant profit to be made from this low-margin ghetto. Given the substandard quality of most house-brand goods, their application was limited to a small number of product categories such as cleansers and bulked canned goods where the customer's trust in the source of the item wasn't a big factor in their buying decision. Generics were ugly ducklings that were stocked on the low shelves. As late as 1986, the top U.S. graphic designer Milton Glaser, fresh from developing a line of private-label goods for the Grand Union chain in the U.S. Northeast, could insist that "generic packaging is supposed to look terrible. Its intention is to produce the impression that no time was spent doing it and no cost."

Nichol's approach was radically different. He thought Loblaw's own products should look as smart as the national brands. He instructed Watt to dress the No Name line in bold graphics that conveyed an image of quality. With the subsequent introduction of the upscale President's Choice line of house-brand goods, the packaging for Loblaw generics was often more effective than for their national-brand equivalents, notable for appetizing photographs of cookies, casseroles and seafood entrees. But the novelty of generics at Loblaw went beyond stylish presentation. There was Nichol's insistence on quality ingredients, which required the use of fancy rather than standard-grade fruit and produce. There was also the enormous breadth of his generics line, which embraced everything from raspberry jam to pantyhose. And there was something else, which Nichol would come to regard as the clinching factor. This was Nichol's role as the grocery world's first house-brand frontman.

In the mid-1970s, Nichol replaced Shatner as the public face of Loblaw. He was soon a ubiquitous shill for products which, he repeatedly emphasized, he had personally travelled the globe to find and bring back for lucky Loblaws shoppers. The beefy Loblaw executive proved to be a highly effective salesman. During one of his infrequent forays into enemy territory, Black had come upon a cluster of senior citizens who appeared to be mesmerized by an in-store video of Nichol extolling his President's Choice exotica. "It had never occurred to me until that moment," said Black, "that anyone could have considered his bumptious self-advertising as an inducement to shop anywhere other than with a competitor. I was mistaken."

The abrasive Nichol, who clipped his fingernails in staff meetings in a show of indifference to ideas that failed to excite him, grated on the subalterns in his own idea factory who conceived the likes of President's Choice Memories of Szechwan Peanut Sauce Stirfry. And he bullied the suppliers who were strong-armed into taking a loss on their production of house-brand items in exchange for the promise of lucrative contracts at some future date.

But Weston, remembering the sad consequences of Metcalf's failure to give talented subordinates a free rein, happily tolerated the eccentricities of his former college roommate. In a break with his father's pursuit of vertical integration, Weston consented to Nichol's use of outside suppliers for his No Name and PC products, a painful slight to the Weston-owned bakeries and canneries. But that enabled Nichol to source his private-label brainwaves as widely as possible, and to be merciless in jawboning suppliers on price.

Weston also signed off on one of corporate Canada's most lavish expense accounts. Voyeuristic readers of Nichol's immensely popular *Insider's Report* (circulation: 10 million), a quirky digest of Loblaw's latest generic "discoveries," launched in 1983, knew that Nichol got his best ideas from hobnobbing with chefs at the Four Seasons restaurant in New York, Taillevent in Paris and Harry's Bar in Venice.

The *Report* was a *cri de coeur* for middle-class foodies, with its barbed commentary on the evils of modern food manufacturing and agricultural methods. In creating an image of himself as a consumer champion, Nichol tapped into mounting consumer awareness about food additives, and their fears about chemicals used by farmers to speed the growth of vegetables and fruit. Nichol expressed such views in his condemnation of "Tennis Ball Tomatoes" an example of the new assembly-line produce that were a tomato-breeder's delight because they could be picked green and boasted a hardiness for travel. "Hardiness? They have skins that would make an armadillo jealous."

Even had Loblaw's rivals succumbed to their own complacency at an earlier point, it's likely that Weston would have backed Nichol's lavish house-brand campaign. Like Nichol, Weston wanted Loblaw to become prodigious as a purveyor of must-have goods that were not available elsewhere. "We've got to get into new, unique merchandise that is fresher, less expensive, more flavoursome and more exciting," Weston said. "There's got to be something to draw people to your store instead of the store down the road — otherwise you'll do no better than the guy down the road."

As Black surmised, Nichol was indeed an advertisement for himself. "I am a walking Loblaw logo," Nichol boasted. He was also a one-man Procter & Gamble of new-product development. Nichol's read on popular tastes was not unerring. His Italian truffles and Texas-style microwaveable chili were too "fashion-forward" for Ontario shoppers in the early 1980s. And a blue corn chip he labelled Suicide Blues had to be withdrawn when shoppers complained about the name. But more often than not, Loblaw was the beneficiary of Nichol's crusade to enable every Loblaw patron to "put a three-star quality meal on your table in only 10 minutes." That and his loud contempt for national brands made Nichol seem less of a salesman than a tireless champion of consumer choice.

It seemed to Nichol that one reason most North Americans were overweight was that they didn't get much of a "flavour hit" from national-brand foods. You could eat a bag of potato chips and never taste a potato. You could down a dozen cups of coffee without tasting a coffee bean. Take the nation's best-selling name-brand cookie. Here was a product that consisted of just 19 per cent chocolate chips. The rest was mostly flour. And the taste, like most brands aimed at a huge audience and formulated to offend as few people as possible, was deliberately bland. In his *Insider's Report*, Nichol proposed that shoppers vote against that outrage by switching to his President's Choice The Decadent, a house-brand cookie that was 40-per-cent-laden with chocolate chips. Within three years of its introduction in 1988, Decadent had overtaken Chips Ahoy! as the bestselling cookie in Canada, despite being available only in Loblaw stores. And given its low overhead — no advertising, no "slotting" or "allowance" fees — The Decadent made more money for Loblaw than Chips Ahoy!, with a gross profit margin of 46 per cent to the 34 per cent that Loblaw and other grocers collected from sales of Nabisco's flagship product.

The pattern was repeated with Memories of Kobe Beef Patties, G.R.E.E.N. motor oil and, most prominently, President's Choice Cola. Nichol considered PC Cola to be his greatest marketing triumph. But the real story of its stunning success had little to do with Nichol. PC Cola was simply the first store-brand cola that tasted like a name-brand soft drink.

Before PC Cola's arrival in 1990, private-label soft drinks tasted just a bit better than G.R.E.E.N. motor oil. That changed after a Loblaw supplier named Cott Corp., a Toronto-based bottler of soft drinks, talked Royal Crown Cola Inc. of Dallas into granting it exclusive private-label rights for use of RC Cola syrup in North America for 25 years. A cola aficionado would be hard-pressed to discern a taste difference between RC and its two entrenched competitors. But after decades of desultory management, RC was a poor also-ran to Coke and Pepsi in market share.

A more quick-witted owner of the RC brand might someday have used it to lead a revolution in generic soft drinks. But it was RC's misfortune to be in the hands of Victor Posner, a perennial target of U.S. fraud investigators, when Cott chief executive Gerry Pencer happened to call on the junk-bond conglomerateur. Posner was in his mid-seventies, and had difficult keeping himself from nodding off in meetings. Over a series of dinners where the paranoid financier and his Canadian guest were surrounded by a dozen or so of Posner's security guards armed with machine guns, Pencer noted Posner's preference for Crown Royal over Royal Crown. Pencer waited for his moment, and struck the deal after Posner "was really in the pail." PC Cola with RC Cola syrup soon overtook Coca-Cola as the market-share leader in Canada.

The snowball effect of private-label merchandising within Loblaw made it a more formidable retailer in unforeseen ways. The budget-priced No Name line, for instance, soon inspired a bare-bones grocery chain, No Frills, with some 80 stores by 2000. President's Choice, the first extensive line of premium house-brand products among North American grocers, begat an in-store banking service called President's Choice Financial. By 2000, after just two years in operation, PC Financial could boast 285,000 customers for its savings accounts, mutual funds,

Visa-President's Choice credit cards and "eatable mortgages" (borrowers who took out a $200,000 mortgage could claim $500 in free groceries). The aura of value and trust built into the PC and No Name brands over two decades could be applied, it became clear, to a remarkably diverse range of goods and services. By the 1990s, one of every three items purchased by Loblaws shoppers was a No Name or PC product. "The irony," said Weston, in a speech to the Toronto Board of Trade in 2000, "is that in the process of bashing the national brands, we created one of the most recognized brands in the country."

Loblaw also spawned a constellation of success stories among its key suppliers. Many of them evolved into major exporters. Riding on Loblaw's coattails, the formerly obscure Cott became the world's largest maker of private-label soft drinks, creating house-brand programs for Wal-Mart, A&P and Safeway in the U.S., and for grocery chains in Spain and Japan. In taking on Coke and Pepsi in the British market with his Virgin Cola, the high-wattage entrepreneur Richard Branson did for Cott in Europe what Nichol had done for Pencer in North America. Menu Foods Ltd., an Ontario pet-food maker that Nichol had approached with a bizarre idea for President's Choice Gourmet Italian Dog Food, was likewise destined to become a gourmet pet-food exporter to Safeway, Wegman's and Amway in the U.S., and grocery chains in Japan, Germany, Italy and Britain. Designer Watt was busy grafting his Loblaws store concept onto Carrefour; Home Depot, the giant Atlanta-based hardware chain; and grocery clients in California, New York and Australia. And the Canadian Imperial Bank of Commerce, Loblaw's partner in PC Financial, custom-designed a similar program for Winn-Dixie's grocery outlets and in 2000 was negotiating a similar contract with Safeway, operator of 1,700 stores.

Loblaw itself had a flourishing sideline in exporting its entire house-brand concept — pricing, packaging, suppliers and all — to about a dozen major grocery networks in the U.S., Australia and Hong Kong. These included Jewel Cos., National's former archrival in Chicago; Lucky's, one of Weston's early role models; and, most notably, Wal-Mart. Founder Sam Walton made the rounds of Loblaws outlets in Toronto, was favourably impressed with what he saw, and gave the green light to a Loblaw-conceived line of house brands dubbed Sam's American Choice. "We don't care where people are from," said Wal-Mart executive Bill Fields, whose firm was based in bucolic Bentonville, Arkansas and was no more a prisoner of the not-invented-here syndrome than Loblaw. The Canadian firm, he told Nichol biographer Anne Kingston, was "the best in the world at what they do. They're visionaries, even though they probably think we're a bunch of hicks." *USA Today*, reporting on the fear they inspired among traditionalists in the U.S. food industry, called them "big league, cross-border terrorists."

So far as the makers of brand-name goods were concerned, Nichol had unleashed a monster. Nabisco was compelled to invest millions of dollars in its

Canadian factories to make them more efficient in order to turn out a lower-priced cookie. It also took aim at Nichol's Decadent cookie with its own choco-late-supercharged product, Chunks Ahoy! Cola-Cola's Canadian arm went into the red for the first time in its history as it slashed prices to arrest its loss of mar-ket share to PC Cola. In every U.S. city where Loblaw had licensed its PC soft drinks, grocery chains accustomed to being dictated to by Coke and Pepsi were treated for the first time to rebates, volume discounts and other incentives from the soft-drink giants, which fattened their bottom lines. Grocers who had never dared to force concessions from national-brand purveyors came to realize, as Loblaw did back in the early 1980s, that they had Nabisco, Nestlé and Colgate-Palmolive on the run — that it was the manufacturers who couldn't afford to alienate the grocers. "Innovation hadn't been there from the national brands," con-ceded Ron McEachern, president of Pepsi-Cola Canada Ltd. "The growth of pre-mium private label is a wake-up call."

The generic revolution rewrote the rules of food manufacturing, marketing and retailing, and was easily the industry's most important innovation in many decades. But unfortunately for Nichol, who had done so much to advance it, the phenomenon of private-label merchandising was also setting the stage for his ulti-mate downfall.

Unlike Nichol, Currie did not regard the holy war against national brands as an end in itself. He had quietly tolerated Nichol's grandstanding only because he seethed at Loblaw's inability to make money from Coke — or, for that matter, cof-fee and any number of other brand-name products where the manufacturer had the upper hand. What Nichol had accomplished with PC was to give Currie the whip hand over the national brands. If Nichol wanted to drive the brand-name marketers out of the temple, Currie simply wanted them to understand that Loblaw was the landlord and, as such, should determine the rent. Currie would quite happily push their goods if only they consented to terms more favourable to Loblaw. By the 1990s, Currie was able to report that Coke, Pepsi and other brand-name food companies were bending to Loblaw's will. They had little choice. As the century drew to a close, Loblaw boasted 33 million square feet of selling space, or about one-third the area of Prince Edward Island. With control of more than one-third of Canadian grocery shelves, Currie could dictate the fee for renting his shelf space.

Early on, that had been a goal of Nichol's, as well. "If you own the theatre and you're writing the play," he had said, "you ought to be able to choose the star." The problem, as time went by, was that Nichol began to see himself as the brand. He had, after all, developed no fewer than 1,700 generic products for Loblaw. For more than a decade, autograph seekers had been hounding him in stores, restau-rants and cinemas. He was better known to schoolchildren than the prime minis-ter, and adults gave him a higher job-approval rating than they did Jean Chrétien.

Under the circumstances, only a miracle could have kept the troika from shattering on the rock of Nichol's ego.

Public perception aside, Nichol was not the Loblaw president. That function
was conducted by Currie, whose talent at working miracles lay in a direction other
than massaging Nichol's ego. Behind the scenes, Currie was using the lion's share
of $1.4 billion in capital spending that Weston had released to him in the 1980s
to shift Loblaw from small- to large-scale stores. In 1984, Loblaw had just eight
stores with more than 60,000 square feet of selling space. Fifteen years later, there
would be 108 such stores, some with more than 100,000 square feet. In total, the
oversized outlets would eventually account for 40 per cent of Loblaw's total selling space. The new emporia were a cost-controller's delight: They were four times
the size of a conventional supermarket, but cost only twice as much to run.

Meanwhile, in a series of flanking moves worthy of the military treatises he
kept at his bedside, Currie had exploited Loblaw's land bank to maximum advantage. One of Dominion's problems had been its reliance on leased land and rented locations, which made it vulnerable to rapacious landlords and gave it no security of tenure over its best sites. But Galen Weston's instincts as a developer, dating from his stint as the Cadillac Fairview of Ireland, were no less sharp than his
feel for merchandising. About half of Loblaw's total retail space was owned outright by Loblaw itself or Wittington Investments, one of the Weston family real-
estate firms.

Over the years, Currie had juggled and rejuggled the Loblaw portfolio of store
formats in order to cater to the varied buying habits of shoppers in inner-city, suburban and small-town neighbourhoods across Canada. He worked tirelessly to
determine precisely the right type of store to operate on each of Weston's abundance of sites. Small towns were favoured with a Zehrs market, a folksy, neighbourhood grocer that often enjoyed monopoly status in a trading zone that could
be measured in scores of square miles. There were franchised, non-union Valu-
marts and Mr. Grocers for low-income neighbourhoods in the inner city. No Frills
outlets appealed to middle-class shoppers who enjoyed upscale bargain hunting.
The Fortinos banner won a loyal following among so-called ethnic consumers in
Ontario's golden horseshoe. (Loblaw grasped earlier than its rivals the importance
of catering to Toronto's Italian population, which was the largest outside of Italy.)
Real Canadian Superstores in Western Canada, launched in 1979, were the country's first successful experiment in combination food and general merchandise
sales. Hangar-sized Loblaws superstores, with a mix of food, housewares and specialized services, were erected in the suburbs and in well-heeled downtown locations. And "pocket" supermarkets like the St. Clair Market in the lobby of the
Weston Centre, the empire's headquarters in midtown Toronto, catered to home-
ward-bound office workers. All 1,065 of those stores carried No Name and PC
products. That gave Loblaw immense clout with suppliers and built consumer loy-

alty for its private-label franchise from coast to coast, and across the entire spectrum of demographic groups.

It seemed to Currie that his unsung victories as field marshall of store planning had rather more to do with Loblaw's ascension than Nichol's "shiny glass pellets" — the PC line over which Nichol was constantly fussing. By the time of Nichol's departure from Loblaw, in 1994, Currie had suffered in the showman's shadow long enough. That much was clear from the way Currie chose to greet the news of Nichol's resignation. "The implication of Dave's leaving," said Currie, who took exacting care with his few public utterances, "is neither negative nor positive. It's neutral." Nichol would not be replaced, he said. With a cruelty that might not have been intentional, but was potent nonetheless, Currie added: "We don't think the business demands a spokesman. Dave needed it, but the business didn't need it."

Currie had not always been successful in hiding his resentment over Nichol's close friendship with Weston, which first blossomed in their college days. Nichol had his own grievances. He was still bitter over Currie's promotion in the 1980s to president and then CEO of Loblaw Cos., ending his status as Currie's coequal dating from 1972. It had seemed to both Weston and Currie that the best way to exploit Nichol's genius was to free him from management responsibilities. Nichol went on to lead the Generic Reformation — a rather obvious confirmation that Weston had been right to give his two closest confidants wholly separate roles. But one which Nichol failed to grasp. In a rare newspaper interview in 1993, Weston had allowed that "Dave Nichol has launched more failed products than anyone I know. On the other hand, he has launched more products than anyone in the history of the world." That too, Nichol chose to regard as a stinging insult.

Everyone acted badly in the end of that affair. The contribution of the Nichol persona in turning Loblaw into a food theatre where there was a new performance each week was underappreciated by his fellow musketeers. But Nichol made the greater error in forgetting that Loblaw had made him. Weston pumped $20 million a year into Nichol's bailiwick, Loblaw International Merchants. That budget paid for 150 product developers, a quality-assurance testing lab and the *Insider's Report*, whose circulation was more than 10 times greater than *TV Guide*'s. True, Nichol had a remarkable success rate: 70 per cent of his private-label offerings were still selling three years after being introduced, while the survival rate for name-brand innovations was a mere 3 per cent. But the dud rate was kept low by Nichol's assurance that he would get eye-level placement in Loblaw stores for his President's Choice Spring Green Bath and Shower Gelee, Exact vitamins and Teddy's Choice plush toys. He could also yank a product immediately upon consulting Loblaw's state-of-the-art inventory control system, which told him on a daily basis how his items were faring in hundreds of stores across the country. It was the absence of such resources that kept grocers like Oshawa Group and the Publix chain in Florida from making a success of their copycat generic programs.

They didn't have the commitment or the buying power of the world's 10th-largest grocery retailer as measured by profits, and the first truly national grocery operation in North America.

Can pettiness and a misplaced sense of mutual betrayal really loom so large in the fortunes of a great corporation? Consider that if he hadn't had a falling out with his superiors at NCR, Thomas Watson would not have gone off to found the modern IBM. If William Shockley hadn't bullied his young lab rats, they wouldn't have left to create Intel. So it goes. At Fort Belevdere, the Weston estate in England where former resident Edward VIII renounced the throne for Wallis Simpson, Galen accepted the abdication of Dave Nichol. Weston had offered Nichol a substantial raise and more autonomy in a bid to keep him. But Nichol was now intent on joining his new best friend Gerry Pencer at Cott, where he was to become, for the first time, a real president.

That would be one of the worst career moves of the century. Pencer was an erratic financier who had never quite lived down rumours of Mafia ties. In the 1980s, he had become a cropper with a scheme to build what he described as the first financial supermarket in Canada. Pencer's handiwork, a $2-billion conglomerate known as Financial Trustco, had collapsed amid allegations of accounting irregularities. Now he was proposing to turn Dave Nichol himself into a "world brand," an assembler of private-label programs for merchants around the globe whom Pencer predicted would soon become "the next General Foods." When Nichol left Loblaw for Cott, then riding high on the PC Cola phenomenon, the latter's stock-market value was several hundred million dollars greater than that of George Weston Ltd., one of the oldest publicly traded companies in Canada. All things seemed possible.

Then the short-sellers began to attack, feeding on rumours that Pencer's former association with fancy bookkeeping had followed him to Cott. Loblaw, perceiving that Cott intended to become its competitor in private-label merchandising, cut back on its orders of Cott soft drinks. Other grocers, in the U.S. and elsewhere, began to wonder if Cott was a bottling company or a stock-market promotion. The firm was wildly overleveraged after rapidly expanding its bottling operations in the U.S., and began to bleed copious amounts of red ink. Less than three years after Nichol's arrival at Cott, Pencer shut down Nichol's international food operation and showed him the door. In a final indignity, the quixotic Pencer, who died in 1998 of brain cancer, publicly rued his own break with Weston. "Why would I do that to my biggest customer?" Pencer wrote in a posthumously published autobiography. "Nichol was a trophy, and until I had the trophy, I wasn't happy."

Nichol had been sorely used. In 2000, he was peddling illuminated dog collars for the Petsmart chain. He couldn't sort out his feelings toward Weston. Nichol had a "profound regret" over the split. But then, he also believed that during his final months at Loblaw, Weston had put the large U.S. detective agency Kroll Associates on his case. Weston had an obsession about prohibiting his executives from trading in the stock of supplier companies. There had been rumours, ultimately proved false, that Nichol had profited by $100 million on secret purchases of Cott stock. Weston would not confirm or deny that he had looked into Nichol's affairs, but Nichol was sure it was true.

"What he was doing," cried Nichol, "was questioning my integrity! I was his best man. He was my best man! I am the godfather to his first child!"

> In every decade there have been a husband and wife blessed with such a concatenation of wealth, looks, power, and style that it seems as though the gods of good fortune have been working overtime on their behalf. Each of these golden couples summed up the aspirations of their peak moment, defining what a pairing of those at the top might be.
> — *Vanity Fair* in 1990, equating Galen and Hilary Weston with Bill and Babe Paley, Jack and Jackie Kennedy, Gianni and Marella Agnelli, and Prince Charles and Princess Diana

WILLIARD GORDON Galen Weston was rich. With an estimated net worth of $4.4 billion in 2000, he was among the 100 richest men in the world. He wasn't in Bill Gates territory, for sure. But rich enough to be among the dozen or so wealthiest people in each of Canada, England and Ireland, the places that meant the most to him.

Weston was also beautiful. Not just in the sense of "the beautiful people," with the social graces and wealthy accoutrements that implies. Acquaintances seldom failed to remark that he was an extraordinarily handsome man, bearing no outward sign of having suffered the rigors of a prolonged corporate turnaround. Trim, tanned and athletic at 60, he was the sort of man who could dominate a room on good looks alone. That was a blessing in more ways than one. For in contrast to a father given to populist bonhomie, Galen could be shy in large gatherings. He fell back on the device of self-deprecation to put himself and others at ease. He stood six-foot-one, and his perfectly coifed sweep of silver hair gave him the aristocratic bearing of a 19th-century Rothschild.

Weston was a product of new money and old. He bridged the era of grasping, guttural tycoons like Roy Thomson ("For enough money, I'd work in hell") and a new age of cybergeek billionaires who often lacked the wit to realize their sudden wealth was in large degree accidental. The absence of worry lines on Weston's face as he entered his seventh decade suggested dynastic power that was both deliberative and sustainable. It also gave some people the idea that Galen Weston was a lightweight. "I think that Galen has been afflicted with the image of being a polo player and the friend of the Prince of Wales," said his wife, Hilary, "as if that's the only thing he's ever done in his life. And that irritates me."

For the longest time, the precise nature of Weston's role at Loblaw was known only to his managers. Never one to seek the limelight, Weston disappeared almost entirely from public view in the 1980s. It wasn't difficult to understand why.

In August 1983, the same Provisional IRA squad that succeeded in murdering Earl Mountbatten was foiled in a kidnap attempt on the Westons at Roundwood Park, the family's 17th-century castle 25 kilometres south of Dublin. Warned in advance, Weston had decamped to Fort Belvedere, his home on the grounds of the Royal Family's Windsor castle. While Ireland's anti-terrorist Garda force was gunning down five of the seven IRA assailants who raided his Irish estate, Weston was playing polo with the Maple Leafs, a team of professionals and amateurs he sponsored and whose best-known member was Prince Charles. Weston tried to downplay the incident by marvelling that the attackers hadn't done their homework. "Everyone knew I'd be in England playing polo this weekend," he offered, noting that the Maple Leafs match had been well advertised. But the Provos soon struck again, holding one of Weston's Irish executives hostage for two weeks.

Weston took to driving about Toronto in a beat-up used car and changing his route to work each day, and well into the 1990s he travelled under aliases. More than ever, he deferred to Currie and Nichol as spokesmen for Loblaw and George Weston Ltd. Which was not to say the Westons had become invisible. No small part of the Weston mystique arose from Hilary's skill at granting strategic interviews to art and architecture publications which could be relied upon to showcase her decorating talents at the Weston homes in England, Forest Hill and Palm Beach without prying into matters the family wished to keep private.

In the pages of upmarket gossip titles such as *Tatler* and *Country Estate*, Hilary Mary Frayne was invariably presented as a rags-to-riches member of the International Best-Dressed List Hall of Fame. In her hard-scrabble teens, the Irish-born waif from the seaside town of Dunleary had turned to modelling to support her family after her father's death. In 1966, she married Ireland's most eligible bachelor, a carpetbagger from Canada who first came to know her from billboards in which she appeared wearing hot pants and Sheer Dynamite stockings. The Westons were also celebrated for their offshore friends — the Begum Aga Khan, Queen Noor of Jordan and, of course, the Prince of Wales, a frequent beneficiary of Weston's largesse. (Galen covered the expense of boarding nine of Charles's ponies at Belvedere Farm, and helped bankroll his quixotic mission to turn back the clock on modern architecture.) Society pages also reported on the offshore education, at Oxford and Harvard, respectively, of the "Irish twins" born to the golden couple in 1972, Alannah and Galen Jr.

Weston did little to dispel his image as an absentee owner. Even when he was on site at Loblaw, which was more often than outsiders realized, so discreet had been his exercise of power that he was sometimes thought to be missing in action. He was unfailingly polite. Certainly he did not like to play the heavy. His name seemed well chosen — Galen is derived from the Greek for "healer, peace." In contrast to his top hired hands, Weston had no taste for confrontations. In the early stages of the Loblaw turnaround, Weston employed consultants as shock troops to visit store managers with a heads-up that they faced summary execution if their numbers didn't improve. Sometime later Weston would appear administering the balm of his personal confidence in those same managers and their ability to help him rescue the company. Much later, when Weston promoted Currie over Nichol's head, he chose not to impart the news to his former college buddy. He gave Currie that delicate task.

The abundance of extraordinarily capable surrogates to whom Weston delegated the task of publicly articulating his turnaround strategy gave Weston's own brother Garry the impression that Galen was something of a loafer. "He has recruited some very good executives and leaves them in charge," said Garry, who had increased the stock-market value of Associated British Foods, the non-North American arm of the Weston family business, from $200 million to $5 billion during a 32-year career at ABF. "That leaves him with a lot of time for his social life."

Garry Weston was a master at creating "shareholder value." He had done that by cutting ABF's losses and retreating from businesses in which his father had once been a significant force — British grocery retailing, for example. He was proud of inventing Wagon Wheels and making them one of the most popular biscuits in Britain. But Garry was not one for lavish spending on businesses that needed to be rebuilt or created from scratch. He had enriched ABF shareholders in large part through the streamlining and astutely timed sale of various chunks of Garfield's legacy.

Garry had not been particularly close to his father. He rejected as "a piece of stupidity" the widely held assumption that Garfield had given his sons an exhaustive tutorial in the family firm. "I taught myself to run the business," he snapped. Galen, by contrast, worshipped his father's memory. He remembered being kept at day schools rather than sent off to boarding school "so that we would hear what my father had been doing during the day, the problems and successes he was having." It had been a charmed life for a child. There had been hot biscuits fresh out of the oven during frequent factory tours. And there were post-theatre visits to Fortnum & Mason after the store had closed, where Galen could make his own ice cream sodas and sundaes. He remembered the affection that Britons had for his father. At the height of the Battle of Britain in 1940, Garfield had donated £100,000 to pay for new Spitfires to replace those lost in dogfights over the English Channel. During the war years, while he served as a member of the British House of Commons for the riding of Macclesfield, Weston donated still more funds for everything from tank-building campaigns to radios for Canadian troops. Weston and New Brunswick native Max Aitken (Lord Beaverbrook), who served as Winston Churchill's minister of war materials production, gave Britons a favourable impression of Canadian business magnates. In contrast, Joseph Kennedy, America's multimillionaire ambassador to Britain, had fled to his native Massachusetts as the Nazis approached, explaining that the island nation was doomed. In 2000, Britons of a certain age could not say Joe Kennedy's name without spitting. Garfield Weston was still remembered as the Canadian food baron who had not sought refuge in his homeland during the worst of the Blitz. "He was determined to keep us all in England and go through the bombs," said Galen, "and if we got hit, we all got hit."

What Galen admired, but also struggled with, was Garfield's indomitable spirit of empire building. "He went over the horizon and planted the flag," said Weston, "and got the whole thing going." Galen, more his father's son than Garry, was happiest when in growth mode. The Loblaw turnaround was showing only the most tentative signs of success in 1979 when Weston made a $488-million bid to acquire 51 per cent of Canada's largest retailer, Hudson's Bay Co. HBC operated the Bay, Simpsons and Zellers department-store chains, and its $7 billion in revenues equalled about 10 per cent of all retail sales in Canada. (Roy Thomson's son, Ken, won the company with a higher bid, and soon regretted his overconfidence in thinking he could revive the ailing firm.) As a consolation prize, Weston settled for repatriating the carriage-trade retailer Holt Renfrew & Co. from its U.S. owners in 1986 for $43 million. "Holts," founded as a fur-trading enterprise in Quebec City in 1838, operated 11 specialty department stores across Canada in 2000, and with deputy chairman Hilary Weston at the helm, it became the nation's premier showcase for designers including Giorgio Armani, Jil Sander, Chloe and Donna Karan. A decade after the Holts purchase, Weston was thwarted in an effort to buy its counterpart in menswear, the upscale Harry Rosen chain, when its namesake founder succeeded in buying back all of the shares he didn't already own.

Weston experienced still more frustration with his foray into luxury real-estate development. In this, he was repeating the misfortunes of his father, whose exclusive resort in Jamaica, Frenchman's Cove, attracted guests such as Picasso, Dylan Thomas and members of the Rockefeller clan in the 1960s, but later succumbed to a prolonged slump in tourism, triggered by political unrest on the island.

Galen Weston seemed to be tempting a similar fate with Windsor, an innovative planned residential project in southern Florida. The 416-acre gated community, eight miles north of Vero Beach on a narrow spit of coastal land between the Atlantic Ocean and the Indian River, was jointly developed by the Westons and a local couple, Geoffrey and Jorie Butler Kent, with Hilary as the project's design director. Notoriety was ensured by the developers' choice of architects — the pioneering town planners Andre Duany and Elizabeth Plater-Zybeck, who were in the vanguard of an architectural movement called the New Urbanism. Most famously at Seaside, a middle-class planned community on Florida's Gulf coast, the Duany and Plater-Zybeck partnership was celebrated in the early 1990s for rejecting the sterility of Modernism with its playful structures that recalled familiar design elements of previous centuries. But it was also accused of conceiving gentrified towns of white-picket-fence conformity whose imagined purity existed only in Disney pictures.

Windsor conformed to the luxury-resort stereotype with such amenities as polo fields, tennis courts, riding trails, a private ocean beach and a golf course designed by Robert Trent Jones. Otherwise, however, Windsor marked a sharp break with standard practice in upscale community development. Its courtyard houses, with enclosed front and side yards, were packed close together on small lots, a sharp break with the prevalent model of low-slung suburban style houses on large lots. The Westons were taking a big risk. Windsor was offering small-town intimacy to a clientele that typically sought privacy. "If successful, Windsor will indicate that affluent home owners have an interest in, and appreciation of, the benefits of community that result from compact planning," said U.S. design consultant Peter Katz. "This theory, once confirmed, will no doubt influence the design of future towns and villages catering to a much broader spectrum of potential buyers — both the affluent and the not-so-affluent."

The Windsor test case got off to a rough start. Vero Beach was becoming overcrowded with luxury residential developments, and the town's former mayor complained that Weston was trying to build "an elite colony of supposedly superior people." Buyers for the Windsor townsites were slow to emerge. With an agonizing sense that he was betraying his friend, even Dave Nichol had resisted Windsor's charms, endlessly putting off his stated plans to buy a house there because he was alienated by its snobbish image.

Finding few takers for Windsor's 300 villa residences, priced at about $1 million each, Weston was forced into some uncharacteristic gaucheries. Prince Charles was prevailed upon to impart some royal cachet by playing a well-publicized polo match at Windsor. And Weston consented to one of Hilary's strategic encounters with the press. Unfortunately, in his determination to build up Galen, a *Vanity Fair* correspondent found it necessary to tear down Garry. The latter was accustomed to learning from media accounts that he lacked Galen's charisma and imagination in business. Until now, however, he had not known that he also lacked friends and wasn't especially likeable. It was then that Garry decided to share with London's *Financial Times* his impression that Galen was a playboy.

Garry had misread his younger brother. The usual sibling rivalry and a considerable geographic remove obscured Garry's view of what was happening in North America. (Well into the 1990s, Garry and Galen sat on each other's boards, but Garry did not attend the directors meetings of the Canadian firms.) The Weston mystique only added to the confusion. It would take the shock of Nichol's departure, and Hilary's appointment in 1997 to the post of Lieutenant-Governor of Ontario — the British Crown's representative in that province — to open the family company and the family itself to greater scrutiny. A more complete picture of this high-society couple began to emerge. More coverage was given, for instance, to the activities of a Weston charitable foundation, which, among other things, had for several years been paying the tuition of dozens of Canadian scholars whose academic promise was not matched by financial means. It now became widely known that Galen's long-standing support of Daily Bread, Canada's biggest food bank, which supplied 80 satellite food banks in Southern Ontario, far outstripped his support for, say, the Prince of Wales's Institute of Architecture in London. In 2000, Weston joined 20 other CEOs in a crusade to shame Ottawa into making good on its 10-year-old promise to eradicate child poverty. In a lower-profile project, Weston tried to rescue the impecunious Canadian architect Arthur Erickson from looming bankruptcy. While he was still reluctant to submit to media interviews, Weston became more willing to make sporadic appearances in the spotlight, campaigning for the landmark free trade agreement between Canada and the U.S. and promoting Toronto's Royal Agricultural Winter Fair during a stint as president of that venerable institution.

All along, Weston had not shied from the difficult task of sacking managers who didn't fall into line behind the turnaround plan. And the tough decisions about which businesses to abandon and which to target for huge doses of expansion capital had always been made by the owner. Nichol had acknowledged as much in a rare expression of candour about the boss many years earlier. "Galen keeps tight control on people decisions, the most important aspect of controlling the company," Nichol said. "He passes on all of them, controls the breeding lines of the organization."

In Nichol's absence, Weston finally took on the role of spokesman for his vision of limitless growth. This he aimed to finance, in large part, with one last purge of chronically mediocre assets. In a sell-off campaign that began in the mid-1990s, Weston shed Loblaw's remaining U.S. stores, the E. B. Eddy forest products operations, the Neilson and Cadbury candy bar lines, and B.C. Packers and its Clover Leaf brand. The proceeds of those sales did not go to Weston and the other shareholders. Instead, Weston commited a staggering $3.3 billion to buying, building and renovating still more stores in Canada, and expanding the food manufacturing side of the business with the purchase of bagel bakeries and pie makers in the U.S.

In 1998, Weston made the largest single investment in his family's history. For $1.7 billion, Loblaw acquired the 348 stores of Provigo Inc., Quebec's largest grocery chain. The deal spoke to Weston's determination to crack Canada's second-largest food market. Beginning with its thwarted bid for Steinberg a decade earlier, Loblaw had been frozen out of the province by nationalist political regimes in Quebec City that preferred to keep local grocery chains in "non-foreign" hands.

Making full use of his considerable diplomatic skills, Weston finally gained his Quebec foothold with commitments not to lay off any employees at the barely profitable Provigo, and to favour local suppliers.

Loblaw's primary focus was still on merchandise. In 2000, it became the first grocery chain in North America to stock foods that had not been genetically modified. But no retailer could match Loblaw in the attention it lavished on the venues in which its merchandise was sold. In the 1990s, Currie was spending hundreds of millions of dollars to create one-stop shopping outlets that boasted cafés, cooking schools, fitness centres and babysitting services. While competitors were still inclined to make neighbourhoods conform to the style of store they wished to operate, Loblaw tried to start from scratch, imagining what type of store a particular community might want. "We do our research to meet the consumers' needs," Currie said, "and then put walls around it."

The enormity of a Loblaws superstore erected in west-end Toronto in the mid-1990s was disguised by red-brick cladding and a false second storey of small square windows, giving the effect of a 1930s series of storefronts, in keeping with the working-class district in which it was located. By contrast, the Queen's Quay Market on the Toronto waterfront, with its cheerful white aluminum façade, large overhanging roof and enormous skylights as a welcome alternative to harsh fluorescent lighting, was meant to evoke the image of a maritime customs house. The first two-storey North American supermarket was ranked in 2000 by the British design magazine *Wallpaper* as one of the world's five top retail outlets. Its design, said Queen's Quay architect Leslie Rebanks, was inspired by the tradition in which shoppers "always had the impulse to treat their markets and public squares as a great meeting place, not just a sanitized box where you buy food wrapped in styrofoam."

In an era of "grazing," when many shoppers were abandoning the big weekly supermarket expedition in favour of dropping into a grocery store several times a week for a few items, Weston was relentless in searching for ways to making that chore less onerous. In 2000, Loblaw began a trial run of electronic checkouts where customers could scan their own purchases. This "cashier-less counter" would speed checkout time and had the estimated potential of trimming labour costs by 0.25 per cent to 0.5 per cent — or as much as $100 million for a company the size of Loblaw.

"I like to believe that at least some of the 12 million customers who shop with us every week actually enjoy the experience," said Weston. He only mused about formalizing Loblaw's growing status as a New Age dating centre. But he had no hestitation about splurging on in-store jazz concerts, and began to put folk singers and tenors on the payroll. Seventy years earlier, band leader Percy Faith launched his career as first violinist with the studio orchestra of Weston's William Neilson Co. "Who knows?" Galen said. "Maybe the next Pavarotti will get his start in a Loblaws store."

There was, to be sure, a cloud on the horizon. It was described best, perhaps, by the Internet enthusiast John Roth. "Imagine what the world will be like when Amazon.com-type companies are the norm," said the CEO of Nortel Networks Corp., a leader in making the fibre-optic networks that most of the world's Internet traffic travelled on. "Why scour local retail outlets for particular goods when you can access dealers across a broad territory, examine quality, compare prices, and have the goods delivered by courier within 24 hours? Why have stores except for their entertainment value or maybe ensuring the right fit?"

In the U.S., Web-based entrepreneurs had already begun to challenge the hegemony of traditional supermarket chains. By 2000, on-line grocery start-ups such as Peapod, Webvan and Priceline were gaining the attention of both shoppers and investors. "Webvan, with sales of only $790,000, just went public with a $4-billion price tag," Weston noted in January 2000. "Incredible! Is there such an opportunity for Loblaw? If there is, we will find it!"

Web food retailing got off to an inauspicious start. Webvan's shares collapsed in the spring of 2000 as its start-up costs mounted, and a similarly troubled Peapod was absorbed by the Dutch grocery giant Royal Ahold. Loblaw's own pilot project in E-grocery retailing, unveiled in February 2000 in Mississauga, Ontario, was a disappointment in the early going. Among other problems, Loblaw found that often no one was at home when it attempted to deliver orders placed by online shoppers.

The venture wasn't scrapped, however. Weston kept experimenting, certain he would develop a winning model. Perhaps, he said, it would make more sense for Web shoppers to pick up their purchases at a traditional Loblaw store or from a new network of mini-warehouses. Eventually, he was sure, money could be made by catering to shoppers who wanted to avoid wandering around a cavernous supermarket. It was for that reason he had pursued a twin-track strategy of building superstores for shoppers who still demanded a cornucopia of selection while continuing to refine his more modest-sized neighbourhood and small-town stores. The latter outlets, said demographic experts, would continue to find favour with on-line shoppers who still preferred to buy certain items, such as fresh meat and produce, in person. The demographers also noted that Web shopping tended to undermine consumer loyalty to national brands. That was a plus for grocers with strong house-brand portfolios.

As usual, Weston was doing his homework. In the U.S., on-line grocery start-ups were faring poorly in comparison with Amazon.com and other Web vendors who dealt in books, music and other non-food items. In Europe, by contrast, traditional grocers such as Tesco, Carrefour and Germany's Metro chain were meeting with considerable success in on-line food sales. Like Loblaw, they had the natural advantage over start-ups in already owning the means of distribution — the warehouses, trucks and computerized inventory control systems (the absence of which was hobbling U.S. Web grocers that were plagued with late delivery problems).

Just as Amazon had branched out from books into music, gifts and other items, it was expected that the dominant on-line grocers would be those that offered more than just food. "Web businesses are most successful," said London grocery analyst Mike Dennis, "where they focus on high net-worth individuals — the time-poor, dual-income families with one or two children." Those shoppers wanted their Web grocer to provide them with such extras as dry-cleaning servic-es and video rentals. The evolution of Loblaw's larger stores into one-stop empo-ria would give it a decided lead over Web start-ups in providing online shoppers with a wide range of non-food goods and services.

IN ITS 118TH YEAR, George Weston Ltd. was still a growth story in an industry that measured progress in single-digit percentage increases in sales. Its revenues had increased fourfold, to more than $20 billion, since Galen's arrival. And sales per square foot at Loblaw Cos.' stores had improved from $100 in the dark days of 1971 to $554 at the turn of the century. In the 1990s, Loblaw's revenues grew at twice the industry average, to $18.8 billion in 1999. In the post-Nichol era, the generic revolution had continued, with sales of private-label goods increasing from $1.5 billion to more than $2 billion by 2000 — or about 16 per cent of the Weston group's total revenues from food distribution. In 1986, there had been 476 No Name and President's Choice items. In 1998 alone, Loblaw embellished its existing generic line with a staggering 750 new products.

In the post-*Garfield* era, profits at George Weston Ltd. hit $670 million in 1998, bettering Garfield's personal best of $17.5 million in 1966. In the last decade of the century, Galen had boosted the stock-market value of George Weston Ltd. from $2 billion to $7 billion. Bay Street expected further gains. "Loblaw is grow-ing faster than the industry because it is a world-class retailer and marketer, in a league with the Europeans and well ahead of its U.S. counterparts," said Patricia A. Baker, retailing analyst at the Montreal office of Merrill Lynch & Co. "This isn't readily appreciated unless one pays a visit to food retailers in the U.S. and the U.K., as I have. The U.S. grocers are relying on 'synergies' from acquisitions. Loblaw is able to generate remarkable growth from its existing stores."

George Weston Ltd. had survived a Depression, two world wars and, as Galen Weston liked to say, "family leadership over three generations, and more especial-ly, some 30 years in the hands of this particular member of the third generation." It had done so because Galen Weston had the daring his grandfather lacked and the patience for administration so little evident in the later stages of his father's stewardship of the firm.

There was that, and a rare humility besides. For his new headquarters, erected in the 1970s, Weston had wanted "a quality-and-value image, something more than a public view of us as just another cheap supermarket outfit." The building, like the redesigned Moore-Bayview store and the packaging for many of the Loblaw house-brand products, won international design awards. A series of photographs of Bulgarian artist Christo's *Running Fence* in the executive suite suggested Weston's own fascination with whimsical variations on familiar icons. Leslie Rebanks, whose long career as a store architect for Loblaw began with the commission to design the Weston Centre, met with his client to plan the octagonal stainless steel tower. "I asked Galen at the outset, 'How does one run a billion-dollar concern?'" Rebanks said. "'I don't know. I'm still learning,' was the reply."

Galen Jr., Weston hoped, would come to regard the family firm with a similar sense of wonder and curiosity. Daughter Alannah was not involved in the business. But at age 30, Galen Jr., nicknamed "G2," was already a junior executive at Loblaw, having undergone an apprenticeship similar to his father's.

From the 21st floor of the Weston tower, where Galen had his office, he could make out the magnificent crypt of the Eaton family in Mount Pleasant Cemetery. It was a scaled-down version of the Lincoln Memorial, with 22 columns and an entrance guarded by a pair of lions. It was the most prominent memorial in Canada's largest burial ground, and one of the few remaining tangible symbols of what had once been the greatest family-owned department store in the world.

In the aftermath of T. Eaton Co.'s bankruptcy in 1999, the great-grandchildren of founder Timothy Eaton explained that they had been victims of demographic forces beyond their control. But in the lassitude of their governance, the boys had simply let the world pass them by. There was no crime in that. The scions of most family enterprises are eventually crushed by the dead weight of inherited wealth. Few manage to elude what Oscar Wilde called "that terrible *taedium vitae* that comes on those to whom life denies nothing."

Directly across from the Eaton memorial in the Mount Pleasant burial grounds was the discreet Weston monument, six slender columns resting on a base inscribed with the family motto. The words had been selected by Garfield: "'Tis not the gales, but the set of your sails that determines the way you go."

Among Galen Weston's natural gifts is a sense of the inevitability of his success, a quality essential in any entrepreneur. But it is matched by an entrepreneurial capacity for hard work, and an iron stomach in tolerating risks. "You put in the hours and apply the virtue of persistence," Weston has said, "and the law of justice says it will come through for you." He conceded Garry's point that their father had not eased their way into the business. And he was grateful. "I was brought up with an ethic that when you got up each morning it was to achieve something," he said. "Otherwise, you're a failure. That's a pretty good background, if it doesn't crack you."

2

MAX WARD

From bush pilot to operator of the
world's classiest charter airline

*"Wardair had thrilled me and nearly killed me,
and I loved it with a passion born of joy and rage."*
— Max Ward

ON JUNE 8, 1968, a sunny clear morning in Edmonton, the Ward household was a happy maelstrom of last-minute preparations. Gai Ward and her bridesmaids were readying themselves for her wedding later that day. The father of the bride, as often happens on these occasions, had elected to keep a safe distance from the hectic home front. Instead, Max Ward spent the better part of the day of his eldest daughter's wedding with Sandy McTaggart, a friend with a hot-air balloon who needed to put in a few more hours of flying time before he could take up paying passengers.

Ward's job was to tag along in the chase car. But the future Companion in the Order of Icarus, and an aviator since age 20, hadn't schlepped out to the hamlet of Wetaskiwin south of Edmonton only to miss the chance to go ballooning for the first time. After a couple of launches and landings, McTaggart was lifting off again when Ward scrambled into the basket, uninvited. He was soon enjoying the sensation of being carried gently in whatever direction the slight wind that day provided.

This blissful journey was to end abruptly, however. Ward noticed that the background hiss of the propane-fired burner that fed hot air into the balloon had stopped. They were out of propane. The fire went out of the burner, and the balloon began an unscheduled descent — straight into a tangle of high-tension wires

55

on a major power line. McTaggart yelled that they'd have to jump. As the wires that joined the basket to the balloon began to spark on contact with the electrical lines, Ward agreed. McTaggart executed a smart dive and roll, and came out standing on the ground below. Ward, not so expert, also went into a roll as he hit the ground. But he caught his left hand underneath him.

Less than a year earlier, Ward had taken his company public with an initial offering of shares in order to convey an image of stability to Wardair Ltd., a former bush-pilot operation that aspired to join the elite ranks of the world's full-fledged scheduled carriers. In the ambulance ride back to town, the CEO of Canada's biggest publicly traded airline was shot full of painkillers for his broken wrist and multiple contusions. But nothing could be done for his two black eyes and wounded dignity.

"That evening, when Gai sailed serenely down the aisle, a vision of beauty," Ward later recalled, "she travelled on the arm of what appeared to be a refugee from a bar-room brawl — black-eyed, bandaged, limping, and unlovely. As we heaved up in front of the minister, he looked from Gai to me, back to Gai, back to me, and broke into a totally unclerical cackle. The last time he had seen me, at the rehearsal the night before, I had looked somewhat different."

Max Ward had built his airline by design, not accident. But mishaps seemed to mark every turning point in Ward's aviation career. He cracked up his very first plane, a two-seater de Havilland Fox Moth, on its maiden flight in 1946. The next four decades would bring an endless series of narrow escapes, two of which nearly cost him his life. The jaws of bankruptcy would open wide many times, poised to finish Ward almost every time he traded in his planes for a new generation of advanced aircraft. And bureaucrats would repeatedly threaten to shut down Wardair. They were provoked by Ward's constant rebellion against rules constraining any upstart who dared to challenge state-owned Air Canada and its only significant rival, CP Air, an arm of the mighty Canadian Pacific Ltd.

But ordeals seemed only to toughen Ward. As an instructor of military aviators in World War Two, he had managed to land safely after a student pilot broke formation and smashed into his flimsy Anson trainer over the farmers' fields of Hagersville, Ontario. As a pioneer bush pilot, Ward had hauled everything from pianos and dog teams to firefighting rigs and the corpses of murder victims across the Far North, and survived a dozen times when a failed engine stranded him on a desolate lake or mountainside. He once landed at his Yellowknife home base to learn that his house had been destroyed. His wife, Marjorie, had spotted flames leaping from a stovepipe just in time to get herself and the two Ward children out of their two-room house before it was gutted. After those trials, what were escalating debt payments, price wars and endless regulatory interference — the worst that life south of the 60th parallel could throw at him?

And by 1985, it appeared that Ward had triumphed over the odds. Wardair carried 1.6 million passengers that year. Its route system stretched from Alert in the Northwest Territories to Venezuela, and from Honolulu to Frankfurt. The financial brinksmanship that characterized so much of Wardair's past had given way to sound profitability. Wardair posted 1985 earnings of $24 million on revenues of $474 million. A chorus of naysayers had insisted that the Wardair formula of first-class amenities at economy-class fares could not work. Now it looked like they were wrong. Ward was not only a financial success, he was one of Canada's most popular businessmen. He was the champion of budget-minded vacationers who had spearheaded the development of the cheap charter market. Ward had also won grudging respect from rivals as the gutsy entrepreneur who risked his company to introduce Boeing and Airbus jetliners to Canadian skies; Wardair had also been the first carrier to take a chance on the Canadian-designed Dash short-takeoff-and-landing aircraft on routes in Canada.

Ward had ferried snow-weary Canadians to the Caribbean and Mexico, carried Muslims to Mecca, rescued Vietnamese refugees from the Far East and shepherded Queen Elizabeth II and Prince Philip on royal tours of the Canadian North. The quality of Wardair's inflight food and cabin service was so outstanding that international aviation authorities repeatedly lauded Wardair as the world's finest airline, ahead of giants like British Airways and the upscale carriers Swissair and Cathay Pacific. When he won Ottawa's approval to become a full-service scheduled airline in 1986, after three decades of relentless lobbying, Ward finally got his chance to go head to head with Air Canada and Canadian Airlines (the old CP Air). And with that, Ward had realized every bush pilot's dream. He had turned a $10,000 investment in his first Fox Moth into an international airline. It was one of the few large carriers in the world still majority-owned and operated by its founder. More than a decade later, an Air Canada captain, Darryl Gunn, would say that "Max Ward is still — will always be — a hero to all pilots."

But having achieved major-league status, Ward would have to pay dearly for the prize. His fleet of enormous Boeing 747s and DC-10s was tailored to the overseas charter market. It was all wrong for short-hop flights among Canadian cities, where Wardair had just been given clearance to compete with Air Canada and Canadian Airlines on the nation's busiest routes. The long wait for Ottawa's blessing to his scheduled-carrier ambitions had held Ward back from buying such planes. He would have to replace his entire fleet. Ward scrambled to trade in his long-range aircraft for smaller, more fuel-efficient Airbus 310s, MD-88s and Fokker F100s. He would need 55 new aircraft, to be purchased at a staggering cost of about $1 billion.

Ward was now pitting himself against two bigger competitors that had operated as scheduled carriers for decades. Their large fleets could easily be reconfigured to put the right-sized plane on each route. Air Canada and Canadian Airlines had a lock on the best terminals and gates at airports. They shared a sophisticated computer reservations system. They had developed frequent flier programs and bonus incentive schemes to woo passengers and travel agents, respectively. And with their deep pockets, Ward's entrenched rivals would be able to absorb the cost of slashing fares to match his own discount prices in any contest over market share.

Ward had no illusions about his chances in that dogfight. "Had we been permitted to compete in scheduled services when the computer-reservations system first came into being, we would have had the necessary strength in place in that area," he said. "Had we been able to build a scheduled airline step by step we would have had public awareness of our service; we would have had a secure base to work upon, because we had by far the best productivity and the dedication to provide a good service."

Yet Ward was pretty much forced to join the big leagues. His success in the charter market, long ignored by Air Canada and Canadian Airlines, was now attracting their predatory attention. And upstart charter firms such as Canada 3000 were also nibbling at his core franchise. If it remained solely in charters, Wardair would be relegated to a supporting role in the industry. "We had not come so far, worked so hard, risked so much, to become a feeder line to someone else's company," Ward said. "So it was obvious our only hope was to turn ourselves into an instant scheduled airline."

And so a new Wardair took to the skies. It quickly won a following among business commuters, for whom Wardair's luxe service came as a delightful surprise. Its speed in taking market share from Air Canada and Canadian Airlines in key Central Canadian cities was all the more startling given that its traditional base was in the West.

But the race to win passengers wasn't being won fast enough. In remaking itself overnight, Wardair had taken on a huge debt load. And the late 1980s was a terrible time for borrowers. In an overheated economy, interest rates on Ward's short-term borrowings had climbed into double digits.

Wardair was about to hit the wall. By the fall of 1988, after just two years as a scheduled carrier, Wardair was bracing for a loss of $100 million. There were all kinds of drains on its cash flow. A prodigious sum had been spent on a promotional blitz. There were costs for retraining pilots and maintenance crews on a new fleet of planes. And price wars had cut deeply into revenue. The big boys on the block were hurting too, victims of overcapacity that was crippling the industry worldwide. But Wardair could not match the financial heft of its archrivals. Ward's bankers began to call their loans. Without a quick capital infusion of $200 million to refinance its debt, Wardair would soon be out of business.

Most mornings, Ward drove from his condominium on the Toronto waterfront to Pearson International Airport. The sprawling Wardair hangar and headquarters complex at Pearson, built a few years earlier for $24 million, never failed to cheer him. It was a symbol of how far he'd come in 30 years from the tent-frame structure on the edge of Yellowknife's Back Bay that Wardair once called home.

On January 18, 1989, however, Ward headed downtown for a planned meeting with an old adversary. On the agenda was the possible sale of his company to Canadian Airlines.

As he made his way along Lakeshore Boulevard, Canada's best-known aviation entrepreneur once again ran through the alternatives to the drastic step he was about to take. "Wardair had given me a good life, and more adventure than I cared to think about," he said. "It had thrilled me and nearly killed me, and I loved it with a passion born of joy and rage, triumph and frustration, pleasure and despair." Through one crisis after another, the remarkable loyalty of his passengers had pulled him through. Maybe Ward could keep them, and his independence, by going bankrupt. Many U.S. airlines had done so. He could work his way back to solvency with court protection from his creditors. But the option repulsed him. Ward had always been in debt. And in 40 years of business, he had never missed a debt payment.

Ward thought again about giving in to the blandishments of American Airlines of Dallas, which had made overtures about buying his airline. He had rejected a takeover offer from Roy Thomson, the press baron, during a particularly rough patch for Wardair in the 1960s. But Wardair was much closer to the brink this time. A deal with American would probably let Ward and his 5,200 employees hold onto their jobs, and keep the Wardair name aloft. But federal restrictions on offshore ownership of Canada's scheduled airlines would require American to accept the status of a minority owner. Even if the giant U.S. airline consented to those terms, the prospect of joining forces with a foreign airline was unpalatable.

Wardair had always been more than a business. Ward's only brush with explosive profits in the business world had come during a two-year hiatus as a homebuilder in the early 1950s. Yet he couldn't wait to plough his real-estate earnings into a new plane. Ward was a flag-waving nationalist. That made him an oddity in an industry that routinely plucked its top-level executives from the U.S. and Britain. Ward had christened his multimillion-dollar planes with the names of Canadian fighter aces and pioneering bush pilots, whom he counted among his earliest mentors. And in his frequent confrontations with Ottawa and the Montreal-based Air Canada, Ward had never disguised the pride he took in proving that an enterprise based in the West could become the class of its field. Say this for Canadian Airlines: It was based in Calgary.

At age 68, Ward was not sure he had the energy to fight another battle to keep his airline flying. This did not prevent him that January morning from wondering if he should turn the car around. "What I had set out to do was to put together one of the largest and finest scheduled airlines in the world," he said. "And if I sold out now — there was no point kidding myself about this — I would have failed."

⧗

In 1937, Trans-Canada Air Lines, now called Air Canada, was created by the federal government. The official reasons were to provide air links with remote areas of Canada which might not be served economically by the private sector, to ensure that Canadians did not have to depend on existing American airlines to travel from coast to coast and, thus, to contribute to the national dream of uniting a geographically and sociologically diverse country. In fact, Air Canada provided very little, if any, service to remote areas, which were actually served by the private sector, while Air Canada was given the best routes as the national carrier, at the expense of private sector development.
— Andrew J. Roman, *Airline Deregulaton in Canada: Why It Failed*

COMMERCIAL AVIATION in Canada began with the bush pilot — a Canadian invention. Stuart Graham became the world's first bush pilot in 1919 with his 645-mile flight from Halifax, Nova Scotia to Lac-à-la-Tortue, Quebec.

There can be no overstating the impact of bush pilots in Canada's economic development. They departed from the traditional east-west trade routes — defined first by the St. Lawrence River and the Great Lakes, then by the railways — and created the first north-south arteries. In doing so, they opened to exploration and development the vast *terra incognita* of the Canadian interior. They were the first to chart rivers and mountain ranges that were unknown to the earlier seafaring voyageurs, whose primitive maps depicted the terrain only a few miles inland from the shores of Hudson Bay and the Arctic Ocean.

These early commercial aviators were mostly retired air-force fliers working in temperatures that varied from 90 F to –65 F. They piloted the only aircraft they could afford — vintage military planes bought from surplus. They were grateful for a gravel runway but more often landed on muskeg, frozen lakes and even baseball fields. Their passengers were prospectors, trappers, lumberjacks and missionaries. And their freight was anything they could cram onto an aircraft — fish, furniture, canoes, fuel drums, diamond drill bits, cows and flour sacks. They hauled construction equipment to isolated mining camps, and made emergency flights to deliver vaccines to flu victims in isolated glacial hamlets.

It was bush pilots who unlocked the treasurehouse of gold, silver, copper and uranium in northern Quebec and Ontario, the Yukon and Northwest Territories. And it was the mining companies, for the most part, that sustained the aviators. But their passion for flying was rarely matched by acumen in business. And the boom-and-bust cycle of mining development conspired against long-term prosperity for commercial pilots. The pattern was set by Laurentide Air Services, Canada's first airline, which transported prospectors from Haileybury, Ontario to

Angliers, Quebec. It folded in 1924 after three years in operation, having never turned a profit.

That left governments to assume a primary role in nurturing the infant industry. In Europe, which was quicker than North America to herald aviation as one of the century's most important new industries, state-owned monopolies in air transport were created in France, Belgium and the Netherlands. By 1926, Weimar Germany's state airline, Luft Hansa, was larger than all of its European counterparts combined. If the future Lufthansa was a tangible expression of Germany's bid to reclaim its prewar international prestige, its former adversaries among the Allies held aviation to be no less strategically important. Britain, for instance, could not abide the destructive competition among the seven airlines operating from London. In 1924, Parliament stepped in to nationalize four of the carriers as Imperial Airways. Six decades would pass before Britain felt confident to entrust the future British Airways to private investors. And at the close of the century, Lufthansa, Air France, Alitalia and most of Europe's other flagship carriers would continue to be wards of government.

The U.S., alone among the major powers, left commercial air transport to the private operators. Washington did foster the development of United Airlines, American Airlines, Eastern Airlines, and Transcontinental and Western (TWA) with air-mail contracts in the 1920s. But it transferred those duties to the air force in the 1930s. That prompted U.S. airlines to pursue a new line of business as passenger carriers long before their peers elsewhere in the world.

Ottawa, too, revoked air-mail contracts, a move which threatened to strangle an infant industry in the cradle. It seemed to Prime Minister R. B. Bennett that civil aviation was an almost pointless novelty. Unprecedented demands were being made on the federal treasury as Canada succumbed to the Great Depression. This was not the time to be fostering an industry based on newfangled flying machines. "With 300,000 of the population receiving some form of relief," Bennett explained later, "there was very little gratification in seeing an aeroplane passing by day after day when the unfortunate owner of the soil could hardly see the aeroplane because his own crop had gone up in dust."

Yet nothing could diminish the enthusiasm of Canada's early aviators. By 1929, they were carrying more tonnage than air-transport operators in any other country. Winnipeg grain baron James Richardson, the father of commercial aviation in Canada, had lost his mail contracts. Yet he could boast in 1934 that his eight-year-old Canadian Airways Ltd. was carrying 60 per cent more freight than the entire U.S. airline industry. Canadian Airways was the world's second-largest air-transport firm, trailing only Imperial Airways in aircraft, employees and routes.

To appreciate the audacity of Ward's later endeavours, it's useful to reflect on the sad fate of Richardson's remarkable aviation firm. It would ultimately be sold to Canadian Pacific, in 1942, and form the basis of the future Canadian Airlines International.

In the 1930s, Richardson was flying into the unknown. He was testing the commercial prospects of a new industry whose primitive status was evident from an early memo to pilots that said: "There will be no stunting or wing walking without approval from Head Office." The pilots were obliged to drain oil from their planes each night to keep it from freezing on the tundra. They slept with oil-pans under their bellies. And they responded to the Winnipeg directive with a ditty of their own. "Air Mail may be lost but must not be delayed. Passengers may be delayed but not lost."

In time, of course, Ottawa did awaken to the importance of the airways. But by then its outlook would be shaped by a Depression-era distrust of business. Bennett's successor, Mackenzie King, feared the encroachment of British and American airlines on Canadian airspace. But he and his new transport minister, Clarence Decatur Howe, chose not to encourage Richardson's ambition to become Canada's flagship carrier. Canadian Airways was already a coast-to-coast operation. But it was a private enterprise at a time when capitalism was out of favour.

In the mid-1930s, Ottawa was stripping banks of the responsibility for issuing currency, and taking a direct role in everything from the marketing of prairie farmers' grain to the creation of comedy shows on the new CBC radio service. Howe, an émigré from Massachusetts who made his name building grain elevators in Northern Ontario and Manitoba, became obsessed with gaining personal control over every aspect of civil aviation in Canada. So much so, that he decided to relegate Richardson's company to the bush, rebuking a man who had commissioned Howe's own company to build grain elevators for James Richardson & Sons.

Ottawa had its reasons for pushing private operators out of the industry they had created. Memories were still fresh of the mess created by overzealous railway promoters — urged on, it must be noted, by federal and local politicians who regarded the iron horse as a spur to economic development. Their bankrupt lines had to be rescued in the early 1920s by Ottawa, which amalgamated them into a new crown corporation called the Canadian National Railways. King saw a parallel between the discredited rail barons and the flyboys. In an earlier career as an industrial consultant in the U.S., King had witnessed the chaotic rivalry among that country's hundreds of fledgling aviation outfits. Many of them were run by barnstormers who made their living from aerial acrobatics. As late as 1925, Washington was classifying all aviators as "entertainers."

King and Howe shared a disdain for the 128 private air companies that were operating in Canada in the mid-1930s. Richardson had national and even global ambitions for his enterprise. But most of Canada's air operations were one-or two-man outfits. They weren't always scrupulous about safety. They were known to overload their aircraft and court disaster by putting off costly repairs. At any given

Max Ward in 1947, newly retired from training fighter pilots for service in Europe in World War II, and his first plane, a $10,000 Fox Moth (above), which he managed to crash on its maiden flight from the factory in Toronto to his home base in Yellowknife. In his twenties, Ward ferried the essentials of life in the North, carrying everything that could be crammed into a plane — food, fuel drums, prospectors, preachers, pianos and dog teams.

Despite efforts by federal bureaucrats to stymie his audacious growth schemes, Ward was soon the top commercial operator in the North. Wardair was commissioned to airlift Queen Elizabeth and the Duke of Edinburgh during a 1978 tour of North Alberta (above). But the North could no longer contain Ward's ambitions by the 1960s when Wardair became Canada's leading champion of affordable air travel for the masses. Crew members of Ward's new Boeing 707 (left) held pineapples aloft at Gatwick Airport to celebrate an historic 7,776-statute-mile flight from Honolulu — the first non-stop flight on that route.

As it evolved from a Far North freight hauler into an international charter operation and then a full-fledged scheduled airline, Wardair outclassed its competitors in the speed at which it upgraded its fleet, trading in existing plans for the most modern aircraft in the industry. Wardair introduced Boeing and Airbus planes to the Canadian market, and was the first Canadian buyer of the Dash 7. Pictured here, at Boeing's headquarters in Seattle when Wardair took delivery of its first 747 jumbo jet in 1973, are other members of the airline's diverse fleet, including a 707 (right) and a 727. The tiny bi-plane is a replica of Ward's original Fox Moth.

time, only two of the planes operated by pioneer bush pilot Grant McConachie (a future head of CP Air) were covered by insurance. He moved the coverage around in the hope that any accident would involve a plane that was insured.

By contrast, the new Trans-Canada Air Lines was to be lavishly financed and run by the book. TCA was created by Howe and chartered with an act of Parliament in 1937. It came into the world with no planes and no staff. Yet this paper airline was to be Canada's "chosen instrument" of aviation policy. To ensure its viability, it was granted a monopoly on intercity routes and international services. TCA was to enjoy a long head start. Not until 1959, two years after Howe lost his seat in the House of Commons, did Ottawa decide to allow just one other operator, CP Air, to assume up to 25 per cent of the nation's scheduled routes. So began a duopoly that would persist for the rest of the century.

It was the private operators, however, that captured the public imagination. For its first two decades, civil aviation had been the more or less exclusive realm of air aces such as Billy Bishop, C. H. "Punch" Dickins and Wilfrid Reid "Wop" May. Every speed, distance and altitude record of these daredevils was splashed across the front pages of newspapers at home and abroad. A teenage Max Ward followed their exploits with growing fascination. But now it was time to turn the industry over to professional managers, and imported ones at that.

Howe appointed an American, former United Airlines president Phil G. Johnson, to be the first head of TCA. Johnson, in turn, recruited a few American colleagues to join him. The message seemed to be that Canadians were not up to the task of developing their own aviation industry. As late as the 1990s, a Canadian aviation historian could write that "the Americans would play an essential part in TCA until there were enough Canadians with the skills and the confidence to take over." There was, as it happened, an abundance of skilled Canadians in 1937. Which was a lucky thing for Johnson as he cobbled together TCA's first fleet of two 10-passenger planes and a crop duster. It's impossible to know how the new airline would have fared if its inaugural captain had been a Canadian. Maybe it's a moot point. The new airline was staffed from top to bottom by Canadians. Johnson spent his first year at TCA raiding Richardson's airline for pilots, and for experts in accounting, scheduling, maintenace and navigation, as well. Many of TCA's first employees reported for work wearing their Canadian Airways uniforms.

There is less ambiguity about Ottawa's early and lasting determination to enforce the favoured status of TCA and its successor, Air Canada. Howe would have been astonished to find that Canada was home to no fewer than three international airlines in the 1980s. Howe doubted even TCA's chances of survival unless it was given the right to rule the airways. "Development of two transcontinental routes across Canada would, of course, be fatal to the success of Trans-Canada," he said. There could be no serious rivals to TCA. Or "my airline," as Howe often called it.

The history of civil aviation after 1937 would be a ceaseless struggle by private operators to assert their right to share the skies with Ottawa's chosen instrument. "Air Canada was the darling of the government, and the government still made the rules," Ward noted. "I couldn't blame Canadian travellers for following the line of least resistance, when the presence of a Crown-owned airline had, for so many years, determined travel habits. We were in a ballgame where the umpire owned the bat and ball — and the home team. Not many calls went the way of the Visitors, and we were always the Visitors."

The Visitors kept showing up for games, however. And they changed the rules for everyone, even TCA.

If you are looking for perfect safety you will do well to sit on a fence and watch the birds, but if you really wish to learn you must mount a machine and become acquainted with its tricks by actual trial.

— Wilbur Wright

MAXWELL WILLIAM WARD grew up in Edmonton in the 1930s, when it was the capital of bush aviation. "The Gateway of the North," as the city billed itself, was at the end of the railway line. It was the jumping-off point to the mineral and oil and gas wealth of the Yukon and Northwest Territories. For Ottawa, it was the southern terminus of federal supply lines to remote Aboriginal communities, whose sustenance was Canada's clearest assertion of sovereignty over the Far North. For Americans, Edmonton was an important junction on the direct route to Alaska. It was also a staging round for the construction of a necklace of radar stations that Washington strung across the roof of Canada in the 1950s to defend the continent from attack by Soviet missiles.

Edmontonians were eager witnesses to the birth of an industry. They watched as the frontiers of both aviation and the Far North were rolled back.

When aviators Wiley Post and Harold Getty circumnavigated the world in eight days in 1931, their last stop before New York was Edmonton. Ward was 10 years old when the celebrated airmen touched down in his hometown. He made the half-hour walk from his home on 104th Street to the downtown thoroughfare of Portage Street (later Kingsway), a newly built avenue whose wide expanse of pavement — a rare thing in those days — had been dressed up as a landing strip for the famous fliers. When it was time for them to complete their voyage, Mounties escorted Post's plane as it taxied down Portage. And it seemed that the whole town was there to see the pair take off for the last leg of their expedition. "I only saw them from a distance through the crowd," said Ward. "But it was a heady experience. Aviators were pretty much the most exciting people in the world."

As a child, Ward built toy airplanes from Meccano pieces and bits of wood he got from a butter-box factory near his home. He hung around Blatchford Field, the future Edmonton Municipal Airport that was named for an aviation-boosting mayor. He watched his bush-pilot heroes getting their planes ready and daydreamed about joining their ranks. He never had the five dollars it cost to take a ride with the barnstorming gypsies who passed through the city. But Ward always knew he'd be a flier.

At the outbreak of World War Two, a 17-year-old Ward signed up for air-force service. "I took naturally to the air — so much so that a number of my instructors insisted, quite wrongly, that I must have had previous flying experience," he said. Ward himself became an instructor. His top marks at flight school had ruled out a tour of duty overseas. He cried all day on learning he'd be staying in Canada to teach other pilots — many of whom, it turned out, would be Englishmen.

But soon enough, Ward would be flying solo. By the time hostilities ceased, Ward had accumulated 2,800 hours of flying time. In 1946, he financed the purchase of a $10,000 Fox Moth with savings from his instructor's pay, together with funds borrowed from his father-in-law and a family friend. The Fox Moth came with wheels, floats and skis, which meant that Ward would be able to land on almost any terrain — provided he could get to the North in the first place. On the return flight from the de Havilland factory in Toronto, bad weather forced Ward down at Kenora, Ontario. In the dark and fog, the Fox Moth smashed into a ridge on the gravel runway. Ward was thrown forward, breaking his nose. His new plane was a wreck. The aircraft was insured, however, and Ward's infant enterprise, Polaris Charter Co. Ltd, was able to obtain its first paying work. Ward carried two prospectors to a lake 70 miles east of Yellowknife. The fare was $63. And Ward, age 25, was in business.

When a valve on his aircraft sprung open in mid-flight one day in the North, grinding the Fox Moth's engines to bits over Spud Arsenault Lake, Ward spent the coldest week of his life installing a new engine shipped from Toronto. Passengers were alarmed when he would have to land abruptly to sweep hoarfrost off the wings. Ward took the frequent mishaps in stride. "The adrenaline was always running," he said, "but pilots were careful to be fully prepared." That meant stocking the plane with plenty of food and blankets for unscheduled stopovers in the bush.

"The problem," Ward conceded, "was that once you cleared Yellowknife there were no maps." He relied on a photographic memory of rivers, glacial outcroppings and other natural landmarks in plotting his route. Those navigational aids were of little use in the dark, of course. Bush pilots tried to avoid flying at night. But that wasn't an option if a flight had been delayed by mechanical problems, or a pilot wanted to get ahead of a storm front. "The thing is," Ward had to admit, "if you're up there in that hostile territory long enough, you're going to get caught." In his own mind, at least, he had led an almost blissful existence. Ward had come away from a string of crashes with nothing worse than the occasional cracked skull and several broken ribs. Sixteen of his fellow pilots from the early days had lost their lives in the bush.

Ward was too young to have an acutely developed sense of danger. And his ego was well fed. He was opening up the North. "Up here at the top of the world, where only bush planes could operate in all seasons, we were more than a part of the transportation system," Ward said. "We were the lifeline of the Arctic."

Consumed with that sense of mission, Ward allowed his rebellious streak to show itself early. A short-lived partnership with another pilot ended when Ward quit rather than share control of the fledgling operation. He was fired from another bush outfit when he rebuffed its suggestion that he manage its Yellowknife operation. For two years, the Wards retreated to Marjorie Ward's hometown of Lethbridge. In that southern Alberta city, Ward made big, fast money for the only time in his life, save for the proceeds he stood to gain from the sale of Wardair some 30 years later. Max built and sold enough houses in Lethbridge to pay off the lingering debts from earlier aircraft purchases. And to return to the air as soon as possible with an innovative new plane, the Otter.

The remarkable Otter was de Havilland Aircraft's encore to its rugged Beaver, the first plane that had been designed expressly for the bush. The Otter could fly faster and further than its illustrious predecessor, and carry a much bigger payload. It was expected to find a market only among the largest airlines. Priced at $100,000, the Otter was ridiculously out of reach for bush pilots. Ward had to have one.

Fortunately for Ward, the Industrial Development Bank felt the same way after hearing him out on the glowing prospects for commercial development in the North that would come about with the introduction of long-haul air freighters. The IDB, a newly created arm of the federal Bank of Canada, decided to overlook a track record that suggested Ward had been something less than a spectacular success at flying smaller aircraft. It financed his purchase of one of the first Otters to emerge from de Havilland's plant in Downsview, Ontario. The IDB would also bankroll Ward in the purchase of his next few planes — a rare instance when he would benefit from an accommodating spirit at a government agency. If the IDB lacked skepticism about Ward's prospects with the Otter, his rivals were quick to step into the breach. "My competitors immediately announced that I would be broke by fall," Ward said. "There was no way, I was assured time and again, that you can fly a $100,000 aircraft around the bush and make money."

The Otter was remarkably efficient, however. Ward and his big airplane were soon in great demand with mining companies that were outfitting their camps far from civilization. They called on Ward to haul building supplies, construction equipment and even firetrucks. Ward's competitors chased after a quick buck from the contractors who were supplying the U.S.-built Distant Early Warning outposts across the Far North. Ward, too, got some of that business. But he chose to dig in at Yellowknife, and bonded with prosaic customers who were in the North for the long term. Among these was the RCMP, which had the grisly task of dealing with the many suicide victims in the North. "On a number of occasions, a new Mountie's stomach wasn't up to the task," Ward remembered. "And I added body-bagging to the list of jobs a bush pilot had to perform."

Ward's young airline helped open the mining communities of Rayrock, Hottah Lake and Taurcanis. It wasn't long before Ward was astonishing his competitors once again by laying out $300,000 for a hulking Bristol Freighter, which could carry six tons of freight or 44 passengers. Ward did not know how to fly the aircraft. "I seemed to have made a habit of buying planes first and learning how to fly them later," he said. Now Ward was able to airlift tractors and entire diesel power-plants. Frontier outposts welcomed the Freighter as it delivered 65 tons of materials for a new school under construction, or touched down at a remote village with a Beaver tucked in its enormous belly. With a growing reputation as the most efficient contractor for large-haul jobs in the North, Ward was also becoming a prime contractor for federal government outposts.

But Ward was making noticeably less progress with Ottawa in persuading it to license him as a scheduled airline. Even the mere purchase of a new airplane was sure to bring on a bureaucratic headache. "My original licence had been for two aircraft only; every time we added a new aircraft to our fleet we faced another long, expensive fight with the federal Air Transport Board [ATB]," said Ward. "More and more of my time was spent, not building and running an increasingly important transportation service, but trying to figure out ways around the thickets of regulations that kept springing up before me."

Yet Ward now identified an even more promising avenue of dynamic growth. That was the emerging market for vacation charter flights in the "South" (the term Northerners use for the rest of Canada). Never mind that the charter business was in its infancy in the early 1960s. Or that a Montreal airline consultant whom Ward canvassed told him that "the big airlines would always use their surplus capacity to run charters, and no small start-up airline could ever compete with them." Ward was not convinced.

TCA and CP Air had shown scant interest in cultivating a market among bargain-minded vacationers. There was no market yet for winter charters. But Ward figured he could fly vacationers to Europe in summer and use his large charter aircraft to haul freight around the North in winter.

After a year's delay, the ATB overcame its initial misgivings. Ward was granted a charter licence. With a Douglas DC-6 leased from CP Air, he flew his first passenger charter in 1962. In its inaugural charter flight, it carried 89 members of the Alberta School Patrol Board from Calgary to Ottawa and back — a seven-hour flight each way in those days. There would also be eight overseas charters that year, including a 20-hour series of flights from Edmonton to Copenhagen. The airline was now known as Wardair Canada Ltd, and was based in Edmonton's Macdonald

Hotel to give it a classy image. It had to undercut the fares of the scheduled carriers to attract business. Wardair lost $350,000 in its first year as a charter company. "In just one year's work," Ward recalled with chagrin, "we had succeeded in wiping out most of the surplus built up so painstakingly over the previous 15 years in the North."

The solution was not to quit. The solution, it seemed obvious to Ward, was to buy one of the new jetliners whose remarkable efficiency held the promise of creating a mass market for air travel. For just $300,000 (U.S.), Ward was able to get a second-hand jet from KLM. That would be one of the few times that he would not insist on a factory-fresh aircraft.

Ward was acutely concerned about his airline's image. "In those days of the early charters, there were a number of fly-by-night operators in the U.S. whose antics were giving the business a very dodgy name," Ward said. "In addition, the customers would inevitably be comparing us to Trans-Canada Air Lines and CP Air. We had to be better and look better, to build up the credibility we required."

In Wardair's first years as a charter operation, its passengers feasted on repasts supplied by the Steak Loft, an upscale restaurant in Edmonton. Wardair cabins began to take on the appearance of a fine dining room. There were linen tablecloths and napkins. Meals were presented on Royal Doulton china with a fresh flower placed on the tray table. At a cost of $15,000 per unit, Ward installed inflight coffeemakers that percolated gourmet java. In later years, each new aircraft was outfitted with one million dollars' worth of galley alterations to provide room for Wardair's expanded array of passenger amenities.

Ward tried to distinguish his airline still further by encouraging a unique esprit de corps among his employees. He couldn't afford to match the salary scales of TCA and CP Air. But then, he also rejected his competitors' practice of laying off workers in winter and during economic downturns. And it helped that for decades TCA and CP Air released female cabin attendants the moment they got married. Ward recruited a great many married ex-cabin attendants who wanted to keep on flying. In the air, passengers were entertained by cabin staff who organized bingo games, calisthenics drills and singalongs. On the ground, Ward, Marjorie and Ward's sister, Lillian, greeted each return flight to Edmonton of Wardair's first DC-6. They pitched in with cleaning and restocking the aircraft. "I wielded a pretty effective vacuum cleaner in those days," said Ward, "and fluffed a pretty pillow." As the Wardair fleet and route network expanded, a flying squad of engineers and cleaners was deployed from city to city to maintain aircraft as soon as required. "The whole point of the operation," Ward explained, "was to keep that aircraft in the air as much as possible."

Wardair evolved into a first-class operation because it had to work harder than its competitors to attract passengers. It was hobbled by regulations aimed at keeping non-scheduled airlines in their place.

At the dawn of charters, carriers were permitted only to fly "affinity" groups. The whole plane had to be filled with people who were members of some club or association for at least six months. "It was ludicrous," said Ward. "We flew the Alberta Judo Club, whose members showed up at the airport with six of their members lined up in wheelchairs for the group photo. Canoe clubs turned up with members who had never seen a paddle. And card-carrying mountaineers from the bald prairie put down their money and took their flight."

Charter passengers were also required to book their flights six months in advance, regardless of whether they were flying with a major carrier or a charter operation. (The rule was soon waived for TCA and CP Air.) "That too was non-sense," Ward said. "I don't think I ever met with a federal cabinet minister who didn't joke with me that his son or daughter had just hopped on a TCA charter they booked the day before."

Wardair and other charter operators were forbidden from advertising their cut-rate fares — "lest the moon turn to blood and civilization perish," said Ward. Regulators ordered him to withdraw one ad for Wardair's $330 round-trip fares that Ward had placed in *Time* magazine: "Fly to Europe for $33,000 — And Take Along 99 Friends."

Yet business was booming. By 1966, Wardair had captured 10 per cent of the trans-Atlantic market for non-scheduled traffic. That year, Wardair took delivery of a $7.4-million Boeing 727 jetliner. The move was seen as folly. The 727 was con-sidered to be a medium-range aircraft. No one had tried to use it on routes from Western Canada to Europe. But in introducing Boeing aircraft to the Canadian market, Ward was able to cut flight times to Europe by more than half, which meant his airline could fly more paying customers on that route than Wardair's competitors. As the 727 overtook the turboprops still commonly used on trans-Atlantic routes, Wardair pilots liked to exchange barbed witticisms with rival airline pilots left behind in the 727's contrails. Ward had to coax them to stop.

In the 1970s, Ward was sufficiently confident in the buoyancy of charters to con-vert most of his fleet to long-haul jetliners. Boeing's 747, which revolutionized mass-market air travel, had been in commercial service for just two years when Wardair took delivery of its first jumbo jet in 1973. The *Phil Garratt* represented the largest aircraft purchase financed entirely in Canada. And the price tag, at $25 million (U.S.), was roughly equal to the value of Wardair Canada prior to the purchase. By the early 1980s, a sudden economic downturn would make Ward wish he hadn't opened his wallet so wide on his frequent shopping sprees for new aircraft.

The recession dealt Wardair a crippling blow. Its revenues sagged just as it com-pleted 250 million dollars' worth of aircraft purchases to upgrade its fleet. But for the patience of his loan officers at Bank of Montreal and Toronto Dominion Bank, Ward would have lost his airline and a good deal more. As part of the financing for Wardair's second 747 acquisition, Max and Marjorie Ward had pledged their family assets. "We were under personal threat of losing everything, our corpora-tion, our home, everything but the clothes we stood in," Ward said.

But Wardair would pull through that nightmarish stretch, entirely on the strength of a growing clientele. By now, Ward had achieved a loyal following among economy-fare travellers. They enjoyed inflight steaks that were cooked to order, and a free bar for the duration of the flight. And they didn't hesitate to swamp their members of parliament with letters expressing a caustic regard for regulations whose intent seemed to be the suppression of affordable air travel. The bureaucrats who enforced the rules gradually turned sympathetic. "High public praise, Ward discovered, carried powerful political clout in Ottawa," wrote aviation historian Peter Piggott. "To bureaucrats whose idea of living dangerously was choosing bran muffins over doughnuts in the government cafeteria, Ward was revered as a romantic throwback, a pioneering hero who, it was said, still answered his own phone. And how many airlines still bore the name of the founder?"

As its passenger count crossed the threshold of one million customers a year, Wardair was also garnering praise outside Canada. "Wardair has earned a reputation that airlines many times its size might envy," *Air International Magazine* would report in 1984. "Passengers receive a standard of service greatly superior to that commonly encountered in the economy-class cabins of long-haul scheduled carriers."

Ward had survived the recession, but feared he was losing the war. Without scheduled routes to subsidize losses in the volatile charter business, the best Wardair could hope for was to keep lurching from crisis to crisis, miraculously emerging each time to tell the tale. So Ward persisted in lobbying for scheduled status. Some 30 years after he began that campaign, his wish was finally granted in 1986. But there could be no real triumph at this late stage of the game unless Ward succeeded in pulling off a rapid transition from charter to full-fledged scheduled airline. The challenge was to gain a foothold against the competition before the next inevitable recession.

That meant Ward would have to create a new major-league airline virtually overnight. He would have to trade in his long-range aircraft for smaller Airbuses that were better suited to intercity travel on Canada's most heavily travelled routes. The new planes were delivered promptly. Europe's Airbus Industrie was grateful for the Canadian's vote of confidence in the young aircraft maker, which was trying to become a credible alternative to Seattle-based Boeing.

Ward immediately applied his airline's distinctive service standards to the commuter market. He stunned the industry by quickly gaining an impressive share of the market for business travellers, who had been largely unfamiliar with Ward's product. And Wardair managed to expand without letting its service standards slip. Annual polling by the prominent British travel-industry journal *Holiday Which?* had cited Wardair as the world's best charter airline in 1985. But charter carriers, with their relatively infrequent flights, face less daunting responsibilities in everything from on-time arrivals to lost baggage than their scheduled cousins. Yet in 1986 and 1987, *Holiday Which?* found that Wardair was regarded as the world's finest operator in the scheduled category, as well.

But for all his exertions, Ward could not overcome the bitter reality that he was graduating to scheduled status 10 years too late. In anticipation of the industry deregulation that would come in the late 1980s, in which airlines could set their rates and routes free of government approval, Air Canada and Canadian Airlines (the old CP Air) had built up networks of regional carriers that fed their systems with passengers. That was a source of revenue that Wardair sorely lacked. To compete with the well-established frequent-flier programs of its two larger competitors, Wardair was obliged to offer passengers four times the normal mileage. And then six times, as Air Canada and Canadian Airlines matched Ward's incentives rather than lose valuable business travellers.

Travel agents were another problem. They earned commissions from Air Canada and Canadian Airlines on a sliding scale, rising from 8 per cent to 13 per cent the more flights they booked. They were loath to place clients on any other carrier. The president of Wardair's own advertising agency reported that his corporate travel agent was stubbornly refusing to book the agency's staff on Wardair.

An industry computer reservations system shared by all of the airlines had a mysterious way of showing Wardair flights to be fully booked when they were not. Travellers who persisted in demanding that they be booked on Wardair faced still more inconvenience at the airport. As a latecomer at many terminals, Wardair was stuck with some of the worst facilities. In Toronto, getting from Wardair's check-in desk to the boarding gate required the stamina of a marathon runner. And passengers in Montreal were obliged to walk across an icy tarmac to get to their plane.

By the fall of 1988, Wardair was bracing for a ruinous loss of $100 million on the year. And it would need at least twice that sum in fresh capital to keep up with payments on its new planes as interest rates skyrocketed. The bankers now had run out of patience. They began to call their loans. And so Ward kept his appointment in January 1989 with Rhys Eyton, the CEO of Canadian Airlines, for exploratory talks about a combination of the two airlines. The finality of what was about to happen didn't sink in until Ward entered the boardroom of the Toronto law office where the meeting was to take place. The walls were lined with Canadian Airlines' top executives and a phalanx of accountants, lawyers and brokers. Eyton was serious, after all.

Eyton's own airline was something of a shambles. In order to create a viable competitor to Air Canada, he had launched Canadian Airlines in the 1980s as an agglomeration of five disparate carriers. These were CP Air; Pacific Western Airlines, a regional carrier based in Calgary; Nordair and Quebecair, regional operators based in Central Canada; and Eastern Provincial Airlines, a regional firm that served Atlantic Canada. The resulting organization, combined with its network of small feeder affiliates, operated an ungainly fleet of a dozen or so different types of aircraft, from puddle-jumping turboprops to 400-seat jumbo jets.

Maintaining that exotic fleet, and training pilots and ground crews for so many different aircraft types, represented a cost burden not shared by Air Canada. And the mishmash of corporate cultures had kept Eyton from exploiting the size advantage of his new airline. Former CP Air flight attendants were accustomed to the cachet their airline enjoyed as a long-haul carrier on Pacific Ocean routes. They were less than enthusiastic about new assignments on the Edmonton to Red Deer run. Veterans of the regional airlines PWA, Nordair, Quebecair and EPA were resentful at the perceived self-importance of their new CP Air colleagues. Lack of cooperation among employees was evident in the rising volume of complaints from passengers, whose level of satisfaction with inflight food service in 1989 was a woeful 6 per cent . The manifest lack of esprit de corps was undermining Eyton's bid to attract more of the full-fare business travellers who account for about 80 per cent of industry revenues.

The primary attraction of Wardair for Eyton was its world-class service standards. At the risk of mongrelizing his airline still further, Eyton hoped that by absorbing Wardair he could impose its customer-centred habits on the dispirited employee population of Canadian Airlines. There were other benefits. Wardair's route system would give Canadian Airlines its long-sought entree to London and Paris. With the addition of Ward's airline, Canadian Airlines finally would achieve relative parity with Air Canada in number of planes and passenger-miles flown. And given the remarkably recent vintage of Ward's 18 jetliners, Eyton would be obtaining the youngest major fleet in the industry.

Ward was flattered by Eyton's logic. He ultimately agreed to a transaction that valued Wardair at about $300 million. "So that was it," Ward said. "After all the years of struggle and uncertainty, and hanging on when there was nothing to hang onto, and building a company, and knowing moments of sheer wonder and sheer terror, Wardair was gone in a few minutes."

Ward retired for good. He would never be tempted to start another airline. "It was fun," he would say many years later. "But, you know, I was a little crazy. To fight for a business like that, you need enormous energy. And you have to be a little bit crazy."

Dipping into his $70-million share of the Wardair sale proceeds, Ward bought one of Bombardier's new Challenger business jets and named it *Marjorie Morningstar* for his wife and career co-pilot. A decade later, at age 78, he was still an active pilot. "I'm playing like mad," he was able to report of his annual transAtlantic flights to Britain in his Challenger, and the snowmobile expeditions he led up North every April. His second home was the Ward campsite at Red Rock Lake in the Coppermine River watershed, about 300 kilometres north of Yellowknife. Thirty or so members of the Ward clan gather there every July and August for extended family get-togethers.

Ward is one of Canada's better-known economic nationalists. He is also a Western Canadian chauvinist. The sale of Wardair prompted him to abandon the Toronto condo and plant himself back in Edmonton. But the loss of Wardair was hardly calculated to arouse his patriotic sentiments. "If I had been an American, if I had moved to the United States," he has said, "I am convinced I could have made it to the very top of this business. No American who had attained the stature internationally that we attained with Wardair could have or would have been blocked from securing a scheduled service for a third of a century."

Without a cent of public subsidies, Ward had built a popular airline, but one that could never quite emerge from the shadow of his country's state-owned flagship carrier. He made no effort to disguise his resentment on that score. "If we had been allowed to operate our business without the constant water-torture of interference, restriction and regulation," he believed, "Wardair could have emerged as one of the premier airlines of the world."

The demise of Wardair raised the curtain on the industry's darkest drama. The Persian Gulf war of 1990-91, followed by the worst economic downturn since the Depression, resulted in total losses of $16 billion (U.S.) for airlines worldwide. In the space of 18 months, the world's airlines lost more money than they had earned in the previous 50 years. The head of American Airlines, the largest carrier on earth, flirted with getting rid of the company's airplanes and reducing the firm to an operator of airline-reservations systems. Omaha investment guru Warren Buffett, who was taking a rare beating on an ill-advised stake in US Airways, confessed that he should have resisted the glamour of an industry whose impact on the 20th century had been profound, but was fundamentally not viable. Citing the 129 airlines that had filed for bankruptcy between 1979 and 1999, Buffett said, "I like to think that if I'd been at Kitty Hawk in 1903 when Orville Wright took off, I would have been far-sighted enough — I owed this to future capitalists — to shoot him down. Karl Marx couldn't have done as much damage to capitalists as Orville did."

In the decade of the 1990s, Air Canada lost money six years out of 10, for a net loss of $381 million. Its shares, first offered to the public in 1988 at $8, were worth a mere $6.50 a decade later, after dipping as low as $2. Canadian Airlines staggered through the 1990s, losing a total of $1.6 billion despite three financial restructurings. One of those rescue schemes included a controversial investment in the carrier by American Airlines that was scorned as a back-door foreign takeover of a vital cog in Canada's transportation system. There were also two government bailouts of Canadian Airlines and repeated wage concessions by its employees that were achieved only by management threats to shut down the company. For a decade, employee morale at Canadian Airlines steadily declined as it became obvious that job security could not be assured at an airline whose massive debts and continued lack of choice routes kept it from gaining any ground against Air Canada. Quite the opposite was happening. By the late 1990s, Canadian Airlines was losing market share to charter carriers and the upstart regional firm WestJet Airlines, whose entire fleet consisted of fuel-efficient Boeing 737s.

Waving a white flag, Canadian Airlines chief executive officer called in early 1999 for an end to the "destructive duopoly" between his company and Air Canada. It was time for the carriers to call off their decade-long price war, he said, and divvy up monopoly routes between themselves. The ploy failed. With Canadian Airlines facing insolvency, Air Canada was able to buy its venerable rival later in the summer of 1999 for just $92 million — about the price of a single long-haul jetliner. In the U.S., meanwhile, of 59 jet airlines that started up after the industry was deregulated in 1978, just two were still flying (America West and Midwest Express).

In the last months of Canadian Airlines existence, the Ward residence was fielding many calls from industry experts. "They all wanted someone to start up another airline," he said. But Ward took note of the chronic industry losses that had culminated in just one carrier ending up with 80 per cent of the Canadian domestic market, and 40 per cent of all international air traffic to and from Canada. He doubted the sanity of anyone who would choose to go into the airline business in the late 1990s. "To get an airline going today, you've got to have a billion dollars," he said. "And if you have a billion dollars, why in the hell would you put it in the airline industry? There's no money in it."

A decade earlier, it had taken Canadian Airlines about 12 months to break its promise to retain the Wardair name, which was scraped off the fuselages of Ward's former planes. The new owner laid off 1,600 of Ward's former employees. It did christen its first new aircraft of the 1990s, a 747 jumbo jet, the *Maxwell W. Ward*. Was there more to Ward's legacy than that? Had he created a model airline which, under different circumstances, might have carried passengers into the 21st century?

THE WORLD's only consistently profitable carrier in the 1990s was a Dallas-based firm called Southwest Airlines, founded in 1971. It was a low-fare operation whose secret to success was to keep its planes in the air, making money, while the planes of rival carriers were languishing at the terminal. Southwest was unequalled at the speed at which it turned its planes around. Restocking the aircraft and exchanging one load of passengers for another took just 20 minutes — half the industry average. The airline's founder, joined by pilots and maintenance crews, helped clean the cabins and fluffed pillows. His cheerful inflight personnel, who had never endured a layoff, dressed as leprechauns on St. Patrick's Day. They organized inflight bowling tournaments with oranges. In 1996, Southwest inspired a Canadian knockoff called WestJet Airlines, launched by a quartet of entrepreneurs led by Calgary real-estate salesman Clive Beddoe. It too was based on a formula that Wardair began to refine in the 1960s, and like Southwest was consistently profitable. "We compete with the car and the couch,"

joked Stephen Smith, the airline's president. "Flying with us is cheaper than staying at home." But those two low-rent operations served no meals, only peanuts and pretzels. They offered no connecting baggage service with other airlines. (Hence no lost luggage.) And passengers were herded onto planes so quickly that it became common for them to grumble that the boarding process resembled a cattle call.

Ward had aimed higher, of course. He sought a level of sophistication in affordable air travel that a five-star innkeeper like Isadore Sharp would emulate. "Max Ward changed the standard for charter flights and the public image of them," said Sharp. "And, by setting new higher standards, he eventually forced airlines many times the size of Wardair to upgrade."

To be sure, Ward was an anachronism. He was a bush-pilot CEO long after the daunting economics of the jet age had pushed aviators like Eddie Rickenbacker and Howard Hughes out of the executive suites of the world's major carriers. "Today aviation is driven more by finance than passion," said historian Piggott. "Or perhaps, as Gloria Swanson put it in *Sunset Boulevard*, the old stars remained big — 'It's the pictures that got small.'"

But Ward was also ahead of his time. The state-of-the-art Airbus jetliners and Dash commuter aircraft whose purchase by Wardair was viewed skeptically by competitors later formed the backbone of Air Canada's fleet. Ward was an exemplar of virtues with which management consultants of the 1990s plied their trade. He was in constant search of new markets, first in the underserved Far North and then on a global scale. Putting air travel within reach of working-class wage earners required him to be ruthless in controlling costs. And he had been quick to grasp the significance of technological breakthroughs. These enabled Wardair to achieve the highest productivity levels in its industry. In some four decades of operation, Wardair never lost a passenger in an accident.

What it never gained was the chance to compete as an equal with its long-established rivals. In 1910, the first powered flight in the British Empire took place at Baddeck, Nova Scotia, when Canadian aviator John Alexander Douglas McCurdy took to the sky in his *Silver Dart*. Ninety years later, Ottawa's policy of insulating its "chosen instrument" from market forces, and its stifling of innovations bred by true competition, had given Canada an aviation industry that could not boast a single carrier of world stature, not one airline that could compete with the world's best in productivity, fare pricing or customer service.

The spirit of Wardair endured, however. On one Alberta flight in the late 1990s, WestJet passengers were addressed by the flight captain: "Ladies and gentlemen, we are about to begin our final descent into Calgary, the nation's entrepreneurial heartland and the home of WestJet Airlines, which believes in the free market and does not need or want government bailouts in order to serve your needs. Please fasten your seatbelts . . ."

3

ISADORE SHARP

Through trial and error, he built
the world's leading luxury hotel chain

"I'm in bed with my customers, almost literally."
— Isadore Sharp

I N THE SAUDI DESERT, Norman Schwarzkopf was assembling the biggest
military strike force since World War Two, to drive Iraqi dictator Saddam
Hussein out of neighbouring Kuwait. The U.S. general, like Dwight
Eisenhower in the tense moments before D-Day, was impatient to unleash his
troops on the enemy. The longer they waited to attack, the greater the toll on
morale as Schwarzkopf's half-million soldiers coped with the intense heat, scorpion bites and the threat of infectious diseases. A television reporter asked
Schwarzkopf about the primitive conditions. "Here you are in the middle of the
desert, General — what are the accommodations like?" Schwarzkopf grimaced.
"Well," he said, "it's not the Four Seasons."

The modern luxury hotel is a 20th-century concept, invented by a Frenchman,
popularized by an American and perfected by a Canadian. Cesar Ritz and his business partner, chef Auguste Escoffier, pioneered opulent innkeeping with the Ritz
Hotel in Paris in 1898, joined the following year by their Carlton Hotel in
London — the origins of today's Ritz-Carlton group and of the idea of a hotel as
celebrity hot spot (expedited by Ritz's decision to allow women on the premises
without an escort). A half-century later, Conrad Hilton at his zenith was presid-
ing over the first multinational lodging empire, a chain of industrial palaces that
teemed with conventioneers. And in the last three decades of the century, hotelier
Isadore Sharp redefined luxury as understated elegance. In 22 countries, Sharp's

more intimate, residential-style hotels attracted the world's most discriminating guests, those who demanded — and could afford — the highest standards of cosseting service the industry had to offer.

By the late 1990s, Sharp's Four Seasons Hotels Inc. was the world's largest firm dedicated exclusively to running luxury hotels. The unequalled variety of its farflung outposts was astonishing. In New York, Four Seasons operated the most expensive hotel ever erected in that city, and also the tallest, at 52 storeys. Designed by I.M. Pei, it was built in the 1990s at a cost of roughly $1 million per room. The company's portfolio also included some of the grande dames of the industry: the George V in Paris, the Ritz in Lisbon, the Pierre in Manhattan and the Beverly Wilshire in Los Angeles.

Four Seasons managed discreet inns nestled in formal state gardens in Tokyo and Dublin, a renovated 14th-century monastery in Milan and the refurbished former Sultanahmet Prison in Istanbul. The Four Seasons flag flew over thatch-roofed villas in the Indonesian rainforest at Bali, each with its own plunge pool and lanai. Four Seasons pampered guests at its teakwood pavilions in the jungle of northern Thailand. It operated a Nevis resort that was accessible only by a private ferry. And it managed a golf retreat at Punta Minta on a desolate stretch of Mexico's Pacific coast where course designer Jack Nicklaus suggested, in all seriousness, that his notorious hole 3A, on an islet 174 yards offshore, was a par three.

Starting with a motor hotel in Toronto's red-light district in the early 1960s, Sharp had painstakingly developed the most powerful global brand-name in its field. Its drawing power was reinforced every time Washington lobbyists gathered to plot legislative strategy at the Four Seasons in Georgetown and high-rolling Arab investors met at the Four Seasons Cairo, within view of the Pyramids in Giza about 16 kilometres to the southwest, to plan the deployment of their oil riches.

Issy Sharp, son of an immigrant Polish plasterer, was host to the world's most prominent people. The semi-annual collections of Chanel were unveiled at the Pierre, and on their European forays Donna Karan and Ralph Lauren camped out at the Four Seasons Milan. Al Gore raised money for his presidential bid with a $1,000-a-plate fundraiser at the Four Seasons Palm Beach, and George W. Bush's troops gathered at the Four Seasons Austin to celebrate his clinching of the G.O.P. presidential nomination. Sir John Browne summoned fellow directors at British Petroleum to a secret meeting at the Four Seasons Berlin to hatch BP's plan for taking over Amoco and Arco. A flustered Jurgen Schrempp, three days before unveiling the biggest industrial merger in history between his Daimler-Benz AG and Chrysler Corp. in 1998, nervously paced his suite at the Four Seasons in Manhattan, rehearsing his announcement of the deal before a group of corporate lawyers and public-relations counsellors.

The International Olympic Committee announced that Sharp's Regent Sydney would be the IOC headquarters for the 2000 Games. In a suite at the Four

Seasons Toronto, unofficial head office for one of the world's biggest film festivals, John Travolta walked a newspaper reporter through some dance steps from *Saturday Night Fever* and savoured a room-service hamburger: "They're so good here at the Four Seasons." In a Boston courtroom, oil billionaire William (Billy) Koch tasted victory when the judge evicted his former mistress, Catherine de Castelbajac, from his apartment at the local Four Seasons. And in Albert Brooks's silver-screen comedy *The Muse*, Martin Scorcese and James Cameron made supplications to Sharon Stone, a material girl with powers to reawaken the creative powers in over-the-hill movie directors. Her price: a hotel suite "on a high floor at the Four Seasons."

Grand hotels have always catered to the exacting demands of High Society, of course. Sharp's genius was to attune himself to the postmodern era of innkeeping, where the goal was to satisfy a new craving for a sort of ascetic hedonism. Ascetic because Sharp's hotels were small (average size: 300 rooms), often unexceptional in their exterior design, and as tranquil as a museum. They were in sync with the less-is-more mentality of upscale consumers in the latter part of the century with their emphasis on health clubs and low-cal, low-sodium meals. Instead of leaving the familiar chocolate on the pillow, housekeeping staff placed an orchid on the pillow and a bottle of mineral water on the bedside table. (Chocolate is "the worst thing to eat before going to sleep," said Sharp, a fitness zealot.) Ask the concierge for a fun way to kill an hour, and you'd probably be handed a jogging map. "Issy taught me how to be classy with simplicity," said John Beier, managing director of the Regency in New York, who built his career at Four Seasons. "He's very clear on the difference between excellence and extravagance. That's the difference between him and everyone else."

But Sharp's hostelries were also hedonistic. The furnishings were exquisite, often selected by Sharp and his wife, the former Rosalie Wise, university graduates in architecture and design, respectively. The atmosphere of a consular residence was evoked by Venetian chandeliers, antique furniture, Royal Doulton and Rosenthal china, Oriental carpets in the elevators and fresh-cut flowers in the lobbies and guest suites (the bill for a year's worth of Thai orchids and other exotic flora at the Toronto Four Seasons: $120,000). Four Seasons didn't pioneer 24-hour room service, 24-hour concierges, minibars, terry cloth bathrobes and hair dryers in every guest room, twice-daily maid service and overnight dry cleaning and shoeshines. But it was the first to make all of those amenities available at every hotel in its chain. It brought North American standards in air conditioning and soundproofed suites to its European hotels, and hired chefs and sommeliers trained in the French school for its downtown hotels in the Western Hemisphere.

Four Seasons had no equal as a restless innovator. It set an industry standard with its greatly improved version of the junior suite, with a seating area separated from the bedroom, usually by French doors, so that businesspeople could hold meetings out of sight of their sleeping area. Many of the chain's guest rooms, often the largest in a given city, were outfitted with three phone lines, for in-room fax and computer hook-ups. An "I Need It Now" service provided for the swift replacement of essential items that guests had lost or left behind.

At Four Seasons, the colour of a napkin was a policy decision. New amenities were rolled out with surgical precision after exhaustive consultation with guests. Each Four Seasons pillow was made from the feathers of seven geese from the Pyrenees. Patrons of the lobby lounge in London had their choice of 60 types of tea. Children were doted on with tot-sized bathrobes, toys from F.A.O. Schwarz and room-service meals that arrived on Winnie the Pooh plates. There was a weight-watchers menu for diet-minded canines, who could select from such plats du jour as German Shepherd's Pie (lean ground beef with potatoes) before napping in wicker bed-baskets provided by the hotel. Window blinds could be adjusted using a bedside switch. Bathroom floors were heated. Bathtubs were equipped with remote-control TV sets and exercise bikes were fitted with VCRs. Hotel rooms in the Middle East had safes. In Tokyo, special spa water was shipped in from the Izu Peninsula, about 100 kilometres away. In Hawaii, guests noticed that the air conditioning shut itself off automatically when they opened the sliding doors to leave. In Chicago, a "compcierge" came to the rescue of laptop-toting patrons with computer problems. "Four Seasons uses the softest toilet paper I've found anywhere," said Stanley Marcus, chairman emeritus of the upscale Neiman-Marcus retail empire. "That tells me they pay attention to the smallest detail."

In a relatively short space of time, Sharp seemed to have attained an early goal. "When I say quality car you immediately think of Rolls-Royce or Mercedes," he had said in the late 1970s. "When quality hotels are mentioned, I want people to think of Four Seasons." Within two decades they did, in almost every part of the world. By the late 1990s, Sharp was managing more than 50 hotels on six continents with total revenues of $2.3 billion (Canadian). The first Four Seasons Motor Hotel, opened in 1961, had employed 200 people, and the room rate was $9 a night. By the turn of the century, Four Seasons was employing 23,000 people and charging $350 to $750 a night for a basic room, ranging up to $5,200 for a sojourn in the presidential suite at the Four Seasons Mandalay Resort in Las Vegas and $11,000 for a night's stay in one of the 4,000-square-foot Royal Suites at the newly renovated George V in Paris.

Sharp's rooms commanded the highest rates in town, typically 20 per cent steeper than the priciest rival. "Every Four Seasons determines the price structure of its city," Sharp said. "And no one can price above us. We are in control of our destiny." He could make that claim because Four Seasons had less difficulty keeping its rooms filled than competitors, giving it a "Revpar," or revenue per available room, nearly 40 per cent higher than its nearest rival. Shares in the company had appreciated from a 1993 low of $11 to $85 in 2000, giving the firm a stock-market worth of about $3 billion and Sharp's controlling stake in Four Seasons a value of more than $300 million. Relative to the size of its revenues and payroll, Four Seasons had a richer stock-market capitalization than the far bigger Marriott International, Hilton Hotels Corp. or Starwood Hotels & Resorts (the Sheraton and Westin chains), and in absolute dollars it was among the half dozen most valuable hotel franchises in the world.

"Cheap doesn't sell anymore," said Sharp, explaining a marketing strategy that distinguished his firm from the likes of Marriott and Hilton, which, with more than 1,000 hotels each to manage, insisted they could not afford to match Sharp's commitment to continual upgrading of facilities or his staffing levels. (The ratio of staff to guests at Four Seasons was 1.7 to 1.0, compared with an industry average of 0.6 to 1.0. At Four Seasons resorts like Bali, there were four employees per guest.) "We live in a time of soaring expectations," Sharp reasoned. "The mass media have communicated the distinction between good and average, and people know the difference. People won't put up with a 25 per cent failure rate, and money-back guarantees are no solution. They want it right the first time around."

After more than 30 years in the business, Sharp sensed that he had gained an unshakeable lock on the luxury market worldwide. "Our core competence, delivering error-free service, is a truly sustainable competitive advantage," he declared. "Combined with our irreplaceable buildings in irreplaceable locations, it creates a signficant barrier to entry for rivals."

With hotels in most of the major cities in North America and Western Europe, Four Seasons was rapidly expanding in 2000 into Central Europe, the Middle East, Asia and South America. It was applying the impeccable standards of its business hotels to a burgeoning collection of exotic resorts, and extending its brand-name franchise into a new field, time-sharing and the outright sale of residential apartments in city-centre hotels and of vacation-residence units in resort destinations. And Sharp was focused on the next challenge: transforming his entrepreneurial success into a durable industrial legacy. "We can earn blue-chip status," he believed. "Not by size, but by what a blue chip truly represents: a global brand name, a dominant market position and a sustainable competitive advantage. The history of great brands says that momentum, once gained, goes on and on. It lasts as long as a company maintains its customers' trust in what built the brand."

But the infection of Sharp's vocabulary with such corporate-speak terms as "core competence," which normally don't fall from the lips of dynamic entrepreneurs, was an ominous sign. In his late 60s, Sharp was confronting the likelihood that none of his three children would carry on the family business. He began to speak the language of a professional manager, realizing that the leadership of his firm would eventually pass to non-family executives. It would be their turn, eventually, to cope with the vicissitudes and setbacks that had always been part of the Four Seasons story.

Even as he spoke confidently of his firm's blue-chip ambitions, Four Seasons was mired in disputes with the owners of the Pierre and a new hotel in Berlin, over the terms of a management contract in the first case, and over who would foot the bill for costly renovations in the second. While those disagreements would ulti- mately be resolved to everyone's satisfaction, they were a reminder that Four Seasons' status as a management company that didn't own its properties — a con- dition it shared with most of its peers, to be sure — meant there could be no assur- ance it would hold onto its best locations indefinitely. Weak local economies in Vancouver, Istanbul and Asia were dragging down the strong performance of the company's U.S. hotels. And there was always the prospect that any of Four Seasons' larger competitors, including Britain's Bass PLC (390,000 rooms) and France's Accord SA (650 hotels), could reposition just 10 per cent of their enor- mous portfolios and create a super-luxury operation that would surpass Four Seasons in size.

If Sharp's firm was to escape the fate of Ritz and Hilton — brand names whose lustre did not outlive their founders — Sharp would have to imbue his profes- sional managers with the same ideals and passion that had guided him in building his company from scratch. The odds against success in that quest were consider- able. The hospitality trade had spawned just a handful of true hoteliers. Instead, hotels were operated by airlines, which regarded them only as collection points for air travellers; by real-estate moguls, who held them for speculative purposes; or by conglomerates, which soon forgot why they had acquired their trophy properties.

Sharp was one of the few career innkeepers. He was also an entrepreneur in a trade that was dominated by corporate bureaucrats. His outward appearance as an urbane, low-key family man belied a gambler's heart. Four Seasons was built on a series of risky propositions beyond the ken of professional managers. Sharp's first three hotels, each ahead of its time in anticipating nascent trends, was initially judged to be a stupendous folly. He defied conventional economics twice again with high-risk expansion drives into the U.S. and the Far East.

More than Sharp cared to admit, Four Seasons was an extension of his per- sonality. And of his contrarian instincts. He did acknowledge that "I have made mistakes, some of them costly. But I've discovered that you must invest to find out if your judgment is right, with no assurance of return. You can ask your market all kinds of theoretical questions about whether or not they will buy the product you are planning to make. But you won't really know until you have built it."

Despite its inauspicious location in Toronto's red-light district, the first Four Seasons (above) was an instant success. Isadore Sharp went international with his third hotel (below), defying experts who warned against the folly of adding to London's glut of luxury lodgings. It was soon the most profitable hotel in Europe, and would help pay for Sharp's future mistakes.

Co-founders Sharp, Eddie Creed and Murray Koffler with Rosalie Sharp and Golda Meir, the Israeli prime minister (above). At left, Sharp, the builder's son, at work on the first Four Seasons. Below, Issy, Rosalie and sons Jordan, Greg, Chris and Tony in 1965, when mounting debt at Four Seasons made Rosalie silently speculate about losing "the house, the silver — everything."

By 2000, Four Seasons was one of the most valuable brand names in the lodging industry, synonymous with five-star luxury on six continents. Room rates had risen over 40 years, from $7 a night at the Four Seasons Motor Hotel in 1960 to a recent $5,000 and more for a night's stay at the best rooms in the house at the George V in Paris or the Mandalay Bay Resort & Casino in Las Vegas. Sharp's 60 inns varied in character if not service, from intimate guest cottages in Bali (above), each outfitted with a private plunge pool, to bustling city centre hotels like the Pierre in the heart of Manhattan, overlooking Central Park (right).

⧗

Our entire business has changed, Warren, since you and I were young in it —
whether we like the fact or not. The days of "mine host" and personal service
are over. Maybe people cared once about such things. They don't any more.
— Curtis O'Keefe, acquisitive chain-hotel operator, reminiscing with Warren
Trent, last of a dying breed of independent hotelier,
in Arthur Hailey's 1965 novel, *Hotel*.

CONRAD HILTON was the first global innkeeper. His father, a
Norwegian immigrant shopkeeper, had failed with several business ventures in his adopted hometown of San Antonio, New Mexico. Hilton himself was thwarted in his ambition to set up a chain of small-town banks in neighbouring Texas. He then, at age 32, began to acquire a modest collection of hotels
in the Lone Star State, only to learn the hard way that innkeeping is one of the
more accurate barometers of economic pressure. Soon after the stock-market crash
of 1929, creditors began to seize his hotels. "The Great Depression of the '30s
tossed my own life's work from a tidy little mound of success into a bottomless pit
of debts, humiliations, and mortgages," Hilton wrote in his 1957 memoir, *Be My
Guest*. "Men were jumping from hotel windows, my hotel windows."

With his unflagging self-confidence, Hilton soon recovered. Exploiting the
same misfortunes that had brought him down, he launched his comeback by snapping up troubled hotels from impatient creditors at distress prices, financing each
new purchase with profits from his success in reviving his most recent acquisition.
He didn't miss a trick in wringing profits from his hotels, going so far as to remove
chairs from the lobbies: If visitors wanted to sit down, they could do so in his bars
and restaurants. As his reputation for brilliant managing and marketing of hotels
spread, Hilton was able to find investors to join him in ever-larger hotel projects,
forging a personal network of banks, insurance companies and commercial land
developers who were eager to ride on his coattails. Eventually his prizes included
the Stevens, the world's biggest hotel (now the Chicago Hilton & Towers) and the
Waldorf-Astoria in New York. In the post-vaudeville era, Hilton found that he was
now the largest employer of supper-club talent in the world. He became a crony
of Benny Goodman, dance partner of Grace Kelly, golfing buddy of Eisenhower
and, most famously, frustrated husband of Zsa Zsa Gabor. With boundless swag-
ger, Hilton created the hotel industry's first global brand-name in the 1950s. He
declared himself to be on a mission to keep the world safe for Free Enterprise.
"Our Hilton house flag is one small flag of freedom which is being waved defi-
antly against Communism," he said. "The international effort of ours is a contribution to world peace."

It would be many years before a hotel company was again associated with the personality of one man. Long before Hilton died, in 1979, the Hilton Hotels Corp. and its imitators had succumbed to mismanagement after falling into the hands of anonymous bean-counters, conglomerateurs and speculators. Hilton's own son, Barron, squandered much of his father's legacy by trading the firm's international division for shares in Trans World Airlines, which promptly lost altitude. By the end of the century, only two major hotel chains were still controlled by their founding families: the one bearing J. Williard Marriott Jr.'s name, and Four Seasons.

Issy Sharp set out not to be a hotelier, but to follow in the footsteps of his father. Max Sharp was a contractor in Toronto, where he built houses and modest apartment blocks. He was one of 10 children of a Polish *shochet* (Orthodox chicken slaughterer). In 1920, Max Sharp fled the pogroms of his native Auschwitz and at age 18 was a pioneer Zionist in the newly established British protectorate of Palestine. As a member of Degania, one of the first *kibbutzim*, Sharp apprenticed in plastering and tilework, and helped build the frontier town of Hadorha Carmel in Galilee amid constant attacks from Arab marauders.

After five years in Israel, Max followed his brother Louis to Toronto, where he worked as a journeyman plasterer for $10 a week and married a Polish immigrant woman named Lena Godfrey. They settled in the Jewish community of Kensington Market, raising a family of three girls and a boy during the bitter years of the Depression. Issy Sharp, born in 1931 in a small house on Major Street, played hockey with hand-me-down figure skates from his sisters that he dyed black. His first entrepreneurial impulse, on learning that a friend was selling sticks of chewing gum for a penny, was to market his gum as "breath fresheners" and pocket a nickel for two sticks.

Issy Sharp's childhood memories were dominated by the image of moving vans. "My father would build a house and we'd move in," he remembered. "Momma would fix it up so nicely that somebody would offer to buy. Then we'd move and the whole process would start again." By the time he was 16, Sharp had lived in 15 houses. "I thought that's how everybody lived."

The Sharps struggled at first. Max's English was poor, and he often didn't understand the terms of the construction contracts he signed. He went broke several times, once from eating the cost overruns on a building project in which he unwittingly bid too low a price but which he completed anyway despite the ruinous terms. At one point late in the Depression, he was selling carnival slot-machine games. But Max at last began to prosper as a contractor when Toronto's postwar building boom gained momentum.

At Toronto's Ryerson Institute of Technology, Issy Sharp was a silver medallist for outstanding academic achievement and athletic prowess in hockey, basketball and football. He studied architecture, not to become a designer but to learn more about the building trades. After spending summer vacations as a plasterer and bricklayer for his father, he doubled the size of the family firm by joining Max Sharp and Son full-time, building apartment units. "When I was a young builder," Sharp would later say, tracing the roots of his hands-on management style, "I worked side by side with my crew, digging ditches, pouring concrete in the rain. And when I had to leave they would go on working as if I were there. That was the attitude of fairness and mutual respect I wanted to establish within Four Seasons."

In the mid-1950s, Max Sharp and Son got a contract to build a 14-room motel in the middle of a spaghetti interchange of Highway 27 and the Queen Elizabeth Way. Issy Sharp would later cringe at the bare-bones budget for construction of this hostelry — about $3,000 a room. "But I was interested because the client thought he and his wife were going to make this thing work as a retirement project. Yet they knew absolutely nothing about the industry." Neither did Sharp, of course. But he soon learned about the growing popularity of roadside attractions when Max Sharp and Son were called back a year later to build an addition for the Motel 27. "The motel was in the middle of nowhere, but he sold out every night. It looked like a lot of fun — certainly more fun than building factories."

Sharp conceived the idea of an inn that would combine the traditional amenities of a downtown business hotel with the convenience of a 1950s phenomenon, the motor hotel. He would need a site large enough for a building where patrons could park their cars in front of their rooms. His scouting turned up an affordable plot at Jarvis and Carlton streets on the eastern fringe of Toronto's downtown. The area was a haven for prostitutes and winos, but close enough to the financial district, Sharp thought, to be viable as a dining and lodging destination for business executives.

It took Sharp, then in his 20s, five years to raise the $1.5 million for his project. Prospective backers were not impressed by Sharp's lack of experience in the hospitality field, or the unpromising site for his planned motor hotel. "When everybody looked at it," Sharp recalled, "they said, 'You are going to blow your brains out with this property.' There didn't seem to be any reason why it would work."

Eventually, Sharp recruited two people with money who believed in him: his brother-in-law Eddie Creed, a scion of Toronto's most prominent carriage-trade apparel retailer; and Creed's close friend Murray Koffler, founder of the fledgling (two stores) Shoppers Drug Mart chain. According to Koffler, though, "From the beginning, Issy was the instrument of genius. Sophisticated hotel people would never have spent as much on amenities and staffing as we did, but Issy was determined to be classy."

The trio did extensive research. They had a name, having rejected an early possibility, Thunderbird Motor Hotel, in favour of a renowned Hamburg restaurant,

Vier Jahreszeiten (Four Seasons). But the concept for the hotel itself took shape slowly. In one U.S. city after another that the budding hoteliers visited, Sharp was put off by the proliferation of banal two-storey motels erected on downtown parking lots. The epiphany was a Phoenix hotel with an interior courtyard. "All the rooms face in, so you control your views, your environment, instead of allowing the street to determine what guests looked at," Sharp said. "In those days, the roadside motel had a swimming pool in the middle of the parking lot. We enclosed the courtyard so we were in charge of the experience that people had."

The 125-room Four Seasons Motor Hotel, built at a cost of $12,000 a room, opened on March 21, 1961, the first day of spring. The new hotel played to the seasons. In winter, there was a frozen sculpture ensemble in the courtyard and Christmas trees on every balcony. In summer, there were outdoor gardens surrounding the courtyard pool. Sharp gave the place an upscale image by yoking it to Toronto's newly vibrant arts scene. The opening-day gala for his modest establishment was a fundraising event for the Toronto Symphony Orchestra and the Art Gallery of Toronto (later the Art Gallery of Ontario). And Koffler's brainwave was to have the hotel play host to an annual outdoor art exhibit and sale, which soon outgrew the Four Seasons courtyard, and four decades later was still an important event on the Toronto arts calendar. With its unusual amenities and its proximity to Maple Leaf Gardens and a CBC Radio studio across the street — Four Seasons' first brush with entertainment celebrities — the motor hotel was an instant success.

At age 29, Sharp had his first hotel. Years later, he would insist that he had no grand plan for a lodging empire. "I was just trying to put one deal together — my vision of the future was hoping to take in enough cash today to pay yesterday's bills." But just as he and his father always had blueprints for the next apartment block in hand even as the foundation was being laid for their current project, Sharp was thinking about his next hotel before registering the first guest on Jarvis Street.

Soon after the motor hotel opening, Sharp and his wife were inspecting the proposed site for a much larger Four Seasons hotel in the barren hinterland of Don Mills. This was a few years before the Reichmann family would bet their young firm, Olympia & York Developments Ltd., on a corporate office park in the remote district, far to the north of downtown Toronto. Rosalie's heart fell as she scanned the forbidding landscape, distinguished by a busy garbage dump, a railway siding and one lonely neighbour, the Canadian head office of IBM Corp. But she kept her doubts to herself. "Years later," Sharp said, "Rosalie told me she resigned herself at that moment to losing the house — the first we had ever owned — hocking the silver and going back to work as a shop clerk. Here she was a mother of three boys, pregnant with the fourth, listening and imagining — and she really has a great imagination. But she could have been right. She usually is."

Yet as the Reichmanns would later do, Sharp had calculated correctly that blue-chip business activity would gravitate north with the scheduled completion in five years of the Don Valley Parkway, making his hotel just a 15-minute drive from downtown. And he was right in thinking that corporate-meeting planners would be attracted to a campus-like setting with no distractions apart from the 500 acres of civic parkland that Sharp's guest suites would overlook. (With many future projects, plans for new hotels would often remain in limbo for years until Sharp could obtain a site adjoining a prominent park.)

Once again, Sharp's aesthetic instincts told him that superior design would give him an edge. He persuaded an ailing Peter Dickinson, architect of two modernist landmarks, Toronto's Benvenuto Place luxury apartment complex and Montreal's CIBC tower, to accept the commission for his first Inn on the Park. Shortly before he died, Dickinson handed Sharp the blueprints he had drafted from his hospital bed of a striking design for the hotel. It was in the shape of a parallelogram, enclosing a courtyard as a big as a good-sized public park. The facility, one of North America's first urban resort-style hotels, was perched on a hill and visible for miles around. It was an instant hit with locals and visiting dignitaries such as frequent guest Alexei Kosygin, the Soviet foreign minister, who appreciated its serene locale. Its arresting architecture served as a magnet, Sharp said; "Some people would come out just to see it." Sharp also exploited an opportunity presented by Toronto's limited selection of fine-dining venues. From the moment of its 1963 opening, the hotel's Café de l'Auberge was hailed by critics as one of the city's top restaurants. Impressed by the popularity of the Inn, Sharp's loan officer at the Bank of Nova Scotia congratulated him on reaching "the pinnacle" of his career. (Grateful for its confidence in him, Sharp would call on Scotiabank to help finance most of his subsequent projects, climaxing in a $120-million loan for Sharp's acquisition in the 1990s of Asia's biggest luxury hotel chain.)

Emboldened by his two early triumphs, Sharp became still more audacious, embarking on what he would later describe as his most important business experience. In the mid-1960s, just three years after the Don Mills debut, he made a leap overseas and began negotiating a hotel project in London with Britain's McAlpine family, which had extensive land holdings in the U.K. and Canada. A chance meeting between Sharp and one of the McAlpines' agents in Canada led to six years of talks about what kind of facility to build on a choice site the McAlpines owned in Mayfair on Hyde Park.

Sharp, whose fascination with London was sparked during a romantic European vacation with Rosalie in the early 1960s, was adamant that his first international project had to be an upscale affair. The McAlpines disagreed. They proposed a Holiday Inn-style operation for the Mayfair site, in the belief that London was oversupplied with luxury lodgings and that a new five-star hotel couldn't hope to compete with established icons such as the nearby Savoy, Dorchester, Connaught and Grosvenor House. "They were trapped in Britain's depressed postwar thinking," Sharp said of his prospective partners. "But coming from a small city like Toronto, I was overwhelmed by London as a capital among capitals, by the sheer hustle of the place. How could it not need another luxury hotel?"

Sharp complicated matters by urging the McAlpines, who already owned the Dorchester, to embrace a new concept of luxury that they could not grasp. "It will be a more personal, down-to-earth hotel," Sharp explained to the Brits. "Not for serving dukes and duchesses, but people who want to be treated like dukes and duchesses. People who are put off by the stuffy formality of the traditional European grand hotel." Sharp offered to pay the rent the McAlpines were expecting to earn from their preferred 320-room structure, but wanted them to build only 230 oversized rooms in the same space. And he wanted air conditioning, a novelty in London. "They said you don't need air conditioning," Sharp recalled. "I said guests from North America need it."

Sharp was hardly dealing from a position of strength. His own consultants sided with the McAlpines in predicting a luxury hotel would fail. "And the British, with apparent good reason, were calling me 'that crazy Canadian'," Sharp said. "All the market research supported their assumption that my concept — modern luxury without formality, service without a class attitude — would never pay for itself." Against the McAlpines' experience with the Dorchester and their many other properties, the 33-year-old Sharp could boast of just two budding hotels that were leveraged to the hilt and had a negative net worth. At that time, Sharp said, "My chief asset was a lack of knowledge and experience, and that gives you the ability to dare." In holding out for his vision of the project, he hoped to exploit the McAlpines' growing impatience with their decade of failure in getting something built on the Mayfair site. And he sensed the McAlpines admired his spunk or they wouldn't still be talking. "I knew their family history. The patriarch had once been asked what collateral he had for an early venture, and he showed up at the bank with his five sons — 'Here's my collateral,' he said."

With his persistence, Sharp did gain the McAlpines' consent to his scheme. They and Four Seasons were soon rewarded. This second Inn on the Park, with its unusually large rooms, European luxury and North American convenience, was popular with international business travellers from the moment it opened in 1970. It turned a profit in its first year. "The place prints money," said Robert Collier, vice-president and director of marketing at Sheraton Corp., who was an executive with British hotel operator Trusthouse Forte in the Inn's early years, when it was fully booked during the 1973 OPEC oil crisis while other London hotels were half empty. "From the beginning, the Inn provided phenomenal service. And because of its small size it was soon turning people away — which just added to the mystique."

The London Inn on the Park was actually a modest venture, even if the money that Sharp sank into it meant it would have to turn a profit almost immediately or he would lose his company. But its location in one of the financial capitals of the world drew wide attention to its 98-per-cent occupancy rate and its status as Europe's most profitable hotel. With just a handful of properties and barely a decade's experience to his credit, Sharp was already being hailed as an innovator with a sixth sense for emerging trends. Researchers at Cornell University in Ithaca, New York, the top hotel-management school in North America, observed that while Sharp's success in Don Mills required merely good business instincts, "London's Inn on the Park demanded clairvoyance." Sharp himself would say that London "not only gave me insight as to what we should do as a company, but it has always generated good profit and has paid for a lot of my mistakes."

Sharp would need the margin for error that London provided. He still had much to learn about the industry, and was not yet even a full-time hotelier. "I'm not sure I even liked the hotel business at the start," said Sharp, who would have to learn how to cope with bomb threats, rock stars who trashed his rooms and last-minute demands from the U.S. Secret Service that he accommodate 200 of its agents on a memorable occasion when President Ronald Reagan and Vice President George Bush decided to make a joint sleep-over at the Four Seasons Houston. "If I'd read *Hotel* or *Be My Guest*, and seen all the problems of running a hotel, I'd never have gone into it." Part of the problem was that Sharp was still his father's son, a builder. "My interest was in putting deals together. If a hotel project was a good real-estate deal, I'd do it." For the longest time, he later confessed, Sharp regarded innkeeping as his "night job."

That much was clear from the unfocused growth that characterized Four Seasons' first 15 years. Hotels bearing its name sprang up in the 1970s in most of Canada's major cities. But many of these inns were large, convention-style places that bore little resemblance to the cashbox in London. Conversely, in Belleville, Ontario (pop. 35,000), Four Seasons opened a facility that was half hotel, half Bell Canada training centre — an innovation that did not set a trend. Sharp spent a year trying to make a success of an underperforming resort in Nassau. And in Netanya, near Tel Aviv, Four Seasons built an opulent but marginally profitable condo-hotel where valued staffers kept being called away to serve in the military. (The project was a sentimental journey for Max Sharp, who helped build it.)

Until the mid-1970s, Sharp ignored the beckoning U.S. market, where the luxury sector was underserved and typified by independent operators and spotty management. Instead, fired by the success of London, Sharp became fixated with Europe, where choice urban sites were rarer than in North America. Four Seasons managed to attract would-be partners for projects on the Continent, including wealthy families in Paris and Athens. But balky local zoning authorities and unreliable financing sabotaged one project after another. In the only instance where ground was broken, in Rome, conservationists scuttled a hotel project when construction workers kept unearthing Roman artifacts.

And in his other career as a land developer, Sharp was devoting much of his energy to schemes with no connection to his young hotel chain. Most of these offended the sensibilities of North America's reform-minded civic officials of the 1970s. They withheld approval for Sharp's residential and office building developments across Canada and in Florida. In perhaps the most painful setback, Sharp gave up on a massive apartment-hotel project on land assembled years earlier by the ill-fated U.S. developer William Zeckendorf on the edge of Vancouver's Stanley Park, after student protesters set up a squatters' commune on the site, dubbed "All Seasons Park." And he retreated from a plan to redevelop the former site of Toronto's Granite Club, a WASP enclave, when well-to-do ratepayers raised a noisy objection to its potentially destructive impact on their neighbourhood. "Four Seasons was like an iceberg," Sharp said. "Beneath our visible accomplishments was a mass of frustration over the dozens of projects we couldn't bring to fruition."

The watershed for Sharp was the Four Seasons Sheraton, an enormous 1,450-room hotel built in partnership with ITT Corp., or, as it turned out, with ITT's new Sheraton division. The U.S. firm wanted to establish a major presence in Canada's principal city; Sharp craved a flagship property in the financial district of his home town. And the city was amenable to a hulking convention hotel going up on a prime site across the street from its new, architecturally renowned city hall, provided that any foreign investment in the complex was fronted by a local partner. But Sharp, having just talked his London partners into building a smaller hotel than they planned for, now found himself playing second fiddle to Sheraton, which proceeded to build a hotel with more rooms than Sharp's entire chain then possessed. "Our later philosophy evolved out of that experience," said Sharp, who sold his passive 49 per cent interest in the Four Seasons Sheraton just four years after it opened in 1972. "Suddenly Four Seasons seemed amorphous, and it had become obvious we weren't going to make a name for ourselves by being all things to all people."

It was during this difficult period that Sharp began to earn a reputation as a class act. "Here was Issy with a public-relations problem in his home town, and he had no control over it," said John Sharpe, the founder's long-time second-in-command at Four Seasons. At the time, Sharpe was assistant manager of the new Sheraton hotel. Its first year of operation was marked by frequent rows with city building inspectors; complaints over the unforeseen way in which the 43-storey hotel tower blocked out the sun for City Hall and Nathan Phillips Square, Toronto's most important civic open space; and a poorly supervised "singles festival" that resulted in an embarrassing suspension of the hotel's liquor licence in time for the arrival of a large contingent of U.S. conventioneers. "Issy was the biggest potential loser in the deal," said Sharpe. "But he never once bad-mouthed Sheraton. He always wanted me to know that all this trouble would pass. I kept thinking, gee, what a hell of a nice attitude."

Sharp, as it happened, was a big winner in his encounter with ITT. "I went to school at ITT," he would say of a process in which he came of age as a dealmaker, gaining a half interest in the Toronto project even though he was shouldering a relatively small portion of the development cost. Decades later, Sharp was still in awe of Harold Geneen's legendary takeover machine. "I was in my mid-30s, negotiating with the most sophisticated conglomerate in the world, the place where all the brightest MBAs in America wanted to work. Academically, I wasn't even close to these people."

ITT, for its part, was sufficiently impressed with the deal Sharp had struck for himself with the Toronto hotel that it tried to buy his company. There were heady suggestions that he would be in line for the top job at Sheraton. "I kept saying no and they kept offering more money, money like I'd never dreamed of having," Sharp recalled. He was powerfully flattered, and did not easily resist these overtures from a corporation that was accustomed to getting what it wanted. "But I had learned that I'd never be a corporate man after those two years of negotiating the Toronto hotel, where it was just me and my lawyer in a room with 20 executives from ITT. They worked around the clock, the pressure on them was fantastic; it was like they were expecting a call from Geneen every minute." Sharp resolved to spare his own managers that punishment.

Sharp was witnessing ITT at its peak. The company was destined to disappear by the mid-1990s, after humbling a succession of CEOs who could not control its disparate parts. The portents of that epic failure were evident during Sharp's partnership with the firm, which was slow to address problems at its new Toronto property. In each of his bet-the-company propositions, Sharp had to ensure from the outset that his hotels in Don Mills and London would be able to stand on their own two feet. But if Sheraton's venture in Toronto didn't pan out it had scores of properties around the world to fall back on. For that matter, if Sheraton itself were to collapse, ITT would scarcely miss it among the other claims on Geneen's attention, which at that time included fibre-optic cable for telephone companies, the Avis rental car system and Hostess Twinkies. As Sharp would later say, "The problem with conglomerates is that after they buy a company, the people who were close to the customer — the founder and his top executives — tend to disappear, they get bought out. At Four Seasons, I'm in bed with my customers, almost literally."

But in the mid-1970s, Sharp himself had distractions he could no longer afford. Even as he was pocketing a handsome gain on the sale of Four Seasons' stake in the Toronto Sheraton, he realized his company was jeopardized by a lack of focus. As a first step in reinventing Four Seasons, Sharp made the controversial move of ending its status as a publicly traded company. Sharp had taken Four Seasons public in the go-go stock market of the 1960s, and its shares had never recovered from their 1969 peak of $22. Sharp's own growth impulse and the demand by investors for deal-generated increases in revenue had proved to be a bad combination, leading Four Seasons down more than one blind alley. In 1977, with the shares trading at less than $4 in a dismal market for real-estate stocks (as Four Seasons was then regarded), Sharp took his company private. The decision won him few friends on Bay Street, where he was accurately seen as having bought back his firm at a bargain price. But then, Sharp had no need to keep the Street happy, having never relied on the stock market to fund his projects. These had been, and would continue to be, financed in the manner that Conrad Hilton pioneered — by insurance companies, pension funds, developers and other institutional investors.

When it entered its next growth phase, in the late 1970s, Four Seasons was a very different company, acutely focused on five-star hotel development. Now guided by his experience in London, Sharp was determined to earn a reputation for unrivalled proficiency in managing small-scale luxury hotels. In executing that strategy to near-perfection, Four Seasons eventually found that it could have its pick of the best sites and properties in the world's leading cities. By the late 1980s, Sharp was turning down dozens of offers each year from hotel owners and institutional investors seeking to have Four Seasons assume the management of their properties.

In place of his former undisciplined expansion, Sharp began to identify "Four Seasons cities" that had an abundance of well-heeled international business travellers. And it gradually withdrew from second-rank towns and from cities where its large properties didn't fit the new formula, including Calgary, Edmonton, Montreal, Ottawa and San Antonio. "A company like Marriott, with hundreds of hotels, can afford to make a mistake," said Roger Garland, executive vice-president of Four Seasons. "But with only a relatively few properties, one bad hotel could infect us like a bacteria."

Attentive service was to be the cornerstone of the Four Seasons franchise. Yet outwardly it also seemed that Sharp's method would be to operate the most lavishly appointed hotel in each Four Seasons city. In his first U.S. foray, in 1976, Sharp had paid $11 million for the Clift Hotel, a 60-year-old San Francisco landmark. He then subjected it to a $4-million facelift — one of the costliest renovations in the history of the U.S. industry. (Within a few years, *Conde Nast Traveler* would pick the Clift as the best hotel in America.) The historic Olympic hotel in Seattle was given the same treatment. Four Seasons was offered the management contract for Chicago's struggling, three-year-old Ritz-Carlton in the glamorous Water Tower complex just off the Magnificent Mile. In another coup, it was given the chance to launch Philadelphia's first new luxury hotel in decades. "With our hotel, which is in one of the most historic parts of the country, Mr. Sharp is having specially designed 18th-century Republic furniture designed for the rooms," said David Perry, explaining why his Philadelphia Investment Corp. chose Four Seasons to operate the facility, which opened in 1983. "He knew how to take our dream for this hotel and make it a reality."

In Washington, D.C., Sharp embarked on one of the most expensive lodging projects ever undertaken in the U.S., spending $102,000 a room to build an intimate hotel on Pennsylvania Avenue six blocks from the White House. The 256-room hotel, opened in 1979, soon became a fixture of the dominant local industry as a hangout for political movers and shakers. And when Sharp finally got his midtown Toronto hotel, refurbishing a former Hyatt Regency to reduce its room count and create larger suites, developer Ken Field, whose company owned the building, was astonished that Four Seasons proposed to spend $40,000 on interlocking bricks for the driveway. "I told Issy, 'You've got to be kidding. Who cares what the driveway is paved with, it's covered with snow half the year anyway.' But he was right. Perhaps his greatest forte is knowing instinctively what each hotel ought to be, down to the last detail."

The crown prince of hotel design at this time was John Portman, a particular favourite of the Pritzker clan's Hyatt chain. Portman's influence accounted for the 1980s trend of soaring, mirror-lined atria trimmed in brass and housed in silo-shaped towers which, in the case of Detroit's Renaissance Center, looked like a nest of ballistic missiles. The antithesis to Portman was Sharp, who was vigilant in nixing overblown aesthetics. "We're selling a feeling of casual elegance," explained Michael Lambert, a Four Seasons executive vice-president. "Our public spaces are less institutional-looking than other chains — much like very grand homes rather than airport terminals."

In January 1981, Sharp was awakened from his sleep with reports of a fire at the Toronto Inn on the Park that would claim six lives and injure 60 other people. The inquest assigned blame all around, including confused municipal fire-inspection procedures and inadequately trained hotel staff. "There can be no excuses, no justification," Sharp said at this lowest point in his career, and immediately upgraded emergency fire procedures at all his hotels, spending $2.5 million in improvements at the Inn on the Park alone. But Four Seasons' reputation survived the tragedy.

Just six weeks after the fire, Sharp kept his appointment with representatives of New York's Hotel Pierre, a granite-and-limestone dowager on Fifth Avenue overlooking Central Park. Opened in 1930 by restaurateur Charles Pierre with the backing of financiers Walter P. Chrysler, E. F. Hutton and Otto Kahn, the building became a cooperative in the 1960s, owned by long-time residents such as the widows of film producer Darryl Zanuck and composer Richard Rodgers. After a falling out with Trusthouse Forte, the British firm was ousted and the Pierre turned to Four Seasons. Over toasts with Dom Perignon in March 1981, Sharp and the Pierre officials toasted the handover of this signature property, which was then treated to a $30-million makeover.

By the 1980s, Four Seasons was winning more accolades, per room, than any other hotel operator in annual reader polls conducted by *Institutional Investor*, *Gourmet* and *Fortune*. Sharp noted with satisfaction that service, and not luxurious appointments, had gained for his company the loyal patronage of globe-trotting bankers, brokers and CEOs. In 1982, at an early stage in Four Seasons' transformation, the authors of *In Search of Excellence* had prefaced their bestselling volume with praise not for the decor of the Four Seasons in Washington, D.C., but for the concierge's alacrity in getting them a room without a reservation — and the fact she remembered Tom Peters and Robert Waterman Jr. from their previous stay at the hotel. "I once read a single sentence by a company president that sums up success," Sharp said at the time. " 'The most important marketer in our company,' he said, 'is the man or woman who decides not to drop the box in the back of the delivery truck.' "

While a Hilton Hotels Corp. could not hope to transform all 1,700 of its outposts into grand hotels, it could, if it chose, outspend Sharp on marble, crystal and reflecting pools in its properties that competed head to head with Four Seasons. But that didn't trouble Sharp. Many of the properties he had collected — the Ritz-Carlton in Chicago and Toronto's Hyatt Regency, for instance — had been mediocre financial performers for their previous owners despite their opulence. This confirmed for Sharp that customer service was his trump card. "We knew we had to set ourselves apart," Sharp said. "We already had the softest towels and the quietest plumbing. Our competitors interpreted luxury chiefly as architecture and decor, but how important was that to our customers? They were mostly executives, often under pressure, fighting jet lag, stress and the clock. We decided to redefine luxury as service, a support system to fill in for the one left behind at home and the office."

By the 1990s, the service culture that evolved at Four Seasons was widely recognized as a paragon of employee initiative and shared understanding of corporate goals. A key factor in that transformation was Sharp's call to arms. His straightforward objective was to create a "fail-safe" experience for patrons of Four Seasons, "so that a company is eager to pay the extra $50 to ensure a hassle-free trip for an executive who might be working on a $50-million deal."

The hardware behind that effort consisted of computer systems that monitored staffing requirements. The quality of service in the hospitality trade is frequently compromised by short-staffing that results from the chronic failure to match staff levels against seasonal fluctuations in business volume. By developing the most accurate forecasting methods in the industry, Four Seasons was able to ensure it always had enough employees on hand at front desks and its dining rooms.

Computers were also used to create "guest histories," a data bank that stored each guest's preferences. These could include everything from a request for hard pillows and vegetarian dishes, to standing orders for theatre tickets, or for exercise equipment to be placed in the suite of a privacy-minded guest who preferred not to mix with other patrons in the hotel's fitness centre. Eventually the system was finetuned to the point where guest histories could be accessed by every hotel and resort in the chain. A patron of the Four Seasons in Palm Beach could be assured of being greeted like an old friend during his first stay at the Four Seasons Berlin.

But computers got a lower priority than the art of personnel management. Innkeeping is, after all, a very labour-intensive business.

In an effort to recruit employees who were motivated to start with, each prospective hire, from dishwasher to comptroller, was screened in four or five separate interviews, including a talk with the hotel's general manager. Staff for a new hotel were assembled over an 18-month period prior to opening. For the early 1990s launch of the flagship Four Seasons hotel in Manhattan, a sister property to the Pierre, 17,000 people were interviewed for 400 jobs. "We rely on character and personality rather than technical expertise," said John Sharpe. "We can always upgrade the skills with training. Unlike other industries, we can't check our product before it's sold."

Results of a confidential employee-attitude questionnaire that each of the company's 23,000 workers filled out once a year were analyzed by the same top management committee, headed by Sharp, that oversaw new hotel projects, ad campaigns and all other major decisions. This data was embellished with reports from a consultant hired to take the pulse of employee morale. These outside monitors asked employees about the quality of working conditions and equipment, and whether there was adequate management feedback to their suggestions for operational improvements. Employee comments had a significant bearing on how their bosses' performance was evaluated, and served as a distant early warning system. When a survey of London employees turned up dissatisfaction with poor staff facilities, the result was quick action to install new flooring, lockers and showers in employee areas. Laundries at Four Seasons hotels were air conditioned. Staff cafeterias often looked more inviting than the commercial variety. The first few millions of dollars spent on upgrading the Pierre went toward new cafeterias, change facilities and uniforms for employees.

Mindful of the limited effectiveness of supervision, Sharp encouraged rank and file employees to be independent. Just as general managers were given unusual latitude in capital spending to replace carpets or panelling the moment it showed signs of wear, housekeepers could free themselves from having their work inspected after they'd achieved a no-fault standard. And extraordinary efforts, such as an incident in which a bellman paid his own airfare to return a briefcase he forgot to send along with a departing patron's luggage, were noted at the top. Sharp spent a great deal of time writing and phoning employees to offer praise. He also enjoyed remarkably harmonious relations with unions in what is a highly organized industry. When hotel owners in New York locked out employees in a dispute with their notoriously combative unions in the early 1980s, the Pierre's general manager set up food carts outside the hotel and personally served coffee and bagels to his employees until an industrywide settlement was reached. A decade later, workers at the newly opened Four Seasons in Milan — a city long controlled by powerful unions — made headlines by ignoring the union leaders' demands that they join a citywide hotel strike, and continued to show up for work.

Monetary compensation for front-line staff included above-average salaries and a profit-sharing scheme that was geared to the performance of individual hotels rather than the company as a whole. Employees of the month received cash rewards and deluxe meals. Employees of the year were rewarded with expenses-paid trips to Four Seasons locations and a cash bonus. *Fortune*, in lauding the company as the only non-U.S. firm to appear on its 1999 ranking of the 100 best companies to work for in America, cited Four Seasons' low employee turnover rate of 23 per cent, about one-third the rate of its competition. "They treat me like a guest at a five-star hotel," an employee told the magazine.

Of course, Four Seasons enjoyed certain advantages in nurturing a high level of job satisfaction. Working in a pleasure palace is more fun than many outposts of the service economy. And the firm's unusual stability in front-line and executive ranks (average tenure for top Four Seasons executives in 2000 was 16 years) result-ed in part from the company's rapid growth. An assistant general manager who was instrumental in the smooth launch of a hotel in Dallas could reasonably hope to preside over the opening of a resort hotel in California or Bali as its general manager. Whole contingents of housekeeping, reservations and banquet managers were periodically airlifted from thriving business hotels in North America to resort start-ups in the Caribbean and renovated historic hotels in the capital cities of Europe. They functioned as "cultural carriers" who imparted the Four Seasons service formula to employees recruited locally. A database that matched job open-ings with employees who had the appropriate skills also listed each worker's next three career moves and a projected date for being qualified for those posts.

The Four Seasons workplace offered up a greater variety of memorable assign-ments than most, given the firm's diverse clientele. Suites used by the Rolling Stones had to be outfitted with blackout curtains. Rocker Rod Stewart required a bagpiper in his room for post-concert reveries. Staff at one Four Seasons facility hand-made a set of canine bathrobes for the pets accompanying tennis star Martina Navratilova. A guest at the Clift set out on a shopping expedition while the concierge took her pet cheetah for a run. And a concierge in Toronto, dissat-isfied with the cage his hotel had rented at Elizabeth Taylor's request for her para-keet, Alvin, hastily ordered the engineering department to repaint and polish it. Employees at the Pierre conspired with Mary Tyler Moore to keep her nuptials at the hotel from nosy reporters; and across town, an obliging staff kept Michael

Jackson's six-month stay at the Four Seasons New York a secret to all but a few friends including Liz Taylor.

Unlike Conrad Hilton, Sharp did not hob nob with his better-known guests. Discretion, he felt, was one of Four Seasons' selling points. Company folklore had it that if Sharp were to bump into Tina Turner in an elevator, he would not introduce himself. "Part of what these people pay for is to be left alone," he said. Sharp once made a joint appearance with Sting to support the rock singer's environmental crusade. He was perhaps the only Canadian on the guest list for publisher Malcolm Forbes's stupendous birthday bash in Morocco. Otherwise, he kept out of the society pages. He engaged in low-key pastimes, notably tennis and heliskiing in the Bugaboos of the Canadian Rockies. Sharp's conversation was seldom enlivened by celebrity encounters. He talked incessantly about employee star turns. Sharp seemed particularly taken with the concierge in San Francisco who responded to the 5:00 p.m. pleading of a guest visiting from Toronto for a Canadian flag to take to a game that evening between the Oakland Athletics and his hometown Blue Jays. The concierge responded by hauling out the spare to the 10-by-12-foot Maple Leaf flying outside the Clift. "So this customer had a huge Canadian flag draped across his box," Sharp said. "It's not a small detail when it's something the customer wants."

Sharp himself was among the most demanding customers. In 2000, Sharp was still spending half the year on the road, staying at 25 or so hotels annually. "Managing a service business through internal reports is like playing tennis while keeping an eye on the scoreboard," he said. More as a request than an order, he would ask that luggage dollies be banished from a lobby, suggest that balcony lights be turned off after 1:00 a.m. ("Last night I couldn't even open the curtains for a bit of air"), express his concern about an elevator door that shut too quickly ("We can't be closing doors on people's dresses") and strategize with a manager over how to reduce the distance that housekeepers were required to lug fresh sheets. Maid carts were forbidden at Four Seasons. "We spend so much money making corridors lovely," Sharp said, "and you don't want to see carts with garbage hanging off them 90 per cent of the time." Nor did he want his hotels showing up on Madonna CD covers. Representatives of the singer — and of Burger King — were denied their requests to use his Pierre as a backdrop.

On full-moon nights in Bali, guests at the Four Seasons Jimbaran Bay could opt for a Hindu karma-cleansing ritual on the black-sand beach at the nearby Tanah Lot Temple, where devotees in sarongs were annointed with holy water and crowned with a tiara of blossoms. Sharp heartily endorsed this sort of thing, for his guests. For himself, Sharp seemed content to find inner peace as his wife's bridge partner.

Two things in particular endeared Sharp to the monied class in Toronto. One was the continuing love affair between Issy Sharp and Rosalie Wise. In the third decade of their marriage, they could still be mistaken for no-shows at black-tie galas in Forest Hill ballrooms, until someone would spot them cuddling in the library. At a time when second and third spouses were cutting a wide swath through the city's higher income brackets, here was a durable union that got people talking about something other than drive-by liaisons. Sharp exulted in his longstanding relationships with key partners; at age 68, his face still took on a warm glow in 2000 as he recounted how older and wiser peers — the McAlpines, the president of Cadillac Fairview, a Big Five bank chairman — had consented to help him despite his youth and inexperience. The greatest of these partners was Rosalie. "At a time in the beginning, when we were surrounded by skeptics," he said, "Rosalie was in a better position than anyone to know how close I was to becoming a ridiculous failure. And that made her support of me especially courageous."

The other thing admired was Sharp's way of handling his personal fortune. Tom Wolfe once observed that Toronto was a city where billionaires made a point of playing down their wealth. Press lord Ken Thomson, for instance, could be relied upon to arrive at swank affairs behind the wheel of his own Subaru hatchback. These things could be carried to extremes, of course. Sharp wasn't precious about his lack of ostentation. And he was a cut-up. At one of the annual Venetian Balls to raise funds for Villa Colombo, a prominent Italian seniors' residence in Toronto, Rosalie showed up wearing a gown with venetian blinds sewn onto her waist. Issy accompanied her as, what else, a blind Venetian, decked out in white suit and cane, panama hat and sunglasses. He was a prominent advocate of ethical reform in corporate governance. He exercised his integrity without being judgmental. When theatre magnate Garth Drabinsky's Livent empire collapsed in the late 1990s, and Drabinsky became a pariah after being charged by the U.S. Securities and Exchange Commission with securities fraud, Sharp quietly raised "Red Cross money" for his legal defence. ("All the great impresarios reached too far — Florenz Ziegfeld had his troubles, too," Sharp said.)

Much more publicly, Sharp was associated with the annual Terry Fox Marathon of Hope. This was the largest single-day fundraising event for cancer research in the world, with runs taking place in several countries and total proceeds by 1999 of $220 million. In 1978, the Sharps lost their 17-year-old son Christopher to cancer. Three years later, before Fox became a media celebrity with his cross-country run in a bid to raise one dollar from every Canadian for cancer research, Sharp had discreetly approached Fox's parents to offer financial support and free accommodation. He then marshalled support on Bay Street to forge a corporate counterpart to the grassroots fundraising effort.

In contrast to the Reichmanns, the Sharps moved easily in non-Jewish circles. But the Sharps' lifestyle, like that of the famous developer family, seemed to be restrained out of respect for agonizing sacrifices in the past. Two of Issy's aunts had died at the hands of the Nazis. And Rosalie, whose family was also from Poland, had lost most of her relatives in the Holocaust. In an era when business was decidedly secular, Sharp did not disguise his faith. "I think being born Jewish is like a blessing," he said. "You may, at various times in your life, be made to feel that you are different. But you are what you are, and you stand up for it as best you can.

"You know, they don't criticize us for being dumb. They're criticizing us for being smart."

There is nothing which has yet been contrived by man by which so much happiness is produced as by a good tavern or inn.
— James Boswell, *Life of Samuel Johnson* (1791)

FROM A PLANNING PERSPECTIVE, hotel development is a hellish proposition. Most new properties consume cash for at least five years before turning a profit, even assuming that the facility turns out to be the right type for the locale. The predictive powers of hotel planners are routinely mocked by recessions, sudden hikes in interest rates, acts of God (Hurricane Hugo interrupted the construction of the Four Seasons in Nevis) and global conflicts such as the Persian Gulf war that depress worldwide travel. Operators of international chains cope with abrupt currency fluctuations. And the diversity of local labour conditions poses a severe challenge to any global hotelier seeking to impose uniform service standards.

Most major hotel firms merely manage, and do not own, their outlets. The revolving-door ownership of properties that characterizes the modern industry plays havoc with relations between hotel owners and managers. (In a three-year span in the early 1990s, the Plaza in New York was owned by Donald Trump and then by Citibank before coming under the stewardship of Saudi Prince al-Waleed bin Talal in partnership with a Singapore-based hotel group; in the late 1990s, management duties at the Plaza were shared by the Fairmont and Canadian Pacific chains.) New and freshly renovated properties, no matter how carefully planned, have an almost magical tendency to open at the top of the economic cycle, and promptly fall victim to periodic overbuilding in the industry. Whenever a real or perceived shortage of rooms appears in a given market, too many opportunists rush to correct it.

For Sharp, who had to be especially selective in choosing locations and suitably intimate premises, the planning process was chequered with delays and disappointments — this despite being at the top of the A-list when managers were sought for new projects. The Four Seasons Motor Hotel had taken six years to develop. In 2000, new properties still took about five years to evolve from concept to reality. It took Sharp five years, for instance, to develop a $300-million hotel that opened in Tokyo in 1992, the chain's first property in Japan. And the 1999 reopening of the refurbished George V as a Four Seasons hotel marked the culmination of more than 20 years of effort by Sharp to plant his flag in Paris. "If you're in a hurry, you shouldn't be in this business," he said.

Yet impatience more than good business sense, it seemed, prompted Sharp in 1992 to spend $188 million on his biggest expansion campaign to date. The Hong Kong-based Regent luxury hotel group, regarded as the Four Seasons of Asia, had suddenly become available with the insolvency of its owner, a Japanese conglomerate. Sharp moved swiftly to close the deal for its acquisition, which almost doubled the size of his portfolio of properties. In one stroke, Four Seasons became the world's first truly international luxury hotel chain. The Regent prize included 10 hotels in prime Asian destinations such as Singapore, Sydney, Hong Kong, Bangkok, Taipei and Kuala Lumpur, plus Regent properties under development in New York, London, Milan, Jakarata and Bali. But most of all, Sharp said eight years later, "Regent was New York." It was getting the Pei palace, then nearing completion, whose stupendous construction costs were absorbed by the previous owner. "We had the benefit of getting this magnificent hotel without having to pay for it; we just have the management contract. True, the hotel industry was troubled in 1992. But this was still New York, 57th Street — you knew the market would turn."

Yet while the price tag might not have reflected the value Four Seasons could hope to eventually derive from the Regent prize, it was arguably more than Sharp could afford to pay at the time. When he grabbed for Regent he was already stretched, with eight new hotels of his own underway in Asia, Europe, the U.S. and the Caribbean. His firm was suffering the worst downturn in business travel in its 30-year history. Operation Desert Storm, to evict Saddam Hussein from Kuwait, along with a worsening recession in North America, had put a crimp in business travel. World airline passenger traffic had plunged more deeply than at any time since statistics were first compiled in the 1940s. And the early 1990s economic downturn, unlike earlier slumps, was characterized by widespread layoffs of white-collar middle managers — a key client group of Four Seasons.

The firm posted a stunning loss of $119.2 million in 1993 as revenues dropped and borrowing costs soared with the Regent transaction. With a debt load almost three times the size of its equity base, serviced at sky-high interest rates, Four Seasons was on the ropes. Investors, who had warmed to the company's prospects from the time Sharp took it public once again in 1986 (to enable Koffler and Creed to each cash out their investments in the firm), now grew twitchy. Short-sellers began to attack Four Seasons stock in early 1994 when an analysis of the company by *The New York Times* accused Sharp of "clever financial alchemy" in his accounting practices.

Yet the crisis soon passed after investors in New York, where Four Seasons stock was listed, got a better grasp of the firm's accounting methods. In truth, its practice of recording its equity stakes in certain hotels off the balance sheet — so that their (poor) performance didn't show up on the firm's profit-and-loss statement — was a legitimate accounting method in Canada. Sharp was also able to cut the debt load of his firm much faster than expected, by selling off many of those same hotel ownership stakes. And the profit picture brightened considerably with a dramatic upturn in the North American economy beginning in 1994.

Yet Sharp seemed to be pushing his luck when he chose that uncertain time to begin a search for a financial partner, one who would inject nourishing capital into Four Seasons without requiring the founder to surrender his control of the firm. Rival hotelier Stephen Bollenbach, then CEO of Host Marriott Corp., was struck by Sharp's seeming chutzpah in submerging his firm in debt and then seeking a lifeline precisely on his own terms. "Having taken this thing on a nightmare journey," he said of Sharp's roll of the dice in purchasing Regent, "now he wants someone to put money in and let him continue to run it. Give me a break. Who would do it?"

Long before the Regent deal, Sharp's glowing reputation as the standard-setter for the luxury sector worldwide had fed a growing resentment of the Canadian upstart. As Four Seasons struggled with indigestion from the Regent acquisition, some of the firm's U.S. competitors took a bit of pleasure from Sharp's apparent comeuppance. This was a time to recall that when former Hilton International chairman Curt Strand was asked if he would ever want to remake his firm in Four Seasons' image, he had said, "We'd love to, we just couldn't afford to."

For all that, Sharp received more than 100 inquiries to invest in his company, many of them from competing hotel chains. He worried, though, that sharing his rooms with another hotelier — shades of the Four Seasons Sheraton debacle — would mean diluting the brand-image he'd worked so hard to develop. There could be no thought of seeking financial refuge in merging with another chain, since that would mean going downmarket, no matter how much autonomy a hotel suitor might promise to grant Four Seasons in a combined entity. "Many of our competitors have tried to mix a five-star company with a three-star company," Sharp said in 2000, citing the luxury operations that some of his bigger rivals had bought or launched internally, which had all failed to gain a serious foothold in the luxury niche. "It's like dentistry and accounting — they just don't mix. Patrons of Holiday Inn don't want to rub shoulders with CEOs; and managers of true luxury operations cannot adapt to a three-star operation, which is driven by volume not quality, no matter what they say."

In cushioning the Regent hit to his balance sheet, Sharp was ultimately drawn to a proposal from Prince al-Waleed. Sharp was the second prominent Jewish businessman from Toronto to visit the nephew of Saudi Arabia's King Kahd in 1994 aboard the *Kingdom*, the Prince's 282-foot yacht anchored in the French Riviera off Cannes. Paul Reichmann came away with an informal agreement that the Prince would help bankroll the O&Y cofounder's ambition to buy back the Canary Wharf project in London. Sharp negotiated a deal in which al-Waleed paid $167 million for 25 per cent of Four Seasons. The founder retained 68 per cent voting control of his firm. Sweeter still, the Prince insisted on investing a further $100 million to buy and develop new hotels for Four Seasons to manage. "What I wanted," said al-Waleed, "was Sharp himself, his expertise, the brain-power within Four Seasons."

Observers like Bollenbach were brought up short by the agreement. Sharp had struck a deal with one of the decade's savviest investors. The Prince had invested in Citibank when the U.S.'s largest bank was flirting with insolvency in the early 1990s, and profited greatly when Citi, and its shares, soon returned to vigorous health. "I was wrong," said Bollenbach on hearing of al-Waleed's partnership with Four Seasons. "I think it's a real vote of confidence for Issy Sharp." As the 1990s bull market fuelled the acquisitive ambitions of CEOs everywhere, pushing up the price of corporate assets, Sharp's 1992 deal began to look like a bargain. An expansion-minded Bollenbach soon moved on to the CEO post at Hilton, where his effort to achieve a Four Seasons-like dominance in the mid-market sector failed when he was outbid for Sheraton in a deal that put an astronomical value on that chain's mixed bag of properties. (Stock in the victorious bidder, Starwood, tanked within two years of the transaction.) The Saudi prince, meanwhile, was rewarded for his faith in Sharp. The Four Seasons shares that al-Waleed bought for $22 a share were worth $85 just six years later. And Sharp got the plum contract to manage the George V, which al-Waleed had picked up in one of his shopping sprees. The Toronto hotelier, a former co-chairman of the local United Jewish Appeal, also found himself in the unexpected role of introducing five-star innkeeping to Damascus, Cairo, Amman, Riyadh, Dubai and Qatar with properties owned by al-Waleed.

In the view of some, Four Seasons occasionally fell short of its founder's standard of perfection. The chain "has tended to believe that the elegance of a hotel room is in direct proportion to the amount of imitation English furniture it contains," said Paul Goldberger, architecture critic at *The New York Times*, who had grown weary of Sharp's widely emulated residential approach to big-city hotels. Praising Four Seasons' break with that style in acquiring Pei's monumental Manhattan tower, Goldberger wrote that "in an age when almost every new luxury hotel seems to be parading domesticity, a hotel that presents itself as a shimmering and urbane presence is a great thing to happen to New York."

While high-level staff defections at Four Seasons were rare, they were not unheard of. The company had a reputation for granting its hotel managers so much autonomy that many considered themselves to be practically independent hoteliers. Yet sometimes, as Sharp fine-tuned his pursuit of chainwide consistency, a manager would balk. "You hear the term 'head-office requirement' much more often now than you did in the past," said one former Four Seasons general manager. "They're not looking for the rugged individualist anymore."

"I have managers who say they couldn't work harder if it was their own hotel," Sharp insisted. But he was candid about his intolerance for executives who didn't hew to his philosophy. "Managers who weren't helping to build team spirit were undermining it," he said of the rationale for a late-1980s purge. "I made cuts at the very top — head office senior executives, general managers of hotels — until all those whom others would copy were playing by the same rules."

If anything, Sharp regretted not acting faster to deal with problem executives. In 2000, he was still angry with himself for dragging his heels three years earlier on the removal of a senior manager who was abusive to workers below him. "I felt I'd grown up with this fellow, a 25-year veteran," Sharp said. "I blame myself for allowing the problem to go on for so long."

"A big part of our culture is storytelling," said Sharp. "People sit down in the cafeteria and one person asks another, 'What's it really like to work here?' And one of the things they talk about is whether we stood on our principles of fair treatment in forcing out people as high as general managers and vice-presidents who were abusing the employees' trust."

In the stock market, Sharp himself was accused of unfair treatment of fellow shareholders by abusing the concept of shareholder democracy in which one share equals one vote. In taking Four Seasons public again in the 1980s, Sharp had endowed himself with a class of "supervoting" shares that carried 12 votes each. He compounded that advantage a decade later in a 1996 share restructuring that was designed to raise expansion capital without diminishing Sharp's control of the firm. The Sharp family's supervoting shares had been converted to "variable voting" stock whose voting power increased proportionately with the number of new shares issued, assuring that the Sharps would keep 67 per cent voting control of Four Seasons.

An outraged Institutional Shareholder Services of Bethesda, Maryland, called the new setup an "egregious capital structure." But Prince al-Waleed, who came out of the 1996 restructuring with the same one-vote shares as ordinary investors, had endorsed the arrangement. And Sharp was unapologetic about it. "There's never been any threat that Four Seasons will be taken over," Sharp said. "Where one person's in control, there's continuity. That means a lot to our employees, who know they can make their career with Four Seasons and they're set, because it's going to be the same company for 10 years. And it means a lot to hotel owners. We were recently chosen over the Ritz-Carlton Co. to manage a hotel in Egypt. The owner told me, 'I don't know what's happening with Ritz in five years.'"

The issue of succession, Sharp realized, was a cloud over Four Seasons. Two of his sons, Gregory and Anthony, had worked in the firm. But each later decided to make their careers elsewhere — in Tony's case, after a 10-year run in which he helped build up Four Seasons' presence in the time-share business. Sharp had determined that the boys would still inherit the firm, however. Tony continued to serve on the board, and made a point of attending several meetings of top management every year. His father, meanwhile, was now basing himself in Palm Springs, California, from January to March. "It gets people in Toronto more and more accustomed to the idea that they're running the show," he explained.

"I used to worry that my shadow was too big, that I have to get everyone to realize that leadership is in place to carry on without me," Sharp said. But in 2000, "the bench strength of executives who have grown up with the company is tremendous." Sharp had just appointed two co-presidents and heirs apparent to the CEO post, Wolf Hengst and Kathleen Taylor, who had respectively, 22 years' and 11 years' tenure with Four Seasons. They were replacing John Sharp (24 years' tenure) and Roger Garland (19 years'). "I think the reason we've been able to keep talent is because everyone sees that the top people have emerged from their own ranks," said Sharp. "And that I believe the best talent we've got will always be better than anyone we could get from outside."

A T THE DAWN of the 21st century, there were no readily discernible limits to Four Seasons' expansion prospects. As a management company, it collected 4 per cent of gross hotel revenues plus incentive fees of 15 per cent to 20 per cent of profits. It left construction, refurbishment and even employee costs to hotel owners to absorb. (Four Seasons carried only 250 or so people on its corporate payroll.) That left the company with ample resources to increase its presence in places like Western Europe and South America, where it had few properties at the close of the century. And to beef up its new sideline of vacation time-sharing and retirement ownership villages, which debuted at Carlsbad, California, in 1997. These were usually located adjacent to a Four Seasons resort and often boasted PGA-calibre golf courses. The cachet of the resorts attracted buyers for the nearby residential properties, whose occupants then provided a steady business for the resorts.

Sharp followed up on that initiative with Four Seasons Residences, urban condos attached to Four Seasons hotels in New York, Boston, Houston, San Francisco and Miami, for a clientele seeking to rent or purchase, for a price of $1 million and up, a home away from home or a corporate apartment. In 2000, Ritz-Carlton was inspired to emulate the concept, but with offerings limited to the U.S. By that point, Sharp was expanding his Residences to places like Alexandria, Egypt and the south of France.

Sharp had reason to like his chances against a competitive threat from any of his larger competitors who might harbour ambitions for a renewed assault on the ultra-luxury segment. Even the best-run hotel management companies were vulnerable to internal upheaval. They were changing hands with all the frequency of hotels themselves. In the space of a decade, the upscale Westin group was owned by United Airlines, then by a Japanese conglomerate and finally by Starwood's Barry Sternlicht, a thirtysomething real-estate speculator and headhunter's delight, given the hectic pace at which his key hotel executives were defecting to rival chains.

As a consequence of their enormous size — Marriott had more than four times the revenues of Four Seasons — the major hotel firms were obliged to diversify in order to satisfy their investors' demands for growth. Even in 2000, the addition of just five new hotels at Four Seasons had the effect of boosting annual revenues by some 20 per cent. To achieve that level of growth, bigger hoteliers were required to buy or launch scores of new properties each year and expand into non-hotel fields. The result was that among the industry's biggest players, Four Seasons was the only focused operator. And his competitors suffered from confused mandates. By the late 1990s, Hilton was generating most of its revenues from casinos, at which point it abruptly decided to quit the gaming business and become a hotel company again. Marriott, ostensibly a mid-market hotelier, also ran school cafeterias, an airline catering business and theme parks, and had bailed out Ritz-Carlton in 1995 after it choked on an expansion drive initiated by its previous owner, an Atlanta developer. France's Accor ran the luxury Novotel inns and deep-discount Motel 6 chain. Britain's Bass PLC, a brewing company, owned both the downmarket Holiday Inn brand and the Intercontinental stable of luxury hotels.

The chief threat to Four Seasons was any diminution of Sharp's operating philosophy. "Sharp's personal stamp becomes corporate mythology," said Toronto developer and Four Seasons director Benjamin Swirsky, underscoring the importance of the founder's touch in motivating employees in some two dozen countries. Sharp, dubbed "razzle-dazzle Issy" by his college newspaper for his basketball prowess, "has an electrifying effect on people because he so obviously concentrates on the positive," added John Young, Four Seasons' director of human resources. That factor was well understood by owners of Four Seasons hotels, who typically signed up with the company on the basis of 50-year management contracts (versus the industry standard of six years). Many of those contracts provided owners with escape clauses in the event that Sharp were to cede control of Four Seasons.

"Some hotel owners once approached us to ask if we'd manage their new hotel," Sharp recalled. "They had copied every aspect of a Four Seasons hotel right down to the pre-opening brochure — and it wasn't working for them. It wasn't working because Four Seasons' most significant aspects are employee esprit de corps and our depth and cohesion of management — what I think of as the 'emotional capital' of the company. It's a product of a culture that can't be copied or bought, only created through collective enthusiasm and belief over many, many years."

But an exacting standard of customer service is the one element of success that is perhaps most difficult to sustain. Sharp couldn't be sure that under someone else's direction, his company would have the resolve to maintain high standards of operation at times of financial difficulty. In one recession after another, Sharp had continued to replace fading curtains and to experiment with food and fitness innovations, enabling some of his hotels to boast of patrons who logged 100 repeat stays in a property's first five years of operation.

So Sharp became an evangelist, devoting increasing amounts of his time to creating a written and spoken record of what he'd learned. One of the more important lessons was that a decision to stoop to cost-cutting in tough times was, wittingly or not, a commitment to a new strategic direction. And one with obvious perils.

"The danger is not that we will suddenly lower our standards," Sharp explained. "The danger is that little changes will creep in on us, especially when they help to reduce cost and save a dollar here and there. At first, nobody much will notice. But, unexpectedly, the accumulation of several minor changes has an incremental effect that will catch up and then suddenly everybody notices. Without meaning it, standards have been lowered, a product or service has been changed, and now someone's not selling the product or service that he used to be selling."

By 2000, Sharp, whose memory was still fresh with being alerted by his night security manager that the Four Seasons Motor Hotel had a problem with couples making out under the grand piano, seemed to have exceeded his most ambitious goals for the company. As Swirsky said, "He's already the host to the elite of the world."

Sharp was not so sure. "We've only just broken the surface of what we can accomplish," he said, noting that perhaps half of his hotels were too new to have achieved anything like their full potential. "I want to make Four Seasons a generic term for quality the way Cesar Ritz did. And his name is now part of the language. The goal is within our reach. All we have to do is impress 20,000 guests each and every day."

4

PAUL REICHMANN

The rise and fall and rise
of the world's greatest property developer

"It is gratifying to build a monument."
— Paul Reichmann

PAUL REICHMANN created and lost the greatest empire in commercial real estate of the 20th century. Had there not been more to his story than that, it might soon have passed from memory. That is, after Reichmann's name had been subjected to the kind of ridicule that a Donald Trump or Robert Campeau endured when the tide of credulity ran out on the high-rollers of the 1980s. Reichmann did, after all, share their near-fatal sense of infallibility. At the groundbreaking ceremony for his massive Canary Wharf office project in London — the scheme that would ultimately tip Olympia & York Developments Ltd. into bankruptcy in one of the biggest corporate collapses of the century — Reichmann had said, "The only question that enters our minds is, Will success happen immediately or later?"

Yet, while the Reichmann name is associated now with epic risk and failure, it also continues to suggest an aura of awesome wealth, breathtaking contrarian bets that usually paid off in spectacular fashion, and a curious, agreeable amalgam of religious adherence and acute entrepreneurial instincts rarely found in a business leader.

Even had he not staged a remarkable comeback just three years after O&Y's bankruptcy, the O&Y debacle would have placed Reichmann in a rarefied class of failure — the kind that commands attention because of its durable legacy. The new industries of the 20th century — automobiles, aviation, computers — each yielded visionaries who blazed a trail of innovation before losing control of their firms for lack of financial discipline. Among these pioneers was William "Billy" Durant, ousted from General Motors, but only after making vertical integration a fact of modern industrial life; Juan Trippe, whose Pan American Airways lost its market dominance, but not before making air travel affordable for the masses; and Steve Jobs, who was forced out of Apple Computer Corp. (and later invited to return as CEO), but only after popularizing the home computer.

Commercial real estate was another industry that came into its own in the 20th century. No one symbolized its potential more than Paul Reichmann, who sought with his private-sector schemes to have the impact once reserved for the greatest public-works projects. He was infused with the same, sometimes arrogant, belief in his own destiny as Baron Haussmann, master planner of 19th-century Paris, and Robert Moses, Haussman's 20th-century counterpart in New York State. Lacking those brazen builders' unlimited access to the public purse, Reichmann managed repeatedly to defy the cruel economics of a volatile industry as he reshaped the sky-lines of a dozen major cities. He built the world's tallest bank tower in Toronto in the midst of a deep recession — and despite the inconvenience of a recently imposed local bylaw restricting the height of all new buildings to 45 feet. He then succeeded in an audacious bid to revitalize the fading Wall Street financial district with a col-lection of neo-classical office towers at the southern tip of Manhattan, launching the biggest construction project in New York history on the eve of the worst economic downturn since the Great Depression. Finally, in the derelict Docklands some two-and-a-half miles from the business centre of London, Reichmann aspired to create the new financial capital of Europe, with a sprawling community of office towers, shopping gallerias, residential buildings and manicured parks that represented the world's largest-ever commercial land development.

Canary Wharf, named for the Docklands wharf on the Thames where 19th-century ships unloaded bananas from the Canary Islands, would be the last Olympia & York megaproject. By the early 1990s, Reichmann had mortgaged O&Y's existing properties to the tune of $5 billion to finance the project's fantas-tic construction costs. But Reichmann had found tenants for just half of the space in Canary Wharf's first few buildings, including the 50-storey One Canada Place, the tallest office tower in Europe. The world was in recession once again, distin-guished by an unprecedented wave of newly unemployed white-collar workers — the target population for O&Y's upscale office space. This time O&Y would not survive. A worldwide glut in office space resulting from rampant overbuilding in the previous decade triggered a "meltdown" in real estate values. In O&Y's key markets of Toronto, New York and London, rents fell by as much as 30 per cent, and vacancy rates soared to 20 per cent as employers trimmed their payrolls. O&Y had borrowed a total of $20 billion to fund its many projects, probably the biggest debt load ever accumulated by a privately held company. Much of it was negoti-ated at short-term interest rates, which had spiralled upward.

As financing costs mounted, and rental revenues shrank, Reichmann was caught in a classic squeeze. By the spring of 1992, O&Y was in default on its debt to several of its 91 banks worldwide, borrowings which were secured against O&Y's empire of office buildings in North America. In May of that year, O&Y's Canadian, British and U.S. operations tumbled into bankruptcy. Reichmann had anticipated a recession, but not its severity or duration. And he was not prepared for the stubborn resistance of prestigious corporate tenants in London who refused to give up their antiquated lodgings in The City for modern digs in the remote Canary Wharf.

The lesson of Waterloo, said Napoleon, is that "there is but one step from triumph to disaster." Reichmann's over-reaching at Canary Wharf obscured his otherwise stunning achievements, making an abrupt end to an unbroken string of triumphs. He had started out building warehouses in suburban Toronto. In the relatively short span of three decades, O&Y assembled a portfolio of 50 million square feet of prime office space at landmark properties in North America's major cities and London. O&Y's vertical integration made it a rarity among developers. It assembled its own land packages, acted as its own general contractor, leasing agent and property manager — allowing it to build on a scale, and at a speed, never before seen in commercial real estate. Competing developers scrambled to adopt the efficient methods of construction that O&Y pioneered. They learned from Reichmann that each new project should be an advertisement for the next one. When it became known that O&Y had quarried marble for Toronto's First Canadian Place, Canada's tallest building, at the same mountain in Italy that provided Michelangelo with the material for his *Pietà*, rival builders grasped the need to upgrade their own aesthetic sensibilities to attract top-drawer corporate tenants.

Paul Reichmann's prescience in forecasting the shift of transient office-worker populations — to the suburbs in the 1960s and 1970s, and back to downtown in the 1980s — was matched by a dexterity in financing that was unheard of among developers. O&Y was the first real-estate company to significantly tap the same commercial-paper and Euro-lending markets that its blue-chip tenants dipped into for expansion capital. And perhaps inevitably, as the Reichmanns' annual rental income topped $500 million, O&Y itself became the industry's first blue-chip firm, a conglomerate that used its burgeoning cash flow to acquire extensive holdings in oil and gas, pipelines, newsprint mills, trust companies and life insurers.

By the late 1980s, lenders, tenants and civic officials who met with Paul Reichmann found themselves negotiating not simply with the head-office landlord for American Express Co., Merrill Lynch & Co. Inc. and the publisher of *The Wall Street Journal*, but a controlling shareholder in Royal Trustco, London Life, Gulf Canada Resources, Consumers Gas Co., Interprovincial Pipe Line and Abitibi-Price Inc., the world's largest newsprint firm and chief supplier to *USA Today*.

But O&Y's blue-chip status would prove to be debilitating. Some years before O&Y's assets peaked in 1989, Paul Reichmann first betrayed a belief in his invincibility when he said that "the health of O&Y is really the health of the tenants." He came to think that as O&Y rapidly matured into a size and diversity similar to that of its deep-pocketed tenants, it would be insulated, as they were, from the notorious volatility of interest and vacancy rates that is the unavoidable curse of the property development business. As economic storm clouds gathered in the late 1980s, Reichmann refused to drop rents to arrest an exodus of tenants to cheaper space, or shed assets to raise cash, or slow the pace of construction at the monstrously expensive Canary Wharf.

At least four times over the previous 30 years, Reichmann had bet the company on his faith that O&Y could make a safe passage through recessionary times without trimming its sails. And his family owed its stupendous wealth to his foresight on each of those occasions. Reichmann would look back on the spring of 1992, when O&Y defaulted on bonds issued by First Canadian Place and some of its prized U.S. buildings, and confess that "the fact that I had never been wrong created character flaws that caused me to make mistakes."

With the 1992 debacle, the O&Y reputation for invincibility — long referred to as "the Reichmann mystique" — appeared to have been shattered. At its height, the Reichmanns' personal wealth had eclipsed that of Britain's Royal Family. And they had built well. In the estimation of architecture writer Ada Louise Huxtable, the Reichmanns' World Financial Center, which now figured prominently in the postcard image of lower Manhattan, was "a first-class urban complex of the standard, significance and size of Rockefeller Center, that will add a spectacular new beauty to the New York skyline. There has been no large scale development of comparable quality since the 1930s." O&Y's transformation of the desolate Docklands was equally dramatic. "From the marbled caverns at the foot of its 50-stories-high central tower to its glass-domed railway station and elegant public spaces, the Canary Wharf development is breathtaking," gushed Britain's *Economist*. "It is already clear that the reclusive Reichmanns have honoured the commitment they made in 1987. They promised that Canary Wharf would be magnificent; and it is."

What did it matter, though, that Margaret Thatcher had said of the Reichmanns that "we have to thank them for their faith in Britain"? The sentiment wasn't shared by prospective tenants in London, whose refusal to embrace a project that Thatcher regarded as an architectural symbol of her Tory revolution had stripped the Reichmanns of their $12.8-billion fortune when the creditors moved in. At U.S. Senate hearings into the collapse of U.S. banks and savings-and-loans institutions in 1992, the Reichmanns and other developers were apportioned a share of the blame for the sorry state of America's financial sector, as conspicuous beneficiaries of feckless lending practices. Experts testified that New York was so overbuilt that the market might never recover. In London, property agents spoke with conviction in pronouncing the half-empty Canary Wharf to be a white elephant of historic proportions.

In Toronto, a funereal silence descended over the financial ruins of O&Y. The Reichmanns, refugees from ethnic and religious persecution in Europe, had settled on Toronto as the base from which to build one of the world's great family fortunes. Their continued residence in the city long after Canada could no longer contain their expansionist impulses fed Toronto's inflated sense of its civility. So did the worldwide acclaim garnered by their projects, which were known to have been largely financed by Canada's largest banks, based in Toronto, and inspired in their design by Toronto's progressive urban-planning practices.

In New York, London and other foreign cities, the Reichmanns had been ambassadors of Canadian engineering expertise and building materials, including the Quebec granite in which the towers of the World Financial Center were clad. The Reichmanns were also the leading patrons of ultra-Orthodox Jewish causes worldwide, having distributed a staggering half a billion dollars to 1,000 haredim schools and other religious institutions in Israel, Eastern Europe and North America, in addition to bankrolling the commercial aspirations of hundreds of haredim entrepreneurs. In doing so, the Reichmanns had shifted the world capital of philanthropic activity in the global haredim community from Brooklyn to the Toronto suburb of North York, where members of the extended Reichmann family lived in close proximity to each other and their synagogues. There was no rush in Toronto to condemn the Reichmanns for Paul's folly. The mood was perhaps best captured by a T-shirt designed by local artist Barbara Klunder. It bore a plaintive inscription: "Owe & Why."

For most of his remarkable career as a developer, Paul Reichmann had promoted an image of himself as merely an equal partner in O&Y with his older brother, Albert, and younger brother, Ralph. But in reality, Ralph had devoted himself exclusively to the family's tile-importing business. And Albert, an administrator in the property operation, functioned chiefly as a sounding board for Paul, the dreamer who conceived the real-estate megadeals and alone among the three had the gritty resolve to make them a reality. "At Olympia & York, I was the guilty party," Paul would say several years after the O&Y collapse. This expression of contrition was Paul's way of asserting that he alone could set things right. From the moment of O&Y's demise, Reichmann was convinced he could restore at least a portion of his earlier reputation for near-omniscience. "The skills people have to build something — even if they make a mistake and lose by it — are not gone forever," he said. "I have to prove I can rebuild and recreate what has been lost by my mistakes."

In a few short years, Reichmann would indeed be vindicated, as North America's leading property markets once again exhibited signs of robust health, and prestigious tenants at last began flocking to Canary Wharf. But Reichmann, now 62, hadn't the patience to wait out the bad times. Amid the climate of fear in 1992, when voters, worried about their job prospects would strip George Bush of *his* job, Reichmann cobbled together a consortium of investors to buy back Canary Wharf. That August 1992 bid, coming just three months after the worldwide O&Y empire was forced into bankruptcy, was rejected out of hand by creditors who weren't quite ready to put the project back into the hands of a man perceived to be the architect of a massive fiasco. Eventually they would have a change of heart. But, Reichmann had wasted no time in taking that important first step, for there was much to reclaim.

S OCIAL HISTORIANS have observed that the 20th century emergence of a secular ethic in North America was signalled by the primacy of commercial buildings over churches. A distinctive feature of the Reichmanns' adopted hometown in 1900 was Toronto's boast of having more places of worship per capita than any city on the continent. Eighty years later, the Toronto skyline was no longer dominated by cathedral spires, but by bank towers.

Developers played only a modest role in the early stages of this triumph of commercial architecture. Tenants, not developers, commissioned the first awe-inspiring skyscrapers. These were often acts of corporate vanity. When Frank W. Woolworth commissioned a head-office tower in lower Manhattan for his five-and-dime empire, his chief instruction to architect Cass Gilbert was to erect a "Cathedral of Commerce" that would be "fifty feet higher than the Metropolitan Tower." Woolworth was still angered by the slight of having once been denied a loan by the Metropolitan Life Insurance Co. His new head office, completed in 1913, was intended to strip the insurer of its claim to occupying the world's tallest building. In 1930, the Woolworth tower was itself overshadowed by Walter Chrysler's $16-million monument to the machine age. The Manhattan landmark, with its 30th-floor frieze of huge hubcaps with winged radiator caps at the corners, was meant to signal the automaker's status as a worthy peer to GM and Ford just five years after the founding of Chrysler Corp.

Because they weren't planned with the idea of generating rental income, private commercial buildings were erected in isolation, paying scant heed to their surroundings. The first major break with that practice came from an unlikely source. The progenitor of the "mixed-use" complex, an ensemble of buildings that incorporated offices, retail shops, restaurants and theatres, wasn't a developer but a scion to America's greatest industrial fortune. Yet it was John D. Rockefeller Jr. who laid the foundations for the modern land-development industry.

Rockefeller conceived the Metropolitan Corp., later Rockefeller Center, not as a glorification of his father's Standard Oil colossus but as an urban reclamation project for midtown Manhattan. In Rockefeller's pioneering vision, a cluster of skyscrapers was meant not merely to provide shelter for office workers but also to function as a magnet for tourists, attracting pedestrian traffic for its stores and restaurants. A piecemeal approach to construction would not do if Rockefeller Center was to draw tenants and shoppers to the unfashionable midtown district. Rockefeller's "city within a city," some 5.5 million square feet of space in 12 buildings, was to be erected all at once. And it would reflect the aesthetic sensibilities of a family whose philanthropic activities had included funding for the restoration of the Rheims Cathedral, the palaces of Fountainbleau and Versailles, and the historic community of Colonial Williamsburg. "While the prime consideration in this enterprise must be its financial success," Rockefeller told his architects, "the importance of a unified and beautiful architectural whole must be constantly kept in mind."

Launched in the late 1920s, Rockefeller Center qualified for mention among the wonders of the free-enterprise world. Its amenities included murals and sculpture commissioned from international artists, the world's largest theatre at Radio City Music Hall, and an ice-skating rink. It also featured a below-ground pedestrian concourse linking some 20 buildings which would inspire similar "underground cities" in downtown cores throughout North America. For all that, Rockefeller's son Nelson, a recent Dartmouth graduate making his career debut as a leasing agent, struggled during the Dirty Thirties to sign up tenants such as RCA, Eastern Airlines and Henry Luce's young stable of magazines. His father's vision was vindicated in time — inspiring the Gershwin brothers' line, "They all laughed at Rockefeller Center" — but the complex suffered heavy losses during its 10-year construction phase. It would have foundered altogether had John Rockefeller Jr. not sold off Standard Oil stock at distress prices to maintain its solvency. Some 50 years would pass before anything so ambitious was again contemplated in New York City, and the driving force behind that project would be a Canadian, not a New Yorker.

Before Paul Reichmann came along, the only career developer to entertain the monumental visions of a John Rockefeller Jr. had been William Zeckendorf. Reichmann's most conspicuous adventures would inevitably be compared with those of Zeckendorf, not only because of the scope of O&Y's projects but the fact that many of them were literally built on the ruins of Zeckendorf's lost empire.

Zeckendorf was a small-town Illinois native who dropped out of college and went to New York to work in his uncle's real-estate office. He eventually gained control of that sleepy firm, Webb & Knapp Inc., and transformed it, in its heyday in the 1950s, into a $300-million stable of properties. Its projects included Century City in Los Angeles, L'Enfant Plaza in Washington, D.C., and Denver's Mile High Center. Zeckendorf also accumulated trophy properties such as the Chrysler Building, and assembled the East River site for the United Nations.

But Zeckendorf fell into the category of developers whose most grandiose visions are not realized. The undoing of Webb & Knapp was the failure of a spectacular Bronx amusement park called Freedomland. Webb Knapp, a firm that was judged to be probably the biggest developer of its day, collapsed in 1965. In Canada, Zeckendorf pioneered suburban shopping centres with his Yorkdale project north of Toronto. But he failed to close deals to develop the city's Eaton Centre and Toronto-Dominion Centre, projects that would be undertaken by others. Nonetheless, Zeckendorf gained lasting renown for succeeding with a string of outsized projects that would have taxed the imagination of his peers, and for making a reality of some of his most unlikely schemes by sheer force of personality. "My observation," Zeckendorf said, "has always been that after a certain key point you must move ahead as if a project were assured — in order to assure it — because if you wait around for all the pieces of the puzzle to fit before closing a deal, you can wait forever." This was to be Paul Reichmann's philosophy as well.

In 1958, Zeckendorf's firm had bought the 500-acre Fleming estate in the path of Toronto's planned Don Valley Parkway for a proposed office, shopping and residential subdivision; and it began work on an office complex in Montreal called Place Ville Marie that was to be the distinctly recognizable new head office for the Royal Bank of Canada. The cruciform-shaped PVM, designed by Ieoh Ming Pei and boasting a novel underground shopping promenade, was an early example of the power of commercial real estate to redefine a city. It caused Montreal's financial district to be relocated several blocks north from Rue St-Jacques to Blvd René Lévesque (the former Dorchester Boulevard), and inspired a boom in signature office towers in city centres across Canada. Zeckendorf had harboured no doubts about the certain success of his project or his own important role in introducing Canada to the future of commercial real-estate development. "Montreal had little wealth, dynamism or modernity," he said. "I took the multimillion-dollar gamble, which nobody else in that country was willing to take. Montreal and Canada will never be quite the same again." Paul Reichmann would make an identical claim for his projects in Manhattan and London.

Reichmann was also making personal history in 1958. Then 28, he embarked on his first real-estate development project. Olympia Floor & Wall Tile, the tile-importing business operated by his brother Ralph, had outgrown its rented premises, and the brothers decided to build a warehouse of their own. They thought the lowest tender, at $125,000, was still too high. Paul was certain he could do better, and acting as his own contractor, put up a one-storey warehouse at a cost of just $70,000. Forty years later, the yellow-brick building at 56-58 Colville Road, tucked behind the North York Plaza, was home to an import-export firm. Oil drums and cube vans lined the sides of the building, which shared the street with a dozen similarly nondescript shelters for plumbing-supply outlets and metal-working shops. Nothing about the scene suggested that Zeckendorf was guilty of exaggeration in thinking he alone was breathing new life into Canadian commercial land development. Paul Reichmann himself, having arrived in Canada just a year earlier, was beyond imagining that he, of all people, might someday transcend Zeckendorf's legacy of audacious gambits.

PAUL WAS the fifth of six children born to Samuel and Renée Reichmann. Prophetically enough, Samuel's Hungarian ancestors had changed the Germanic family name, early in the 19th century, from Feldmann ("peasant") to Reichmann ("rich man"). Renée Gestetner Reichmann was descended from one of the founding families of Orthodox Judaism in Hungary. In their native Oberland district in western Hungary, Samuel and Renée had a large poultry business that exported eggs throughout Europe. In 1928, fearing that the Russian Revolution would spread, Samuel relocated the family to Vienna, where their youngest children, Albert, Paul and Ralph, were born. Ten years later, the family fled Austria after the Nazi invasion and spent two chaotic years in Paris. A consequence of that nomadic existence was that the Reichmann children learned seven languages (English, French, German, Italian, Spanish, Hungarian and Hebrew). In Morocco, the family's last stop before North America, Samuel flourished as a currency trader. And the children were inspired by the heroism of their mother. Renée recruited a network of women to prepare food packages that were dispatched under the auspices of the Spanish Red Cross to prisoners in Nazi concentration camps. They managed also to periodically slip behind enemy lines to distribute Spanish passports among Jews on the Western Front — a rescue mission that saved an estimated 1,500 lives. The Reichmanns were powerless, however, to assist their own relatives in Hungary, deep inside Nazi-occupied Europe. More than 60 of Samuel and Renée's aunts, uncles and cousins perished at the hands of the Nazis.

The experience of those wartime horrors sharpened Samuel's resolve, passed along to his sons, to accumulate wealth as a firewall against persecution. His sons would also keep faith with their mother's example of communitarianism. In the late 1990s, charitable donations by the average major Canadian corporation seldom reached even 1 per cent of annual profits, and total yearly giving by the most generous corporate donors, Imperial Oil Ltd. and the Royal Bank of Canada, ranged between $7 million and $15 million depending on the health of the firms' profits. From its beginnings in the early 1960s, O&Y commited roughly 30 per cent of profits to charitable activities, and its total yearly donations rose steadily from $3 million in the 1960s to more than $60 million at the peak of O&Y's fortunes in the late 1980s. On rare occasions when the Reichmanns contemplated taking O&Y public, charity was always a stumbling block: the family imagined that investors in a public company would not tolerate such a liberal donations policy.

From their father, who died in 1975, Albert, Paul and Ralph inherited an austere lifestyle. In contrast to the flamboyant dealmakers who dominated the real-estate scene in North America during the span of O&Y's ascent, the Reichmann brothers dressed conservatively (narrow-lapelled charcoal suits, white shirts, thin black ties). They shunned publicity. But their shy demeanour in rare public appearances belied the increasingly ambitious reach of their projects.

Negotiators meeting Paul for the first time were invariably taken aback at this bear of a man — broad-shouldered and six-foot-two, with a genial smile largely hidden in a flowing black beard. He spoke in a barely audible whisper and was unfailingly polite, exuding an aura of Old World courtliness. Paul would prove to be a tough, even defiant, negotiator. But his even temper and propensity for self-effacing comments often gave dealmakers on the other side of the negotiating table reason to wonder if it wasn't they who were being unreasonable. The Reichmanns "are warm people who don't lose their sense of humour just because a billion dollars or so are at stake," was how the brothers struck John Cushman III, one of New York's top realty brokers in the 1980s. "You can't appreciate those qualities unless you've been in this world of upper-end real estate. It is filled with very strange, very nasty creatures."

At Talmudic schools in Vienna, Tangier, Antwerp and London, Paul had shown great promise as a scholar. He became a rabbi, and although he would never use that title, his parents had reason to believe he would devote his life to teaching. While his brothers, less academically inclined than Paul, showed entrepreneurial instincts from an early age, Paul resisted joining Samuel's merchant banking operation in Tangier and became a social worker, setting up Talmudic study centres in Casablanca. It was the eldest son, Edward, who would spearhead the family's New World forays. Samuel, who feared the rising tide of nationalism in Morocco, sent Edward to America in 1954 to seek out business opportunities. Edward landed first in New York City. This should have been the Reichmanns' new home across the Atlantic, given that the family had relatives in the city, and Brooklyn was the capital of the haredim diaspora. But Edward was alienated by the McCarthy-era obsession with Communist witch-hunts, which reminded him of the persecutorial zeal of the Nazis.

The Reichmanns also had relatives in Montreal, a city with a vibrant Jewish community numbering 100,000 people, and in that city Edward spent hours in public libraries studying up on Canada's economic prospects. He quickly warmed to the apparent promise of Canada, the world's fastest-growing industrial nation in the postwar era. Edward learned that in the 15 years prior to his arrival, Canada had become the world's fourth-largest economy, its GNP having quintupled since the outbreak of World War II. Edward couldn't know that the economy would keep on booming, tripling over the next 15 years, but the pattern seemed a positive one nonetheless. With backing from Samuel, Edward set up a business in Montreal just weeks after arriving in the city, importing ceramic tiles from Italy to feed the explosive demand for postwar housing. Edward was still living out of his luggage at the time. When his incorporation lawyer needed to know the name of Reichmann's fledgling enterprise, Edward responded with Olympia, the brand-name of a pair of socks in his open suitcase.

One by one, Edward's siblings followed him to Canada. Second-oldest son Louis, soon joined by Ralph, opened a Toronto branch of the tile business. Paul, a newlywed in 1955, came to the realization that his meagre earnings as an itiner-ant teacher would not enable him to raise a large family — a condition of the haredim life. In the late 1950s, Paul and Albert settled in Toronto, Paul to launch Olympia Steel Products, a firm that imported construction materials. Albert, who had helped his father build Tangier's stock exchange building, went into property development as York Factory Developments Ltd., named for the county sur-rounding Toronto. In the early 1960s, soon after Samuel and Renée joined their children in Canada, the patriarch encouraged Paul and Ralph to join forces, cre-ating Olympia & York Industrial Development.

Like his brothers, Paul had learned something of the complexities of currency and commodities trading from Samuel. Impressed that he could undercut the low-est bidder on that first showroom-warehouse for Olympia Floor & Wall Tile and still come out with a 50 per cent profit, Paul began erecting 60,000-square-foot warehouses and small industrial buildings at a cost of $125,000 to $250,000 each throughout the Toronto suburb of North York, more than 100 buildings in all during O&Y's first decade. The Reichmanns could scarcely have chosen more fer-tile ground for a property development enterprise. On a per capita basis, the value of building permits issued by North York in the 1960s outstripped that of any other city on the continent. And Toronto as a whole, dubbed the "The New Great City" in a 1974 *Fortune* magazine cover story, was gaining a reputation as the con-struction capital of North America. "Toronto is really a new city," Paul Reichmann said a decade later, "built in a very short time."

The boom was characterized in large degree by sloppy work by unsophisticat-ed contractors. Delays and cost overruns were common. O&Y distinguished itself by getting its projects built ahead of schedule and by absorbing the cost of last-minute alterations requested by clients. O&Y was unusual, too, in perceiving an advantage to be gained from above-average aesthetics. Given the hectic pace of demand, rival contractors could be forgiven their cookie-cutter, utilitarian build-ings. But O&Y prided itself on custom design. "We felt it looked horrible," Paul Reichmann said of the dominant industrial design of that time. "Typically, indus-trial buildings then consisted of a brick wall in front and concrete block. We made it brick all around and did some landscaping in front. This made quite a differ-ence in appearance but it did not cost us a lot. The extra cost was more than worth it because people would pay more in rent to be in a better environment."

While most developers hired a general contractor to oversee their projects, O&Y functioned as its own general contractor in order to hold subcontractors to exacting cost and completion schedules, O&Y coped with a self-imposed penalty of shutting down its work sites during 64 or 65 Sabbath and other Jewish holy days, roughly doubling to 120 its annual number of lost work days, given that it could hardly require subcontractors to operate on Saturdays and Christian holidays. The combination of Rosh Hashanah, Yom Kippur, Sukkoth and Simchat Torah, along with Labour Day, meant O&Y sites were idle for most of September — a critical month for contractors in Canada, given the early onset of harsh weather. But the Reichmanns got their projects built on time just the same, a sign to early observers that perhaps the family gained special powers from its strict religious observance.

In 1964, O&Y's reputation for speed and quality resulted in an invitation from Mutual Life Insurance Co. of Canada (MONY) to build a four-storey office tower on a patch of farmland at Don Mills Road and Eglinton Avenue East. Seeing an opportunity for O&Y to make its mark as a developer of first-class office accommodations, Paul Reichmann startled MONY by proposing a 16-storey tower which, upon completion in 1967, would be the first high-quality office building outside downtown Toronto. It would also prove to be the site of O&Y's first megaproject of sorts. In 1965, Paul had persuaded his reluctant brothers to bet the entire company on the $18-million purchase of the Flemingdon Park estate from the ailing Zeckendorf empire. The deal, which would see O&Y take possession of hundreds of acres surrounding its planned MONY tower, required the family firm to borrow against every building in its portfolio in the hope that prestigious tenants could be lured to the pastoral wilderness of Don Mills.

The transaction also marked Paul's emergence as the leader among the Reichmann brothers. For within six months, his gamble paid off, when O&Y was able to recover its initial $3-million cash outlay by selling off small parcels of the Flemingdon tract. And over the next few years, O&Y would erect 13 towers for head-office tenants such as Nestlé, Texaco Canada, Blue Cross and the Ontario Federation of Labour. Those buildings, which formed the largest suburban office park in Canada, would be a passport to still bigger and more far-flung projects. An O&Y data centre in Don Mills for oil giant Shell Canada led to a commission to erect Shell's 33-storey head-office building in Calgary. The speed with which O&Y completed Bell Canada's data centre prompted the firm's CEO, Robert Scrivener, to commission O&Y to build the enormous 1.5-million-square-foot Place Bell Canada tower in Ottawa. Scrivener, arguably the most powerful businessman in Canada at the time, fretted about a $250,000 cost overrun on the building—until Reichmann informed him that O&Y would absorb the extra cost. Scrivener also put in a good word for the young developer with the *Toronto Star's* Beland Honderich. The publisher of Canada's largest newspaper gave O&Y the nod over rival bidders to build a new home for the *Star* on the Toronto waterfront. On the site of the old *Star* building at 80 King St. W., obtained in the deal with

Honderich, Reichmann hatched a plan for an office tower complex that would forever mark O&Y as being in a class of its own among developers.

With Toronto overtaking Montreal as the financial capital of Canada, O&Y was drawn to the city centre, where the Big Five banks, Canada's most prestigious tenants, had their monumental head offices. In securing Bank of Montreal (BMO), Canada's oldest bank, as the lead tenant in O&Y's proposed First Canadian Place at King and Bay streets — the focal point of corporate power in Canada — Paul Reichmann obtained incomparable cachet for O&Y as developer of choice among elite clients. The building would claim the status of world's tallest bank tower previously held by Zeckendorf's Chase Manhattan Plaza in New York. And while BMO's rivals would sneer at the huge illuminated blue "M" atop the building, the bank's U.S.-born chairman, William Mulholland, was delighted to have the world's tallest neon advertisement on his tower, supplanting the RCA sign at Rockefeller Center.

In appearance, the white marble-clad building was handsome but not remarkable, eliciting none of the love-hate commentary directed at Mies Van der Rohe's ensemble of black glass Toronto-Dominion bank towers across the street, known locally as "the coffins." At Paul Reichmann's insistence, Edward Durrell Stone, the U.S. architect who had designed O&Y's acclaimed Place Bell Canada, opted for a classic, streamlined style much in favour with big-league corporate tenants. The features that assured the destiny of First Canadian Place as a cash machine were its vast expanses of unobstructed floor space — the largest pillar-free spaces of any office building in Canada — and its 12-sided exterior shell, which gave each floor the potential for no fewer than eight corner offices.

Obscured by superlatives that were highlighted in O&Y's promotional material for the complex, (16 miles of marble, 9,300 windows, 284 miles of wiring — all records for an office building in Canada) was the enormity of the risk assumed by the Reichmanns. O&Y was once again required to pledge the entirety of its assets to obtain financing for the five-million-square-foot project. It would have to build Canada's greatest skyscraper, one of the 10 tallest buildings in the world, with unprecedented speed if it was to install tenants and begin collecting rental income before debt payments came due.

The Reichmanns would also have to cope with a 1973 bylaw, heralded throughout North America as a radical step in controlling runaway development, that placed a moratorium on new buildings more than five storeys high. Fortunately for O&Y, Toronto city council's reformers did not impose their edict retroactively, although it would affect a planned twin tower to the Bank of Montreal tower, thus undermining the economic logic of the entire project.

Local developers engaged in a war of words with the reform council, led by newly elected mayor David Crombie. But Paul Reichmann sensed that confrontation was pointless. He met with Crombie a dozen times and collaborated with the young turks in Crombie's progressive planning department. O&Y secured the necessary exemptions for its flagship project by overhauling its design, scrapping plans for a twin tower that would rival the height of the BMO building in favour of a 36-storey tower, and placing a park and neighbouring four-storey pavilion (future home of the Toronto Stock Exchange) at street level, where it would be used by the public, rather than on top of a three-storey podium. The alterations were costly, but in Reichmann's estimation they enhanced the project's value as a showcase of O&Y's design capabilities and its harmonious dealings with civic officials.

First Canadian Place became a laboratory for "fast-track" construction techniques that would be widely copied elsewhere in North America. O&Y installed a 45-ton truck elevator in the core of the structure so that the 500,000 tons of materials used in construction could be brought directly to each floor, eliminating manual unloading of pallets and cutting labour time by 1.3 million person-hours. Novel "kangaroo" cranes that scaled the exterior of the building were able to assemble three floors of steel frame in six days — triple the usual pace. The 72-storey tower was outfitted with double-decker elevator cars that could serve two floors at once — a first in Canada — to cut transit time for the building's population of 20,000 people. The building was equipped with innovative energy conservation and air-recycling systems, and the country's first automatic window-washing system, which could clean the tower in an hour — a job that would have taken a month if done manually.

When tenants moved into the lower 22 floors in May 1975, just 18 months after construction began, the market for Toronto office space was glutted. But Paul Reichmann refused to slash rents. The building took four years to fill, or twice what O&Y expected. But by patiently enduring negative cash flow in the early years, Reichmann was able to sign up late arrivals to long-term leases at more than $40 a square foot as the market strengthened, compared with the $12 paid by early birds.

O&Y was still looking for tenants to fill its flagship Canadian property when Paul Reichmann bet the company again. In 1977 he seized on an opportunity to buy eight Manhattan office towers in a single transaction that would come to be regarded as the savviest real-estate deal of the century. For an upfront cash payment of just $46 million and the assumption of $288 million in mortgages, O&Y was able to acquire about 10 million square feet of prime office space, including the head offices of ITT Corp., Harper & Row and American Brands.

The upfront cost to O&Y seemed modest relative even to the depressed value of the buildings at that time, but the Reichmanns had to take out a bank loan for half of that amount, and could not be sure that rental incomes in the weak New York market would cover the mortgages they were taking on.

The timing seemed to be dreadful. The New York economy was mired in a decade-long slump. Blue-chip corporations were fleeing Manhattan's crime and high taxes. The city had narrowly averted bankruptcy only two years earlier. Even

The world's greatest developer with a scale model of Canary Wharf, the biggest office project in European history. "I want to do something which others consider difficult if not impossible," said Paul Reichmann. His colossal bet on London would pay off, but not soon enough to save Olympia & York from bankruptcy.

Paul Reichmann's first development (below), in 1958, was a yellow-brick warehouse for the family tile-importing business at 56-58 Colville Road in the Toronto suburb of North York — the first of some 100 modest industrial buildings that O&Y would erect over the next few years. In the mid-1970s, O&Y first gained national attention by raising the world's tallest bank head office, in downtown Toronto, for the Bank of Montreal (the white tower in the photo at left). O&Y's First Canadian Place inspired Robert Campeau's nearby Scotia Plaza, and O&Y found itself in posession of both buildings when it rescued a tapped-out Campeau in the late 1980s. Reichmann's own eclipse was not far off.

O&Y's World Trade Center (right) at the tip of Manhattan island, the most ambitious real estate project since the Rockefeller Center in the Dirty Thirties, breathed new life into a fading Wall Street district. Like Canary Wharf (below), it attracted blue-chip tenants. Merrill Lynch, American Express and *The Wall Street Journal* took up residence at WTC. By 2000, the tenant roster at Canary Wharf, dismissed as a white elephant a decade earlier, included the head office of one of the world's biggest banks, HSBC Holding; the European headquarters of Bank of New York and Boston's State Street Bank; and the newsroom of *The Daily Telegraph*, Britain's leading upmarket newspaper. The Reichmanns had "promised that Canary Wharf would be magnificent," noted Britain's *Economist*. "And it is."

Washington had been unsympathetic to the Big Apple's woes. In expressing reluctance to bail it out, President Gerald Ford in 1975 inspired a famous New York *Daily News* headline, FORD TO NEW YORK: DROP DEAD.

Many prospective buyers had passed on the so-called Uris package of buildings, named for Percy and Harold Uris, the old-line Latvian-American development family that had painstakingly assembled them. They didn't share Paul Reichmann's belief that the overwrought obituaries being written for the world's financial capital were fanciful, and that a powerful turnaround was imminent. "A boom in New York rents wasn't a hope," he later said, "it was a conviction."

The Uris deal was the sort of large-scale endeavour from which U.S. developers typically shrank. The U.S. industry was characterized by local developers who seldom strayed from their regional fiefdoms. The only developers in North America with national, and later global, ambitions hailed from Canada, where strict zoning laws had nurtured the evolution of development firms that were substantial enough to tap Canada's Big Five banks for what seemed like unlimited amounts of financing. They alone could field large teams of experts in land assembly, urban planning principles and trends in office, residential and retail-store design. By the 1970s, giant Canadian development firms such as Oxford, Nu-West, Daon, Bramalea, Cadillac Fairview and Trizec were heading south, where they figured among the biggest commercial landlords in Minneapolis, Denver and the sunbelt cities of Dallas, Houston and Atlanta. Yet even they were sobered by the enormity of risk in the Uris properties. O&Y was a closely held firm with eight shareholders, all named Reichmann. Most of its Canadian peers were publicly traded companies. At least one of them, Cadillac Fairview, had pulled back from bidding on the Uris package. As its CEO explained, his shareholders wouldn't sit still for the 10 years that would likely be required for a payback on the Manhattan buildings.

With its big bet on Manhattan, O&Y was about to become one of the best-known private companies in North America. If he was looking for a prominent stage on which to exhibit his forecasting skills, Reichmann couldn't have chosen better than the Big Apple. Even in its depressed state, New York boasted an unrivalled concentration of the world's top real-estate developers and financiers. They noticed, of course, when rents jumped almost immediately, just as Reichmann had forecast, when New York began to reassert itself in the late 1970s as the undisputed business capital of the world's most powerful economy. They were chagrined by the tripling in value of the Uris buildings within a few years; in the space of a decade the value of the buildings would increase tenfold to an astounding $3.5 billion.

The sudden windfall, outstripping even Reichmann's expectations, spurred O&Y in a campaign to build major office and mixed-use properties across North America in the late 1970s, extending the Reichmanns' reach into Chicago, Boston, Dallas, Miami, San Francisco, Seattle and other cities. O&Y also channelled some of its Niagara of cash flow, for the first time, into non-real estate assets, with Paul

Reichmann's decision to make substantial investments in oil, mining, forest products and financial services. "There's just more money coming into O&Y than the Reichmanns — or anyone — would know what to do with," Toronto real-estate analyst Harry Rannala of Merrill Lynch said in 1983. The boundless confidence that bankers would invest in Paul Reichmann late into the spring of 1992 traced its roots to the fateful Uris deal. In the estimation of Meyer Frucher, president of New York's Battery Park City Authority, there had been two great transactions in the city's history. "The first was when the Dutch bought the island of Manhattan," he said. "The second was when the Canadians bought the island again."

Soon enough, Battery Park itself was stimulating Paul Reichmann's imagination. For more than a decade, the Battery Park City Authority, a creation of the state of New York, had been trying in vain to develop a 92-acre sandbar on the Hudson River shoreline at the southern tip of Manhattan, which consisted of landfill from the adjacent twin towers of the World Trade Center. The scheme for reclaiming the waterfront had been hatched in 1966 by Nelson Rockefeller, then governor of New York. Over the years, developers such as Robert Tishman, Harry Helmsley and Cadillac Fairview, had come forward with proposals that were both grandiose and banal, and none had been feasible. With the collapse of the Manhattan real-estate market in the 1970s, all hope of redeveloping the site seemed to disappear. By 1979, the state and city governments were panic-stricken over the approaching insolvency of the Battery Park City Authority. "Nothing could have started worse, taken longer, or had so many strikes against it than this stop-and-go (mostly stop), large-scale urban dream," wrote Ada Louise Huxatable, architecture critic for *The New York Times*.

At this bleak moment, Reichmann introduced himself to the Authority as its rescuing angel. Alone among the 12 developers to submit proposals to the Authority in 1980, O&Y rejected the familiar approach of erecting one building at a time in order to test the market. Reichmann instead committed O&Y to putting up a dozen buildings all at once with a total of six million square feet, and to have the project completed by 1987 — twice as fast as anyone else. Before the state officials could catch their breath, Reichmann also offered to guarantee payment of the Authority's bonds. He alone seemed to realize that the looming maturity dates on that debt — and the embarrassing prospect of default — was the issue that most concerned the New York State bureaucrats.

World Financial Center, as it came to be known, was a breathtaking proposition. For its design, Reichmann recruited Cesar Pelli from his perch as dean of Yale University's graduate school of architecture. Pelli conceived an ensemble of neo-classical towers that turned the page on the stark anonymity of the International Style. Pelli's four main buildings, ranging in height from 33 to 51 storeys, rejected the flat-roofed edict of modernism. His rooftops featured whimsical pyramids and cones sculpted from copper, which were to be lit at night. The towers — on lower levels sheathed in granite, which melded into reflective glass in the upper reaches — were designed to change colours depending on the sun's position in the sky. The project's dazzling centrepiece was a "winter garden" retail galleria nearly the size of the concourse at Grand Central Station. Public amenities, by now a trademark of O&Y projects that helped the company win favour with municipal officials, included a three-acre plaza and a mile-long pedestrian promenade along the Hudson River shoreline. To obtain exactly the right hue and cut of granite panels for the principal buildings, O&Y shipped granite quarried at Bagotville, Quebec, to Italy, where stonecutters formed it into one-and-a-quarter-inch-thick panels before sending them off to Ireland, where they were attached to frames and then sent on to New York for installation.

New York was booming, for the moment. So much so that O&Y would be hard-pressed in the early 1980s to round up the 120 subcontractors and 4,000 workers needed to complete the biggest commercial building project that New York had ever seen. But scarcely a year after construction began, the North American economy tumbled into what would prove to be the most severe downturn since the Depression. The malaise diminished the flow of rental income from O&Y's existing buildings. It also shaved hundreds of millions of dollars from the value of O&Y's non-real estate holdings, such as Abitibi-Price, the world's largest newsprint maker, which was dazed by a sudden collapse in commodity prices.

Under the circumstances — similar to what O&Y had encountered at Flemingdon Park and First Canadian Place — Paul Reichmann was certain that the proper course for O&Y was not to suspend the Battery Park project. He chose to proceed with the hectic pace of construction at World Financial Center in order to give his project the force of inevitability. The key to the project's viability, and the spur to his personal salesmanship, was the pursuit of elite tenants who would secure the complex's status as a first-class corporate address, even while it was still a 14-acre hole in the ground. Reichmann could think of no better expression of his own confidence in the project than to buy, at a steep premium, the New York head-office buildings of American Express, Merrill Lynch and the City Investing conglomerate as an inducement for them to take huge portions of space on the Hudson River waterfront. In 1977, the Reichmanns were unknown in New York real estate, a world dominated by venerable families — the Dursts, Tishmans, Urises, Rudins and Helmsleys — that quietly exercised their power through backroom arm-twisting. Five years later, O&Y, a foreign upstart that publicly embraced deals of unimaginable risk, owned and was developing about 20 million square feet in the city, or 8 per cent of the city's total inventory of office space. This amounted to twice the property holdings boasted by Manhattan's second-largest landlord, the Rockefeller family.

By the mid-1980s, the North American economy had rebounded and Wall Street, whose denizens were O&Y's most highly coveted prospective tenants, was embarked on the greatest bull market in history. The American Express and Merrill Lynch towers at World Financial Center were filling up nicely, even before the lobbies and landscaping were completed, and the complex welcomed a new big-league tenant in Dow Jones & Co., which relocated the newsroom of its *Wall Street Journal* to one of Pelli's towers. By 1989, the complex would be valued at about $3 billion, or twice O&Y's construction costs. Long before that, Paul Reichmann had been invited onto the board of the Canadian Imperial Bank of Commerce. In Canada, membership on a Big Five bank board conferred the status of a corporate knighthood. Reichmann also joined David Rockefeller's five-man board at Rockefeller Center Properties Inc., an acknowledgement by John D. Rockefeller Jr.'s youngest son that Paul Reichmann was America's most important developer.

Reichmann hardly rejected the corporate establishment's warm embrace. But he and his brothers added to their mystique by remaining aloof. "When they leave the office at night, it's not only that the public doesn't see the Reichmanns," said Marshall "Mickey" Cohen, who oversaw the family's enormous portfolio of non-real estate assets. "I don't see them — not at parties, movies or the theatre. They are wrapped in a small, tight world of family and a few friends, strangers in a strange land who don't venture into the secular world."

To Mulholland's annoyance, Paul Reichmann repeatedly declined the banker's invitations to travel the short distance from O&Y's headquarters in First Canadian Place to the Bank of Montreal's executive dining room on the 68th floor of that building to sup with the likes of Henry Kissinger, a barnstorming windbag who was a particular favourite of Toronto's corporate elite in the 1980s. When the Toronto Club, notorious as a WASP enclave, deigned for the first time to invite Albert and Paul Reichmann to an intimate pow-wow of three dozen Establishment leaders, the brothers failed to turn up.

The Reichmanns were not known for deliberate snubs. They were simply too busy to socialize. In 1988, more than 50,000 people toured World Financial Center during a five-day promotional event to mark the opening of the project's polished-marble lobbies and shopping gallerias. Among the guests at an O&Y-sponsored black-tie event in honour of Nancy Reagan was the billionaire media mogul John Kluge. He said that "the center reminds me of Egypt and the pyramids." But Kluge was unable to share his impressions with Paul Reichmann. O&Y's chief strategist was busy with a project far more ambitious than World Financial Center, one that was taking shape on the other side of the Atlantic, at a notorious peninsula jutting into the Thames River.

J UST AS THE Battery Park officials hoped to rejuvenate a rundown Wall Street district by approving O&Y's design for their landfill site, the Thatcher government had placed its hopes with Paul Reichmann for reclaiming a miserable stretch of the Thames waterfront known as the Isle of Dogs. It was not an island, in fact, but a sizable peninsula. It was also one of the least desirable neighbourhoods in London, or in all of Britain, for that matter.

Once the shipbuilding capital of Europe in the mid-1800s, the Docklands a century later was a 5,000-acre no man's land of abandoned wharves, factories and warehouses fringed by crime-ridden public housing. If they thought of it at all, the Oxbridge graduates who toiled in the City's banks and brokerages knew the Docklands as the hunting ground for Jack the Ripper and home to the Limehouse opium dens that had been an object of fascination for Charles Dickens.

As late as 1984, Reichmann himself was no fan of London. During his Talmudic studies there some 30 years earlier he had been alienated by a rigid British class structure that discouraged upward mobility. And in the early 1980s, the absence of "North American drive" in London accounted for its tepid rate of economic growth and lack of appetite for the modern office towers to which O&Y was committed. The Brits were a curious lot, said Reichmann, willing to put up with decrepit office buildings in London that "in New York you couldn't rent as a slum."

But in 1987, Paul Reichmann was convinced that O&Y was running out of expansion opportunities in North America. And he now believed that London was destined to enjoy a new age of prosperity with the advent of European trade and currency union, set to take place in 1992. He estimated that two-thirds of the City's existing supply of office space was antiquated by the standards of North American tenants, who demanded buildings that were energy efficient, copiously wired for massive computer banks, and could boast pillar-free floor plans that would accommodate enormous trading rooms. More than Londoners themselves, Reichmann believed in their city's future as "the strongest commercial real estate market — in both Europe and North America." London's emergence as the capital of a unified Europe, like the dramatic turnaround in the New York property market in the late 1970s, was not a hope but a conviction. "The confidence in the political stability and democratic tradition of England will cause international companies to choose the U.K. as the base and location of their expansion," Reichmann said in the late 1980s.

"Each time I go to London, the more enthusiastic I become as I meet the younger people," said Reichmann, in evident accord with Thatcher that her revolution to return the stewardship of Britain to private-sector hands was working a delayed version of the economic miracle that rejuvenated postwar Germany and Japan. When he had been a student in London in the early postwar years, his peers aspired to careers in government. Now, Reichmann said, "Young graduates want to be entrepreneurs, to go into a business where they can be creative."

On that basis, Reichmann signed up for the generous tax breaks and cheap land offered by the government authority that had been attempting without success to kick-start development in the Docklands. Imagining that the "Canary Wharf District" could be made over as a London version of Manhattan's Park Avenue, Reichmann stunned the Canary Wharf bureaucrats by expanding on their already hugely ambitious scheme for 22 buildings with 10 million square feet. To give it a "critical mass," Reichmann reconceived the project as 24 buildings with more than 12 million square feet on a 71-acre site, plus three million more square feet of housing, shopping and hotel development on an adjoining 22 acres, all to be completed in just seven to 10 years.

No one had ever built on this scale in Europe. Reichmann's construction chief warned that Britain did not have the engineering know-how to build a North American-style office megaproject. O&Y's leasing experts worried about the absence of adequate subway, light-rail and highway connections to central London, all of which would be lacking at Canary Wharf until the late 1990s at best. Without them, it would be enormously difficult to find tenants quickly enough to match rental income with payment schedules on the debt O&Y would be taking on in order to finance the $5-billion project. Reichmann himself had canvassed local opinion about Canary Wharf. He spoke with three dozen or so CEOs of blue-chip British corporations. They all agreed with his assessment of the woeful inadequacy of current City accommodations. But not one of them was prepared to relocate to the unfashionable Docklands if Reichmann went ahead with his plans to revitalize Canary Wharf.

Prince Charles tried to kill Reichmann's scheme at the blueprint stage. The Reichmanns figured prominently in Charles's late-1980s crusade against what he described as the brutality of modern architecture. Charles had first gained attention by pronouncing that the Luftwaffe had done less damage to London than the postwar architects of dehumanizing office and apartment blocks. Now he selected Cesar Pelli's concept for the massive Isle of Dogs reclamation project as a target worthy of special condemnation. In his controversial TV documentary, "A Vision of Britain," later a book with the same title that was a best seller in Britain and North America, the Prince of Wales expressed scorn for the 50-storey obelisk of One Canada Place. The tower was the centrepiece of the proposed Canary Wharf scheme. It would be the tallest building in Europe, and visible from Kent, some 20 miles away. "The monstrous Canary Wharf is a monument to the wrong-thinking of the 1960s," Charles said. "I personally would go mad if I had to work in a building like that. The tragedy is that it will cast its shadow over generations of Londoners who have suffered enough from towers of architectural arrogance."

In truth, the skyscrapers in Pelli's conception were modest by the standards of North America. Or, for that matter, of Asia. In the 1990s, Pelli's twin Petronas

Towers in Kuala Lumpur, which looked like a pair of corn cobs sprouting from the financial district of the Malaysian capital, eclipsed the Sears Tower in Chicago for bragging rights as the world's tallest office buildings. One Canada Place, by contrast, was a stately obelisk, a traditional four-sided tower topped off by the familiar Pelli pyramid. Reichmann had actually scaled down the outward grandiosity of the scheme he inherited from the Canary Wharf bureaucrats. He rejected the three 850-foot towers called for in their original plan in favour of the single, 800-foot One Canada Place, which would be partnered with two towers of 40 and 39 storeys, respectively. Reichmann had also scrapped the original proposal's call for roads, parking lots and mechanical systems to be enclosed in a massive podium. He thought that was dehumanizing. Instead, Reichmann put most of this infrastructure underground, placing Canary Wharf's expansive allotment of gardens, plazas and other open spaces closer to the level of the encircling Thames.

As a counterpoint to Pelli's New World-style central office tower, Reichmann recruited other celebrated architects, including I. M. Pei, Aldo Rossi and Sir Norman Foster, future designer of Germany's born-again Reichstag and the Millennium Dome in London, to design the project's other buildings, its gallerias and tree-lined promenades. Historical experts, including the former director of the Victoria and Albert Museum, were enlisted to assist Canary Wharf planners in evoking the character of venerable London neighbourhoods, such as Grosvenor and Berkeley Squares and the Bloomsbury Estates. Like many other features at Canary Wharf, Reichmann had chosen a name with a Canadian connection, Cabot Square, for one of the project's principal open spaces. Cabot Square was, however, lined with buildings whose domes, columns and pediments echoed the most common design elements of traditional London buildings. At the risk of upsetting his own fast-track construction schedule, Reichmann intervened time and again to call for refinements to Canary Wharf's highly detailed public spaces. Even the most minor items — lampposts, handrails, telephone boxes and litter bins — were custom-designed.

But these efforts would be lost on Britain's architectural elite. Architect Francis Tibbalds, who spoke on behalf of the design establishment as head of the Royal Town Planning Institute, was an early and persistent ally of Charles in objecting to the Reichmann atrocity on the Thames. And as the first phase of Canary Wharf neared completion he asserted that "it's every bit as bad as I had feared it would be. Future generations will wonder how we allowed it to happen."

By the mid-1990s, when its first phase had been completed according to the schedule Reichmann proposed at the outset, Canary Wharf would prove to be an engineering triumph. As there was no vacant land adjacent to the Phase I site — it was completely surrounded by water, and devoid of power, sewer or telephone connections — O&Y was obliged to surround the peninsula with temporary floating roads. A dozen barges were used as on-site office and storage space. A floating cement plant was brought in from Norway. Slate and marble from suppliers in

Canada, Italy, India, Brazil and Finland were floated up the Thames, along with a small forest of nursery-grown trees.

And by 1995, the first eight buildings at Canary Wharf, with a total of 4.5 million square feet, would also be a budding commercial success, having attracted Citibank, Morgan Stanley Dean Witter, Credit Suisse First Boston, Conrad Black's *Daily Telegraph* and many more of the blue-chip refugees from the City whom Reichmann had initially wooed. But the early deep-seated resistance to Canary Wharf presented an obstacle that Reichmann could not overcome, ultimately causing his family to lose much of what it had built since it left Tangier.

Having obtained the Docklands site from the Thatcher government at rock-bottom prices — £50 per square foot, compared with £500 in the City — Reichmann felt the project could not fail. In fact, "this is not a risky project," he announced. "On a scale of one to 10 — if the risk of Battery Park was a nine — here it would be one." That was an outrageous claim, to be sure. But it was Reichmann's job to be buoyant; and those who had doubted his prophetic gifts in the past had reason now to be cautious in forecasting disaster at Canary Wharf lest they be embarrassed again.

By now the "Reichmann mystique" — almost a cliché, endlessly repeated in glowing media accounts about the man who was rewriting the rules of real estate development — was doing yeoman service in keeping all but the hardiest skeptics at bay. It fed on Paul Reichmann's audacity. "What sets O&Y apart from every other developer is that they think that by their actions they can actually change real-estate markets," said James Allwin, head of real estate at New York brokerage Morgan Stanley in 1989. "Often they are right." Yet the Reichmanns, with so much to crow about, were self-effacing. "They are very strange, reticent people," a veteran Manhattan developer told *New York* magazine in 1986. "If Donald Trump had a project like their World Financial Center, you'd think it was the biggest construction job since the Pyramids. Manhattan Island would be tilting over from people rushing downtown to be part of it."

The delicate matter of religion was at the heart of the Reichmann aura of mystery. The private lives of the Reichmanns were just that, private. Paul did allow, however, that none of his worldly achievements could match the fulfillment he had derived from establishing Talmudic schools in North Africa.

"The most intense part of my life was long ago," Reichmann said, "in the eight years before I turned 25. In those years, my most formative, I worked night and day on my scripture studies and in social education, setting up schools. If I have succeeded since then, I think it is because I vowed to challenge the belief that, when you hunger for something, you have to compromise. I was not going to be enslaved by the popular image of the entrepreneur who is consumed with his success."

By the late 1980s, the Reichmann brothers had each lavished millions of dollars on renovations to their North York homes, and there was now a corporate jet to ease the strain of attending to Canary Wharf. Yet an image persisted of Paul

Reichmann heading for the nearest subway entrance at the close of a negotiating session while his lawyers hailed cabs. His one known indulgence was a passion for collecting rare Talmudic manuscripts. It was Reichmann who made this known.

In the haredim world, Paul explained, a scholar who abandons study for secular pursuits is thought to have sold out. In the 1980s, Reichmann became increasingly candid about his regret at turning away from his rabbinical calling. He was still devout, certainly, and this gave a sheen of noble purpose to his temporal strivings. It made Reichmann's bankers and other business partners swallow hard before asking for a thorough accounting of O&Y's internal finances, and to apologize when these requests were politely but firmly turned down. Credulous observers wanted to believe that the Reichmanns' word was as good as a legal contract, even if Paul often followed up a handshake deal by haggling for better terms.

Reichmann, then, was an enigma. A supercapitalist who was reluctant about his almost accidental status. But how much of this was a pose?

O&Y worksites were closed on Jewish holidays. It was not unheard-of, though, for a business associate to be summoned on a holy day for a meeting at the home of Paul and his wife, Lea, there to find that two or three other visitors were ahead of him in line. Though Reichmann had agonized about no longer having sufficient time for the mitzvah of religious study, his regret was not especially noticeable to those closest to him until well into his third decade as a developer.

"I never want to be subservient to my wealth, to have it running my life instead of the other way around," Reichmann said in 1986, evidently troubled that he might become vainglorious. "The things I'm proudest of are things I do outside of business." Yet Reichmann seldom attended the kollel he founded in his North York neighbourhood in 1970. In time, he delegated his share of responsibility for the family's philanthropy to brother Albert, who made community work his chief occupation after meeting with one disappointment after another in stalled O&Y projects under his supervision. Paul himself was worn down by criticism in the 1980s of his stock-market activities, notably O&Y's hostile takeover of Hiram Walker, maker of Canadian Club whisky, and its acquisition of Western Canadian oil producer Gulf Canada Resources, a transaction that was greased by a controversial $500-million federal tax break. On more than one occcasion, the sublime defiance of adversity for which Reichmann had long been admired gave way to abrasive outbursts. "While it is a pity that so many people misunderstand the things we're trying to do, this will not stop us from doing them," Reichmann vowed in 1986 when he was under fire over planned layoffs at Gulf Canada. "If a businessman — or a scientist or an artist — has that attitude, he simply vegetates."

As the early 1990s economic maelstrom gathered force, pushing up vacancy rates and choking off rental income in London and O&Y's key North American markets, Reichmann once again refused to cut rents to staunch tenant defections, a repeat performance of the gambit that had worked 15 years earlier at First

Canadian Place. He did entertain offers on some of O&Y's buildings and stock-market holdings, but rejected them as too low, even as the value of Abitibi-Price, Gulf Canada and O&Y's other equity holdings dropped by some 20 per cent, or $2 billion, in 1990-91. As the recession deepened, and with Canary Wharf's first phase just 14 per cent leased, Reichmann squandered an opportunity to land a "bell-cow" tenant — one whose prominence would attract others to follow its example — by haggling too long with Britain's Midland Bank over rental rates.

To Reichmann's few close friends, it seemed apparent that he was acting increasingly like a riverboat gambler, not only certain of his winning hand, but determined to triumph on his own terms and humiliate everyone at the table. The most astute observers, particularly those old enough to have seen prominent real-estate dynasties wiped out by a sudden interest-rate spiral, were apt to conclude that Reichmann had developed a penchant for betting the house on schemes that gave him a chance — as at Flemingdon Park, World Financial Center and now Canary Wharf — to succeed where others had failed. There was, Reichmann him-self once admitted, a sirenic appeal to "do something which others consider diffi-cult if not impossible." Reichmann was "a shrewd player but a true gambler," said Toronto financier Andrew Sarlos. Another friend recalled Paul having told him that "my religion won't let me go to Las Vegas. This is my Las Vegas."

Yet Reichmann had succeeded in cultivating an image of himself as the antithesis of the flamboyant speculator, even though only the most difficult schemes held much attraction for him. It wouldn't help his cause for bankers and other suppliers to know about the enormity of risk he was prepared to assume; quite the contrary, it would narrow his ambit to be second-guessed by creditors. O&Y's status as a private company had been of great use in disguising the enor-mity of risk that Reichmann was willing to tolerate. It also kept rivals guessing about O&Y's progress in making its big bets pay off. That gave rise to such curi-ous incidents as the reaction to a minor fire at First Canadian Place in 1983. Analysts combed newspaper accounts to see how many people had evacuated the building, hoping they could guess how successful Reichmann had been in signing up tenants. But in time, Reichmann took to granting strategic interviews with prestigious financial journals in what can best be described as an effort to take his firm public through the media, rather than the usual device of an initial public offering. To his delight, Reichmann found that the earliest journalists he encoun-tered in that campaign, grateful for an audience with the reclusive billionaire, duti-fully passed along the nuggets of information he selectively doled out, each of them, to be sure, a genuine scoop. It was more his mannerisms in these sessions than the information that changed hands that impressed Reichmann's visitors. He was not to be mistaken for Jimmy Stewart, certainly. But Reichmann's evident bemusement that things were going so well — his bafflement, even, that things were turning out so much better than even he expected — seldom failed to convince even the most skeptical interlocutors that Reichmann was more obsessed with protecting O&Y from downside risk than making a name for himself as a latter-day Haussmann. In the 1980s, an image of Reichmann as one of history's most judicious planners of large-scale urban projects began to take shape in the pages of *Fortune* and *The Wall Street Journal*. His real genius, as reported in those accounts, was his novel ability to apply the same common-sense rationality to real-estate transactions that had made heroes of Peter Lynch and Warren Buffett to a generation of Main Street stockpickers. Real estate is easy, Reichmann kept saying: Just plan for the long term, like the Japanese, and don't lose your nerve.

As well, any temptation to see Reichmann's grandest schemes as reckless had to be matched against his reputation for calculated risk aversion. He had, for instance, shelved plans in the 1970s for a twin tower to rise alongside the Bank of Montreal skyscraper, wisely postponing the Exchange Tower until the Toronto office market firmed up in the early 1980s. And O&Y was a model of frugality. Although it was twice the asset size of Cadillac Fairview and Trizec, it employed just half as many people as those firms. Tenants sometimes complained about a lack of the customary hand-holding expected of a developer, which resulted from chronic understaffing in O&Y's property management division. But a crucial aspect of O&Y's success had been Reichmann's ruthless suppression of costs. And the firm's notable lack of bureaucracy helped account for the speed with which Reichmann was able to make decisions. That was a cardinal virtue in a game where the planetary alignment of land, money, prospective tenants and obliging zoning authorities was seldom favourable except for the briefest flashes of time.

Reichmann's most grievous error, it would later be said, was his failure to take sound advice even from those closest to him, arising from a conviction that he was singularly endowed with the power to work miracles. "I would not be surprised if he believed his own mystique" of infallibility, said Reichmann observer Rabbi Arthur Hertzberg, "because I've seen the movie. I've seen *Citizen Kane*." But Reichmann had not plied his trade with mounting success over 30 years by ignorning his hired hands or subjecting them to cruelty. He had a talent for heeding the advice of outstanding people, notably construction chief Keith Roberts, a brilliant former British Army officer who was given carte blanche to devise his own solutions to the impossible challenges that Paul handed him; and the triumvirate of Michael Dennis, Ron Soskolne and Anthony Coombes, savvy urban planners whom Reichmann had poached from the City of Toronto. If anything, Reichmann was overly deferential to the managers of Abitibi-Price and Gulf Canada; they were doing a mediocre job, but Reichmann did not replace them, feeling unqualified to make personnel decisions outside of real estate. On his home ground, he had reason to be confident in his judgments. In a now-famous warning about Canary Wharf, Otto Blau, an O&Y executive, told Albert that the colossal venture was "against our religion. It's a poor location." Blau was misinformed. "Poor" locations — Don Mills and Battery Park, for instance — were something of an O&Y specialty. And the conservative Albert, decidedly cool to the London project, was not a reliable source of wisdom in such matters. He had been a less than zealous conscript to the earlier audacious projects by which his younger brother had bolstered O&Y's treasury; and the troubles that dogged many of Albert's own projects at the firm undermined his credibility.

By the late 1980s there was a large cheering section for Paul Reichmann in his mission at O&Y to make a "permanent imprint," as he put it, on the world's most famous skylines. In New York, San Francisco and Mexico City, civic officials sought O&Y's expertise in spearheading ever more ambitious urban revival schemes. O&Y's project manager for the gargantuan Tokyo Teleport Town, a proposal for 30 million square feet of office space and a huge residential project besides, was often stymied by the language barrier in trying to grasp exactly what his Japanese partners wanted for their planned transformation of Tokyo Bay. Whenever that happened, the Japanese officials would pull out glossy photographs of the World Financial Center. "Build this, build this!" they would say.

Success is more dangerous than failure. The ripples break over a wider coastline.
— Graham Greene

AT CANARY WHARF, Paul Reichmann came remarkably close to triumphing over the odds one last time. But the next upturn in real-estate values, and the resulting salvation of fresh liquidity, would come 18 months too late. The debacle of O&Y's bankruptcy in 1992 — a year in which the firm posted a staggering loss of $2 billion — erased a reported Reichmann family fortune of close to $13 billion as creditors seized its property and stock-market holdings. The brothers were left with their tile company and a handful of obscure, heavily mortgaged properties such as Toronto's Queen's Quay Terminal and the Charlottetown Mall, worth perhaps $100 million all told.

How did one of the world's great fortunes disappear so quickly? In a word, deflation. The Reichmanns' outlook was shaped by the hyper-inflation and volatile currency rates that characterized their European homeland. Paul's unshakeable belief that inflation would always be a fact of life served him exceptionally well until late in his career. Deficit financing by governments in the West and the oil shocks of the 1970s had reinforced Reichmann's conviction that prices would keep marching upward at double-digit rates into the future. The focus of his investment activities, real estate and shares in natural resources firms, had been were the time-honoured hedges against inflation.

Reichmann was hardly alone in greeting with some disbelief the success of Paul Volcker, chairman of the U.S. Federal Reserve Board, in clubbing inflation into submission in the early 1980s, a mission that was continued with even greater zeal in Canada a decade later by John Crow, governor of the Bank of Canada. Pierre Trudeau had been famously premature in the mid-1970s in his declaration that "We have won the war against inflation." Most businesspeople imagined that the war would never truly be joined, much less won. Yet governments eventually did find the resolve to curb inflation. By the mid-1980s, inflation was inconsequential; and in the grim economic downturn of the early 1990s, prices were actually falling. With stunning speed and fury, traditional inflation hedges were beaten down in value as investors reduced the price they were willing to pay for real-estate, gold, oil and gas, forest products and other commodities. The combination of its land holdings and stock-market investments in commodities producers like Abitibi-Price, Gulf Canada and Noranda Inc. exposed O&Y to the full fury of the new phenomenon of disinflation.

There is some evidence that Reichmann sensed as early as the late 1980s that economic trends were moving against him. But he was trapped. The prudent thing to do, in the overheated market of 1988 and 1989, would be to sell off some buildings and portions of O&Y's stock-market portfolio, and realize a sizable profit. Reichmann could not take any of his winnings off the table, however, because he had borrowed against all of O&Y's assets to finance Canary Wharf. When the unrealistically high appraised value of everything from World Financial Center to O&Y's shares in Abitibi-Price and Gulf Canada fell by 30 per cent to 50 per cent in the space of a few months in the money-tight climate of 1990, Reichmann was obliged to hang on, hoping for the salve of a smart recovery that had followed earlier downturns. But real-estate values continued to fall in 1991, and dropped still more in 1992. This was catastrophic, as Reichmann had left himself no room for error. He had long been in the habit of keeping his borrowing costs as low as possible by taking out short-term loans rather than locking in 25-year mortgages with their higher rates of interest. When money suddenly got tight, and rates on short-term loans soared, Reichmann had to scramble to refinance $1 billion or so in short-term borrowing at the very moment when lenders were slamming shut the credit window as the recession deepened. The cash squeeze only worsened, of course, with the flight of cost-conscious tenants to cheaper space, with a resulting shortfall in rental income. By the spring of 1992, the once mighty O&Y was out of cash, and no longer able to honour its loan obligations or pay the contractors at Canary Wharf.

The losses from the eclipse of O&Y ran deeper than money. Paul Reichmann had noted a few years earlier that "I am proud our family has been at the forefront of major undertakings, such as the largest development projects in the world, and yet has adhered to principles and has not compromised." But in his desperate bid to stave off the ignominy of an O&Y collapse, Reichmann had compromised one of his firm's most valuable assets — the trust placed in it by creditors. Reichmann had misled the company's scores of bankers and suppliers about the true, perilous state of O&Y's internal finances, and some creditors were provoked to sue for redress. He had exploited O&Y's status as a private company that was not required to disclose its financial performance to investors; he had not been candid with bankers about the degree to which he had borrowed against properties whose appraised worth had plummeted in the sudden worldwide meltdown of real-estate values. O&Y was preceded into the abyss by just about every major developer in North America, including the venerable Trammel Crow of Texas and Chicago's JMB Realty, along with Canada's Trizec, Campeau Corp. and Bramalea Ltd. The Japanese syndicate that bought the Rockefeller Center at sky-high prices in the 1980s — inspired by the Reichmanns' 1997 coup and themselves inspiring populist fears of an Asian takeover of American icons — watched helplessly as the value of its investment abruptly plummeted.

Only O&Y, however, had traded on a reputation of otherworldly sophistication in financial management, and unstinting integrity besides. That this reputation was well-earned over three decades couldn't excuse Reichmann's 11th-hour dissembling about the frightful degree of cross-collateralization of O&Y's assets on the eve of its demise. Anthony Bianco, author of a largely admiring biography of the century's greatest property developer, acknowledged that "rarely has extreme commercial ambition come as demurely packaged as in the person of Paul Reichmann, whose religiosity did not blunt his secular ambitions but rather seemed to feed a self-assurance that swelled into megalomania."

When his first, impetuous bid to reclaim Canary Wharf in the summer of 1992 was rejected, Reichmann turned to small-bore pursuits. In partnership with George Soros, the world's most prominent currency speculator, he managed a "vulture fund" that picked over the ruins of failed real-estate empires. But the fund had a short run: Soros quietly folded it after investors complained about subpar returns. For several years, Mexican government officials flirted with Reichmann's proposals for three ambitious office and residential projects, all aimed at rejuvenating rundown parts of the city. But peso crises and chronic political upheaval kept the projects from being realized.

Reichmann also nurtured the dynastic ambitions of his nephew Philip Reichmann and son-in-law Frank Hauer, who successfully bid in 1993 for the contract to manage many of O&Y's former properties on behalf of the creditors who now owned them. Within a few years, their young firm, O&Y Properties Corp., was the largest manager of office space in Canada. It had also eased itself into property ownership, accumulating a $700-million portfolio of buildings in Ottawa, Calgary and Winnipeg. By 1999, the firm had achieved sufficient heft to buy back the 72-storey First Canadian Place for the Reichmann family, paying just $368 million, or less than half the appraised value of the landmark building in the overheated market of the late 1980s. Unlike O&Y Developments at its peak, said

Philip Reichmann, the new firm was modest enough in size that "we don't have to buy a small Eastern European country to meet our growth targets." Paul and his son, Barry, meanwhile, had built up Canada's largest nursing home operator, CPL (Central Park Lodges) Long Term Care Real Estate Investment Trust, a firm with 92 nursing homes in Canada and the U.S.

Reichmann himself was still intent on reclaiming Canary Wharf, certain that only he was capable of managing it to its full potential. His next two bids to reacquire the project, like the first, were rejected as too low. He then heard from a contact at Citibank that one of the bank's major shareholders, Saudi Prince al-Waleed bin Talal, had also been a disappointed suitor for Canary Wharf in the latest round of sealed bids. In 1994, Reichmann invited himself aboard al-Waleed's yacht, *Kingdom*, moored off Cannes, where the Prince told him that had his own bid succeeded, he had planned to tap Reichmann's managerial expertise.

With this encouraging news, Reichmann spent the next few months putting together an odd combination of investors to take yet another run at Canary Wharf. It would consist of himself, the most prominent haredim entrepreneur in the world; al-Waleed, the grandson of the founder of Saudi Arabia; former CBS owner Laurence Tisch; and some institutional investors in the U.S. On the fourth try Reichmann prevailed: in 1995, his investor group bought Canary Wharf from its lenders for $1.4 billion, or about the amount of its debt. Four years later, the investor consortium took its holdings public as Canary Wharf PLC, securing a stock-market listing for what became, overnight, the second-largest publicly traded real-estate firm in Britain. Reichmann confessed that this newfound experience with managing a company that was subjected to the rigors of public scrutiny was humbling but instructive. "One of the lessons I have learned about risk is the benefits of a public company," he said. "One tends to develop strong management in a public company and be less reliant on one individual."

The chairman of Canary Wharf PLC was a chastened man. But in one telling respect, Reichmann had not changed. At his showcase on the Thames, Reichmann was still experimenting, still taking risks. By erecting its buildings on an assembly-line basis, Canary Wharf PLC was able to extract concessions from suppliers hoping to secure repeat business, which in turn enabled Reichmann to underprice rents in the City by 30 per cent. And without waiting to line up new tenants, the company had started foundation work for buildings that would supply up to 2.5 million square feet. Once a building reached street level, it could be completed in just 18 months, compared with three-and-a-half years to build from scratch. That flexibility, and the blanket zoning approvals already in place for the entire site, enabled Canary Wharf to provide new space more quickly than competitors. Citing red tape in the City, the West End and other rival districts, London property analyst Nan Rogers of CCF-Charterhouse said that prospective tenants "know Canary Wharf can deliver space to them. They have no idea what will happen elsewhere." The company's reputation for catering to the precise demands of blue-chip renters of corporate space accounted for the robust health in 2000 of Canary Wharf's shares, which held their value during a periodic slump in shares of other publicly traded developers.

Reichmann had launched Canary Wharf with a haunting assertion. The only question, he had said in 1988, was "will success happen immediately or later?" By the close of the century, Canary Wharf signed its first significant British tenant. Hongkong and Shanghai Banking Corp. (HSBC), one of the five largest banks in the world, and the biggest controlled by British interests, had installed its head-quarters in a building erected by the Reichmann-operated Canary Wharf PLC. It joined recent arrivals from overseas such as Bank of New York and Boston's State Street Bank. With 11 buildings completed and seven more under development, representing 8.3 million square feet of space, the population of the complex had reached 25,000 people. That was expected to double by 2001, and to double again to 100,000 when the project expanded to a total of 30 buildings with 13.7 million square feet — the outer limits of Reichmann's original conception of Europe's new epicentre of financial activity. Within four years of Reichmann's regaining an ownership stake in Canary Wharf, the project's value had more than tripled, to an estimated $5 billion. That made Reichmann's 10 per cent holding in Canary Wharf PLC worth about $500 million — a fraction of its likely value ten years hence as the site's river of rental income swelled in the first decade of the 21st century. At the posh Canary Riverside, walking distance from aging kiosks that continued to thrive on the sale of Jack the Ripper merchandise, realty agents were peddling Thames-view apartments at prices ranging from $380,000 to $4.3 million. The Four Seasons chain had settled on Canary Wharf as the site for its second luxury inn in London, three decades after founder Isadore Sharp opened his first hotel in the city. Noting the proximity of the short-haul City Airport three miles from Canary Wharf, a spokeswoman for the new hotel said, "The worry that there had been about location is no longer there."

"Reichmann has certainly been vindicated," said David Tunstall, a London property analyst with the Dutch bank ABN Amro. "Five or six years ago people had written it off. There was no incentive to go there." That was before the mid-1990s boom in the British economy, of course, fuelled in part by the launch of the Euro, Europe's new common currency. And before the completion of the long-delayed Jubilee extension of the underground in 1999, which cut the commuting time between Canary Wharf and central London to 20 minutes. In 1999, Reichmann was confident that "the ultimate value of Canary Wharf will be double the highest value of Olympia & York at its peak." It had been wrong for anyone to imagine that any project of this scope, no matter how well conceived, would establish its viability in short order, said Tom Curly, head of urban design at Chicago-based Skidmore Owings & Merrill, the most prolific design house for blue-chip corporate clients in the second half of the 20th century. Curly saw a parallel between Canary Wharf and the new corporate suburb of La Defense on the western fringe of Paris, which had the benefit of sitting on the nexus of three high-speed rail lines. He also noted that Pierre L'Enfant, designer of Washington, D.C., laid out plans for a city much larger than George Washington could have envisioned. "Cities take time," Curly said. "They don't just take off and they do need pioneers."

After Donald Trump crawled out of the wreckage of the early 1990s recession with only a few casinos to show for what had been a formidable collection of hotels, airlines and luxury yachts, he appeared on the bestseller list with *Trump: The Art of the Comeback*. Trump used the memoir to excoriate the many adversaries he fingered as the cause of his near-destruction. Perhaps the ultimate indignity of O&Y's eclipse was the solace Trump took from the spectacular implosion of a much larger player. "At the awesome O&Y, Paul Reichmann made a huge error — he let his ego get in the way of his financial recovery," wrote the promoter of the Trump Shuttle, the Trump Castle, the Trump World Tower and the Trump Taj Mahal. "I guess Paul just couldn't put his ego aside for a second and tell the banks how much trouble he was really in. It ended up hurting him badly."

Paul Reichmann, whose family had never attached its name to the facade of an O&Y building, went about his comeback noiselessly. He had wit enough to take the measure of his own hubris. He now regretted having inadvertently denigrated his peers by asserting that his own triumphs had come from taking advantage of opportunties that were "obvious for a six-year-old child to see." He keenly felt the loss of his power. "Today," he said, "if I visit one of my former buildings and the elevator is not working I feel my blood pressure rise until I remember I have nothing to do with this property any more."

But he was determined to keep building. Reichmann returned to Mexico City yet again in 1999 to unveil a proposal for Latin America's tallest office tower. He seemed oblivious to a Mexican credit crisis that had most of the nation's banks scrambling to maintain their solvency. The new structure was still looking for a principal tenant. Yet there was no disguising Reichmann's paternal pride in showing off his glittering 55-floor tower, eventually to rise on Paseo de la Reforma, the city's principal thoroughfare. It would boast a 10-storey atrium, a novel system for triple-filtering the city's polluted air and giant shock absorbers to withstand an earthquake.

The former Talmudic scholar tried to explain why he was so powerfully drawn to the task of turning dirt and money into landmark buildings and still more money. "Maimonides preferred that his students pursue the intellectual rather than the material," Reichmann said. "But some of his students asked him, 'Who then shall develop the material world?' And Maimonides said, 'Don't worry, there are enough crazies out there who will take care of that.'

"I'm probably one of the crazies."

5

ANDREW SARLOS

Adventures in high finance with the
nicest guy on Bay Street

"Failure has its place — otherwise trees would grow to the sky, and they don't."
— Andrew Sarlos

O F ALL THE CLASS ACTS in the history of the Exchange, none compare with Andy Sarlos. In 1978, an elderly woman phoned Sarlos to tell him, "Young man, I have owned shares of Abitibi Paper Co. for 28 years. And I am delighted you have just purchased 10 per cent of the company. I hope you will do something."

Sarlos paused for a moment. Then his face broke into a pixie grin. "I will."

That scene of a mirthful man at work was in contrast with his early public image as an intimidating investment genius. One couldn't take his measure over the phone, because he was so soft-spoken he was only barely audible. Neither would a printed account of that conversation between a frustrated investor and a former Hungarian freedom fighter now making his mark on Bay Street soften the image, circa 1978, of Sarlos as a shakedown artist. Someone who was demanding that Abitibi either dip into its treasury to buy back his stealthily acquired shares — at a handsome premium, of course — or else he would oust Abitibi's sleepy management team and break up the world's biggest newsprint maker for a quick profit.

In person, it was plain that Sarlos was only sabre-rattling. He didn't resemble the piratic characterization of him offered up by executives at Abitibi — or conglomerate Brascan Ltd, distiller Hiram Walker-Gooderham & Worts Ltd and the other firms in which Sarlos had suddenly made his presence known as a major investor. Managers of these dead-in-the-water companies were transported into

Handmaiden to some of the greatest corporate combinations of the century, Andrew Sarlos was philosophical about reversals of fortune: "You have to have the courage to go through disappointments, and to change your mind when your vision is wrong."

fits of bellicosity by Sarlos's penchant for publishing open letters about his views on abysmal corporate stewardship. In one, he noted that "Brascan's record of earnings on its existing North American assets has been one of the worst in North America for the past five years." This was in the late 1970s, when Brascan, a pillar of the Toronto business establishment, still commanded respect for its long-ago exploits in building some of Brazil's first railways, and its current status as controlling shareholder in blue-chip icons such as the Labatt brewing empire. But Sarlos was no respecter of past performance. The laurels on which some of Canada's most venerable firms rested, Sarlos thought, would make good kindling.

Proteges of his investment style would soon grasp, however, that a "hostile takeover," as conducted by Andrew Sarlos, was not the exercise in pyrotechnic demolition which that term now connotes. In the Sarlos version, it meant simply that his decision to invest in a given firm was not welcomed by its management. The worst outcome that such managers could expect was a forthcoming series of newspaper accounts in which Sarlos would explain to reporters the various examples of managerial ineptitude that prompted him to buy the understandably cheap stock of a particular firm, in the hope that someday *quite soon* its leaders would start attending to their duties with a heightened sense of urgency.

And they did. Which was remarkable, given that institutional investors twenty-two years later, with their multibillion-dollar pension and mutual fund portfolios, can't seem to light a fire under mediocre managers the way Sarlos could back then. And what he was doing was new at the time, and he never had more than a few million dollars to play with — a quaint sum from the perspective of the early 21st century, when the table ante for a takeover deal of any consequence was measured in the hundreds of millions, if not billions, of dollars. Still more remarkable was that Sarlos, for all his activity in upsetting the comfortable status quo, would soon become a friend of the people who ran Brascan, Abitibi and the rest. Indeed, Sarlos came to be liked, trusted and sought out for advice by more members of the Canadian corporate elite than any financier before or since.

Curious about this influential investor who often accounted for more than 10 per cent of trading volume on the Toronto Stock Exchange, visitors would seek out his war room in the sky with its panoramic view of the financial district that lay at Sarlos's feet. Well, there was no war room. The first clue that Sarlos was not an arrogant master of the universe was that he operated out of other people's head offices. Yes, he was saving on rent, but the important thing was that he always have someone to talk to. After all, Sarlos's own staff numbered just three, a minimalist personnel policy later made famous by U.S. superinvestor Warren Buffett. Like Sarlos, Buffett has found it a useful means of ensuring that his team spends its time monitoring his investments, and not managing each other.

There were other hints of inverted grandeur. In a familiar ritual for greeting guests, Sarlos would jump up from the side table where he kept the paperwork for big deals in the works. He didn't like to have a desk between himself and another person. He also worried about putting people in his shadow. So he'd drag a chair, smaller than his visitor's, to within six inches of where his guest was sitting. Even then, one still had to strain to make him out, what with the whispered voice and undisguised accent, as Sarlos explained that with his habit of provoking corporate shakeups, he certainly was hoping for a handsome profit, but also meant no harm.

And people immediately believed him. Maybe it was his elfin frame, the slight stoop. The perpetual smile. Mostly it was Sarlos's obvious love of business, an affection that grew as he learned it from the outside in, toiling as an auditor for mining developments in Northern Ontario and power projects in Labrador. If one happened to visit on a Monday at lunch hour, two blocks away from Sarlos's TD Centre office, a CEO would no doubt be complaining to a Canadian Club audience about the twin evils of taxes and government regulation. And at that same moment, Sarlos would lean into his visitor's face, his laced fingers resting on his knees, and start explaining how business was not about sitting on your duff waiting for the government, the competition and the unions to stop giving CEOs a hard time. "Whether it's building a hydroelectric project such as Churchill Falls or an iron ore project like Labrador City or building a financial empire," Sarlos would say, citing his own curriculum vitae, "the ingredients are very similar. You have to have guts to pursue it against difficult odds. And you have to have the courage to go through disappointments, and to change your mind when your vision is wrong."

Sarlos thought he was merely prodding CEOs to be more daring in their vision. But in 1978, at the dawn of Sarlos's career as a midwife to takeovers that would reshape the Canadian corporate landscape for the next 20 years, there was no track record to show that Sarlos never would "bust up" a company. Or ever obtain for himself the requisite hangar-sized corner office befitting a creature of the TSE milieu, whose network of personal friends in high places constituted a sort of parallel exchange. Back then, as he began to make and lose a succession of stock-market fortunes, it was easy to marvel at the idea that Andy — it was always "Andy" — would finish his career without having accumulated a long list of enemies.

Back in 1978, Sarlos's elderly caller was rewarded: Abitibi got serious about drumming up new business — *USA Today* would soon make its debut, printed on Abitibi newsprint — and shares in the company flew heavenward. The bigger triumph, though — and this would become something of a pattern in Andy's long reign as the insider's insider on Bay Street — was that once Abitibi was delivered into the hands of a new buyer, the executives who lost control of their firm were seeking his counsel in plotting their comebacks.

⧗

THE POINT of Andrew (Endre) Sarlos's maximum impact as a stock-market icon was a span of four or five years beginning in the late 1970s, a period during which the price of a TSE seat leapt from $12,000 to $165,000. In this golden era of the Exchange, the value of trading climbed to a 1983 high of $400 million, making the TSE, in the 131st year of formal equity trading in Toronto, the world's eighth-largest venue for stock trading.

It was during this time that Sarlos introduced Canada to the concept of hostile takeovers. He was also Canada's pioneer of risk arbitrage, the practice of investing in potential takeover dramas. And he blazed a trail for reformers in corporate governance, giving today's institutional investors their first lessons in how to call entrenched managers to account for chronically mediocre performance. In doing so, he ran up the assets of his merchant banking firm, HCI Holdings Ltd, from $9.7 million to $130 million between 1977 and 1981; at his peak in the early 1980s, Sarlos was managing more than 700 million dollars' worth of investments through HCI and other portfolios in his care. When Sarlos finally faded from the scene more than a decade later, and was replaced by a new breed of hit-and-run investors who wrecked companies for a quick buck before taking refuge in offshore tax havens, he left behind some indelible rules about how profits can be reaped from responsible speculation and shareholder agitation. And he exhibited survival skills, grounded in his own near-perfect manners, the absence of which accounts for such flame-outs as Frank Lorenzo, T. Boone Pickens, Al Dunlap and other wrecking-ball operators who have only briefly commanded attention.

Sarlos was an exotic specimen. It would later seem that he was preordained to transform his adopted hometown from a backwater of dull-witted dividend reapers.

A bookkeeper's son born in Budapest in 1931, Sarlos earned a degree in economics at the University of Budapest, signed up with the youth wing of the Communist Party in order to advance his career prospects and was an officer in training in the Hungarian Air Force. When his squadron was targeted in one of Hungary's periodic Stalinist purges, Sarlos found himself in prison, with no way to tell his family he was still alive. Emerging after a year's confinement, a victim of beatings and racked with pneumonia, he turned against the Communist leadership, joining in the spontaneous uprising of 1956. His poorly armed National Guard unit was no match for the Red Army forces that poured into Budapest that year, and Sarlos escaped on foot to Austria, then Genoa, before making his way to Canada, where he arrived, 25 and penniless, after finding passage on a freighter bound for Saint John, New Brunswick.

Hungarian friends in Canada steered him to a $600-a-month accounting position in the mining town of Capreol, Ontario, near Sudbury, the beginning of a 10-year career with the giant engineering firm Bechtel. As the chief financial officer at another legendary engineering firm, Acres Ltd, Sarlos used the company's investment kitty to mastermind a string of audacious takeovers, including Inter-City Gas, Great Lakes Power and Traders Group, the second-biggest financial company in Canada and controlling shareholder of Guaranty Trust. In that last, most spectacular deal in 1970, Sarlos used a sliver of real money — paying $5.1 million for an obscure holding company — to gain control of an enterprise with assets of $569 million. Striking out on his own, he later rolled his Acres winnings into a new investment vehicle, HCI.

Thus began an era, lasting about two decades, when Andy Sarlos was Canada's fifth business. This is the stage term for the actor who, seen only fleetingly, is the catalyst of events. Sarlos was the catalytic agent who helped broker deals that created today's industrial giants, companies such as Norcen Energy Resources and Abitibi-Consolidated. Barely visible in the wings, he was the line prompter for a callow Upper Canada College graduate named Trevor Eyton during the opening act of the EdperBrascan extravaganza — which would rapidly evolve into one of the biggest, most diverse industrial conglomerates in world history. In the small-business arena, he gave a push to the publishing empire that grew out of Ron Hume's budding investment newsletter, *The MoneyLetter*, where as Canada's best-known stockpicker he boosted subscriptions by contributing a column.

Sarlos was befriended equally by establishment bluebloods like Conrad Black and scrappers such as the coroner-turned-investor Morty Shulman. The phone would ring, and it would be the yet-to-be-disgraced financier Ivan Boesky seeking or imparting advice on takeover candidates. Or impresario Robert Lantos or Garth Drabinsky, needing to be reassured that Canada could support their global ambitions. Or superstar investor George Soros, the man who broke the Bank of England with his multibillion-dollar correct guess on the direction of the pound, confirming travel arrangements for the next phase of the personal post-Communist reconstruction project that these two Hungarian émigrés, Soros and Sarlos, launched in the late 1980s.

Andy was often wrong in his market timing, but people trusted him all the same. At one time or another, he handled the personal finances of Maurice Strong, Sam Belzberg, Max Tanenbaum and Peter Munk, ran hulking investment portfolios for corporations and the comparatively small endowment of Dalhousie University.

He was the class act of Bay Street. Sarlos was known in the press as an investment wizard, the Buddha of Bay Street — an inevitable consequence of making a $9-million profit one day on shares in Hiram Walker-Gooderham & Worts Ltd. in the early going of his investment practice. But he was more of a financial-markets Metternich. He arranged the defection of pretty much the entire trading staff of Wood Gundy's young boutique trading arm, 42 Street, to the rival Walwyn Inc. Only he could have drawn start-up funds for one of his many comeback bids from both of the estranged Montreal and Toronto branches of the Bronfman family. And only Sarlos, perhaps, could get the chief executives of Nova Corp. and Polysar Energy & Chemical to suppress their warring egos long enough to consummate a $4-billion merger that became one of the Street's biggest paydays in commission fees.

The Street loved him. He should have been tarred with lasting embarrassment over the implosion of HCI, the former Hand Chemical Industries, which began life in 1873 as a maker of fireworks. Having turned HCI into one of the most powerful investment firms on the continent, Sarlos developed an exaggerated sense of his invulnerability to capricious turns in the market. HCI was leveraged to the hilt to finance its purchase of stocks that Sarlos counted on to make a swift recovery once the early 1980s recession had passed. But the recession dragged on, and Sarlos watched helplessly as HCI's shares plunged from $20 to less than 50 cents in the prolonged stock-market swoon. Yet the HCI debacle was quickly forgiven and largely forgotten by an investment community that had thrived on the commission income that Sarlos generated for them with his non-stop trading. Indeed, the Street fuelled his comeback as he painstakingly rebuilt HCI. It was a symbiotic relationship. Sarlos boosted year-end bonus pools at selected brokerages, and in turn, brokerage analysts and traders tipped him to the Street's most lucrative deals before the less-smart money crowded in. By Sarlos's reckoning, if you spent only $2,000 a year on commissions with a particular broker, "you buy his cup of coffee a day." And what kind of friend does that make you? "If a guy has 70 names to call" with potentially lucrative deals in the works, Sarlos would ask rhetorically, "will he call them alphabetically or by commission income?"

Sarlos was one friend the Street would never betray. Sarlos kept bouncing back — from being tortured in a Hungarian prison as an anti-Soviet dissident, and then in rebuilding after the HCI disaster, and still later in staging a prompt recovery after the Crash of '87. By definition, investor supernovas tend to be one-shot wonders who disappear after briefly lighting up the sky.

But after his stock-market humblings, Sarlos stuck around to sweep out the ruins. He'd pay off all his markers. Then Sarlos would do that rarest of all things: he'd offer heartfelt thanks, in public, to his bankers and shareholders for giving him a chance in the first place, and for letting him try to sort out the mess so everybody but him got some, and often all, of their money back. "There wasn't one segment of the financial community that was out to destroy us," Sarlos marvelled after the HCI meltdown. "And many had the opportunity to do so." Lawrence Bloomberg, who would go on to stardom in the 1990s with his First Marathon brokerage, was astonished that Sarlos and his partners in the crippled HCI struggled to pay off every cent of HCI's $150 million in debt before closing the partnership. "They didn't shrink from their responsibilities," Bloomberg said in 1984. "He's the only man I know," said Peter Munk, "who went bust, and I never saw a negative comment about him." At the culmination of that 18-month ordeal, Sarlos suffered a heart attack the day after HCI made its final debt repayment. "One of the things I learned is that people tend to have heart attacks after they have solved problems, not while they're dealing with them," Sarlos said.

As he mounted his next comeback attempt, Sarlos would decline to insult anyone's intelligence by swearing — as is commonly done by today's celebrity investors — that nothing would go wrong this time. Sarlos would rather warn than promise. The man regarded by many as the Street's most upbeat players was in fact a closet cynic, another legacy of his Budapest youth. He remembered that the Soviets did not seem to fear the Americans so much as view them with contempt, and he remembered why. The Americans would tell Sarlos and his freedom-fighter compatriots, "'Hold on another day, we are going to come,' " Sarlos recalls. "Then I realized they had no intention of coming. You come to the conclusion you can't trust anyone."

One of the things Andy warned people not to expect from him was talent for the day-to-day operation of the businesses in which he invested on their behalf. Sarlos was a financier, after all. And financiers raise money for businesses, they don't run them. Even the best financiers won't offer more than a cursory forecast of how the new corporate enterprises they are constructing will perform.

It was not so surprising, then, that some of the deals of which Sarlos was proudest looked their best on the day of their announcement. Then, with varying degrees of rapidity, things went south. The Polysar deal was the ruination of CEO Bob Blair's career at Nova, a firm where he had earlier won great praise for converting a stodgy provincial utility into a dynamic multinational enterprise. The grossly mismanaged EdperBrascan was history's biggest missed opportunity to place a Canadian firm, for the first time, among the exalted ranks of diversified global powerhouses such as General Electric, Mitsubishi or Nestlé. In the 1990s, Sarlos and his fellow directors at Ontario Hydro did not, so far as anyone can tell, do anything to call management to account over safety and debt-management practices. These culminated in Hydro being forced, a year after Sarlos's death in 1997, to take a multibillion-dollar write-off that marked Hydro as one of the biggest fiscal basketcases in the global nuclear-power industry.

"The only question is to what degree we are leveraged," was the motto of Sarlos's own firm. So perhaps it's no coincidence that each of the nightmares cited above was brought on by delusions of debt-carrying capacity. But in the Sarlos playbook, if you weren't prepared to overextend yourself, you weren't in the game. "You have to learn one thing in the game: the rule of the casino," Sarlos once explained in *The Financial Post*. "You go into the casino and you have $5; the likelihood is that you'll walk out of the casino broke. If you play the game of the house, the house has a hell of a lot more money than $5 against you. The more money you can bring to bear on a situation, the closer you can come to the amount of money held by the major player or players in the game, and the odds improve in your favour." Maybe so. But as Sarlos himself might say, business is about more than luck and a fat wallet.

Sarlos could also be spectacularly wrong as a seer. By the mid-1980s, The Buddha of Bay Street was predicting that both the takeover boom and the bull market in equities that began in 1982 had peaked. But both trends were still going strong by 2000. In 1984, Sarlos predicted a lengthy reign of perhaps 16 years for the newly elected Canadian prime minister Brian Mulroney, whose privatization reforms and conciliatory approach to Quebec nationalists were sure to win him enduring popularity. Sarlos severely underestimated the resolve of fiscal authorities at home and in the U.S. in their fight against inflation. Which also made Sarlos a goldbug to the end. Inflation stubbornly refused to re-emerge as a threat to world economies, but Sarlos stuck with gold — the ultimate hedge against inflation — as its price kept sinking.

That pattern carried over to Sarlos's personal life. At the market top for fine art in 1980, Sarlos accumulated works by Jean-Paul Riopelle, Milton Avery and A.Y. Jackson, unloading them just one year later in a bid for solvency as HCI collapsed. Sarlos was not the only expert who didn't follow his own advice. He had warned readers of his *MoneyLetter* column of impending doom as October 1987 approached, but stayed in the market himself, losing yet another fortune. Fiercely Canadian, he could nonetheless be blinded by passionate attachment to the land of his birth, dismissing the Poles, especially, as having much further to go than Hungary in reaching a state of capitalistic grace. (By the 1990s, Poland had outdistanced all of its former Communist Bloc cousins in the pace of its economic modernization.)

Yet Sarlos managed to keep his credibility in good order. You could not accuse this emperor of having no clothes. For there he was, naked in the public square, acknowledging with candor and wit that he had been wrong, and exploring the depths of his intellectual deficiencies for the reasons why — hoping, always, that others could learn from both his successes and missteps. "Failure has a good attribute," he said. It prompts one to abandon obsolete methods which once worked so well, and to start anew. "Failure has its place — otherwise trees would grow to the sky, and they don't."

Sarlos mined his personal misfortunes for conversational ice-breakers. In a meeting with Czech leader Vaclav Havel, who, like Sarlos, had once been a political prisoner, Sarlos quickly made it clear that he did not come bearing New World wisdom to the intellectually impoverished Czechs. Having thus distinguished himself from most North American visitors to Eastern Europe in the 1980s, Sarlos then put Havel even more at ease with a joke about the multitude of Mulroney ministers whose political careers had been curtailed by ethics inquiries. "In Czechoslovakia, people come out of jail and go into the cabinet. In Canada, it is the opposite."

It was Andy's prescience, rather than his bad calls, that close friends and mere spectators tended to keep uppermost in mind. After all, as Trevor Eyton would say of Sarlos, "If he has any problem, it's that he tends to be ahead of things."

And there were, of course, many good calls. Sarlos liked General Electric Co. in the 1980s, a decade before it emerged as the world's most valuable company in terms of market capitalization. He bought into Gillette Co. before the razor maker became one of Warren Buffett's favourite investments. Sarlos started predicting disaster for Japan's overleveraged economy several years before that reversal of fortune came to pass in the mid-1990s. And he had good reason to express sorrow over the woes that would soon overtake the Western firms that imagined China could somehow become a lucrative market for consumer goods, before satisfying its more basic needs for decent roads and modern irrigation systems.

Not that Sarlos was an isolationist; quite the opposite. Noting that Europeans, with their pioneering multinational enterprises of old, such as the East India Co. and the Hudson's Bay Co., had eagerly financed the new economies of North America and Asia, Sarlos would express his despair at the homebody caution that still characterized most Western investors. "European fund managers and individual investors have always known that investing in one's own domestic economy is not sufficient," Sarlos told a gathering of Canada's top brokerage-house analysts in 1993. "But unlike their European counterparts, North American investors have been typically isolationist." For several years beginning in the late 1980s, most conversations with Andy touched at least briefly on how his good friend Soros had, in the short space of 20 years, managed to turn a $250,000 grubstake into an $8-billion investment empire. Soros had done so largely with his bet, back in the late 1960s, that "Made in Japan" would lose its connotation of inferior goods and evolve into a label of quality and efficiency. "Imagine," Sarlos would gush, exhilarated by Soros's success, "an empire built around one single guideline — that global investments are out there for the taking."

By the late 1970s, Canadian industrialists were beginning to expand offshore, and were searching the world for innovative practices to apply at home in fields as varied as engineering, telecommunications and retailing. But stock-market investors in both Canada and the U.S. were still reluctant to take a bet on foreign ventures.

Sarlos conceded that one reason Canadians were reluctant to join in the global fun was that too many of them had reason to rue at least one plunge on Filippino diamond mines and Nigerian offshore oil projects — bets, more often then not, based on knowledge that investors had gleaned from a broker's report or the business pages of Saskatoon's *Star Phoenix*.

Sarlos himself collected his most profitable insights by getting out in the world — a practice he exhorted others to adopt. He would tartly observe that some of his peers imagined they had a grasp of the Japanese investment scene based on their experiences at the upscale sushi bars of Toronto. Better that they should feast on Western food in a Yokohama diner, Sarlos would say, recounting that one of his correct calls on the Canadian dollar's imminent advance against the yen followed close on the heels of a restaurant summit meeting in Tokyo where he had enjoyed a $100 steak dinner.

"*Being there* is crucial for generating successful investment strategies," Sarlos wrote in an open letter to the Canadian investment community in 1987, about five years before Main Street investors in North America began to exhibit an insatiable appetite for developing world stocks. Brokers who led their clients into these stocks, and CEOs who led their companies into exotic locales, were counselled by Sarlos to first check out these remote arenas in person. "Glasnost is one thing when you read about it in the newspapers; it's easy to believe it's nothing more than a propaganda ploy, empty words," Sarlos said, several years before the final and utter collapse of the Soviet Union in 1991. "But while relaxing in Armenia or walking the streets of Moscow, I felt the new openness." He would talk about his tours of China, with its "omnipresent bicycles rattling along the streets" and its "minimal infrastructure of roads, airports and railways for transportation and its [lack of] an effective communications system." His travels convinced Sarlos that North America marketers who dreamed of peddling their wares in this market of one billion people were trapped in a fantasy. In China, Sarlos said in an observation that continues to be true in the early 21st century, "opportunities for Canadian business lie not in mass marketing our products — nor even in selling the technological expertise and component parts for modernizing production — but in helping develop that infrastructure" of phones, canals and highways.

In the arena of global investing, if not always in the domestic stock market, Sarlos did follow his own advice. He and Soros launched what Andy described as the Canada-Hungary frequent flier club. In fact, the two men travelled often and widely throughout all the East European economies. Yet Sarlos could seldom free himself of his parochial biases. A visit with Havel reconfirmed, in Sarlos's mind, the superior business habits of Hungarians. And to be sure, any prospective investor would been taken aback by the surreal scene at the presidential digs in Prague. Installed in a setting of marble floors and pillars, and rooms lit by crystal chandeliers, Havel, the renowned author and philosopher, presided as probably the only Western leader to wear jeans when greeting foreign visitors. Toiling at his side were advisers dressed like college students at a donut shop. There were fax machines, Sarlos noted, "but nobody seems to know how to use them."

No such gentle mocking was in evidence when Sarlos reported on his progress in Hungary, however. This despite an episode worthy of the Marx Brothers that Sarlos and Soros had experienced in launching one of Hungary's first mutual funds. "We had to start from scratch, and I mean right from the beginning," Sarlos admitted. "New laws had to be written and, to ensure their passage, we had to collect the signatures of over 1,000 officials. And our legal bill hit $1.2 million. A substantial fee just to launch one fund!"

M ARKETS ARE ANIMATED by a sense of great and rising expectations. But Sarlos never denied that hopes might be dashed on the morrow. Markets turn, fortunes are lost, sages become fools — the important thing was to be breathing. "When you've been in prison, when you've been threatened with execution," said author and friend Peter C. Newman of Sarlos's ability to calm those around him, "you realize that it's only money."

At every turning point he witnessed, whether an isolated incident such as a handshake on a merger deal or a student's graduation at a school he had endowed, or an entire era such as the Runaway Inflation Period or the Junk Bond Years, Andy was happy just to be there. The enjoyment was heightened, admittedly, when he was helping to direct events, sight unseen. "He knew who the bidders were, who the gamblers were, and who would be the losers," said Anna Porter, a fellow Hungarian émigré whose Key Porter Books Ltd. published Sarlos's memoirs. "Often he knew all this even before the participants themselves realized what their roles were in Andy's script." He was not above promotional gimmicks, once inviting a *Toronto Star* photographer to capture an image of him strapped to a hospital gurney while undergoing tests soon after his heart surgery in the mid-1980s. Sarlos wanted to reassure people who had bought shares in his investment counselling firm — had bought shares in *him* — that both he and their investment were on the mend. And he continued to tutor Main Street investors in the verity of the market:

> It's easier to make money in a bad market than in a good market because the downside risks are much lower. If you can minimize the downside risk, you have won half the battle.
>
> Unless there is a certain amount of fear in a stock, it probably doesn't have great capital gains potential.
>
> Avoid most popular stocks and fad industries; also, avoid most new ventures.
>
> Instead of aiming to hold a lot of good investments, it's far better to hold a few outstanding ones.
>
> Avoid "inside information" as you would the plague.

Sarlos was one of his era's most-quoted experts on the stock market. He didn't pretend to know everything, but he did seem to know everybody. For all his prominence in Canada, his profile was still higher, perhaps unavoidably, in Hungary. This was rarely a blessing. Sarlos backed out of a deal to revive a commercial district in Prague because of unfounded accusations, widely disseminated in the local media, that he was a New World carpetbagger out to make a quick buck by purchasing distressed real estate on the cheap.

It was always himself that Sarlos saw in T. E. Lawrence's self-description: "I was, and am, ridiculously over-estimated." Characteristically, Sarlos opened a 1993 speech by apologizing for not being someone more important. "I think the conference organizers were under the impression that George Soros had been booked to deliver today's address," Sarlos began. "Well, it is an easy mistake to make: Both of our names start and end with the letter 's,' we are . . . about the same age, and we are both Hungarians working in the same profession. What makes us different is that if you gave George $10,000 in 1969, when he started his Quantum Fund, you would be $10 million richer today. Unfortunately, I can't say I have matched his performance."

It may have been that Andy's lack of pretence was his strongest ally in keeping hubris at bay. Into the late 1980s, Sarlos was still making some of the biggest bets in the casino, waging $100 million a throw. Yet he clung to the modest suburban home and aging Jaguar bought in his earliest Bay Street days. To the end, Sarlos held himself to the lifestyle of the junior accountant he once was. He did not relate to the concept of the trophy wife, a fixture of both Wall and Bay streets since the 1980s. Sarlos lost his first wife, a university sweetheart, when he was imprisoned by the Soviets. She was forcibly kept behind and instructed by Communist Party apparatchiks to sue for divorce. Having been torn from his first love, Sarlos revelled at the duration of his 47-year union with Mary, his second, whom he first met at a church dance in Sudbury in 1958. It ended only when, as his church would put it, Sarlos was called away for the last time.

Sarlos was forever protesting that he wanted to be regarded as a moneymaker — not so much out of greed, he would say, as from a desire to dampen memories of a hard-scrabble childhood in Budapest, and the tough early years in Canada. A Canadian friend had dissuaded him from defecting to Australia. He cursed this friend on putting ashore at Saint John in February 1957, finding Canada in the depths of an economic recession. He was accustomed to bleak financial prospects; it was the bitter cold that was a novelty.

For all of his later protestations that he had been on a lifelong mission to secure his financial freedom, it was non-profit endeavours that claimed the greater portion of Sarlos's energies.

Out of gratitude, perhaps, for being granted second, third and fourth chances after his own financial reversals, Sarlos was the one who linked a discredited Paul Reichmann with Soros in the former's first comeback stirrings after the shattering demise of Reichmann's Olympia & York property empire. For old times' sake, he rounded up domestic and international advisers to pump $1 billion into the tottering EdperBrascan empire in the early 1990s, so that it wouldn't have to unload prized assets at fire-sale prices. But Jack Cockwell, master architect of that conglomeration, declined the lifeline. Cockwell feared losing control of the firm in any reorganization, and his was one ego that Sarlos could not tame. (EdperBrascan was subsequently forced to part with crown jewels Noranda Inc., London Life and Canadian Hunter Exploration, among others.)

Many tycoons, prompted by an awakened sense of their mortality, turn late in life to good works in the community. Sarlos was different. As a student indoctrinated in Communist ideology, Sarlos formed a lasting kinship with socialistic principles of community. In Budapest it had not been Communism that sparked his revolt against the state, but Russian nationalism. He could not bear the harsh colonization of his beloved homeland by an occupying force of Moscow-trained idealogues.

Thus Sarlos delivered $100,000 each year to Toronto Hospital, and said that a chief regret over the HCI implosion was that he had to scale back on donations to the Art Gallery of Ontario. He kept describing his activities in Hungary, into which he channelled millions of Western investment dollars in the 1980s, as a venture from which he hoped to extract a profit. And some of his ventures did bear an entrepreneurial mark. Among them was the Polus Centre, Budapest's first shopping mall. There was a new office building in Budapest, one of the first to introduce the city to air conditioning. Sarlos's Western-style mutual fund, designed to finance new Hungarian companies, was emulated by other funds throughout Eastern Europe.

There was no flood of dividends from these upstart ventures, however. And no readily discernible payoff, either, from Sarlos's work in helping to reopen the Hungary Stock Exchange. Or in raising funds to launch the International Management Centre (IMC) in Budapest in the late 1980s, one of Hungary's first private-sector business schools, a Harvard on the Danube that is now the premier MBA mill in Eastern Europe and draws about 90 per cent of its 200 or so students from outside Hungary. Or from that teary moment in the mid-1990s when, on Parliament Square in the heart of Budapest, where the submachine-gun-toting Sarlos and his hopelessly outnumbered air-force buddies had once taken up positions against the Red Army, Sarlos unveiled a statue of Irme Nagy, former prime minister and national hero.

By the time ill health eased him out of money management for good in 1995, Andy Sarlos had knocked much of the stuffiness out of Bay Street. And he had imparted some compelling lessons in loyalty and the power of humility. A pioneer to the end, Sarlos became, in 1996, the first North American to be treated with an innovation in open-heart surgery. Called ventricular volume restriction, the procedure reduces in size a damaged heart, the object being to help the heart overcome its inefficiencies. No eulogist put it better than Anna Porter, in describing how even this trailblazing medical advance could not quite keep up with Andy, who died about a year after the operation.

"Twice before, Andy had faced death and won," Porter wrote in *The Globe and Mail*, May 19, 1997, a few days after his passing. "This time, he knew he could not win. It is sadly ironic that it was, in the end, only his big heart that failed him."

6

FRANK STRONACH

The restless drive of Magna's auto-parts czar

"This is my morning, my day begins."
— *Frank Stronach*

I N THE ROLLING COUNTRYSIDE north of Toronto, a latter-day John Singer Sargent might do a thriving business painting portraits of fading third-generation industrial barons and hustling immigrant tycoons — each camp regarding the other with feigned indifference, each drawing its wealth from the explosive growth of North America's fourth-largest metropolis. Here, in 1997, within sight of his 400-acre horse-breeding operation, Frank Stronach built the new headquarters for an empire of auto-parts plants that spanned four continents.

It was an odd place. You could stand on this gentle rise of land, surrounded by fields dotted with barns and horse paddocks, and marvel at a replica of an 18th-century castle with fortress enclosures, brashly transplanted in the New World. This homage to European monarchs conceived by an Austrian immigrant industrialist was a handsome ensemble of château-style buildings, all dormers and fretwork, and vaguely suggestive of the orderly arrangement of the Parliament buildings in Ottawa. It was also the nerve centre for 164 metal-bashing factories — plants that existed to serve the age of the automobile. Yet you could wander till dusk among the formal lawns and low stone walls, a tableau that called to mind Sargent's *Luxembourg Gardens at Twilight*, and not see a car. A vast network of underground parking lots with unobtrusive ramps far from the main buildings kept automobiles out of sight. In the cathedral hush above ground, one heard only the efficient working of stately fountains, which came to life and fell silent according to the dictates of a distant computer.

The effect was unsettling. There was, after all, no order or stateliness to Frank Stronach. He was a cocksure visionary who had bullied his lieutenants into submitting to the countless doubtful schemes from which his $13.6 billion enterprise had emerged. The founder of Canada's biggest auto-parts firm, the sixth-largest in the world, was also a quixotic dabbler in thoroughbred racing, nightclubs, publishing, European theme parks and soccer teams. He was given to unintentional self-parody, having once sought a seat in Parliament on a platform of balancing the national accounts even as the overleveraged Magna was hurtling toward near-insolvency.

The scene of pastoral serenity in Aurora, Ontario had to be a put-on, the conceit of a rich man seeking to create his own reality. It was a relief to approach the elegant stone facade of these buildings, and peering inside, to see a shiny sport-utility vehicle on a hoist with its metal and plastic guts strewn on the floor. Casting a glance upward to the top storey, one could imagine a replay of that oft-recalled Magna board meeting which began with one of the directors commenting on what a beautiful day it was for the board members to be launching their day's deliberations. From his seat at the head of the board table, Chairman Stronach had thundered: "This is *my* morning, *my* day begins."

But he was no simple autocrat, and this kept Stronach from being celebrated as a wildly successful capitalist in an era that venerated entrepreneurs as the one true source of wealth creation. He never quoted Ayn Rand, but his lectures on the paramount virtue of individualism put some detractors — and not just the union leaders who tried with little success to organize Magna's plants — in mind of the grasping Howard Roark. Yet neither did Stronach find favour with devotees of Rand, for he was a meddlesome social engineer who sought to impose Magna's holistic pay-and-benefits scheme on the entire body politic. Free-market purists could hardly embrace a soft-headed mogul bent on reforming a capitalist system that was, in Stronach's view, "from time to time self-destroying, with the lowest suffering the most." There was more of a consensus about Stronach's flair for self-indulgence, which his many critics in the budding "shareholders rights" movement saw as Ozymandian. Certainly, Stronach was not a lonely pioneer of campus-style head offices on the fringes of major cities. In these earnestly "worker-friendly" iterations of the company town, employees were spared any distractions save the occasional deer sighting. The Magna retreat at Aurora had its counterpart in the Microsoft enclave in the Seattle suburb of Redmond, Washington, the Nortel Networks' executive offices at Brampton, Ontario, and the Nike campus in Beaverton, Oregon, where Phil Knight had named each of the buildings after his favourite basketball and track stars. But the *two* Magna castles — the firm's European operations were run from a 400-year-old fortress outside Vienna — seemed to push at the boundaries of acceptable excess.

Yet if one were to adhere to the guidelines for Harvard case studies, which carefully strip out all of the speculative character insights in order to measure only tangible achievement, one could make the case that Stronach was a great builder, after all. This would mean falling in line with *Forbes*, which in 1999 included Magna and just one other Canadian firm, Bombardier Inc., among the world's 20 best-managed global enterprises.

Stronach had arrived in Canada in 1954 with $40 in his pocket and built from scratch one of the world's leading companies of its kind, mounting a campaign for global dominance no less successful than that of Bombardier in aviation and mass-transit equipment and Nortel in telecommunications gear. Long before North American manufacturers woke up in the 1980s to the quality and innovation threat posed by Japanese and European interlopers, Stronach created a business model for managing sustained growth based on those principles. The model insulated Magna from both the whims of Stronach himself and the feast-and-famine business cycle of the auto industry, which had humbled General Motors and stripped Nissan and Volvo of their independence.

Stronach had also furnished a blueprint for survival to Detroit's Big Three automakers, Magna's biggest clients, by devising a means of providing them with just-in-time delivery of high-quality engineered parts. He could turn out parts faster and cheaper than the automakers themselves. Eventually, he was supplying vehicle manufacturers with complete subassemblies and entire vehicles. In doing so, Magna contributed mightily to the dynamism of Canada's most important industry, the auto sector that was concentrated in Southern Ontario. Magna created thousands of new jobs for highly trained workers in Canada, who were beneficiaries of a European-style emphasis on apprenticeship and engineering skills that Stronach had brought to Canada from his homeland. It was also a paragon of international expansion. At a time when Canadians were exhorted to make themselves globally competitive, Stronach had already expanded his network of factories into the U.S., Europe, Brazil, Korea and China.

By the late 1990s, the issues that Stronach had championed — including government deficit reduction, tax cuts, higher R&D spending and touchy-feely values in the corporate workplace — had gained widespread public acceptance. And he had engineered one of the greatest business comebacks of the century, pulling his $2-billion company back from the brink after a 1990-91 brush with bankruptcy that followed a decade of debt-financed overexpansion. As a silver-lining legacy of that near disaster, Magna emerged with the industry's most modern plants and a two- or three-year lead over its rivals in key manufacturing technologies. Magna stock had rocketed from $2 at the start of the decade to $113 by 1998, giving Stronach's personal stake in the firm a value of more than $400 million. Magna already controlled 2.5 per cent of the world market in auto parts. Now it was poised to climb to still greater heights by exploiting the biggest transformation in auto history since the assembly line. By 2000, automakers were outsourcing ever larger portions of their design and manufacturing operations. And the most sophisticated of these transfers of technological responsibility were going to Magna.

Yet these were unhappy times for Stronach. In 40 years, he had never exaggerated Magna's growth potential. But his vow to double and perhaps even triple its sales in the early years of the 21st century was greeted with disbelief. In 1999, skittish sellers of Magna shares chopped about 40 per cent off the company's stock-market value, alienated by the founder's new vision of a "second Magna" of race-tracks, theme parks and European off-track betting services. Stronach had done much to invite this chorus of derision. In 1990, he had equated saving Magna with saving the country, and preventing Canada from becoming "a nation of warehouse operators." Back then, Stronach believed that manufacturing enterprises like Magna were the underpinning of the economy, because "changing linen and making hamburgers is not wealth creation. We've got to make things." He'd been proven right on that score. But now, a decade later, Stronach was pinning his hopes on the humble "service" economy of tourism, sports and entertainment. Why? Because, he explained, "the Western world will lose a lot of industrial jobs." That was hardly a ringing endorsement of Magna's core business.

But there was something uglier behind the dubious regard for Stronach, something hinted at by his chroniclers' unfailing habit of referring to his "thick Austrian accent," even his "slithering Austrian accent." Warren Buffett, the Oracle of Omaha, could get away with investing in both the august Washington Post Co. and the profit-challenged Dairy Queen, operator of roadside ice-cream stands that were closed half the year. But the eccentric machinations of a refugee from Nazi-occupied Austria were always clouded with suspicion. Stronach had become a whipping boy for the shortsighted Bay Street brokers and institutional investors who had dismissed him as a shooting star in the 1980s and hastily pronounced last rites on Magna at the end of that decade. They once had faulted him for attempting to micromanage every aspect of Magna's operations. Now, even as Magna was reporting a record profit of $430 million (U.S.) for 1999 on record sales of $9.4 billion (U.S.), they were slamming him for letting his attention wander from auto parts.

As the century drew to a close, Stronach felt a growing alienation from his adopted homeland. A top Canadian business historian, asked by a national newspaper to rank Stronach among the country's 20 leading business figures of the century, had replied: "Is Stronach a serious businessman? I've always thought of him as a phony." At age 67, when the legacy of most successful business people is secure, Stronach could still be presented as an enigma in *Maclean's*, one of Canada's most widely read magazines. It noted that "twenty years after he and Magna came to the attention of the Canadian business scene, people are still asking the same questions. Is Stronach a genius or a total flake?"

Stronach himself, usually the most talkative person in any gathering, seemed at last to grow weary of explaining himself. At a shareholders meeting in 1998, all of the questions were directed at his former son-in-law, Magna chief executive Donald Walker. No one wanted to hear from Stronach, who had once offered that he was "always available to help the economy of Canada." He retreated in disgust. "So, who needs to ask questions of a chairman, anyway?" In Aurora, both his daughter, Belinda, and his son, Andy, were erecting mansions next door to the newly built mansion shared by Stronach and his wife, Frieda. But the Magna founder was making only token appearances at a head-office facility that some locals ridiculed as a faux Versailles. Mostly he was at the other castle, in Vienna, building Magna's European operations into a $1.6-billion business and sparking accusations back in Canada that he had become a tax exile. He was not widely popular in Austria, either. Stronach's schemes to shower prosperity on the burghers of Vienna with proposals for amusement parks and racetracks met with the same sort of skepticism that greeted him in Canada. But at this unsettled time in his life, Stronach needed to return to his roots, and the wellspring of his undeniable accomplishments.

FRANK STRONACH would always be called a maverick — a descriptive term, often derisory, for people whose actions are poorly understood. Stronach sometimes gave the impression of being an egotistic grasper. He offered no apology when it was revealed in 1987 that with a salary of $2.2 million, he was paying himself the highest salary of any CEO in the land. Yet he was a caustic observer of the corporate scene, a scold who faulted his peers for their insensitivity to the welfare of their workers. Stronach seemed to regard Magna, with its elaborate profit-sharing plans and employee benefits, and its commitment to lavish spending on R&D and charitable donations, as an instrument of socio-economic policy. To Stronach's constant chagrin, the Canadian corporate elite could no more applaud that vision of bastardized capitalism than conceive of the Horatio Alger stories as written by Sidney and Beatrice Webb. But in his own mind, at least, Stronach's ideas were a bridge between the old and new worlds of free enterprise. As a young man, Stronach had traded his homeland for a continent that celebrated raw capitalism. Yet he would always be influenced by the way that capitalism was practised in Europe, which placed a high value on apprenticeship and long-range planning over the pursuit of a quick buck. Late in the 20th century, Europe still adhered to a social contract between capital and labour which saw many of the largest business enterprises owned by the state, with significant labour representation on corporate boards of directors.

Stronach was born Frank Strohsach, which means "straw sack," in 1933 in the town of Weiz, near the border with Hungary and Yugoslavia. He is the second-most-famous product of the southeastern Austrian foothills, after Arnold Schwarzenegger, another émigré who made good in the New World.

Magna employees Stacy Jimmerskog and Michael Whitfield assemble components for the Chrysler 300 family sedan (above) and the racy BMW Z3 (below). While rival firms were still turning out bolts, body panels or headlamps for the big automakers, Magna was pushing its clients for the chance to build entire subassemblies. With its success in developing ways to build ever more sophisticated components, and to make them faster, cheaper and with fewer defects than the automakers could, Magna became a leading supplier to almost all of the world's two dozen major vehicle manufacturers.

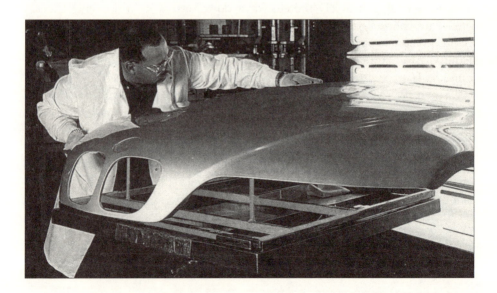

Was he a genius or a total flake? Magna's opulent head office in Aurora (below), north of Toronto, was merely one of Frank Stronach's (left) many extravagances. Castle Frank was paired with Magna's European headquarters, lodged in a 400-year-old fortress outside Vienna. Stronach seemed to encourage his reputation as an oddball visionary with his improbable schemes to launch an executive airline (Magna Air) and to build theme parks, soccer academies and a network of betting salons in his native Austria. He answered critics by saying, "People forget that when it was first built, the Eiffel Tower was unpopular too." Obscured by the fanciful ideas, which seldom saw the light of day, was Stronach's real success in building a second Magna empire of racetracks which by 2000 accounted for roughly one-quarter of all parimutuel betting in North America.

Stronach and his two sisters endured the Depression and the successive occupations of the Nazis, the Russians and the British. Stronach's father, a factory worker and ardent Communist, argued with his son at the dinner table about the merits of socialism. It was Stronach's mother who kindled the fire of their son's ambition. Eager to have him learn a trade, she pulled him out of school at 14 and packed him off to Elin Inc., a maker of hydro-electric generators and Weiz's biggest employer. The young tool-and-die apprentice was given a block of steel and a metal file and told he had one month to turn it into a piece of electrical machinery. Over the next eight years, Stronach worked at other factories in Austria and Switzerland. His proficiency on company soccer fields led to offers to play the game as a professional. But Stronach was impatient to escape postwar Europe. "I was restless," he later recalled, "and the atmosphere was confining. The whole pattern of life in Europe, the whole business structure, was too set in its ways for me to advance the way I wanted."

In 1954, at age 22, Stronach sailed for Montreal. He arrived with no money to speak of. He anglicized his name and took a series of odd jobs. In Montreal, he retrieved golf balls at a driving range. He soon moved to Kitchener, Ontario, a town that had changed its name from Berlin as war loomed in Europe and which still had a large German population. There he toiled as a dishwasher at a local hospital before getting a chance to put his toolmaking skills to work at a factory that made airplane parts. Within a year, Stronach had been laid off after the factory suffered a loss of orders. Stronach's prospects brightened in Toronto, where he found work as a toolmaker and eventually was given a chance to become a partner in a machine shop. But he wanted to be his own boss.

By 1957, Stronach had saved up enough money to finally launch himself in business. In a garage on gritty Dupont Street near Dufferin Street in Toronto, Stronach used a $2,000 bank overdraft to finance $15,000 worth of equipment, consisting of a band saw, a drill press, a lathe, a milling machine and a surface grinder. The first order landed by his infant enterprise, Accurate Tool and Die, was for a metal bracket for American Standard, a maker of toilets located around the corner. For the first few years, Stronach slept in that garage, on a cot next to his lathe. Total sales in his first year were $8,200.

In subsequent years, Stronach's larger-than-life persona would give outsiders the impression that Magna was, and had always been, a one-man show. But this would never be the case. As Magna evolved into a multibillion-dollar firm, Stronach would rely on a team of plant managers, financial experts and super-salesmen. With his natural ebullience, Stronach was able to recruit top-notch talent. The earliest lieutenants often shared his Central European background and high regard for engineering skills and quality workmanship. Few were put off by Stronach's hard-charging ways, because they shared his fierce ambition.

Early on, Stronach was joined by Anton Czapka, a fellow tool-and-die maker and erstwhile soccer opponent from Weiz, who invested all but $12 of his weekly earnings from his day job at Canadian General Electric Co. in Stronach's fledgling company, soon renamed Diamatic Ltd. Helmut Hofmann, a German émigré who would later be the architect for Magna's first major expansion drive as an auto-parts supplier, helped the struggling firm by feeding it orders from the engineering firm which employed him at the time. As it developed a reputation for making high-quality tools, Diamatic attracted the attention of Burton Pabst, a former high-school track star from Detroit who ran the Ajax, Ontario branch plant of a U.S. maker of auto-trim components. Pabst struck a 50-50 partnership with Stronach, who needed a frontman with better English than his. Pabst, a high-powered salesman, soon used his contacts with the Big Three automakers to land Stronach's first auto-parts deal, a $30,000 contract in 1960 to supply General Motors of Canada Ltd. with the metal arms for sun visors. Within a decade, a single machine shop with 10 workaholic German and Austrian tool-and-die makers had grown into four factories in the Toronto area.

In the 1990s, when Stronach began to hatch grandiose projects in his native country, Bay Street critics took this as a sign that the founder had become easily distracted. But Stronach had never cut his ties with Austria. When prosperity first shone on him in the 1960s, Stronach bought a brand new Pontiac and had it shipped to Weiz, where he returned in triumph to give friends a spin around town. He returned again to marry Elfriede Sallmutter, the daughter of a local furniture maker. Stronach's relationship with Elfriede would endure. He had taken a methodical approach to selecting a mate. His biographer Martin O'Malley would relate that, in pursuing the teenaged Elfriede, Stronach was hoping she would grow up to be as pleasant and attractive as her mother, and had selected Elfriede "for her bone structure and breeding possibilities, like choosing a thoroughbred." By the late 1960s, Stronach and his young family were living on a farm in Aurora with several thoroughbred horses, and was entertaining thoughts of semi-retirement. He decided to sell his interest in his thriving auto-parts firm to Magna Electronics Corp., a publicly traded defence contractor, for $500,000 and a 9 per cent stake in the new company. Stronach celebrated the transaction by purchasing a grey Corvette coupe. He seemed content with a demotion to a mere vice-president of someone else's firm.

Soon enough, however, Stronach was back to getting just four hours of sleep each night. The future lightning rod for critics of corporate diversification was alarmed with Magna's plans to go into the business of computer manufacturing. Taking a plunge on electronics was a favoured method by which stagnant firms of that era attempted to mask deeper problems with their core business. It was also a means of courting faddish investors in the go-go stock market of the late

1960s. But Stronach wanted no part of that. With Pabst and his other fellow partner-employees from the old days, Stronach regained control of the firm. He dumped the computer division but kept the Magna name and the firm's status as a publicly traded company. The stock-market listing was of immense value. It would soon become a key element of Stronach's "Fair Enterprise" system of incentives for outstanding employee performance. And that system would help to ensure Magna's emergence as the world's fastest-growing major auto-parts maker.

Stronach's Fair Enterprise gradually evolved into a corporate constitution and charter of employee rights that dictated every aspect of Magna's operating philosophy. It took root in the late 1950s, when Anton Czapka had abruptly announced he was leaving Diamatic to start his own firm. Stronach could sympathize. He'd done the same thing in quitting his post at that Toronto machine shop. But he couldn't afford to lose his valuable foreman, much less find himself in competition with Czapka. So Stronach built a new factory for Czapka, and gave him the opportunity to buy a stake in it with the profits he earned.

The auto sector has traditionally been a textbook example of labour relations at their worst. Workers at GM, Ford, Chrysler and the parts firms that supplied them were treated for the most part as potentially mutinous automatons whose only incentive was a union-negotiated contract often obtained at the cost of a punishing strike. Conditions were quite different at Magna. As it grew with the booming auto industry in the 1960s and 1970s, its top managers were cast in the Czapka mould. Almost all would be former tool-and-die makers whom Stronach promoted to foreman, then plant manager, and then group manager, in control of several plants. At each step of the way, these compatriots got a cut of the profits from their plants. By 1984, the so-called "Magna Carta" called for all employees, rank-and-file as well as managers, to share in Magna's booming profits. This was the chief means by which Magna was able to underprice the in-house parts divisions of the automakers — and ultimately to be entrusted by the Big Three as a favoured outside supplier. It also helped keep the unions at bay. Magna's hourly workers were paid only two-thirds or so of what their unionized counterparts received at other firms. But they garnered 10 per cent of each year's corporate profit. Three per cent of that was in cash, amounting to about $3,000 for each hourly worker in 1998. The balance was in Magna shares, which exposed the firm's 54,000 employees to the unsentimental assessment of their performance by stock-market investors. But long-time employees did well in that bargain. They suffered as Magna stock plunged from $36 to $2 between 1987 and 1990, but reaped enormous gains when the shares subsequently recovered to a 1998 high of $113.

⧗

TRADITIONALLY, AUTOMAKERS have regarded their suppliers with disdain, rather like the contempt that Hollywood producers have for movie-house operators. What could the man who ends his day by picking gum off theatre seats know about the magic of making a motion picture?

Yet the movie studios had begun as offshoots of cinema chains, which needed product to fill their theatres. In the early days of the auto industry, parts suppliers regarded the first automakers as mere assemblers of vehicles, put together with doors, fenders and windshields whose design often originated with the auto-parts makers. The earliest automakers were, after all, primitive operations. In Southern Ontario at the turn of the century, there were hundreds of garage mechanics who conceived new-fangled automobiles. The more successful of these tinkerers might turn out all of a dozen vehicles each year. The progress of those pioneers was largely dictated by the technological advances achieved by parts makers. Notable among that group were the carriage craftsmen, including the Massey and McLaughlin enterprises in Ontario, and the Fisher brothers in the U.S. It was Fisher Body Corp. that made the horseless carriage more widely popular by perfecting the closed body for automobiles — a decided boon at a time when hardy motoring enthusiasts were exposed to the elements. By 1927, when closed bodies accounted for 85 per cent of industry sales, the pace of GM's growth was set by the speed at which Fisher could turn out bodies. Realizing it could not control its own destiny if it continued to rely so heavily on outside suppliers like Fisher Body, GM bought out the six Fisher brothers between 1919 and 1926. GM also absorbed Delco Light, Remy Electric, AC Spark Plug and various other key suppliers, and launched the General Motors Acceptance Corp. to help buyers finance car purchases. The early Ford, Chrysler, Studebaker, Packard and Nash enterprises all bought up many of their leading suppliers, as well. To be sure, the principle of vertical integration stopped at the steel mill and the gas pump. By the 1940s, Henry Ford had proved the folly of taking vertical integration to extremes by feeding his own blast furnaces with his own coal carried on his own ships to Ford Motor Co.'s massive River Rouge plant on the outskirts of Detroit, a company town that employed 100,000 people at its height in the 1930s and was one of the great industrial boondoggles of the 20th century. Still, it would be 60 years after the disappearance of Fisher Body before the world's automakers turned once again to outsiders for critical components.

All along, of course, automakers did rely on outside suppliers for many of the 15,000 or so parts in each car or truck. But the vehicle assemblers built their own engines, chassis, powertrains and other major components. And for lesser parts, they did not trust their suppliers with design responsibilities. Until the 1980s, parts makers worked almost exclusively from engineering blueprints provided by the automakers. As Japanese vehicle manufacturers, who enjoyed an edge in quality and price, began to steal market share from the Big Three, Detroit's automakers found themselves in a near-fatal bind. With both their assembly plants and parts-making factories locked into long-term labour contracts that gave workers a guarantee of high wages and job security, the Big Three were unable to match their Japanese rivals in quick styling changes. And given the Japanese innovations in making cars more cheaply, Detroit could no longer pass rising production costs onto consumers without driving them into the showrooms of Toyota and Honda. The only way out of this dilemma was to relax their zealous grip on control over parts making. And Magna, steeped in Old World engineering expertise, and boasting lower costs than the automakers, was well positioned to exploit this lucrative trend. But first, Stronach would have to endure a crisis that would nearly destroy his company.

By 1990, Magna was making close to 5,000 different auto parts at 125 factories in Canada and the U.S. But it was also on the brink of insolvency. Stronach was struggling to make payments on about $1 billion in debt accumulated during a huge expansion campaign over the previous few years. Magna was a victim of its own success. In order to win the automakers' business, Stronach had complied with their demands that he help them achieve efficiency gains through just-in-time delivery of parts — a method for cutting down on costly inventory. That required Magna's own new factories to be located near, and often right next door to, the Big Three's assembly plants. In the short space of six years in the 1980s, Stronach had scrambled to build a new chain of parts factories that replicated the sprawling network of the automakers' own assembly plants across North America.

There were additional factors that drove up Magna's expenditures at that time. As the cost-conscious automakers stopped sending blueprints along with their orders, pushing design responsibility onto Magna, Stronach was required to go on a hiring spree for engineers and support staff. Many of the new Magna plants represented a gamble on the popularity of a particular vehicle, and Magna lost a few of those bets. Among the disappointments was the $187 million that Magna spent to build a stamping plant at Milton, Ontario to supply the new Eagle/Premier line of sedans, which turned out to be a flop for the (now defunct) American Motors Corp. Making matters worse was Stronach's determined effort to supply the new "transplants" — assembly plants that the Japanese automakers were setting up in Canada and the U.S. to get around import quotas imposed by Washington. Nissan, Honda and Toyota were notorious for sticking with suppliers brought with them from Japan. To win even a fraction of that business, Stronach had to cut his prices so deeply that Magna lost money on almost every contract with a Japanese automaker.

Magna's timing could not have been much worse for taking on a debt load that was twice the company's equity. In 1990, the world auto industry plunged into its deepest slump since the early 1980s. As the tide went out, it became apparent that Magna was bloated with overhead as a byproduct of its expansion drive, when it was opening a new factory every three weeks. In the pell-mell rush to fill the new orders it eagerly booked, Magna had accumulated multiple levels of managerial bureaucracy, with attendant perks. And Stronach had picked this same crucial period to become distracted with a failed 1988 bid for a Liberal seat in Parliament. He had also embarked on such non-auto-related ventures as a general-interest magazine called *Vista* that was to disseminate his Fair Enterprise ideas (it closed after three years). There were Magna condo development projects, a start-up business that sold tennis equipment, and a restaurant called Belinda's, named for Stronach's daughter.

To stave off receivership, Stronach took writedowns of $150 million on his plants, many of which were operating at just 50 per cent of capacity due to the downturn in auto sales. Yet Magna was still in breach of the performance tests on most of its debt, although it was just barely able to stay current with scheduled payments. Stronach's 16 bank lenders, led by Bank of Nova Scotia, began pushing for the closure or sale of many Magna factories. Fearing, correctly, that Stronach would balk at such a drastic restructuring, the bankers wanted him removed from power, at least temporarily. And Magna's Big Three clients were urging him to follow their example by shifting jobs to low-wage jurisdictions in the U.S. South and Mexico.

Stronach, his attention now fully engaged on Magna's founding business, promptly sold 20 older factories. He pushed a few plants into joint ventures, and merged or closed another 16 plants. This triage operation resulted in a 17 per cent reduction in the workforce, or almost 3,000 employees (many of whom continued to work at the same facility but for a new, non-Magna owner). Stronach also laid off about 500 mid-level managers, closed executive dining rooms, took back the keys for company cars and sold corporate jets. He acknowledged that "when you grow quickly, you do get a little sloppy."

What Stronach didn't do in these dark hours was abandon his best factories or lose his grip on power — which amounted to the same thing, and turned out to be a blessing for all concerned. With 60 per cent or so of the voting stock, Stronach was able to block any debt-restructuring scheme that meant giving up his newest and most efficient plants. Stronach's ace in the hole was his ability, if the bankers tried to squeeze him too hard, to simply put his company into bankruptcy. That would have meant disaster for Magna's Big Three clients, which didn't relish the prospect of scrambling to replace so much lost production. "When Magna nearly bought the farm in 1990," said Neil DeKoker, a senior vice-president at Magna in the 1980s, "the Big Three automakers had to figure out which Magna plant each of those would be taking over, so that their supply lines wouldn't be cut." By this point, Magna was supplying $1,000 worth of parts for each of DaimlerChrysler's minivans, which were then among the best-selling vehicles in the world. Magna had become too important to fail. By the fall of 1990, Scotiabank chairman Cedric Ritchie conceded the point. He acknowledged that Stronach would have to be the one to stage Magna's resurrection, even if he had also loomed large in its calamity. The Big Three automakers agreed to assist by making their payments on parts every two weeks rather than waiting the traditional 45 days.

As things turned out, Magna rebounded much more quickly than its automaker clients, who lost a collective $7 billion or so in the prolonged recession of the early 1990s. Magna's debt holders were paid off. Stronach then swore off debt for all time. He financed Magna's next round of expansion — larger than the last — from cash flow and funds raised in the stock market. With its remaining modern plants, few of them more than seven years old, Magna was able to strengthen its hold on existing clients. And it hustled for new ones. By the end of the decade Magna was a key supplier to most of the world's 20 or so major automakers. Its roster of clients now ranged from assemblers of compact cars and sport-utility vehicles to luxury marques such as Jaguar and Rolls-Royce. And its reliance on Detroit's Big Three was gradually easing as Stronach began to consolidate his early beachhead with the Japanese vehicle makers.

By betting the company in the 1980s on Magna's ability to crack new markets such as the seating business, Stronach became the single largest supplier to DaimlerChrysler AG, whose every minivan contained about $1,600 worth of Magna parts by the early 1990s. Stronach's huge investments in new factories, and Magna's unstinting commitment to R&D, had given the company a head start of more than two years over its competitors in leading-edge design and manufacturing technologies. Prominent among these was hydroforming, a revolutionary manufacturing process that replaced traditional welding with a system in which water pressure was used to form parts. These parts were lighter, stronger and of more consistent quality than welded parts. By the late 1990s, GM was entrusting Magna with the task of supplying hydroformed frames for its new pickup trucks and sport-utility vehicles. Ford gave Magna the even more prestigious assignment of designing the complete interior and exterior of its hot-selling Lincoln Navigator luxury sport-utility vehicle. That job likely would have taken Ford's own development team about three years to pull off, compared with the 24 months required by Magna. Stronach's firm also supplied an astonishing $6,500 worth of parts for each Navigator. An admiring GM delegated similar responsibilities to Magna for its high-end Cadillac Catera.

On the strength of rising cash flow from its North American operations, Stronach sought to replicate Magna's success in Europe by investing heavily in new plants on the Continent. Beginning in 1992, he spent about $1 billion over the next eight years on a dozen or so acquisitions that created a $1.8-billion-a-year European business. In short order, Magna was able to add Fiat, Saab, Volvo, Peugeot-Citroen and GM's Opel division in Germany to its client list. By beating out rival bidders Dana Corp. and Borg-Warner Automotive of the U.S. for the acquisition of Steyr-Daimler-Puch Group, an Austrian maker of cars and parts, Magna became the world's first independent auto-parts supplier that was capable of building an entire vehicle. The Steyr facility assembled Jeep Cherokees for the European market, along with Mercedes G and E class sedans and the M class sport-utility vehicle.

By the 1990s, Magna was leading a revolution among auto-parts suppliers, the largest of which no longer answered to the description of mere stampers and bashers of metal. Industry giants such as Dana, Lear and Johnson Controls — U.S. firms much older than Magna — began to specialize in niches such as seating and electrical controls. They sought to emulate Magna's example of turning out parts more efficiently than the automakers' in-house operations. Alone among its peers, however, Magna resisted the specialization trend. It opted to continue making almost every part to be found in a vehicle, from prosaic oil pans, water pumps, sunroofs and carpeting, to sophisticated instrument panels, infrared anti-theft mirror systems and electronic sliding doors that could be opened by remote control. Where other suppliers might turn out a lamp or a fender, Magna blazed a trail in "integrated" components. It won orders for complete front-end assemblies that incorporated a bumper, grille, headlights and parking lamps, and all the connecting struts and wires.

Magna's dedication to above-average spending on R&D — which amounted to 7 per cent of annual sales in times of robust and disappointing profits alike — began to pay off as the company turned the old relationship between supplier and automaker on its head. Rather than wait for orders and specs from automakers, Magna turned increasingly to its 21 R&D sites in Canada, the U.S., Europe and Japan to invent new parts and complete subassemblies that it could then shop around to the world's leading automakers. For DaimlerChrysler, Magna designed a child seat that was integrated into a traditional passenger bench seat. Magna scored industry firsts with a lightweight all-aluminum seat frame for the Plymouth Prowler hot rod, and minivan seats that swung up into the roof for self-storage. For the Navigator, it sold Ford on the idea of an elegant running board that lit up at night. Magna's laboratories came out with patented mirrors that rotated to improve rear viewing around trailers and campers, warning bells to tell the driver he was about to back into an obstacle, and cupholders that maintained beverages at desired hot and cold temperatures.

In the late 1980s, Stronach had been ridiculed for investing $8 million in a vanity bid to design and build a vehicle of his own, a four-wheel-drive sports car. There were no takers for the $200,000 Torerro as the auto industry plunged into recession. Still, Magna clung to its vision of someday turning out complete vehicles, even after automakers rejected its concept of a "Martha Stewart wagon" that provided ample room in the back for kids to work on crafts. Eventually its persistence would be rewarded, though, when DaimlerChrysler gave Magna unprecedented design responsibilities for its daring "microcar," the so-called Smart subcompact designed in partnership with Swatch, the Swiss watchmaker. By this point, Stronach was able to boast that "Magna is a virtual car company, except that we don't make cars." With the Steyr acquisition, even that description was proving to be an understatement.

FEW ENTREPRENEURS were more in tune with their times than Stronach. And few entrepreneurs of similar accomplishment got less credit for their progressive ideas.

"Spinning," or projecting a desired truth via the media, was widely scorned in the 1990s as a talent peculiar to manipulative politicians. In truth, the most ubiquitous spinners were corporate helmsmen. And their track records were rarely subject to the same exacting scrutiny as political figures. One of the most celebrated CEOs of the era, Jack Welch of General Electric Co., was essentially a cheerleader. His chief occupation at GE was to preside over New-Age encounter sessions among management recruits at GE's fabled training retreat at Croton-on-Hudson, New York, and to make carefully timed appearances in *Fortune* and *Business Week* as a cover boy for the GE vision of "employee empowerment." Beyond the fashionable rhetoric, however, Welch and his fellow CEO-statesmen were known to fall back on familiar expedients in tough times. Rather than think hard about how to reinvent a business for the long term, they sometimes gave in to the temptation to boost profits with a sudden layoff announcement or a reduction in the R&D budget, or to make a flashy acquisition that masked problems in the underlying business.

Stronach would never be mistaken for one of those glib operators. He had been transparently ruthless in consolidating his control of Magna, forcing out executives who didn't buy into his risky growth strategy. "Whatever Frank wants, Frank gets," said Bob Krever, a former Magna manager who left to run his own Toronto plastics firm. "If he wants to see someone come or go, he does it. If he wants to say 'Off with their heads,' it's off with their heads." Wayne German, an Iowan who ran Magna's profitable operations in his state, was one of those who left. He had made the mistake in 1987 of objecting to Stronach's reorganization of the Iowa division, and eventually quit in exchange for a handsome goodbye package. "The thing about Magna is they shit on you," German said, "but they make you so rich you don't mind it so much."

Such departures had become rare by the 1990s, when Magna was recognized as having one of the most stable and competent management groups in the industry. And Stronach's earlier rough-house tactics with wayward subordinates had disguised a consistent pursuit of laudable long-term objectives. He had rejected quick fixes, and had focused instead on internal growth, through R&D, new-product development and continual improvement of manufacturing methods. His takeovers were a natural extension of Magna's existing operations rather than a crowd-pleasing move designed to jolt some life into the company's stock. And even when he had resorted to layoffs in the crisis of 1990, Stronach had refused to cut the payroll anywhere near as deeply as his bankers and stock-market analysts had demanded.

In the 1970s, when Welch was still recovering from a shaky career start after accidentally blowing up a GE pilot plant, Stronach had begun to delegate key financial and manufacturing duties in a bid to develop a large corps of talented managers. And he devised the outlines of a model workplace that would later be recognizable to readers of the *Harvard Business Review* as "employee centred" and "family friendly." On cheap land he amassed north of Toronto, Stronach created an industrial campus whose holistic approach to employee needs resembled the 19th-century experiments in economic self-sufficiency that began with New York State's Oneida Community. Among the small-scale Magna plants scattered about Newmarket, Ontario, where the intimate employee populations seldom topped 100 people, Stronach set up training centres and medical facilities to serve Magna workers. His Newpark Day Care Centre was candidly an experiment in corporate social welfare. "We want to be part of your child's formative years," explained Magna literature of the time, "providing child care which lays the foundation for children to grow into caring, contributing adults." Stronach personally designed Simeon Park, a sprawling recreation area for Magna employees with an artificial lake, barbecue pits, a huge outdoor swimming pool, volleyball and tennis courts and fishing docks. Employee rights and responsibilities were codified in a formal constitution that exhorted workers to complain about inefficiencies or poor working conditions in their plants (by means of a confidential company hotline, if necessary), and rewarded them with the most elaborate profit-sharing plan in the industry. Signs posted at Magna plants told the departing shift: "Drive carefully. We need you."

By the mid-1980s, Stronach was popping up on Peter Gzowski's popular CBC radio program, *Morningside*, to campaign for reforms in traditional capitalism. In his view, free enterprise in North America was hobbled by regulatory and taxation restraints, a refrain familiar to any habitué of chamber-of-commerce conclaves. But Stronach went far beyond that, insisting that modern capitalism also deprived workers of a fair share of corporate profits and denied them sufficient incentive to work smarter. He said the entire country needed to adopt Magna's strategy of outsized R&D spending, manufacturing efficiency and harmonious labour-management relations. "There are only three economic models in the world," Stronach would explain, giving voice to a primitive version of what would someday become a lucrative branch of the management-consulting trade. "Those are socialist, totalitarianism and free-enterprise systems." Magna, he would explain, had created a fourth model of sharing capitalism. "We still believe in entrepreneurship," he said, "but what we're telling the entrepreneurs is: for God's sake, you can't take it all."

Over the next 15 years, Stronach's internal role as corporate cheerleader would find expression in inspirational videos from the chairman that were distributed to thousands of employees. As an external ambassador for the Magna Way, Stronach set up chairs in entrepreneurship at leading Canadian universities, at $75,000 to $100,000 a pop; the $1-million Magna for Canada Scholarships for ambitious but financially pinched students; the Fair Enterprise Institute to disseminate the Stronach doctrine of cooperative capitalism; and a series of books called *As Prime Minister, I Would . . .* , in which the iconoclastic views of ordinary Canadians impatient for reform were given a national forum.

By any objective assessment, Stronach could claim an impressive legacy as he entered his seventh decade. In 2000, Magna controlled 2.5 per cent of the world's highly fragmented auto-parts market, having used relentless innovation to thrive in a new and unforgiving era of international competition that Stronach had foretold two decades earlier as a coming time of "economic global warfare." At Magna itself, the founder's ideas had translated into a 25-year record of average annual growth in sales and earnings of 29 per cent and 17 per cent, respectively, a performance that was unequalled among traditional North American manufacturers. Alone among its competitors, Magna had the international reach and astonishingly wide range of products to serve an industry no longer dominated by Detroit's Big Three, but by a new global "Big Seven" consisting of combinations such as GM-Fiat-Saab, DaimlerChrysler, Renault-Nissan and Ford-Volvo-Jaguar-Mazda. These recent agglomerations were lavishing their most important outsourcing contracts on Magna because it could feed the automakers' plants on several continents. And few of its production facilities were vulnerable to the threat of strikes. Just 12 of Magna's 164 plants were unionized, and employee turnover was only 3 per cent, well below the industry average. (Most of the union contracts were inherited with Magna's acquisition of factories in Europe, where Magna did endure a work stoppage called by a Communist-led union at one of its newly acquired French plants in the late 1990s.) More important, perhaps, was Stronach's success in becoming a purveyor of "value-added" engineered products who created thousands of jobs at home while expanding rapidly abroad, in accordance with his own exhortations to others, and the now widely accepted corporate mantra of the times. This made him, in contrast to the easy rhetoric of corporate leaders who preached but did not always practice that approach to business, a genuine model citizen.

Yet Stronach was not embraced as a fresh thinker.

He had accepted federal appointments to serve on advisory panels to examine trade issues and schemes for rejuvenating the crippled economy of Cape Breton, and directorships on two crown corporations, the Canada Development Investment Corp. and Fishery Products International Corp. But Stronach was not accorded the status of an industrial statesman.

Horses wearing the Stronach colours — black diamonds on a light blue field — had won the prestigious Queen's Plate and the Breeder's Stakes. And thoroughbreds from Stronach's stables in Ontario, Kentucky and Florida won $7.2 million (U.S.) in 1998, topping the list of North American breeders in prize winnings, and prompting the *Daily Racing Form* to name Stronach as its outstanding owner the following year. But in Canada he was not celebrated as an upholder of E. P. Taylor's legacy with Northern Dancer. Some 25 years after he bought his first horse at auction for $700, Stronach was finally accepted as a director of the snooty Ontario Jockey Club, whose outlook had scarcely changed since Taylor ran it as a personal fief in the 1960s. He was destined to be one of the shortest-serving directors of that tradition-bound institution. Stronach made himself unwelcome at board meetings after insisting that his fellow directors privatize and overhaul its Woodbine racetrack in Toronto, the creaking flagship of the OJC circuit. (Belated renovations began only after Stronach's departure.)

He was scarcely less controversial in Austria. Stronach was a prodigal son who in his 60s was using his Magna profits to promote economic development in his homeland. But many of those schemes met with hostility. Local zoning authorities objected to his proposal for a $1.1-billion restoration of the dilapidated Prater park in Vienna, the setting for the ferris-wheel scene in Graham Greene's *The Third Man*. Stronach's plan for a "World of Wonders" theme park south of Vienna was decried by Green Party activists as "an architectural Chernobyl." Closer to home, Stronach's pledge of $100,000 to a delegation of Canadian Olympians including Mark Tewksbury and Susan Auch to press for reforms in the scandal-plagued International Olympic Committee was mocked as "a belly flop." That slap didn't originate with Juan Samaranch, the autocratic Spaniard who had long run the IOC as a private club, but with Canada's own Richard Pound, the IOC's backroom financial wizard and a staunch upholder of the Olympics status quo.

Yet Stronach continued to pursue his digressions. There were several motives. Chief among these was the alluring challenge of trying to replicate his mastery of auto-parts in new pursuits where once again Stronach was required to start from scratch. He also widened his ambit of acquaintances. Not many auto executives could claim to have received from Queen Elizabeth herself the 50-guinea purse for winning the Queen's Plate.

And there was also the issue of succession. Behind his entertaining assertions that he intended to run Magna past the age of 150, Stronach was worried about succession. In a triumph of domestic diplomacy, Stronach had decided to retain Donald Walker as Magna's CEO after Walker's 1998 divorce from Belinda Stronach, the mother of their two children. Walker was highly regarded by Stronach and Magna's peers in the industry. And Belinda, appointed to the Magna board while still in her early 20s, had continued to serve as a director for the firm alongside her former husband. But Belinda's involvement in Magna had always been minimal, limited to advice on human resources policy and liaison work with the town of Aurora. She was less interested in auto parts than fashion merchandising, having bankrolled Misura Inc., a Toronto couture house founded by Toronto designer Joeffer Caoc. At age 33, Belinda seemed to drift even further away from Magna with her second marriage, on the last day of 1999, to Johann Olav Koss, an Olympics speed-skating medal winner from Norway, whom she had first met when she lobbied for his support of Tewksbury's mission to clean up the IOC. She was now mostly occupied with homemaking and IOC reform. At about that same time, Stronach had recruited his son Andy, at age 31, to Magna's executive ranks. But Andy was not involved in auto parts. He headed the umbrella company that his father created for Magna's racetracks and other sports and entertainment ventures. In 2000, it looked like this non-auto parts aspect of the Magna legacy would have to function as the chief vehicle of dynastic progression.

F RANK STRONACH paid a price for the showmanship that marked his career. But he was incurably stagestruck.

At shareholder meetings, held at Toronto's elegant Roy Thomson Hall, comparisons with another F. S. were inevitable. The house lights would dim, and a white spot would hit the chairman. Almost from the back of the hall one could see his blue eyes flashing. A red carnation was pinned to the left lapel of his immaculately tailored suit, usually a grey double-breasted number that showed off a physique that Stronach kept in good repair with mogul-skiing expeditions in Colorado and tennis matches with partners half his age. Working without notes, Stronach would pace the stage, clutching a cordless microphone held close to his chest. His name was emblazoned in huge letters on a backlit screen behind him. When he began to talk, Stronach didn't so much speak as croon in a deep baritone that indeed bore a certain likeness to Sinatra's. Even his public-relations minions half-expected him to offer a rendition of "My Way."

Stronach did not regard these encounters as an opportunity to calm shareholders who fretted about the $2 billion or so worth of non-auto schemes he had hatched, including executive resorts in Ontario and Europe, a luxury airline with private cabins and oversized beds (Magna Air) and the proposed theme park near Magna's headquarters in a Vienna suburb to which Greenpeace had pledged its wholehearted resistance. The centrepiece of that project was to be a 60-storey globe braced by enormous statues of the Greek god Atlantis, the proportions of which were so huge that the sexual organ of each figure would be six metres long. At least one agitated shareholder, Montreal money manager Roch Bedard, was threatening to sue Magna if Stronach proceeded with Magna Air and his other loony projects. "If he wants to go ahead with this crazy stunt of flying bedrooms and resort hideaways, let him do it with his own money," Bedard had said, complaining that "I don't see why we should pay for this man's late-life crisis." Missing his chance to allay investor concerns, Stronach instead chose to fuel them. Sure, the Austrian theme-park concept might seem like a boondoggle to critics of stunted vision. But "people forget that when it was first built, the Eiffel Tower was unpopular too," Stronach said. He had no qualms about having spent $324 million of Magna's money to buy horseracing tracks in Los Angeles, San Francisco, Cleveland, Oklahoma and southern Florida — a sum that eclipsed Magna's outlay on all but the largest of its auto-parts acquisitions. Which was not to deny, Stronach cheerfully confessed, that you mention racetracks to bankers "and they would shit their pants."

But was Stronach ignoring Magna's basic business? In the late 1990s, with no fanfare, Magna had opened the world's most advanced auto-parts factory in St. Thomas, Ontario, where 650 robots turned out frames for GM's popular Sierra and Silverado trucks at the rate of one every 10 seconds. Laser devices checked every part for defects, a break with the past practice of subjecting only a few parts at random to spot checks. And hundreds of kilometres of fibre-optic cable were strung throughout the facility so that every function from precision-cutting of tiny parts to payroll management was conducted on an intranet. In 1999, the Smithsonian Institution in Washington, D.C., added this world's first Web-based metal-bending factory to its roster of historic breakthroughs in computing technology. But the more remarkable thing about Magna's newest facility was GM's reliance on it. St. Thomas was the sole supplier of truck frames to GM assembly plants in Ontario, Michigan, Wisconsin, Indiana, and Mexico. "Being sole supplier means if we shut down, we would shut down six GM plants," said John Burwash, manager of the Southern Ontario facility. "For General Motors to put all its eggs in one basket, there had to be a lot of trust on its part." This was the sort of initiative that won raves from industry experts. "Magna is the best auto-parts company in the world," said analyst Paul Fricke of Prudential Securities in New York. "In terms of its product diversification and growth prospects, it's without peer."

But the breakthrough in St. Thomas could not hope to compete for media attention with the flying beds that the proposed Magna Air would be shuttling between London and New York. If, that is, the carrier ever got off the ground. Stronach almost invariably followed through with his bold plans in the auto-parts trade. He often did not do so with his other schemes. Magna had yet to take delivery of any planes, the chain of executive resorts was in limbo, and there had been no progress in his plans to convert one of Vienna's most prestigious religious schools into a soccer academy.

Horse racing was the only passion outside of the auto-parts world to which Stronach had actually committed himself. And in this realm, too, he was very successful. Magna Entertainment Corp. (MEC) made its debut on a publicly trade spin-off by reporting a profit of $12 million (U.S.) in the first quarter of 2000 — and a Stronach thoroughbred, Red Bullet, won the Preakness Stakes. MEC's seven racetracks, all in the U.S., accounted for 23 per cent of wagering on parimutuel racing in the U.S., or a total of $1.59 billion (U.S.) in the first quarter of 2000 alone.

Genius is a curious amalgam, equal parts prescience and eccentricity. Thomas Edison went to his grave arrogantly claiming the superiority of his appliances that ran on direct current, refusing to join in the widespread acceptance of alternating current. Magna vice-chairman James Nichol, who quit the company and returned not once, but twice, in the 1990s, compared his boss's brainstorming with that of Edison. The famous inventor would file for 10 patents, nine of which would amount to nothing, and the 10th would be the lightbulb. "This is what Frank is like," Nichol told *Maclean's* writer Kimberley Noble in 1999. "He has an inquisitive mind and tremendous youthful energy. It annoys people at times. But we never know when he's going to invent another lightbulb."

Stronach seemed to delight in presenting himself as a bundle of contradictions. He wouldn't be much of an oracle if everyone could readily see the common sense of his ideas. So he went on nurturing his image as an oddball visionary. Even if that meant inviting detractors to put him in a league with crackpots such as Ross Perot, with Stronach's promise to bankroll any Austrian willing to launch a new political party based on the Magna Carta. Even if it meant undermining his legacy of executing, with admirable determination and acumen, business plans that were grounded in an astute grasp of trends. At times, Stronach seemed to work at not being taken seriously. He did not doubt that Fair Enterprise was "perhaps the most important chapter in Western industrial society in many years." Then again, as he also conceded, "I constantly have 100 projects and ideas ready for examination on my desk. Ninety-nine per cent of them are junk."

Only on the most infrequent occasions did Stronach accept limits to his imagination. In 1998, Magna acquired the Santa Anita racetrack in California. The course, in the shadow of the San Gabriel Mountains east of Pasadena, was one of the oldest tracks in North America and a long-time haunt of Hollywood celebrities. On the opening day of Santa Anita's 1998-99 season, Stronach told local reporters about his plans to totally rebuild — some would say desecrate — the venerable facility. He would soon be gutting its clubhouse, paddock, gardens and the derelict housing for employees, and installing a hotel, shops, a horse-racing museum and an IMAX-format cinema on the hallowed site.

Was there anything he intended to leave alone, someone had to ask. Stronach thought about that. "The mountains will stay," he said.

7

LAURENT BEAUDOIN

How a snowmobile maker achieved world dominance
in mass transit and civil aviation

*"With any new product, I'm excited. I like to touch it, to feel it, to be part of
the process."*
— Laurent Beaudoin

L AURENT BEAUDOIN did not set out to build one of the biggest
Francophone enterprises in the world, and the largest outside of
France.

Indeed, not long after he assumed the presidency of Bombardier Inc. at the
tender age of 27, it appeared that Beaudoin had fumbled the legacy handed to him
in 1966. The oil crises of the 1970s had pretty much killed the snowmobile market. They threatened to destroy the enterprise founded some 30 years earlier by
Beaudoin's father-in-law, Joseph-Armand Bombardier, a mechanical genius who
was one of the most indefatigable inventors of the century.

Beaudoin, however, proved to be as tenacious as the founder, and perhaps more
resourceful. He experimented with new lines of business, refusing to give up even as
he met with defeat in many of his early efforts to diversify into different modes of
transportation. His boldest strokes were contrarian gambles that took Bombardier
into rail transport and aerospace, troubled industries in which it had no experience.
And even as he worked to make good on those bets, Beaudoin refused to abandon
Bombardier's original business, pumping scarce R&D funds into new products such
as an aquatic version of the snowmobile, dubbed the Sea-Doo.

But fortune smiled on Laurent Beaudoin. The same oil shocks that dealt a crippling blow to the gasoline-guzzling snowmobile also triggered a revival in mass tran-

sit equipment. With Canadair Ltd, Beaudoin's first stake in aviation, Bombardier obtained a firm that was poised to exploit the most important air-travel phenomenon in the 1990s — the emergence of regional jets as an alternative to noisy turboprops on the world's busiest commuter routes. And as luck would have it, Bombardier's Sea-Doo caught a wave of young "Generation X" outdoor enthusiasts, who made it the most successful recreational product of the 1990s.

But fortuitous opportunities are often squandered by undisciplined CEOs. On closer examination, Beaudoin was revealed as a master of calculated risk. In 2000, Bombardier operated 44 factories on three continents and was one of the largest employers of engineers and research technicians in the transportation industry worldwide. But it was not in the habit of erecting new factories, or assembling teams of skilled personnel from scratch. Beaudoin had obtained much of the R&D prowess and manufacturing capacity to match his expanding ambitions by acquiring, at bargain prices, a score of once-formidable railcar and aerospace firms that had fallen on hard times.

Once he had identified a promising market for a new type of aircraft, passenger train or recreational vehicle, Beaudoin goaded his engineers to rush new products to market and gain a head start over potential rivals. He had a genius for wringing maximum value from a new technology. Through a series of refinements over the span of a decade, the eight-passenger Challenger business jet acquired in the purchase of Canadair morphed into a 90-seat regional jetliner. To speed up the innovation process, Beaudoin insisted that his aviation companies — Canadair, Learjet, Short Brothers and de Havilland — share technology breakthroughs with each other, and with their railcar and recreational siblings, which were ruled by a similar edict. Each division was kept busy making components for sister firms and with subcontracting work for the likes of Boeing Co. and Airbus Industrie.

At the dawn of the 21st century, Bombardier was poised to achieve lasting dominance in its chosen niches. It was now the world's third-largest maker of civilian aircraft, after Boeing and Airbus, and the undisputed leader in business and commuter planes. Beaudoin had created the global market for commuter jets. His Canadair Regional Jet was the backbone of fleets at dozens of regional airlines on five continents. Wealthy commuters such as Oprah Winfrey and John Travolta were opting for the fastest business plane in the skies, Bombardier's $50-million Global Express, which could fly non-stop from New York to Tokyo at Mach .88, just under the speed of sound; the ultimate luxury aircraft was outfitted with dressing rooms, divan beds and conference facilities. Bombardier's rivals trumpeted their own plans for new aircraft to compete in the lucrative markets that Bombardier had pioneered. But Robert Brown, Bombardier's new CEO, couldn't resist a pointed reference to his company's formidable lead over pretenders to its crown. "Our planes are already there, they have already flown," he said. "All the others — where are they?"

If anything, Bombardier's position in rail transport was even more commanding. By the late 1990s, it had overtaken its sole remaining competitor, Germany's ABB Daimler-Benz Transportation GmbH, to become the world's largest maker of railway rolling stock. Bombardier engineers had developed elevated monorails at Walt Disney World; low-maintenance subway cars for the London Underground and Paris Métro; innovative railcars for the English Channel tunnel and the Eurostar cross-country service in Western Europe; and driverless robot cars for Kuala Lumpur's commuter trains.

In one of the most prominent displays of Bombardier's R&D prowess, top U.S. transportation officials gathered at a 1999 unveiling ceremony in Washington for the Acela high-speed train that Beaudoin's firm had designed for Amtrak, the U.S. passenger rail service. Jolene M. Molitoris, head of the U.S. Federal Railroad Administration, hugged the contoured snout of Bombardier's newest locomotive. She predicted that the Acela Express, designed to be the fastest train in North America, would bring high-speed passenger rail service to remote communities in the U.S. Interior. Officials at the state-subsidized Amtrak, the U.S. passenger rail monopoly, had more modest expectations. They merely hoped that the Acela would attract 2.5 million additional riders annually, and make Amtrak a viable alternative to air transport on the New York-Boston-Washington corridor before Congress acted on its threat to kill the railroad, citing Amtrak's chronic insolvency. "The promise of European-style high-speed service has been part of our campaign to rebuild the passenger train into a serious component of our national transportation system," said an Amtrak spokesman. "When these slick trains are fully deployed on the entire Northeast corridor, the ripple effect will be felt across the nation."

There had been a time when luck was thought to have played an outsized role in Bombardier's reinvention of itself. But in the 1990s, when its profits increased six-fold, to $554 million, and its stock-market value crossed the $15-billion threshold, Bombardier's transformation from a small maker of snowmobiles into a diversified transportation giant was perceived as anything but accidental. Beaudoin's commitment to R&D, export markets and innovative manufacturing techniques was a nuanced strategy that powerfully recommended itself to entrepreneurs striving for success in an unforgiving new era of global competition.

Yet even as he set a new goal of doubling revenues to $23 billion by 2004, Beaudoin had reason to expect that the next few years would be a rough ride. Fifty per cent of his sales, and an even bigger portion of total profit, were hostage to the volatile airline industry, where too many planes were chasing too few passengers. The railcar business, overly reliant on sales to mass-transit authorities, was vulnerable to political instability. A showpiece Bombardier project to develop a high-speed commuter system linking Miami, Orlando and Tampa fell victim to local political infighting over spending priorities. The Acela project was delayed by technical glitches, triggering late-delivery penalties to Amtrak. And Bombardier was losing money in recreational products as the Sea-Doo faded in popularity and record warm winters had sabotaged snowmobile sales.

Yet for Bombardier's fans on Bay Street, the most troubling development of 1999 was Beaudoin's decision at age 60 to step down as CEO. He was doing so at the top of his game, having turned a $20-million firm into an $11.5-billion multinational during his 33 years at the helm.

As chairman and controlling shareholder of the company, Beaudoin would continue to set Bombardier's strategic direction. And his chosen successor, former aerospace head Robert Brown, had been a conspicuous success in running Bombardier's biggest division. But Brown, a soft-spoken former federal government bureaucrat, lacked his predecessor's ebullience. And Brown's capacity for risk-taking and high-stakes salesmanship was untested. Having joined Bombardier only 12 years earlier, he had not been toughened by the crises that Beaudoin endured in his first two decades at the helm. For all that Brown was held in high regard, said Montreal investment fund manager Stephen Jarislowsky, but "Everyone would prefer to have Beaudoin back in there at age 40."

The import of Beaudoin's remarkable run extended beyond his success at enriching shareholders. His decision to kick himself upstairs called attention to his rare achievement in creating a durable francophone enterprise. The boom years of Bombardier had roughly paralleled Quebec's so-called Quiet Revolution, a glorious 25-year era beginning with the election of Jean Lesage's reform-minded Liberal government in 1960 when francophones asserted their claim to stewardship over Quebec's economy. But Bombardier's golden decade of the 1990s, when it emerged as a world-class power, also marked the eclipse of many hothouse tycoons whose reliance on Quebec government subsidies ill prepared them for the competitive rigours of the free trade era. By 2000, the only francophone business enterprises of any global consquence were the media giant Quebecor Inc., the engineering firm SNC-Lavalin and Bombardier.

While he was sharply at odds with the separatist outlook of many of his francophone business peers, Beaudoin had championed the new class of homegrown industrialists. He was fluently bilingual. But after years of dealing with English-speaking bankers, politicians and factory workers, Beaudoin still often had trouble finding the right English word. Running a multinational firm with 80 per cent of its sales outside of Canada had not diminished Beaudoin's concern about the fragility of the French fact in North America. He was sharply disappointed that so many of his peers had proved unable to project the culture of francophone enterprise on a world stage. But he was not altogether surprised.

In a society that traditionally had not encouraged entrepreneurialism — indeed, had actively discouraged it well into the 20th century — Beaudoin's own career had been occupied less with empire-building than *la survivance*. Truth be told, his leaps into unknown realms, at least in the early going, had been largely defensive actions. Beaudoin recognized that the career of Armand Bombardier had been something of an anomoly. Nothing drove Beaudoin more powerfully than an ambition to protect his father-in-law's living legacy. "My main goal at Bombardier," he said, "is to build something permanent."

Let us beware how we allow the establishment of manufactures in Canada. She would become proud and mutinous like the English colonies. So long as France is a nursery to Canada, let not the Canadians be allowed to trade, but keep to their wandering, laborious life with the savages, and to their military exercises.
— Marquis de Montcalm, in a 1759 letter written shortly before the fall of New France

W HEN JOSEPH-ARMAND BOMBARDIER was born in 1907, young Quebec francophones with intellectual promise were still directed by tradition and exhortations from Roman Catholic pulpits to pursue careers in law, medicine, politics or the priesthood. Business was suspect, the province of *les maudits anglais*. Notwithstanding the eventual commercial success of his most famous invention, Bombardier was a lifelong mechanical tinkerer drawn into business only of necessity. It would fall to his son-in-law to turn Bombardier's machine shop and remarkable 40-odd patents into a dynamic corporate enterprise.

As the Olympic torch made its way from Greece to the site of the 1988 Winter Games at Calgary, it was transported by snowmobile across a one-kilometre stretch of Canada's Far North by a Catholic priest named Maurice Ouimet. The Oblate preacher, who had dedicated his life to working with Native communities in the North, had received the very first Ski-Doo some 30 years earlier from Armand Bombardier. That Bombardier chose a missionary to inaugurate his favourite invention said a great deal about his own mission. The animating spirit of Bombardier's restless experimentation was an ambition to open up the isolated rural and remote regions of Quebec, snow-locked for more than half the year, to the civilizing influence of doctors and veterinarians, merchants and schoolteachers, installers of telephone and power lines, and itinerant pastors.

Bombardier was a descendant of André Bombardier, a soldier in the French army and one of the founders of Detroit. The oldest of eight children, Bombardier was born on a farm near the Eastern Townships hamlet of Valcourt, 120 kilometres southeast of Montreal. He could easily have ended up a farmer. But any thought of his inheriting the farm ended when his father sold it and moved to Valcourt, where he bought the general store. Bombardier could have been drawn into the priesthood, but he was bored with the classical studies in Latin and ancient Greek at St. Charles Borromee Seminary in Sherbooke.

From early childhood, Bombardier's head was crammed with images of all things mechanical — wheels, gears, clockworks and engines. He had a team of steamfitters in Valcourt run steam into his prototype for a tiny engine, which promptly exploded. He nearly blew himself up with a homemade welding torch that consisted of a tin can and a tire pump to provide pressure, into which he poured gasoline.

At age 15, Bombardier tested his first crude snowmobile. It was hideous to look at. Bombardier had lashed an engine from a Model T Ford salvaged from the junkyard onto the metal skeleton of a dismantled sleigh. Sticking out of the back end of this motorized sled was an enormous propeller, nearly the height of the vehicle, that Bombardier had carved from a piece of wood. His inspiration had been the variable pitch propeller, a recent invention of the New Brunswick engineer W. R. Turnbull that had revolutionized aviation by enabling pilots to adjust the propeller's angle for much safer takeoffs. But Turnbull's device was more suited to air than ground transport. It was something of a miracle that as Bombardier manoeuvred his sleigh down the length of Valcourt's main street, blowing up furious gusts of wind, no one was injured by the whirling blades that sent him flying, as legend had it, into the side of a barn. His father ordered him to dismantle the frightening machine.

His goal was to breach the great snowdrifts that blocked his escape to the bright lights of Sherbrooke, and beyond that Montreal. Later, as a young father, Bombardier's drive to perfect a motorized replacement for the sled-dog team would be heightened by a family tragedy, when his two-year-old son, Yvon, died of appendicitis because country doctors were unable to cross Quebec's rough winter terrain. Asked to explain his obsession with motorized transport over snow, Bombardier said, "*Car mon pays, c'est hiver.*" Because in my country it is always winter.

Bombardier polished his gift of natural technical wizardry by toiling as a mechanical apprentice in the town of South Stukely, and later in Montreal. He took correspondence courses in electrical engineering, and scoured the libraries for scientific journals that carried news of breakthroughs in automation and aerodynamics. With that knowledge, Bombardier improved on his first contraption. In the late 1920s, he turned out a dozen snowmobiles that were modified Model T Fords with skis out front and tracked wheels in back. And by 1933, he was no longer converting cars but designing vehicles from the ground up.

Bombardier's propeller-driven sled of 1922 was not the first motorized over-snow vehicle in the world. Indeed, mythology aside, Bombardier wasn't the sole inventor of snow-going machines. Three brothers in Crested Butte, Colorado, received a patent in 1896 for a "power-sled" to be driven across ice and snow; and in 1906, an intrepid doctor trekked from Quebec City to Boston aboard a tracked vehicle that he had designed. Inventors in the U.S. were developing motorized toboggans in the 1920s at the same time as Bombardier. In the 1930s, Carl Eliason of Sayner, Wisconsin, sold his design for a toboggan powered by a Johnson outboard motor to a U.S. firm, Four Wheel Drive Corp. The Canadian subsidiary of that firm, based in Kitchener, Ontario, turned out some one thousand machines based on Eliason's design, mostly for government survey-work in the Far North. But the vehicle was never more than a sideline to FWD's truck business, and production of the "motor toboggans" was discontinued in 1963. That decision, as FWD's own managers would concede only a few years later, was to earn a high ranking among the missed business opportunities of the century.

Bombardier, then, would be the one to perfect the design of the over-snow vehicle, and his company would be the first to manufacture it in mass quantities and popularize it around the world. Indeed, the vehicles didn't become practical until Bombardier, at age 28, conceived a revolutionary rear-wheel drive and suspension system for his machines. Its key component was a rubber-coated cog, or sprocket. Sixty years later, Bombardier's most important innovation could still be seen in the Bombardier logo, a stylized sprocket that adorned Manila subway cars and Lufthansa jetliners.

Still, the personal snowmobile would have to wait until the arrival of a suitably light but powerful engine. Until the Ski-Doo finally came along, the *auto-neiges* to which Bombardier devoted himself were variations of a snow bus. His first commercial success, in 1936, was the seven-passenger B7, which boasted a sheet-metal body, looked like an oversized VW Bug, and sold for $1,700. Six years later he introduced the B12, a hump-backed mechanical monster that looked like something out of *Voyage From the Deep*. Imagine an even larger Bug with four portholes on each side and you have the idea. But these sinister-looking machines were blessedly rugged, a match for snowbanks and ice-rutted roads.

Those early successes begat more commodious versions of the *auto-neige* that made the countryside accessible year-round for foresters, prospectors, game wardens and RCMP rescue patrols. At a factory he built in Valcourt — where he would spend his entire life, having long since lost interest in big cities — Bombardier turned out a succession of ski-cars, ski-trucks and ski-buses. He built mammoth snow cruisers for school boards, the post office and for ambulance operators, and adapted the cruisers for service in World War II as armoured troop transports. Laurent Beaudoin would recall that his own father, a wholesaler outside Quebec City, owned a few snowmobiles for making grocery deliveries to rural customers.

When the Quebec government launched a snow-removal service in the late 1940s to open up rural roads, a development that reduced demand for snowmobiles, Bombardier lost no time conceiving a series of new products that diversified his client base. He developed specialized vehicles for transporting workers to remote logging camps, muskeg tractors for navigating swamp lands, all-terrain machines for mining and oil development and a "steel lumberjack" for tree cutting. Bombardier's handy Muskeg, a tracked snow cruiser, was used by Sir Vivian Fuchs on his 1957 expedition to Antarctica. In many cases, the essential technology of those machines was still the standard for such vehicles in the 1990s. And Bombardier Inc.'s export orientation dates from that time as well. Bombardier machines were used on Peruvian sugar plantations, for laying pipelines in Scotland and by the French Foreign Legion in the Sahara Desert.

Lacking formal training in finance, engineering or modern manufacturing methods, Bombardier gave the impression of being a backwoods mechanic. True, he didn't believe in big-budget advertising, offering credit or shipping on consignment. He put new products on the market once he felt they were worthy, often in the absence of any obvious demand for them. But his obscure operation in Valcourt was using assembly-line methods in the 1930s; and the output of that factory met with the approval of customers from Japan to Venezuela, and from Lapland to Antarctica.

Bombardier spent most of his time in the factory, seldom using the heated swimming pool that was his sole luxury indulgence. ("I don't think well when I am wet," he explained.) Wes McGill, a business friend, said Bombardier "had a typical president's office but the door was usually locked and you'd find him down at the factory standing over an old oak desk covered in gears and sprockets and bearings. He was obsessed with ensuring that his products were light in weight and low in cost. He was attracted to the things that other people couldn't do."

For more than three decades after his parents erected a garage for their teenage son to build his prototypes in, Bombardier himself was frustrated in not realizing his own earliest dream of a personal snowmobile. Finally, 36 years after that first trial run on Valcourt's main drag, the small vehicle that most people would come to associate with the word snowmobile began to take shape, as Bombardier integrated recently developed lighter engines with a continuous rubber tread that was reinforced with hidden metal bars.

The first commercial version of the Ski-Doo, introduced in 1959, was outfitted with wood skis and could reach a top speed of 40 kph. The bright yellow machine was not intended for urban thrill-seekers. It was a utilitarian vehicle that eased the working lives of government surveyors, Inuit hunters and Métis trappers. It was to be called the "Ski Dog," since it was intended as a replacement for the sled-dog team. But when the tail of the "g" broke off the lettering on a prototype model, the resulting name stuck.

By century's end, the snowmobile would prompt the creation of more than 900 snowmobile clubs in Canada and 132,000 kilometres of snowmobile trails across the country. But the Ski-Doo had been on the market for just five years when Bombardier was stricken with cancer. It was only after he died, at age 57, that the Ski-Doo soared in popularity, and created the first new winter sport that Canada would give to the world since ice hockey.

Restless tinkerer Joseph-Armand Bombardier, honoured by Canada Post in the late 1990s (above), gave the world one of its most popular winter recreations, snowmobiling. In transforming the maker of Ski-Doos into a world leader in aerospace and mass-transit equipment, Laurent Beaudoin (left) was focused only on the survival of his father-in-law's company, after the energy crisis of the 1970s dealt a devastating blow to the snowmobile market. "My main goal at Bombardier," said Beaudoin, "is to build something permanent."

By the 1990s, Bombardier was in command of the world market for business planes, offering a wider range of aircraft than any competitor, with new models constantly emerging from the hangars of subsidiaries Canadair, de Havilland, Learjet and Short Brothers. The firm's regional jet (below), snapped up by commuter airlines around the world, revolutionized civil aviation by displacing noisy turboprops, boosting traffic on short-haul routes, and introducing direct service by jet among smaller "second-tier" cities, enabling travellers to bypass overcrowded "hub" airports.

Bombardier built subway cars, trams, monorails and cross-country passenger coaches for clients as varied as the Eurotunnel, the Toronto Transit Commission, the city of Kuala Lumpur, Richard Branson's Virgin Rail and Walt Disney World. In 2000, it was working out technical glitches in the Acela (above), North America's fastest train, designed to whisk travellers along the Boston-New York-Washington, D.C. corridor at speeds of up to 240 kph.

⧖

EVERY FEW YEARS, Laurent Beaudoin would be invited to accept another honorary degree from universities in Canada and Europe. But none of these mattered as much to him as his commerce degree from the University of Sherbrooke. Not just because he earned it. At Sherbrooke he met, and soon married, a fellow commerce student named Claire Bombardier.

Years later, Beaudoin would tell visitors to his executive suite in Montreal's Canada Trust tower that "Bombardier was not part of my career plans. I never thought I would be running a company of this size." He had positioned a photo portrait of Claire on the credenza behind his desk in such a way that you couldn't talk to him without meeting the level gaze of the founder's daughter. (In 2000, the family firm was controlled by Claire and her sisters, Janine and Huguette, and her brother, André.)

There was reason to take Beaudoin at his word. He was easily the least voluble builder of a multibillion-dollar enterprise in recent Canadian history, and notoriously shy. It would take an event as momentous as Bombardier's watershed contract to design a monorail for Walt Disney World to lure Beaudoin into the limelight, posing awkwardly for a photograph in front of an elevated train with Mickey Mouse at his side. He tried to delegate public relations to others. He did so with ever diminishing success as Bombardier's heightened prominence forced him to grow into the role of corporate statesman.

But Beaudoin's low-key persona was at least in some degree calculated. He was, after all, an outsider in Valcourt, a company town where half the working population was employed by Bombardier. Compounding the geographic isolation of Valcourt was Armand Bombardier's aversion to outside influences. The inventor had built his own factory because he did not trust subcontractors to make good copies of his prototypes. He had designed and built his own parts, and even the machines that made them, rather than turn to potentially unreliable outsiders.

The company was intensely familial. It had always been managed by the founder and his brothers. Long before Armand Bombardier's death, at which point ownership of the firm passed to his five children, the founder's two sons had also joined in running the company. Apart from marrying the boss's daughter, Beaudoin had no obvious qualifications for trumping the claims on succession of brothers Germain and André Bombardier. When the company's board of directors handed the presidency to Beaudoin in 1966, he was just 27 years old. He was a trained accountant with scant knowledge of engineering and no experience in managing a large enterprise. Before joining Bombardier just three years earlier, Beaudoin seemed determined to make a career in management consulting. Was

Armand Bombardier, who today would be described as a micromanager, to be replaced by a hands-off dilettante?

Yet the decision of the board, which was dominated by Bombardier family members, was not wholly inexplicable. Germain Bombardier, a gifted mechanic with several patents to his credit, had toiled at his father's side for 15 years, and succeeded him as president in 1964 on an interim basis. But he had only a high-school education and seemed uncomfortable with the firm's evolution from heavy industrial vehicles to Ski-Doos (so much so that he had sold his shares in the company). André was four years younger than Beaudoin; he was content to play a nominal role in the firm. For the next two decades there would be rumours about Beaudoin's stunning elevation to the presidency and his apparent grasping for the brass ring. They abated, finally, in the mid-1980s, when a Quebec-based rubber company in which Germain and André Bombardier were involved came close to bankruptcy, and had to be rescued by a $1-million cash infusion by its shareholders.

What the board saw in Beaudoin was a quiet dynamism that reminded them of Armand Bombardier, but without the founder's stubbornness. He was a team player with a sixth sense for hiring the right people, and was more suited than the founder to guiding Bombardier's evolution into a major corporation. "I'm not a religious man," said Beaudoin's close friend Charles Leblanc. "But I sometimes think it must have been the hand of God that caused Bombardier's daughter to marry Laurent, and brought him into the company."

Beaudoin was born in the French-speaking town of Laurier Station, near Quebec City. But he was fluent in English owing to his parents' decision to enroll him at age 10 at Ste. Anne College, a Catholic school in Church Point, Nova Scotia. Not long after he set up his management consulting practice in Quebec City, Beaudoin was invited by his father-in-law to offer an opinion on a struggling sawmill in which he had invested. Together with Leblanc, a young Sherbrooke lawyer who tended to the Bombardier family's legal matters, Beaudoin examined the operation and came away thinking it could be fixed. Beaudoin and Leblanc asked Bombardier to hold off on placing it into bankruptcy. With his blessing, they overhauled the mill's management practices. It had failed to collect on its accounts receivable, and was wasting wood by cutting the wrong sizes for each cycle of the building trade. Six months later, the two young men were able to report that the operation was turning a profit for the first time in five years.

Impressed with that rescue, Bombardier then asked Beaudoin and Leblanc to rearrange his personal estate. He acted on their recommendation that he buy out his three brothers, who then owned almost 25 per cent of the firm. Without quite realizing it, Beaudoin had allowed himself to be drawn into a family business he had never wanted to join. And soon after accepting his father-in-law's invitation to become the comptroller at L'Auto-Neige Bombardier Ltee., as the firm was then called, he found himself wanting to quit time and time again.

While he shared in the general admiration of the founder, Beaudoin was frustrated by his refusal to delegate authority. One visitor to Bombardier's office recalled that a small cement floor was being added that day in a far corner of the shop. "The old man dropped everything," the visitor said, "and spent half an hour telling the guy who was laying the floor exactly how the concrete should be brushed — telling the contractor, in other words, how to do his job." Beaudoin, who had been given authority for the administrative affairs of the company, would later acknowledge that his work was often meddled with. "Mr. Bombardier was a very strong character," he said. "Everything had to go across his desk. Every time I made a decision, he'd ask me: 'Why did you do that?' I'd tell him, 'Well, that's what you hired me for.'" Leblanc offered a more blunt description of the fractious relationship. "Laurent used to come to me and say, 'He gives me authority one day and takes it away the next!' I'd tell him: 'Hang on. If you quit, there'll be a real mess.'"

Beaudoin found Bombardier to be particularly immoveable on the matter of advertising. His father-in-law's idea of marketing had been to drive his snow machines into towns across Quebec and invite local newspaper editors to take a ride. On one celebrated occasion, he had driven one of his vehicles backward up the famous tobaggan chute next to Château Frontenac hotel in Quebec City. But the potential of the Ski-Doo could not be realized, Beaudoin argued, as long as the machines were expected to sell by word of mouth. After he was promoted to general manager, Beaudoin had pushed even harder for an aggressive marketing campaign to boost Ski-Doo sales. In time, the board came to share Beaudoin's passion for reinventing the family firm as a maker of consumer goods, its future pinned to the Ski-Doo.

Beaudoin hardly created the boom in snowmobiling, which had attracted a cult following in Quebec, Ontario and New England in the first half of the 1960s. But the new president of Bombardier soon began to test the outer limits of its commercial potential.

He assembled a new team of thirtysomething managers whose outlook was similar to that of the most zealous snowmobilers. Machines previously identified with model codes (B7, C18 and the like) were given evocative names — Alpine, Olympic, Élan, Blizzard. The budget for mass-media advertising was boosted from $32,000 in 1964 to $5 million by decade's end. Beaudoin financed high-profile expeditions to the North Pole that showcased the snowmobile's power and endurance. He sponsored regional races and a World Snowmobile Championship. The latter took place not in Quebec, but in the important export market of the U.S., at Eagle River, Wisconsin.

The growing popularity of snowmobiling — or Ski-Dooing, as Bombardier dealers were instructed to call it — was boosted by the unprecedented consumer prosperity of the late 1960s. As industry sales doubled year after year, more than 100 competing manufacturers quickly emerged, hailing from Canada, the U.S., Europe and Japan. As in the early days of the auto industry, it seemed as if every garage mechanic in Quebec and the northern U.S. states had ambitions to design his own line of snowmobiles. In short order, there was a proliferation of competing brands, including Skiroule, Sno Jet, Alouette, Sno-Prince, Starcraft, Scorpion and the Johnson Skee-Horse. But most of these upstarts were intent only on exploiting a regional market. Beaudoin, by contrast, had bet his company on a strategy of "going everywhere at once." He wanted nothing less than to be the dominant player in every North American market. So it was Bombardier that fostered the network of groomed trails across the continent, and established the industry-wide standards for safe use of the machines. Beaudoin was relentless in exploiting Bombardier's head start. He used feedback from the races and snowmobile clubs that Bombardier sponsored to keep the market supplied with a steady stream of upgraded models. The new machines were supported by the industry's strongest dealer network. The dealers, in turn, were backed by Bombardier-supplied credit and inventory financing schemes that would have made Armand Bombardier blanch.

Bombardier's response to the phenomenon of snowmobiling should have found a place in the annals of business-school case studies as a brilliantly executed strategy of marketing, new-product development and continuous improvement in manufacturing methods. Instead, the snowmobile came to be regarded, with reason, as a cautionary tale in the folly of commiting an entire company to the caprice of a consumer fad. Save for the fact that people were still buying Ski-Doos into the 21st century, there was little to distinguish the sales trajectory of the snowmobile between 1966 and 1974 from the boom-and-bust cycles for Cuisinart food processors or Cabbage Patch dolls.

At the snowmobile's zenith as a must-have toy in 1971, Valcourt turned out 210,000 Ski-Doos, up from 23,000 in 1966. Those same early years of Beaudoin's presidency were marked by an explosion in revenues, which increased ten-fold, to $183 million. To be sure, Beaudoin was no more comfortable with Bombardier's new reliance on the snowmobile than he'd been with its earlier dependence on heavy equipment. He bought a Montreal-based maker of aircraft landing gear. And he diversified into fibreglass sailboats and off-road motorcycles. But a camper and an aqua-scooter dubbed the Sea-Doo were pulled from the market after meeting with a tepid response. The Sea-Doo, based on the design of a California inventor, was a notable fiasco. Beaudoin lost between $2 million and $3 million on the ill-fated venture.

Meanwhile, Beaudoin had doubled his bet on snowmobiles. Bombardier acquired the Austrian tramway maker Lohnerwerke GmbH — not for its mass-transit expertise but its Rotax-Werk AG affiliate, a key supplier of engines for the Ski-Doo. Beaudoin bought one of his chief snowmobile rivals, Moto-Ski Ltd. of La Pocatiére, Quebec. Bombardier introduced a Skidozer for use in grooming snowmobile trails. No less a believer in vertical integration than his father-in-law,

Beaudoin snapped up a string of suppliers that made parts for the Ski-Doo. Leaving nothing to chance in its bid to dominate the industry, Bombardier even bought a couple of firms that made snowmobile jumpsuits, gloves and other accessories.

The decision of Arab oil producers in the Organization of Petroleum Exporting Countries (OPEC) to jack up petroleum prices in the wake of 1973's Yom Kippur War hastened a decline in snowmobile sales that had begun in the previous 18 months. The novelty of line-ups at gasoline stations across the U.S. reinforced the pleas of government officials for consumers to cut back on their use of gasoline-powered vehicles for the sake of "energy security." Snowmobiling was a luxury that could no longer be indulged when Middle East oil ministers were piloting the North American economy, which slipped into a seven-year despond of "stagflation" — the freakish curse of simultaneous inflation and recession.

The lack of hype that characterized Bombardier in later years can be traced to the misplaced bravado of its 1970 annual report. "Some economists have referred to snowmobiles as riding the crest of the leisure market, but the wave shows no signs of cresting," Bombardier told its shareholders that year. "All forecasts point to a positive and continuing upsweep of the trend well into the 21st century." But in the space of just two years beginning in 1973, world production of snowmobiles would plummet from 500,000 to 170,000 units. In Valcourt, annual output shrank to 60,000 Ski-Doos — little more than one-quarter of peak production. With more than 90 per cent of its business tied to snowmobiling, Bombardier was now in severe difficulty. For, as Beaudoin conceded, "the Ski-Doo era was obviously over." So was the Bombardier era, at least on Bay Street. Shares in the former high-flier, once valued at $22, slid all the way down to $2. "They used to call me a hero," said Beaudoin, who was no longer being wooed by investment bankers urging him to issue more stock. "Now they call me a zero."

But Beaudoin did not panic. It wasn't so long ago that Quebec's snow-removal program for rural roads had abruptly chopped Bombardier's sales in half. The 1950s were lean years for Bombardier as it struggled to diversify. But eventually it made a complete recovery, its sales having tripled even before the arrival of the Ski-Doo. As the number of snowmobile makers rapidly dwindled to six in the early 1970s, Bombardier dominated the industry as never before. By 2000, Bombardier would have just three snowmobile rivals: Arctic Cat, Polaris and Yamaha. If Beaudoin was willing to shed some production facilities and cut the payroll, a truncated Bombardier could survive by catering to the frontier medics, prospectors and missionaries for whom Armand Bombardier had originally designed his Ski-Doo.

Beaudoin used the crisis as an opportunity to trim some managerial deadwood. He cut some 30 executives from the payroll. But he could not bring himself to contemplate layoffs in Valcourt. Beaudoin felt the same way about La Pocatiére, another remote community on the south shore of the St. Lawrence River about 125 kilometres northeast of Quebec City, whose livelihood depended on the former Moto-Ski plant. And Beaudoin had already shown his determination not to join the ranks of proud Canadian firms that reached a certain size and then petered out or were sold to foreign interests. In the late 1960s, when Ski-Doo sales were booming, the Bombardier family had been tempted by takeover overtures from Ford Motor Co., Chrysler Corp., Massey-Ferguson Ltd and Outboard Marine Corp., maker of Mercury and Johnson outboard motors. But Beaudoin, remembering that Armand Bombardier had resisted several U.S. takeover offers, persuaded the family to instead take Bombardier public, and raise expansion funds from minority investors while retaining control of its namesake company. "You had this $8-million company being run by a bunch of kids, and everybody tried to buy it," said John Hethrington, Bombardier's head of marketing in the boom years. "Well, the tradition in Quebec is that you sell out to the Americans. So these guys had two choices: go clip coupons on the Riviera, or do it. They did it."

Beaudoin now brainstormed with his skeletal management team. He asked them to help him bet the company again, this time in a field that was alien to Bombardier. Montreal was caught up at this time in hectic preparations for the 1976 Olympic summer games. That would require a large expansion of the city's subway system. In 1974, the Quebec government invited Bombardier to join the bidding for a contract to supply 423 new subway cars over five years, with a significant portion to be delivered by 1976.

Beaudoin was unenthusiastic at first. Britain's Vickers Ltd had supplied the inaugural series of rubber-wheeled cars for the Montreal Métro, based on technology it licensed from a French company, and it seemed to have a lock on the follow-up order. A more practical concern was that while Bombardier's founder had been a pioneer in developing rubber wheels and traction devices, Bombardier had no experience in mass transit. It lacked both the technology and production facilities to carry out such an enormous project. And with the games just two years away, there almost certainly would be cost overruns in the rush to meet an inflexible deadline.

Then again, Bombardier had surprised even itself at the speed with which it was able to boost its output of Ski-Doos by a factor of 10 in a few short years, even as it added performance-enhancing features to each new model. Given the nationalist tenor of the times, the high-profile Métro contest seemed to favour a local bidder. Then Beaudoin learned that Vickers had not renewed its technology agreement with its French partner, CIMT-Lorraine. What happened next set the pattern for Bombardier's transformation into the world leader in railway equipment.

Beaudoin deftly recruited the jilted CIMT as Bombardier's technology partner. He submitted a $117.8-million bid to supply the Métro cars, which was accepted when the Vickers design was found to contain flaws with its coupling system for linking the subway coaches. At La Pocatiére, which was destined to become one of the world's biggest centres for railcar production, Beaudoin scrambled to expand

and retool the old Moto-Ski plant to turn out subway cars. And for the power component of the contract, he bought MLW-Worthington Ltd. The former Montreal Locomotive Works, a 73-year-old manufacturing operation located in east-end Montreal, gave Beaudoin needed expertise in locomotives and diesel engines.

The MLW deal would prove to be a near-disaster. The far smaller Bombardier had challenge enough in trying to digest the huge MLW operation. Making matters worse was the discovery that MLW was what merger and acquisition specialists call "a bag of snakes." In his haste, Beaudoin had purchased a firm where almost everything was in a shambles — "management, labour relations, equipment, engineering, product quality, customer service, you name it," Beaudoin said. MLW was bleeding red ink and its treasury was exhausted. Things got more complicated when the same Quebec government agencies that had encouraged Bombardier to assume responsibility for the ailing MLW tried to lure it into a misguided scheme to yoke Bombardier with Marine Industries, a chronically insolvent Montreal shipyard. Having accepted a $6.8-million government investment in Bombardier shares to help buffer the company from the unforeseen MLW liabilities, Beaudoin felt obliged to waste precious time on the negotiations. He was fortunate when the plan fell through.

Beaudoin moved quickly to amputate the obsolete assets at MLW. And he lured Raymond Royer from snowmobile maker Skiroule Ltd. to head up Bombardier's nascent mass-transit division. Royer, who would eventually become president of Bombardier, was a brilliant salesman. With the technology and production capacity for railcar manufacturing in hand, Beaudoin and Royer assembled a team of managers to ride herd on the Métro project.

For all the start-up woes it was obliged to endure, Bombardier was also gaining valuable expertise in a new field, and a skill at turning around ailing manufacturing operations that would serve it exceptionally well in the future. Its first Montreal subway cars were delivered in June 1976, a few weeks before the opening ceremonies at the Olympics. By the time the contract was completed, on schedule, in 1978, Bombardier had already signed its first U.S. order — 36 commuter cars for a Chicago transit authority.

But to be a major force in this new industry, Beaudoin reasoned, his company would have to offer the widest possible range of mass-transit equipment. Specifications for rail transport varied from one city and region to the next. To expand its base of potential clients, Bombardier needed to become a proficient maker of subway cars, tramways, streetcars, self-propelled and double-decker commuter cars and intercity passenger coaches. It would have to develop expertise in both electric- and diesel-powered locomotion. It would also be required to help cash-strapped public transit authorities finance their big-ticket purchases.

The decades following World War II had been cruel to the makers of railway rolling stock, as commercial aviation triumphed over passenger rail, and trucking asserted its supremacy as a cost-efficient alternative to railways in freight haulage. Many famous names in rail equipment had fallen by the wayside. Others were ripe for acquisition by a bargain hunter with faith in the future of rail transport. Bombardier seemed poised to duplicate its position in snowmobiles, as a major player in an industry that was a shadow of its former self. But Beaudoin had even bigger hopes. He had elected not to abandon snowmobiles, out of a conviction that the market would recover, and now Beaudoin had a similar belief that rail was on the verge of a renaissance.

Over the next several years, Bombardier spent judicious sums to acquire technology licences and entire companies rich in R&D from investors who didn't share Beaudoin's unconventional view. Every few months, the company would generate headlines by landing another order to supply railcar equipment to a large foreign transit authority. Beaudoin did nothing to discourage the impression that his improbable strategy was working — that his snowmobile company, as if touched by the wand of a fairy princess, had suddenly become an ambassador of Canadian high-tech ability. The strategy *was* working; and it didn't matter that a good deal of Bombardier's technological know-how was imported. But the real story was Bombardier's quiet but rapid accumulation of design and manufacturing expertise, as well as assembly plants in 11 countries in North America, Europe and Asia.

That gambit dated from 1975. Within a few months of winning the first Montreal Métro order, Beaudoin had signed technology licensing agreements with Pullman Inc., the venerable U.S. passenger railcar maker, and with Belgium's BN Constructions Ferroviaires et Métalliques S.A., one of Europe's design and manufacturing leaders in urban transit and intercity rail equipment, and a supplier of passenger railcars for the Docklands Light Railway that would link downtown London with Olympia & York's future office suburb at Canary Wharf. Eventually Bombardier would buy those firms outright, along with the mass-transit division of Budd Co., its chief U.S. competitor. In fairly short order, Bombardier put itself in the running for railcar orders around the world.

During its first five years in the rail-transport field, Bombardier won contracts to supply LRC (for light, rapid and comfortable) railcars to Via Rail Canada, commuter cars for New Jersey Transit, tramways for Portland, Oregon, and subway cars for Mexico City. And in 1982, Beaudoin landed the contract that would establish Bombardier as the North America leader in rail transport when the Metropolitan Transportation Authority (MTA) of New York granted it a $1-billion order for 825 graffiti-resistant subway cars. That was the largest export contract ever awarded to a Canadian manufacturer, and carried the same risk as the Montreal project. It specified steep penalties in the event of design flaws or late delivery. But the subway cars were delivered ahead of time. They would earn the highest performance ratings of any railcars in the MTA fleet. They triggered a new wave of orders from commuter-train operators in Pennsylvania and the Metro-North Commuter Railroad serving

New York's northern suburbs and Connecticut. And Bombardier managed to clear a $135-million profit on the MTA contract.

Back in 1982, Beaudoin, Royer and the negotiating team they created to put a full-court press on the MTA officials had toasted their success with reheated coffee over plates of stale sandwiches at a gritty all-night Manhattan diner. Lavish celebrations were not Beaudoin's style. He was a cost-controller who taught by personal example. But he ruled by consensus rather than fiat, and was gentle with subordinates. With his aquiline nose, strong chin and dark eyes — always focused intently on interlocutors to create a bond of intimacy — Beaudoin had the bearing of an Old World patrician. Save when unruly locks of hair would fall onto his forehead. Then he was the kid president who still looked like the photo that appeared above his name in the University of Sherbrooke yearbook.

This was the Big Man on Campus era for francophone entrepreneurs in Montreal. In the 1960s, Montreal-based Power Corp., an investment vehicle for Sudbury, Ontario, native Paul Desmarais, had begun to repatriate firms such as Canada Steamship Lines, Consolidated-Bathurst Inc. and Imperial Life Assurance Co. from their Anglo owners. His bold example was an inspiration for a new generation of French-speaking tycoons that was asserting itself in the city's political and cultural life. Their Anglo counterparts in Toronto, "big swinging dicks" in local parlance, congratulated themselves on coaxing taxpayers to finance the SkyDome and other vanity boondoggles in the 1980s. Montreal's francophone business elite, accorded heroic status for its role in fostering Quebec's growing economic self-reliance, was even less restrained during that heady decade. Bernard Lamarre of engineering firm Lavalin Inc. made over the Musee des Beaux-Arts according to his own vision. Claude Castonguay, a distinguished former Quebec cabinet minister and architect of the Laurentian Group financial services conglomerate, was embraced as a guru on the restructuring of constitutional arrangements between Quebec and Canada. Having installed one of their own at 24 Sussex Drive in Ottawa, the francophone entrepreneurs who had guided former Iron Ore of Canada president Brian Mulroney in his political ascension now devoted less and less time to their day jobs. They became preoccupied with counselling their compatriots in the National Assembly on everything from language purity laws to methods of restoring the depressed francophone fertility rate to 19th-century levels.

Beaudoin missed out on that phenomenon, although he despaired in the early 1990s when Lavalin, Laurentian Group, Provigo, Steinberg and other francophone enterprises came to ruin, all victims of inept or absentee management. By then, he was spending more time in Quebec after having established Bombardier's bona fides from Paris to Santiago. Concerned about the province's downward economic spiral, Beaudoin finally emerged as a public figure. But he limited his observations to a call for sensible policies in deficit reduction, apprenticeship training and R&D. By this point he was something of a rarity among his peers in being able to address an audience without fear of embarrassment. (Bombardier's sales and profits increased each year during the 1990s recession.) The novelty in Beaudoin's comments was the absence of any nationalist *cri de coeur*. That was a stinging rebuke to the separatist government in Quebec City, which hoped for better from the one CEO recognized across Canada as a remarkable success story in francophone entrepreneurialism. (Things would get worse for the Parti Québécois when Beaudoin took an uncharacteristically public stand on a political issue. For an excerpt of his speech calling for a "No" vote in the 1995 Quebec referendum on sovereignty, see the Appendices.)

Beaudoin had tried to steer clear of politics. Given the enormity of his ambitions, Beaudoin was compelled to focus on the business at hand. And his co-workers couldn't help but absorb his competitive spirit. This showed itself in Beaudoin's determination to win not only at the negotiating table but on the tennis court, in gin games and at his only peculiar pastime, fox hunting. Beaudoin kept thoroughbreds at his home near the Eastern Townships village of Knowlton, where he indulged in a British sport that was utterly alien to French Canada. His explanation was simply that "it keeps me in shape."

Beaudoin's horses were often lonely. Their peripatetic owner was preoccupied with seizing one of the better business opportunities of the century. To do so, he would have to act quickly to consolidate Bombardier's hold on the international market for rail-transport products before the revival in passenger rail drove up acquisition prices and lured new competitors into the market.

In order to comply with the U.S.'s protectionist "Buy America Act" of 1978, Bombardier had opened its first plant outside of Canada, at Barre, Vermont. It built a factory in Dublin to fulfill a contract to build buses for that city. But Beaudoin preferred not to build from scratch. With modest outlays of cash, he bought the rights to monorail technology developed by Walt Disney Co.; and from Europe's GEC Alsthom he acquired the North American licence for its Train à Grande Vitesse (TGV), the fastest train in the world.

As it established credibility for on-time delivery and product reliability, Bombardier was able to create a stable base of revenues from new orders and long-term maintenance contracts, which tended to generate high-margin repeat orders. The assured revenue stream, in turn, enabled Beaudoin to pounce whenever a For Sale sign went up at a rail-transport maker. Many of those firms were in financial distress. All could be acquired cheaply. And some were in countries where state-owned transit systems were required by law to buy from local suppliers, providing Bombardier with an edge against competitors.

In time, Bombardier was in possession of the largest share of rail-transit production capacity in North America and Europe. It bought Mexico's leading maker of railway rolling stock; a British supplier of railcar and locomotive components; and Canada's Urban Transportation Development Corp. (UTDC), which made the world's largest double-decker passenger cars of their kind for Ontario's GO Transit. The purchase of France's 107-year-old ANF-Industrie, a maker of commuter railcars with clients in Amsterdam, London, Venezuela and Chile, also brought contracts to supply the English Channel tunnel and TGV projects in France. With its 1999 purchase of Germany's Deutsche Waggonbau AG, a major supplier of subway and intercity passenger coaches, Bombardier became the largest rail equipment firm in the world.

That was proving to be a lucrative distinction. Beaudoin's faith in rail had not been misplaced. If anything, the crush of orders from public transit authorities was a chronic strain on Bombardier's overtaxed plants, which accounted for Beaudoin's persistent sleuthing for takeover prospects. As state and municipal governments around the world made progress in getting their deficits under control during the last two decades of the century, they finally had money to overhaul their deteriorating mass transit systems. Pressure to do so grew in tandem with growing concerns about global warming, and mounting traffic congestion that threatened to bring commercial activity in cities from Rio to Bangkok to a standstill. Among the lobbyists for upgraded public transit were business leaders. The 1990s corporate obsession with computerized "just-in-time" inventory control systems, a critical element of an Internet economy where customers demanded overnight delivery of goods, was a distant dream as long as parcels kept getting trapped in vehicular gridlock.

Yet long before the milestone achieved with the Deutsche Waggonbau transaction, Bombardier had undergone one more gut-wrenching transformation. By the mid-1990s, Beaudoin was convinced that his company looked too much like the single-suited enterprise that had come to grief a decade earlier. The company that was staring at extinction not long ago was now generating annual sales of more than half a billion dollars, roughly three times more than its best performance before the snowmobile market collapsed. But almost all of those revenues were derived from the one field. Mass transit was not a fad. Yet Beaudoin wondered if there was another realm in which Bombardier could exploit its skill at turning inefficient factories into money-spinners.

In Ottawa, meanwhile, Mulroney was preparing in the mid-1980s to auction off Air Canada, Canadian National Railways, Petro-Canada and several other crown corporations that had long ago ceased to be relevant to Canada's industrial development policy. He was particularly keen to unload a blighted enterprise named Canadair Ltd.

Canadair was one of the world's oldest and most prolific airplane makers, having turned out more than 4,000 aircraft by 1986. It traced its roots to 1923, when it was founded as a branch plant of Britain's Vickers. For three decades following World War II, it was owned by the U.S. defence contractor General Dynamics Corp. and was primarily a maker of military planes. These included the Sabre fighter, the Argus marine patrol plane, and the Tutor trainers used by Canada's renowned Snowbirds aerobatics team. Canadair's Yukon cargo planes had been used extensively by freight haulers in the Pacific Rim, and were converted by some carriers into 214-passenger airliners. And Canadair's CL-215 was the world's only purpose-built water bomber, used for aerial firefighting on five continents.

But Canadair lost altitude in the 1970s, when the market for military aircraft went into decline. Ottawa took Canadair off General Dynamics' hands with the idea of rescuing this showcase of Canadian aerospace know-how. In a bid to reinvent itself as a maker of civilian planes, Canadair spent more than $1.5 billion to develop a new executive jet. The project was a fiasco. The Challenger program was marred by delays, cost overruns and poor marketing. And there were few buyers for business jets when the Challenger made its debut in the early 1980s recession. With no prospect of recovering its development costs for the plane, Canadair took a $1.4-billion write-off in 1983, a record loss for a Canadian corporation at the time.

But where Ottawa saw an albatross, Beaudoin sensed opportunity. The Challenger, he thought, was a good plane that was a victim of bad timing. Canadair also had a large pool of skilled technicians, a modern aircraft assembly plant in Montreal, and a healthy sideline as a supplier of components to the U.S. aircraft makers Boeing and McDonnell Douglas Co. And the price was right. Mulroney was eager to kick off his privatization campaign with an improbable victory in finding a buyer for one of Ottawa's least attractive assets. In 1986, Bombardier paid the deep-discount price of $120 million for a company whose debts had been absorbed by the taxpayer.

Beaudoin's top managers were preoccupied with rail transport, of course, and could ill afford the distraction of Canadair. Beaudoin scored a coup in tapping an outsider named Donald Lowe to head Bombardier's newest division. At Montreal's Pratt & Whitney Canada Ltd, a world leader in making engines for small aircraft, and later at the fabled Kidd Creek Mines Ltd in Northern Ontario, Lowe had proved to be a turnaround expert of rare ability. At Canadair, Lowe quickly eliminated overlapping layers of management. He created a new team of marketing and manufacturing experts that matched Royer's young lions in mass transit.

Within two years Canadair had bolstered its subcontracting arm with one billion dollars' worth of orders to supply components to Europe's Airbus consortium. And as the economy shifted back into high gear, sales of a more competently promoted Challenger began to take off. But Beaudoin was not content to rely on the volatile market for business aircraft. He pushed Canadair to develop a regional version of the Challenger for the commuter market.

The Canadair Regional Jet (CRJ) would not be ready for three years. In the meantime, Beaudoin sought to widen Bombardier's product range in aircraft as he had done in rail equipment. In the space of four years, Bombardier's revenues doubled to 1992's $3.1 billion as Beaudoin shopped for distressed aircraft makers.

He bought the state-owned Short Brothers PLC (Shorts) of Belfast, which received the first aircraft production order from Wilbur and Orville Wright in 1909. Like Mulroney, British prime minister Margaret Thatcher was eager to sell off her government's aerospace interests. For just $60 million, Bombardier acquired a leading maker of regional airplanes whose production facilities had recently been overhauled at great expense by the British government. In return for agreeing to keep Northern Ireland's biggest industrial employer in business for at least four years, Beaudoin got a company with a clean balance sheet and $1.5 billion in back orders, including contracts to supply wing components for Boeing jetliners. "Shorts" was also one of the world's top makers of nascelles, the housings for jet-aircraft engines. Nascelles made by Shorts were fitted under the wings of Airbus jetliners, where they suspended engines made by Rolls-Royce and BMW.

To fill out Bombardier's portfolio of business planes, Beaudoin bought Learjet Corp. of Wichita, Kansas, from its insolvent parent company. In addition to its pioneering executive jets, Learjet made components for U.S. defence contractors and the NASA Space Shuttle. And Beaudoin thought it wise, as production of the CRJ was gearing up in Montreal, to add more production capacity by purchasing de Havilland Inc. That last deal raised a lot of eyebrows.

By this point, the investment community was applauding Beaudoin's acquisition strategy. "Beaudoin made a decision to search for the best technology and the best designs, and either get the exclusive licenses or buy the companies," said a Toronto aerospace analyst. "Bombardier's expertise was always manufacturing and marketing. Why not build on those strengths?" By this point, Canadair had proved to be an inspired purchase. But the de Havilland deal struck many observers as holding little promise of a repeat performance.

The venerable de Havilland, founded in 1928 in Downsview, Ontario, to build aircraft for its British parent, was responsible for a Canadian export as famous as the snowmobile. Prior to World War II, de Havilland had been a branch plant that merely turned out copies of Geoffrey de Havilland's Tiger Moth biplanes and Mosquito bombers. But in the late 1940s and early 1950s, Downsview made design history of its own by inventing a series of aerial workhorses.

The six-passenger Beaver was the world's first aircraft designed specifically for use as a bush plane by frontier aviators such as Max Ward, and at the close of the century it was still in commercial use in deserts, jungles and mountainous regions around the globe. De Havilland followed up that triumph with the Otter and Twin Otter, the principal aircraft used in opening up the Canadian North, along with the rugged Caribou and Buffalo cargo planes. In the 1970s, de Havilland Canada had also pioneered the development of short takeoff and landing (STOL) commuter aircraft, which were designed for short runways at city-centre airports and crude landing fields in remote areas. But sales of the Dash line-up of STOL planes were slow to materialize, prompting a federal bailout that saw Ottawa gain control of the firm in 1974. And after a boomlet in the late 1970s caused by deregulation of the U.S. airline industry, the STOL market collapsed in the 1980s as airlines around the world flew into the worst financial turbulence in the history of commercial aviation.

Even a modest purchase price of $51 million for de Havilland looked overly rich to admirers of Bombardier on Bay Street, who questioned Beaudoin's rationale in acquiring a firm that had not earned a profit in the previous 10 years. Back in 1986, the same year it sold Canadair to Bombardier, Ottawa had dealt de Havilland to Boeing. But the $400 million spent by Boeing to modernize the Downsview facility was money down the drain for the Seattle aerospace giant, which came late to the realization that it didn't understand the commuter airline business.

Beaudoin, however, thought de Havilland was a prize. The talent-rich company, Toronto's largest industrial employer, had more than 600 engineers on staff. Its modern plant could accommodate spillover work from the Canadair facilities in Montreal — a cheap alternative to adding capacity from scratch. De Havilland had 40 years' experience in export markets. And its Dash series of STOL turboprops, a complement to the regional jet under development at Canadair, would give Bombardier the industry's widest range of commuter planes. Beaudoin promptly put de Havilland to work refurbishing Canadair water bombers and painting the exteriors of Canadair Regional Jets.

The CRJ represented the biggest gamble in Canadian aviation since the ill-fated Avro Arrow, the space-age jet interceptor that the government of John Diefenbaker killed off in the late 1950s before its commercial viability could be determined. To the fantastic sum that Ottawa had already spent on developing the eight-passenger Challenger, Bombardier added another $300 million in development spending to expand the plane into a 50-seat aircraft. The CRJ would be the world's first commuter jet.

The evolution of what would turn out to be one of the most successful new aircraft of the late 20th century was marked by a series of crises prior to Bombardier's arrival on the scene. They had their inception in a feud between Canadair management and the plane's inventor. The Challenger concept sprang from the mind of William P. Lear. The business-jet pioneer had sold his Learjet operation in the 1970s, and then met with frustration as he shopped his idea for a long-range business jet to several aircraft makers. There were no takers until Lear knocked on the door at Canadair. The Montreal firm seized on Lear's idea as the centrepiece of its project to reinvent itself as a producer of civilian aircraft.

But consultant Lear soon clashed with Canadair managers, who wisely sought to increase the diameter of Lear's fuselage. In designing a cabin that wealthy airplane owners could stand up in, Canadair was refashioning Lear's prototype into the world's first widebody business plane. "Corporate executives don't want to sit in the prenatal position in an executive mailing tube," explained a Canadair marketing expert. Lear was scornful of the new design, which he called the Fat Albert. But as Bombardier's marketers realized, the Challenger's "stand-up" cabin would prove to be one of the most effective selling points of the aircraft with buyers such as Bill Gates, Warren Buffett and Saudi investor Prince al-Waleed bin Talal. And the widebody design would make the Challenger's later modification into a commuter plane a realistic option.

Yet in turning that proposition into a reality with the scheduled debut of the CRJ in 1992, Beaudoin was launching the plane in the same dismal economic conditions that nearly grounded the Challenger for good a decade earlier. Money-losing airlines around the world were cancelling orders for proven aircraft in the midst of the industry's worst downturn on record. Who, skeptics argued, would want an untested and costly jet for prosaic commuter runs between Des Moines and Baltimore when a cheaper turboprop would do?

The doubters could foresee neither the dramatic upturn in the North American economy that would begin in the mid-1990s, nor the pent-up demand for new planes at airlines that had not upgraded their fleets in more than a decade.

The CRJ turned out to be one of the most successful planes ever produced. The 50-seat CRJ was an instant hit with independent regional airlines on five continents. Orders also poured in from the new commuter offshoots of major airlines such as Lufthansa, American and Delta, which were impatient to tap a regional market that now accounted for more than half of all flights. The quiet, comfortable CRJ was a passenger-pleasing improvement over noisy turboprops. "There is the perception among some passengers that turboprops are not safe," said Glen Hauenstein, a vice-president at Houston-based Continental Airlines, which was not alone in capturing a whole new market of travellers in small cities who had previously refused to fly because their community airports were served only by turboprops. "Turboprops vibrate and the passengers can see the propellers." Turboprops were safe, with an accident rate of just 3.62 per 100,000 miles flown. But that was twice the accident rate for jets.

Once they got over the sticker shock from the CRJ's $20-million (U.S.) selling price, airlines calculated they could realize a higher profit per passenger from the fuel-efficient jet. The high-speed CRJ could make more flights each day on a given route. And its extended range was instrumental in creating dozens of new commuter routes that enabled passengers to fly "point to point." For the first time, commuters could fly direct between many so-called second-tier cities, and no longer have to change planes at busy "hub" airports. Turboprop-hating business executives in small centres who once drove two to five hours to a major airport to avoid using them could now fly out of towns like Greenville, South Carolina, by jet. And such unlikely non-stop routes as Atlanta–Grand Rapids suddenly became commercially feasible. "The important thing about regional jets is not [simply] that they are more cost efficient than turboprops," said Samuel Buttrick, an airline analyst at PaineWebber. "The airlines expect to get more revenue from region-al jets by selling more seats in what is a preferred product." Less than a decade after their introduction, regional jets accounted for 11 per cent of daily jet departures in the U.S. domestic market in 2000. It was forecast that between 1999 and 2008, carriers would take delivery of 3,750 regional jets, worth an estimated $6 billion (U.S.).

Within seven years of introducing the 50-seat CRJ, Bombardier had sold more than 550 of the planes, worth $14 billion. By the late 1990s, it had booked six bil-lion dollars' worth of orders for a 70-seat model. And it was contemplating a 90-seat version for a market with an estimated value of $25 billion to the year 2015. With their $2-billion investment in the Challenger and the CRJ, for which Bombardier received modest government assistance, Ottawa and Quebec had financed an aircraft program that was now poised to rack up sales of $45 billion. It would also do for Montreal what rail transport had done for La Pocatiére. Bombardier Aerospace's network of assembly plants, centred on Dorval, was now a world capital of aircraft production.

The only blot on this record of success was Bombardier's reputation in some quarters as a glutton for government handouts. Given its prominence and prove-nance, Bombardier was more widely regarded as a favoured child of government than perhaps any other company in Canada.

To be sure, many of Bombardier's earliest snowmobiles, subway cars and aircraft had been purchased by public agencies. (The first Challengers were used by the Canadian military to ferry VIPs including the prime minister, an example soon copied by heads of state in Europe and Asia.) And accusations of sweetheart deals marred almost every Bombardier acquisition and many of its largest contracts.

The allegation of favouritism was hard to refute. Bombardier had not gained renown outside Quebec, after all, until Ottawa commissioned it to make armoured snow buses for use in Europe during World War II. That would be pos-sibly the last Bombardier contract that failed to spark a controversy.

Having just handed Canadair to Bombardier in 1986 at what seemed like a giveaway price, Mulroney then stripped Winnipeg's Bristol Aerospace Ltd. of the contract to overhaul CF-18 military aircraft, and gave it to Bombardier. The move triggered outrage in Western Canada over Ottawa's perceived support of Quebec companies at the expense of the rest of the country. And as with Canadair, there was a sense that de Havilland was a federal donation to Bombardier. (In the latter case, the Ontario government also ponied up $200 million in loans and subsidies, and took a 49 per cent equity stake in the com-pany for $49 million.)

The public largesse was not limited to Canada. John Major, the former British prime minister, recalled in his memoir that as a junior cabinet minister with responsibility for Shorts, he had been driven to thoughts of tendering his resignation in order to force Thatcher to submit to Bombardier's demands in acquiring the troubled aircraft maker. "Bombardier would not buy Shorts without a substantial dowry," Major said, "but Margaret objected to the terms I proposed." Beaudoin wanted the British government to waive a $780-million loan to Shorts and contribute $550 million toward the firm's rejuvenation, only a portion of which was a repayable subsidy. "We had a two-hour confrontation that ended in fierce rowing, and I was determined to resign if I was overruled," said Major. The next day, Thatcher accepted Beaudoin's terms.

But for all that, critics rarely appreciated the traditional role of governments worldwide in subsidizing transportation. This ranged from the taxpayer-funded highways used by the trucking industry to airport construction and air-traffic control. Every major aircraft maker in the world was government-owned, suckled on state subsidies or bolstered with defence contracts. Often it was all three, as with the members of Europe's Airbus consortium. And there was more than a hint of patriotism in the Bombardier story, although it was rarely commented upon. In the case of the Montreal subway, Canadair, de Havilland and the CF-18 contract, governments in Canada were now subsidizing activities that had been repatriated from foreign owners who themselves had been the beneficiaries of support from goverments in Canada.

An early attack on special government treatment for Bombardier arose from the $750 million in financing that Canada's Export Development Corp. provided to New York's MTA in 1982. But Bombardier's two closest rivals for that watershed subway-car contract had lined up similar assistance from government agencies in Europe and the U.S. The pattern repeated itself in aviation. Bombardier's chief competitors in commuter aircraft, the German-U.S. partnership of Dornier-Fairchild and Brazil's Empresa Brasileira de Aeronautic (Embraer), were largely owned by state entities. To a greater extent than was the case at Bombardier, government-supplied financing for buyers was critical in greasing the sale of products by those two firms.

Given the abysmal track record of such diverse ventures as the Bricklin sports-car and the bailout of Massey-Ferguson (which soon defected to the U.S.), Canadians had reason to be wary of "chosen instruments." That was the term for private-sector ventures that were expected to brighten the country's industrial prospects in return for lavish outlays of taxpayer support. In contrast to Air Canada and Petro-Canada, however, Bombardier never did seek or gain the status of a cosseted champion of industrial development.

In an ironic twist, the sharpest criticism of Bombardier came from Quebec's separatist government in response to Beaudoin's defence of national unity in the province's 1995 referendum on sovereignty. Quebec City, which had participated in more than one Bombardier project, now accused the company of being a puppet of its alleged masters in Ottawa. Some separatists "who scarcely a moment ago used the Bombardier name to illustrate what Quebec is capable of achieving now want to strip us of any credit and deny our unquestionable success," Beaudoin said in a Montreal Board of Trade speech three weeks before the crucial vote. Beaudoin, who turned caustic only when confronting allegations of government favouritism to his company, acknowledged that "without the support of the federal government's export financing programs, we would not have developed as we have." He then noted that of Bombardier's $2.3 billion worth of investments in Quebec over the previous decade, just $99 million was in the form of non-repayable assistance. And that sum represented R&D and other industrial-development financing to which companies of every description availed themselves.

In acquiring so many cast-offs in the fields of aviation and mass transit, Beaudoin had also come to be regarded as something of a junkyard dog. But he had rescued a string of ailing companies that previous owners, all recipients of copious government subsidies, had failed to revive. In Bombardier's care, the workforce at Canadair had doubled in size, to 8,000 employees. With a slight decrease in its payroll, the now profitable Shorts had tripled its output of aircraft components; Bombardier had invested $1.9 billion in the firm by 2000. Beaudoin had been urged by experts to rationalize de Havilland, reducing it in status to a mere subcontractor of parts to Canadair, Shorts and Learjet. The firm's workers did indeed supply de Havilland's sister airplane makers. But Beaudoin also invested heavily in de Havilland's long-standing Dash program. Once they reached cruising speed, regional jets were much more fuel-efficient than turboprops, costing only 10 cents per air mile on longer routes of between 500 and 1,000 miles long, versus 19 cents a mile for turboprops. But on routes of less than 500 miles, turboprops were still much cheaper to operate than jets, which explained why in 2000 there were 1,400 turboprops in service in the U.S., compared with 410 regional jets. At a time when de Havilland's turboprop sales were declining, Bombardier spent six years in the 1990s to develop an antivibration system to reduce cabin noise by 10 decibels to 75, or the same level as its regional jets. Beaudoin hoped that a new generation of quieter turboprops, for which Bombardier was the only supplier, would attract buyers in need of a commuter aircraft that could boast lower operating costs than jets on ultra-short-range flights.

By the late 1990s, neo-conservative commentators in academe and the media, vaguely frustrated with Bombardier's emergence as an equal to Nortel Networks Corp. as a world-beater in its industry, continued to argue that its triumphs were a freak of nature. People who actually ran businesses had a different view. In its annual poll of CEOs who were asked to identify Canada's most respected firms, *The Globe and Mail* reported that Beaudoin's peers regarded Bombardier as the best-managed company in the country.

⧗

A T THE TEST TRACK in the desert near Pueblo, Colorado, the fastest train on the continent was undergoing trials for reliability. The landscape was studded by cholla cactus and overrun with rattlesnakes. After reaching speeds of 260 kph on its most recent lap, the Acela Express abruptly ground to a halt after hitting an antelope. A test controller joined the engineer who was inspecting the undercarriage of the train, looking for remains of the animal. "Finding enough for the barbecue tonight?" said the controller.

From time to time, when the mercury soared past 95 on the Fahrenheit scale, the Acela was forced to slow to a 130-kph crawl. Federal regulations dictated the reduced speed because welded steel rail changes shape at high temperatures. That wasn't going to be a problem in the U.S. Northeast. The $1.5-billion train, designed by a partnership of Bombardier and Europe's GEC Alsthom, was planned to be ready for high-speed service in the antelope-free urban corridors from New York to Boston and Washington by October 1999.

Bombardier had designed North America's fastest train to move at speeds of up to 240 kph on existing Amtrak rail lines, cutting travel time between New York and Boston by an hour and a half, to three hours and eight minutes. The Acela, a word Amtrak invented by combining "acceleration" and "excellence," would not match the speed of the world's fastest trains. But unlike the European TGV and Japan's bullet trains, which ran on specially designed straightaways with no level crossings, Bombardier's train would be capable of running on Amtrak's antiquated trackage, which was in notoriously poor condition by international standards. Since upgrading those tracks was a financial impossibility, so was high-speed passenger rail travel in North America. That changed with the Bombardier-GEC partnership's success in the 1990s in developing "tilting" railcars that leaned into turns without inducing the rail equivalent of seasickness among passengers.

In anticipation of the scheduled launch, Amtrak had already begun a $27-million publicity campaign, blanketing Boston and the nation's capital with advertisements that boasted about the Acela Express's creature comforts. These included microbrews on tap, modem jacks for laptop computers at every seat and overhead luggage bins that were twice the size of those found on most passenger jets. Alluding to the aroma of gourmet coffee and amenities not available to the air traveller, Amtrak was trumpeting the Acela experience as one in which "Inner children travel free."

But a few weeks shy of the expected delivery date for the first 20 train sets, Amtrak officials were told the Acela's hyped inaugural run would have to be postponed by at least six months. Late in the test trials, a problem had been detected with the wheels on the passenger cars. They vibrated at high speed and were wearing out too quickly.

Publicly, Amtrak and Bombardier tried to downplay the bad news. Amtrak insisted the Acela would still spearhead the railway's daring bid to steal upscale business travellers from airlines on the U.S.'s busiest short-haul commuter routes. Bombardier explained that the problem wasn't related to safety but only a desire to reduce maintenance costs. Privately, though, Amtrak was furious over the embarrassing delay of its ballyhooed renaissance, which already had attracted skepticism. And Bombardier was quietly getting the word out that the wheel design was GEC Alsthom's responsibility.

In its own bids to reinvent itself, Bombardier had battled through one setback after another. Sometimes the problems were technological. Prominent among those debacles was Bombardier's LRC train for VIA Rail in the 1970s, which had been plagued with glitches.

There had been disputes with customers. A series of last-minute changes to the design specifications for railcars ordered by the English Channel tunnel authority caused Bombardier to lose money on the contract.

Politics made long-term planning a mug's game. In awarding a contract for 1,200 buses to General Motors, the new separatist government of Quebec premier René Lévesque had passed over local employer Bombardier. Lévesque was trying to send a signal that the province was still open to foreign investment. "The PQ had such a negative image internationally, and it was looking for some credibility," Beaudoin said.

And for all his skill at timing the market, Beaudoin had courted disappointment more than once. That would be the case with Bombardier's three-cylinder microcar, to be developed jointly with Japan's Daihatsu Motor Co. That project had to be abandoned in 1987, after four years of planning had failed to identify sufficient demand for such a curiosity. (A decade later, DaimlerChrysler, Suzuki, Honda and other automakers were still struggling to make a profit with their own microcars.)

Arguably, the project closest to Beaudoin's heart was a high-speed TGV train in the Windsor-Quebec City corridor. The train was to be a symbolic bridge between Canada's two linguistic solitudes, and would serve more than half the country's population. But after 20 years of persistent lobbying, Beaudoin could not get governments to commit to the $5-billion scheme.

Yet Beaudoin had ample reason to be confident about his company's prospects as he handed day-to-day management to Robert Brown, whose acumen Beaudoin had first come to admire when Brown helped Ottawa negotiate its sale of Canadair to Bombardier. Beaudoin could not realistically complain about hard luck. In 2000 his company had overtaken Gulfstream as the world's top maker of executive aircraft. Bombardier was looking at $9 billion in potential sales for its Global Express ultra-long-range executive plane, whose advanced avionics were being compared to those of a fighter jet. Bombardier Aerospace had just secured a record $1.9-billion order in 1999 from Northwest Airlines Corp. of Eagan, Minnesota for 54 CRJs. The deal was topped in May 2000 by a $2.92-billion order from Delta Air Lines Inc. for 94 regional jets, with options to buy as many as 406 more aircraft — a deal that was expected to create 1,000 new jobs in Montreal. Bombardier was studying the feasibility of developing a 110-seat super-regional jet to replace aging DC-9 and 727 aircraft in use among many large airlines. And Beaudoin's faith in the turboprop market seemed to have been vindicated with a $1.2-billion order in March 2000 from Spain's Air Nostrum for 29 Dash 8 turboprops and 15 CRJs.

The Bombardier Transportation group was nailing down record $2.7-billion orders from the Long Island Rail Road and Richard Branson's Virgin Rail. More than half of the value of the Virgin deal was a 20-year contract to provide ongoing maintenance services. Maintenance contracts were a reliable source of steady cash flow that Bombardier was trying to build into more of its contracts to guard against the volatility in the markets for new aircraft and rail equipment. Another reliable source of income was FlexJet, a fleet of 90 jets Bombardier operated on behalf of owners who bought only a fractional share of one or more planes. Clients got access to an entire fleet of aircraft without the cost of owning a single plane.

With an order backlog of $28.3 billion in the spring of 2000, there seemed to be little doubt that Bombardier would meet Beaudoin's target of doubling its annual sales to $23 billion by 2005. And the company was aiming to squeeze a few cents' more profit from each of those sales dollars. The rapid pace of Bombardier's expansion had not made Beaudoin less averse to debt, which amounted to only one-seventh of total equity. Nor had it dimmed his obsession with cost control. Beaudoin was an early disciple of the Six Sigma program for conceiving new methods of continuous improvement, a sophisticated strategy of setting steadily higher rates of efficiency and quality that was promoted by Arizona consultant Mikel Harry and perfected in the mid-1990s by General Electric Co. By enlisting employees' support in finding ways of wringing costs out of everything from advertising budgets to precision-grinding of the 35,000 rivets in each wing of a commuter jet, Beaudoin expected to reap at least $400 million in annual savings.

Bombardier already boasted one of the industry's best labour-relations records. This dated from the paternalism of the founder, who built libraries, fishing camps, golf courses, skating rinks and cultural centres for his workers in Valcourt. And its exemplary human-relations policies continued to be a distinction of the company. Labour harmony was crucial to Bombardier. Without it, Beaudoin could not hope to integrate the diverse cultures of the companies he acquired. And time-sensitive contracts were seldom won by strike-prone manufacturers.

In the 1970s, when Quebec suffered from the most violent industrial relations scene on the continent, Bombardier was creating committees of workers and managers to address shop-floor concerns. Strategic decisions were put to a vote in employee referendums. Above-average wages and benefits, profit-sharing and personalized training programs all contributed to the failure of unions to make inroads at Bombardier facilities where unions had not existed prior to a company's acquisition by Bombardier. They also held turnover to less than 1 per cent. A stock-purchase scheme for employees meant that workers shared in the stunning 34 per cent average annual increase in the value of Bombardier shares in the second half of the 1990s. An investor who bought 1,000 Bombardier shares in 1989, for a total value of $15,750, could have sold them in 2000 for about $250,000.

By the turn of the century, Beaudoin and Brown were thought by some industry experts to be entering uncharted territory. Bombardier was said to be running out of acquisition opportunities in its core businesses. And to be sure, Beaudoin was now flirting with the idea of entering still more new industries, the identity of which he would not disclose.

But there was scant reason to question his faith in Bombardier's ability to prosper from internal growth. The firm was constantly turning out new products, and usually finding markets for them. "As Bombardier has achieved critical mass in the past five years," said a Toronto stock-market analyst, "it has undergone an impressive shift from buying technology to developing its own." In his restless search for new markets, Beaudoin was determined to keep Bombardier from slipping into the complacency that had been the undoing of so many of the firms it had acquired. "You can never be stagnant," he said. "If you think you're pleased with a plateau you've reached, by the time you stop to think about it, somebody's ahead of you."

Bombardier seemed to be in little danger on that score. Its skills in mass transit had evolved to the point where it was now invited to design entire commuter systems for clients in the U.S., Europe and Asia. Among those so-called "turnkey" projects was a Bombardier contract to build a rail line to link John F. Kennedy International Airport with Manhattan and Long Island. The JFK project pointed the way to more airport business. Once GEC Alsthom got the bugs out of the Acela's suspension system, Beaudoin was certain that demand for high-speed passenger rail would make itself felt in as many as 20 U.S. transit corridors that were likely markets for the TGV technology to which Bombardier held North American rights. By most estimates, the North American market for less glamorous forms of mass-transit equipment was expected to grow by 50 per cent in the early years of the 21st century. And while Bombardier's chief competitors in commuter aircraft, Embraer and Dornier-Fairchild, were vowing to bring out their own 70- and 90-seat regional jets, Bombardier enjoyed a head start over its rivals of at least two years. "If the stampede starts to buy those airplanes, and it will," said a Canadian aviation analyst, "and if Bombardier is the only game in town, they're going to lock up a huge chunk of the market."

Even the recreational products operation was seeing renewed signs of vitality, after two years of losses. That was important to Beaudoin because the $1.1-billion division was headed by his son, Pierre. At his father's suggestion, Pierre had dusted off the 20-year-old prototype of the Sea-Doo in 1988, and launched a revamped model that quickly grabbed half of a market that had been dominated by Japanese firms.

Beaudoin wasn't coy about his aspirations for 36-year-old Pierre, who was expected to make a bid for his father's job. "I hope it could happen one day," Beaudoin said, "but it's not something that should happen overnight." When Pierre's career prospects seemed to fade as the recreational-products division dipped into the red in the late-1990s, Beaudoin was quick to signal his succession hopes. Pierre's bailiwick, he reminded shareholders, "has made an exceptional contribution to Bombardier's profitability in recent years, generating 35 per cent of total pretax profit in 1997." By the first quarter of fiscal 2000, the recreational division was back in the black, with a pretax profit of $9.1 million.

Almost everything Bombardier built was designed for speed. Which explained why, despite the vagaries of the market, the company was still turning out high-powered toys for outdoor-thrill-seekers some 80 years after Armand Bombardier shattered the Sunday silence of downtown Valcourt with his first experiment in snowmobiling. Speed and entrepreneurial risk-taking seemed to go hand in hand for CEOs at Bombardier. That augured poorly for incoming CEO Robert Brown, who liked to relax with a poky Bombardier-built powerboat.

Armand Bombardier was a snowmobile racer who startled companions by standing up at the controls of his machine, guiding it with ease over bumps and dips that threw less skilled enthusiasts head first into the snowdrifts. Pierre Beaudoin was a speed demon. Usually he could be found on the shop floor, examining blueprints. Otherwise, Pierre was outdoors, testing a parade of high-speed jet boats, snow racers and all-terrain vehicles that issued from the prodigious R&D works at Valcourt.

His father, too, was always in motion. A dozen years after undergoing sextuple heart-bypass surgery in 1986, Beaudoin was still careening at daredevil speeds across the ice of Lac Brome near his Eastern Townships home on a souped-up Ski-Doo.

Beaudoin also enjoyed challenging fellow board members to outrace him in Sea-Doo expeditions down the treacherous Saguenay River. He wasn't given to bragging about those exploits. As his machine hit speeds of 100 kph, it seemed enough for Beaudoin to look over his shoulder every so often, and catch a glimpse of his competitors as they receded into the distance.

8

ROBERT SCRIVENER AND
JOHN ROTH

How one man played midwife to a multinational,
and another got Nortel to move at the speed of light

*"There isn't anything any other manufacturer in the world
can do better than we can."*
— Robert Scrivener

"You know why great companies fail?
Suddenly, one morning, their chief asset becomes their chief liability."
— John Roth

THE PUBLIC FLOGGING of John Roth lasted for several weeks in the fall of
1998. By the time it was over, you understood why most CEOs would rather
stick pins in their eyes than try to lead a revolution at a large company.

It had been less than a year since Roth assumed the leadership of Northern
Telecom Ltd., Canada's biggest and most important high-tech firm, and the second-largest maker of telecommunications equipment in the world. The future
Nortel Networks Corp., as it was soon to be renamed, did not look like a company in need of a transformation. A few months after becoming CEO in October
1997, Roth was able to report that Nortel had enjoyed its best year ever, posting
record profits of $812 million (U.S.) on record sales of $15.4 billion.

By that point, however, Roth had committed Nortel to a wrenching transition,
betting the future of his Brampton, Ontario-based firm on its ability to become a

prime contractor in building a new and improved Internet. "The promise of the Internet," he said, "is that anyone in the world can access all the world's information, anytime they want it, from wherever they are — and do it in real time. Now, maybe it doesn't fulfill that promise today, but that's the vision we're moving toward." Put more crudely, the reinvention of the world's biggest industry, telecommunications, was the most substantial business opportunity of the 21st century. The Internet at this early stage in its development was a gold rush, and John Roth was emerging as one of its most formidable claim-stakers.

Roth had not yet told his employees that they were on a mission to reinvent the Internet. He didn't think they were quite ready to hear that. The so-called "Webtone" strategy he unveiled in December 1997, just two months after becoming CEO, was startling enough. In an internal memo to Nortel's 70,000 employees, he warned them that their company's star was fading as dynamic young firms in California's Silicon Valley and elsewhere took the lead in creating the communications networks of the future. In order to survive, the novice CEO asserted, Nortel would have to make a "right-angle turn" into Internet technology. The 116-year-old Nortel would have to reinvent itself from a safe and steady maker of old-line voice equipment for a handful of the world's largest phone companies, or telcos, into an aggressive supplier of data-networking gear for thousands of Internet-related network operators. Roth, a graduate in microwave engineering, exhorted his fellow engineers at Nortel to move at "Webspeed" instead of old-world telecom speed in racing to market with Internet-oriented products that would prove the company's new capabilities. To hammer home his point about the need for urgency, Roth had followed up the Webtone memo by going out and buying one of those daring Silicon Valley companies he wanted Nortel to emulate, paying $6.9 billion (U.S.) for Bay Networks Inc. of Santa Clara, California, a firm that specialized in data-networking equipment for the Internet age.

The stock market, however, was still operating at Nortel speed. It respected Nortel, but as a maker of conventional switching equipment for a relatively small client-base of big telephone companies around the world. When sales of that bread-and-butter product line appeared to soften in the summer of 1998, investors got nervous about Nortel's prospects. And they panned the deal for Bay, regarded as an also-ran in Web technology to another Silicon Valley firm, Cisco Systems Inc. If Nortel's core franchise in old-world telecom equipment was slumping, perhaps Roth's bid to merge his slow-moving Canadian telecom supplier with a troubled California networking company was a sign of desperation.

For many years, Nortel's stock had been listed in New York and many other offshore exchanges, along with those in Canada, as a means of raising the firm's profile with both investors and potential clients abroad.

On September 28, 1998, Roth hosted Nortel's annual investor conference in New York for hundreds of securities analysts and fund managers who followed his company and were in a position to influence the price of its stock. At Manhattan's Essex House hotel that day, Roth had wanted to set investors straight on the merits of the Bay acquisition. His audience, however, simply wanted reassurance that Nortel's basic telecom supply business wasn't going down the toilet. "We didn't handle that meeting right," Roth would say later, "trying to allay concerns about Bay without also anticipating concerns about the older business."

Roth had opened the New York meeting with a methodical dissertation on Bay as Nortel's response to the enormous commercial possibilities of the Internet. No one seemed to be listening. Then his chief financial officer took over. The audience strained to hear him. The CFO began his presentation by saying something about how the modest increase in sales of traditional telecom gear that Nortel had previously forecast was not going to be quite as strong as expected. The CFO didn't get a chance to finish that sentence.

"At 10:06 a.m. of that meeting," Roth remembered, "our CFO mumbled something about a sales uptick that might fail to materialize. At 10:07 a.m., our stock had lost $3 billion." Analysts and brokers had fled the conference hall to place sell orders, and those who remained in the room and were equipped with cellphones sold the stock without rising from their seats as Roth and his CFO exchanged bewildered glances. As he watched the stock jockeys yelling into their mobile phones, Roth had a heretical thought. "It was the one time," he recalled, "that I might have wished for something less than the reliability for phone systems that Nortel is known for." He couldn't help thinking that the sell orders were going out over the lines of Bell Atlantic Corp., one of Nortel's loyal clients, and were being executed at the New York Stock Exchange, which relied on equipment it had purchased from Bay Networks.

Over the next few days, the selling continued until $9.1 billion (U.S.) of Nortel's share value had been erased, and the company's stock had fallen 58 per cent from the record high set earlier that year. And over the next few months, it seemed there wasn't a constituency whose confidence Roth hadn't lost.

On Bay Street, where "Nortel is pretty much hated right now," in the words of a pension fund manager at Canada Trust, emotions were running high. "Our investor clients are livid," said Robert MacLellan of Kearns Capital Ltd. Many institutional investors, reported that Toronto money-manager, were clamouring for heads to roll, starting with Roth and his CFO. "Nortel has lost all credibility," MacLellan said. "Starting with the Bay deal, every time investors have bought back into Nortel on weakness, they've caught a falling knife by the blade."

Investors, Roth had to admit, were not buying into his vision the way he had expected them to. "They were telling me, 'John, why don't you keep making switches?' " Roth would later say. "Their problem was that Nortel has become a very unpredictable company." Nortel's own employees, who received a large portion of their compensation in company stock, were among the disaffected. Design director John Tyson, who gained fame with his Contempra phone in the 1960s, complained that the plunge in Nortel shares had done frightful damage to his retirement nest egg. And in Silicon Valley, some of Roth's newest employees doubted his ability to revive the prospects of Bay, a firm that was alien to Nortel's cozy telecom world. "I'd give Nortel an 'F' for marketing," said an ex-Bay employee.

The Bay deal had been the costliest takeover of foreign assets in Canadian history. And it was the Bay takeover, in particular, that raised doubts about Roth's strategy of using takeovers to become an Internet contender almost overnight. Bay was said to have a weak client list. And its chronic failure to speed new products to market suggested that maybe the technology in its new-product pipeline was not very good. "Bay is a handyman's special," griped one Toronto analyst, "and it won't provide Nortel with any decent products to put on the market for at least a year, yet Roth paid a small fortune for it." Ian Angus, a top industry-analyst based near Toronto, doubted that Nortel or any other company could use takeovers to become a powerhouse of Internet technology. "I almost think all tech takeovers are doomed to fail," Angus said. "They so often bring a culture clash between traditional firms in old-line industries with the brash start-ups in the Web world."

Roth had pounced on Bay because he knew he hadn't much time to put Nortel in the vanguard of making the Internet a ubiquitous appliance that people would someday take for granted, like running water. Nortel was in the business of making equipment for transmitting voice messages, and the volume of voice traffic was growing at just 3 per cent a year, while growth in data traffic was something like 30 to 40 per cent per quarter. "It's getting to the point," Roth said, "where who cares about voice?" Since the burgeoning traffic in data was taking place mostly on the Internet, there was a race to deliver the technologies that eliminated the "World Wide Wait" of its infamous bottlenecks and breakdowns. It would be a contest with few winners. Only the firms that played the biggest role in shaping those standards would enjoy the kind of dominance that Bill Gates had reaped from bringing order to the once-chaotic world of personal computing.

He also knew that Nortel had at least one big advantage over Cisco and the other upstarts in the telecommunications field. Unlike those interlopers, Nortel could boast a blue-chip client roster of the world's leading telephone companies, plus scores of major corporate customers. And with its broad array of products and its know-how in systems integration, Nortel was one of the few companies that could design, manufacture, and sell and service an entire network. In the jargon of the industry, that gave Nortel an above-average chance of becoming an "end-to-end" supplier to its customers — providing them with everything from handsets to the room-sized computer switches that dispatched voice and data traffic around the globe — all of it Web-friendly, if Roth's ambitions were realized.

But that holistic advantage would hold only if Nortel could rush to market with technological innovations at a pace that kept it ahead of its rivals. Roth could perhaps be excused for thinking that his only shot at achieving dominance as an Internet player lay with reinventing his company into a unique, and untested, hybrid: a firm with the heft of a telco supplier but infused with the urgency and technological street smarts of Cisco and the other hot firms in data networking. Yet his strategy had an ungainly look to it. "Telco suppliers like Nortel are trying to become supermarkets that offer something of everything — and supermarkets are rarely cutting edge at anything they do," noted Angus.

Roth's peers in the fraternity of telecom suppliers, giant firms such as Siemens, Ericsson and Lucent, were baffled by his ambitions. They had done their best to ignore the tinkerers in Silicon Valley who were designing on-ramps to the "information highway." That was to be expected. The Internet was anathema to veterans of the traditional phone industry, who worshipped at the altar of reliability. They had been ignoring the Internet for years.

The Interent was older than it looked. It was a child of the Cold War, tracing its roots to the creation in 1958 of the Advanced Research Projects Agency (ARPA) by U.S. president Dwight Eisenhower in response to the Russians' triumphant launch of the Sputnik satellite a year earlier. In its mission to spur the Free World exchange of scientific information, ARPA was given $1 million in U.S. government funding to create a computer network that would survive a nuclear attack by automatically routing digital messages to their proper destinations. The early users of the ARPAnet were pen-pal researchers who exchanged notes on a crude network that linked mainframe computers at universities, government agencies and defence installations around the world. The first message between nodes on the ARPAnet was sent on September 2, 1969. That was also the date of the first ARPAnet crash.

The Internet took a quantam leap forward in 1990, when a 35-year-old English physicist named Tim Berners-Lee perfected a set of protocols for addressing and transferring documents on that network, and called his invention the World Wide Web. But 10 years later, the Internet was still in its infancy as a practical means of communication. In 2000, it remained a congeries of old and new technologies. These included everything from fibre-optic pulsing devices that set data zipping along at 1 trillion bits a second across slender strands of glass, to wooden plug-hole switchboards and rusty cross-bar relays that first made their appearance in the 1920s. It was held together by a jerry-built superstructure of venerable telephone trunk lines, glitch-prone switching devices and bug-ridden software. And the databases that Internet "surfers" hoped to access varied from hulking mainframe computers operated by governments, universities and large corporations to PC disk-drives owned by home-based Internet businesses, religious cults and professional UFO sighters.

In the old world of telephone networks, phone utilities that ruled over region- al and national monopolies had sole discretion over how and when to upgrade their systems, invariably with equipment that had been field-tested for five years or more. In the new world of the Internet, every crackpot Edison with a clever idea for a device to access all the world's atmospheric monitoring stations, or a software program for routing Mother's Day greetings around the globe, or a Website for downloading memorable images from the personal archives of Larry Flynt was welcome to simply bolt his invention onto the Internet.

For decades, the Internet had been a primitive grapevine that linked computer databases at universities, government agencies and military institutions. Its sudden, explosive growth in the 1990s resulted from the proliferation of personal comput- ers, by which millions of people around the world could access information from remote databases, and from the perfection of the World Wide Web, a roadmap for locating obscure files in those databases. But the anarchy of free access that inspired the creation of the Internet in the first place continued to define it at the turn of the century, inviting comparisons to the early days of the automobile, whose annals record that the first two vehicles to approach a particular crossroads outside Kansas City managed to crash into each other. Similar pile-ups were a common occurance at the intersections among the roughly 100,000 networks that made up the Internet at the time of Roth's appointment as CEO of Nortel.

After decades of clubby relations with their key customers, the big telco sup- pliers were not especially interested in catering to the thousands of upstart opera- tors of Web-based businesses whose roots in the computer culture, with its casual regard for reliability, made them highly suspect to veterans of the slow-but-sure phone industry. The telcos themselves, including such key Nortel clients as its cor- porate sibling, Bell Canada, and the so-called Baby Bells in the U.S., had invest- ed $1 trillion (U.S.) in traditional switching equipment. It was true that voice transmissions now accounted for just 5 per cent of total traffic on the world's telecommunications networks, thanks to the stupendous increase in data traffic during the 1990s. The dilemma was that the telcos continued to derive four-fifths of their revenues from voice signals, which were carried on secure, industrial- strength pipelines that were costly to maintain. By contrast, the 900-page merger document that made its leisurely way from a law office in Boston to a securities dealer in San Francisco by means of electronic transmission was relegated to a sec- ond-tier system. The cost of sending the document that way was minuscule com- pared to secure voice transmission, but faster than conventional couriers, and that explained the frenzied rush beginning in the mid-1990s to commit reams of data to the electronic post. But that merger document was obliged to traverse a spider's web of new and old and public and private networks as it was slowly transported across the continent, appearing more or less intact on arrival.

The telcos and their equipment suppliers had been struggling with that cost-reward equation for decades. In theory, you could upgrade the telephone system to carry high-quality, high-speed data messages. But who was going to pay for this new railroad?

That was the kind of thinking that sorely tested Roth's considerable patience. He was breaking with his industry's most hallowed traditions in embracing the Internet, but there was little about Roth's manner or appearance that suggested a disturber of the peace. In his mid-50s, Nortel's newest CEO was a quiet man with a folksy grin who could be relied on to give out a great laugh over jokes told at his own expense. In time, Roth would emerge as the most Net-savvy executive in the telecom field, a man whose true contemporaries were said to be the tech zealots in California rather than his fellow CEOs in telecom equipment.

For all that, Roth still derived a good deal of pleasure from a celebrated ability to translate jargon into layman's terms. Casual Fridays posed no challenge for Roth, who easily dressed the part of the weekend farmer mildly anxious to get away to his 20-hectare tree farm in the Caledon Hills north of Toronto, where he lived with his wife and two daughters. ("It's very therapeutic ripping out tree stumps.") A scale model in his office of a fire-engine-red Plymouth Prowler was the one clue to Roth's secret life. At a local raceway, he hit speeds of 160 mph. His predecessors had bonded with clients by capping off a plant tour with preferred seating at a restaurant, theatre or sports stadium. Roth tried to haul clients off to speedways. In the fall of 1998, he managed to put a gang of 40 customers through their paces at Pennsylvania's Pocono Raceway, where they dawdled around the lap at just 90 mph.

He had urged his clients to go faster, particularly in adapting to the Internet. Roth was obsessed with speed. Companies that derive their success from reliable technology tend to make speed a low priority. While Nortel had a deserved reputation for lighting a fire under its engineers, it was still an old-world telephone equipment company. Those who had praised its alacrity in developing new products did so after comparing Nortel with other telco suppliers, which disdained the breakneck pace of innovation in the computer world. In this respect, the fraternity of Nortel, Lucent, Alcatel, Ericsson and Siemens was no less insular than Detroit, where auto executives all lived in the same neighbourhoods, belonged to the same golf clubs, and even wintered together in the same Caribbean sunspots. Truth be told, the California computing scene was little better; its adolescent and testosterone-charged environment was accurately conveyed in the title of Robert X. Cringley's 1992 bestseller, *Accidental Empires: How the Boys of Silicon Valley Make Their Millions, Battle Foreign Competition, and Still Can't Get a Date*. In 2000, Roth's colleagues at Nortel still took the occasional swipe at "Silly Valley," which, among its many failures, had missed the boat on fibre-optics. But Roth loved the place. He resisted some of the Web-head vocabulary, but this is where he picked up terms like Webtone (the name Java crusader Scott McNealy of Sun Microsystems had given one of his prototype products) and Right-Angle Turn, Gates's abject call to arms in 1995 when he confessed to Microsoft's employees up and down the West Coast that he had underestimated the impact of the Internet and that Microsoft would have to reinvent itself quickly in order to recover from his error.

When something new did penetrate their consciousness, Roth noticed, the Valley people were quick to repudiate their own most cherished tenets in order to capture the high ground in an emerging technology. He knew that much from his long tenure at Nortel's R&D arm, Bell-Northern Research, which had a laboratory in Palo Alto, California, dating from 1975. Roth himself had made a career of challenging the engineering and telco culture in which he worked. He shared with hot-shot technicians in California an impatience with "over-engineered" projects that had been designed well beyond the point of perfection, and with those that missed their market altogether for having languished too long in the lab.

Of course, it helped that every time Roth had broken with orthodoxy he had been right. Drawing on his own experience with satellites, he had warned Nortel not to accept an invitation to join the U.S.-based Iridium consortium that was proposing in the late 1980s to build a constellation of telecommunications satellites. (Iridium, the brainchild of Motorola Inc., collapsed in a $5-billion (U.S.) bankruptcy in 2000, and released its 88 satellites to burn up in the Earth's atmosphere.) Conversely, in the early 1990s Roth had urged his skeptical superiors to embrace wireless communications, believing that cellphones were about to graduate from a novelty to a necessity. The wireless episode said something about Nortel's ability to execute on a vision. From a standing start in 1993, the firm managed in less than five years to eclipse all but two of the world's leading makers of cellphone equipment. It even overtook Motorola, which practically invented that business. Long before that episode, it was Roth's knack for spotting a lucrative invention and speeding it to market that won him the presidency of Bell-Northern Research by age 39. The tactics that marked his career ascent at BNR and later at Nortel also happened to be the defining characteristics of the Internet — which were fast-paced innovation, technological breakthroughs, and seemed to have a shelf-life of more than six months.

Roth was a 30-year veteran of the phone industry, and had a scientist's appreciation of the beauty of perfection in engineering design. He did not, however, share the widely held view in his industry that the Internet was the biggest Rube Goldberg contraption ever to heave itself up over the horizon. You could bitch about the Internet's imperfections, but you couldn't deny that it was going to be the transformative event of the early 21st century. Within a decade, Roth was predicting, virtually all telecommunications would take place on the Internet. And so would a huge portion of the world's business transactions. The CEO of Nortel put his faith in studies that said Internet activity would amount to $2.8 trillion (U.S.) by 2003, or 7 per cent of the world economy.

The Internet was changing how the world did business. Major enterprises like J.C. Penney and Citibank were scrambling to transform themselves into Kings of electronic commerce, while Tom Lowe, son of the man who invented Kitty Litter, was going on-line with Praying Manits Inc., a Web-based business that peddled reissued toys from the 1960s. Stephen King, the thriller writer, bypassed his publisher and the bookstores by publishing a ghost-story novella on the Web. What had begun as a cult — people meeting and marrying at Internet "chat rooms" and cybercafés in the mid-1990s — had become a mass-market phenomenon, touching off a *fin de siècle* rush among investors seeking to cash in on the riches sure to be reaped by Internet-related companies. The so-called panic buying of dot com stocks crested in the early months of 2000 — about the time when it was reported that Queen Elizabeth II had made a one-day, $1.4-million (U.S.) killing on Getmapping.com, a firm that posted 3-D aerial maps of her realm on its Web site, and whose stock posted an opening day gain of almost 1,000 per cent.

More ominously, for those who still disputed the Internet's commercial possibilities, Detroit's Big Three automakers were forming an alliance to buy their parts on the Internet; Pratt & Whitney began hawking airplane engines on-line; and Wal-Mart was rushing to put the world's biggest inventory control system on the Web. In an oft-told anecdote, Roth said his epiphany came when he succeeded in using the Web to track down a supplier of glovebox linings for a vintage 1966 Jaguar E-Type he was restoring. The supplier was a four-man operation in England. "I sat there afterward, thinking, 'This is powerful. How could I have found this supplier if the Web didn't exist? This is so powerful that a garage in London can carry out a real-time business transaction with a guy north of Toronto,'" Anybody with a rudimentary $1,000 computer set-up could put up a Web page and go into business flogging stock-market advice or Pez dispenser collectibles on-line. Entrepreneurs who wouldn't dream of competing with the physical branch network of a Bank of America or a Sears Roebuck could blithely go head to head with them on the Internet. "A specialty business like this," said Roth, who also used the Web to buy a 1950s jukebox and a pool table, "now has an inexpensive and easy-to-use channel to a market covering the entire world."

Yes, Internet crashes were still common. All told, various branches of the ungainly system were down for a total of some 88 hours a year in the late 1990s, compared with less than five minutes for the traditional phone system. But the economics of the Internet were irresistible. The new medium was incomparably cheaper and faster than alternative methods of conveying bulky legal documents, elaborate technical blueprints and medical diagnostic images from one point on the globe to another.

The architects of the Internet were making fantastic promises for it, which at first only served to feed the conventional telephone world's sense of disbelief. Innovations in fibre-optics technology, which greatly expanded the capacity of telephone-system trunk lines that carried Internet traffic and vastly improved the quality of signals, opened the door to "convergence." That was the prospect of blending voice, data and video signals, which would be carried at unheard-of speed and volume over the same line with no distortion of their quality. The result was a stunning reduction in the cost of transmission. By the late 1990s, the cost to telephone utilities of transmitting a long-distance call had already been reduced by 99 per cent. By 2001, said the makers of fibre-optic equipment, it would be possible to take all of the voice and data traffic in the U.S. in a given 24-hour period and reduce it to just one second of transmission time. They planned to double this performance in each following year. The public was spellbound by the idea of a global village that was shrinking to a town square. In 2000 there were already 475 million Internet users worldwide, up from 40 million just four years earlier; and the volume of Internet traffic was doubling every 100 days, or tenfold each year. Canadians had a reputation, dating from the 1950s, of being among the most telephone-happy people in the world. It was no different with the Internet. They and the Americans had taken the Internet to heart with equal passion. About 60 per cent of adults in each country reported that they were chronic Internet users — far ahead of the residents in the other G-7 industrial nations, Japan and Britain (33 per cent), Germany (29 per cent), France (22 per cent) and Italy (15 per cent).

It was the breakthroughs in fibre optics, which promised to fuel the E-commerce boom by making the Internet faster and more reliable, that put an abrupt end to the punishment of John Roth. It wasn't a classic turnaround in the financial sense, for in the wake of the Essex House P.R. disaster Nortel had gone on to post 1998 results that surpassed the previous year's record. What happened to Nortel over the next 18 months was the biggest turnaround in perception in Canadian corporate history.

Fibre optics was a phenomenon that historians would later equate with the advent of steam, railways and the telephone. It supplanted Alexander Graham Bell's invention by using light rather than electricity to conduct voice and other signals. The signals travelled across slender strands of glass rather than copper wires. Converted into photons, these signals moved at exceptionally faster speeds than electrons over a copper wire, since they encountered far less resistance travelling over glass. In 2000, one optical fibre could carry 130,000 simultaneous phone calls; hundreds of these fibres were bundled together to form the so-called backbones by which network operators were able to transmit vast amounts of data, voice and video signals around the world at low cost. And researchers were finding ways to divide light wavelengths into a spectrum of colours in order to cram still more signals into each optical fibre. In the closing months of the 20th century, it suddenly was perceived that fibre optics was the silver bullet that sped the progress of E-commerce. Late in 1999, Wall Street got religion about fibre optics, and discovered that Nortel was the world's leading supplier of optical systems that moved voice and data at the speed of light. At which point, it embraced Nortel with the fervour of a convert, and sent its shares soaring to the moon.

There was nothing particularly new about fibre optics, or Canada's leading role in the technology. Alexander Graham Bell had experimented in 1880 with a "photophone," a device for sending sound messages as photons across a sunbeam. The concept's practicality was established after a series of technical breakthroughs: the invention of the laser at Bell Labs in 1958, British scientist Charles Kao's experimental fibre-optic system in 1966; the production of the first glass fibres, each thinner than a human hair, for use in telecommunications by Corning Inc. in 1970; and the success of Kenneth Hill, working in a government-funded lab in Ottawa, in solving the problem of splicing optical lines together in 1975, a technology used by Nortel in its first fibre-optic trials, in Montreal and Toronto, in 1977. Five years later, Nortel built what was then the world's largest fibre-optic network for Saskatchewan Telecommunications. In the early 1980s, it unveiled the industry's first comprehensive range of optical networking products, dubbed Fibre World.

Fibre optics had long been deemed too costly to be commercially viable. But constant refinements in the technology, notably by Nortel and Lucent Technologies, demonstrated its potential to greatly increase the capacity of existing copper phone lines. By the mid 1990s, most of the world's major telephone trunk lines — those that crossed continents, and those that linked continents by undersea cable — had been upgraded to glass fibre. But a nagging problem remained. It was called "the first mile." The miracle of fibre did not extend into urban neighbourhoods or the remote countryside. It stopped at the nearest big transmission station. Fibre-optic lines were still too expensive to run up to every home, school and business, which continued to be linked to the worldwide telecommunications system by old-fashioned copper wire. This was why the condo dweller in Boulder, Colorado taking an Internet tour of the Rijksmuseum in Amsterdam was obliged to wait 20 minutes for her PC to download Rembrandt's *Night Watch*.

The fibre-optics pipelines had been built at fantastic cost by the telcos, and were the preserve of voice signals. Voice was the only market where customers were willing to pay the steep fees, or tariffs, that telcos charged for long-distance calls. By the turn of the century, however, further advances in the technology had reduced transmission costs over fibre-optic networks to ridiculously low levels. A transcontinental trunk line that cost $100,000 in the 1980s could be had for $2.50 in 2000. In the new math of telecommunications, transmission costs kept dropping as more and more signals were crammed into an existing pipeline. Operators of fibre-optics networks now had a powerful incentive to carry as much voice — and data and video — traffic as they could attract.

Meanwhile, of course, the volume of that traffic was soaring, placing enormous burdens on the more primitive components of the communications system. And the junctions where old and new components met, notably the transfer points where analog transmissions were converted into photons, were the scene of bottlenecks. Meanwhile, corporations that were eager to cut costs began to wonder why they needed two sets of wires — one for traditional phone links to the outside world, and another for the in-house networks that companies had been building at a frantic pace ever since the 1980s to link their various operations. It was also now apparent that those internal networks, or "intranets," would have to be plugged into the Internet if they were going to be of any use in the new world of E-commerce.

In 1999, the disruptive event that Roth had been warning of took place. Almost overnight, it seemed, every client of the telecommunications industry — the telcos, TV networks, private corporations, government agencies, Website operators — all began to book passage on the new fibre-optics Internet. Pressure was enormous now for someone to rebuild the Internet and the traditional arteries of the telecommunications network into a fibre-optics superhighway.

Very few firms were in a position to take on this colossal project. One was Cisco, but its expertise was in routing devices for private data networks. It had almost no expertise in fibre optics, although by 2000 it would be scrambling to make up for lost ground. Another was Lucent, which was rich in fibre-optics know-how. But late into the 1990s, it was not an aggressive promoter of optical networking, out of a conviction that there were few commercial applications for the technology. It, too, would soon be playing catch-up. As for Nortel, it had never lost its belief, dating from the 1970s, that fibre optics would ultimately be the dominant technology in global telecommunications.

At several of its R&D labs, and especially in Ottawa — destined to become the world capital of fibre-optics research, and host to the optical-networking labs of Nortel, Nokia, Cisco, JDS Uniphase and Newbridge/Alcatel — Nortel had been working furiously throughout the 1990s to develop "high-performance networks." These were based on higher-capacity glass fibres and ultra-fast lasers for moving signals at ever greater speeds. In a 1995 watershed decision made when he was still second-in-command at Nortel, Roth invested heavily in a super-sophisticated optical system. There was no apparent market for it yet. But someday, Roth was certain, Nortel would be rewarded for being the first on the market with a 1.6 terabit system that could carry 1.6 trillion bits of data per second.

Nortel's periodic breakthroughs in optical networking had attracted little notice outside the tech community. In 1996, it scored an industry first by unveiling a laser device that operated at 10 billion pulses a second, or 10 giga-bits of data, quadrupling the speed of fibre-optics transmission. The industry yawned. It couldn't conceive that the market might someday crave an improve-ment over the current standard of lasers that blinked on and off 2.5 billion times a second.

A few years later, however, there was reason to fear that without a massive increase in cheap, reliable transmission capacity, referred to as "bandwidth," E-commerce would be a stillborn revolution. So the industry paid attention in 1999 when MCI Worldcom Sprint, the giant long-distance phone company, reported that it had completed field-testing of Nortel's 1.6 terabit system — and it worked. With a system that transmitted 1.6 trillion bits per second, a network operator could send the data equivalent of the Library of Congress across the U.S. on a sin-gle strand of glass fibre in just 14 seconds. Nortel immediately vowed to bring a 6.4 terabit product to market by 2001. This was Dick Tracy stuff, except it was real. A 6.4 terabit system would boost the carrying capacity of existing fibre-optics pipelines by a factor of 128,000 times. The cost of transmitting voice and data sig-nals would fall to practically nothing.

Few doubted Nortel's ability to make good on its promise. It had established itself as the standard-setter in ultra-high-speed optical networking, with a 90 per cent share of the global market for 10-gigabit systems. By 2000, Nortel had installed 12 million optical wavelengths, equal to 480 times the circumference of the earth. An estimated 75 per cent of the Internet traffic in North America trav-elled on the heavy-duty "backbones" that Nortel had built for the continent's largest phone companies.

Events moved quickly now. With a two-year lead on its rivals for the most sophisticated optical networking gear, Nortel began to win huge orders in 1999 from major telco clients in North America and Europe, stealing business from both Lucent and Cisco. Nortel's order book also fattened up with contracts to build private networks for corporate, or "enterprise," clients such as Dell Computer, the leading U.S. drugstore chain Walgreen and the British news agency Reuters. In early 2000, Lucent admitted it had not anticipated the sudden switch by its clients to optical equipment, and that its sales had suffered from its inabili-ty to keep up with orders. The CEO of Cisco told a meeting of securities analysts that it was now Nortel, not Lucent, that disturbed his sleep. "I have a lot of respect for John Roth," said Cisco's chief executive, John Chambers. "I just wish he'd retire or go into a different industry."

Wall Street took another look at Nortel and saw a company that relied on its traditional telco clients for only 18 per cent of its revenues, down from 70 per cent just a few years earlier. Nortel now derived most of its revenues from the fastest growing segments of the telecommunications industry. These were from wireless telephone equipment, which it had quickly built into a $4 billion (U.S.) business in the 1990s; optical networking, now a $5.5 billion (U.S.) business that was growing at the rate of 70 per cent a year; and access products, a segment in which Nortel was suddenly booking $1 billion (U.S.) in sales for products that enabled clients to plug into the Internet and other data networks, where business was growing at the rate of 125 per cent a year. As CEO of the only firm with leading technology in both wireless and optical-networking, Roth was uniquely suited to make good on his vow to seize the high ground in the "next next thing," as well: the wireless Internet. Certainly that was Wall Street's view. In 1999, Nortel stock began spiraling upward, roughly quadrupling in price giving the company a stock-market value of $203 billion (U.S.) by June 2000.

After 32 months on the job, Roth had "enhanced shareholder value," as the saying goes, by $176 billion (U.S.). That was a record unmatched in speed by such legends as Jack Welch of General Electric, Michael Eisner of Disney or the late Robert Goizueta of Coca-Cola. For $176 billion (U.S.), Roth could go out and buy General Motors, Sears Roebuck, J. P. Morgan, Nike, Mattel, Quaker Oats, Bethlehem Steel and the entire U.S. airline industry, and still have enough left over to build five new Millennium Domes for London, England.

Instead, Roth bought a string of outfits with unfamiliar names like Aptis, Cambrian, Shasta, Clarify, Qtera, Promatory, Xros and CoreTek. Those firms, many of them start-ups, were going to be subcontractors on the project to rebuild the Internet. With little fanfare, they had been experimenting with arcane devices for connecting traditional networks to an optical Internet, and with exotic accessories like all-optic call centres for direct marketing firms, and all-optic inventory control systems for retailers. One was even working on a gadget that would make copper wires mimic the behaviour of glass fibre.

As an aspiring general contractor, Nortel could have stuck to the task of building the fibre-optics pipelines and the more important pieces of data-networking gear that kept traffic moving through those pipes at the speed of light. But Roth had grander designs. He bought those key subcontractors in order to give Nortel the status of a one-stop shop. Roth was convinced that the upstart local phone operator in, say, Tuscaloosa who was battling the mighty BellSouth Corp. would not want to hire a dozen suppliers to help him conceive a network that had to be up and running in a matter of weeks. Equally important to Roth, there would likely be a profitable cross-pollination among the Web-oriented engineers at the likes of Aptis, Clarify and Xros with his own army of telecom researchers at Nortel. The worldwide shortage of engineers had reached crisis proportions by 2000; the easiest way to gain a competitive edge was to buy the companies that employed them.

And so, with the found money provided by Nortel's soaring stock price, Roth had financed his unprecedented talent raid on the U.S. tech community. Between 1998 and 2000, Roth was able to make several lonely laps around the Monopoly board of optical-networking properties. While Cisco and Lucent were still deciding whether they wanted to play, Roth spent a total of about $18 billion (U.S.) in Nortel stock to snap up some of the best properties on the board. In doing so, Roth was bolstering a company that was already one of the world's top R&D shops, blessed with 20,000 researchers who were collectively filing an average of three patents a day.

Having once headed that R&D operation, Roth knew exactly what Nortel was still lacking in Internet capability, and had a trained engineer's sense of how much to pay for the expertise he was acquiring. By early 2000, he had most of the pieces he wanted. In the meantime, investors had bid up the prices of the remaining fibre-optic boutiques. They anticipated that Cisco and Lucent would follow in Roth's wake. They would not be disappointed. Between the two of them, Cisco and Lucent managed to spend $40 billion (U.S.) in their own buying binge of optical networking firms. Soon it would be Lucent, which paid $25 billion (U.S.) for one company alone (a Bay rival named Ascend Communications), that would be faulted by Wall Street for overpaying on acquisitions. Lucent's CEO, Richard McGinn, insisted that the move was necessary. His firm had been caught napping. But Lucent was now wide awake to the Internet's possibilities, said McGinn, who was vowing that "we intend to lead the networking revolution."

Vindication had come more swiftly and powerfully than Roth had expected. He had, after all, been a novice CEO when the storm of criticism began. It had occurred to him that winning clients, investors and his own employees to his point of view would take time. That was a precious commodity, of course, but he had reason to wonder if he was pushing his change agenda too fast. There had been no calls for the resignation of Robert Scrivener, the last man to reinvent Nortel, some 30 years earlier. But then, Scrivener had directed Nortel's previous transformation from his perch as CEO of Bell Canada, then its parent, which gave him enormous stature as a senior statesman of Canadian business.

As well, Nortel's new CEO was not cut from the same cloth as his predecessors. In Nortel's long history, Roth had been only the second product of Nortel itself to be given the chance to run the company. Since the 1960s, Bell had plucked all of Nortel's CEOs from its own ranks, or imported them from the U.S. The selection of Roth, a Lethbridge, Alberta native, was a signal that Nortel was about to gain its genuine independence. Indeed, less than three years after Roth's appointment, the Bell Canada holding company, BCE Inc., cut its last ties with Nortel by spinning off its remaining Nortel shares. But in 1998, even Roth had to wonder if Nortel was ready to go it alone.

Months after the promulgation of his Webtone strategy in 1997, Roth knew his firm still lacked a sufficient sense of urgency. How could he doubt it, when even the slow-moving telcos were showing more restlessness than his own troops? Roth was troubled by a conversation in 1998 with the CEO of a major U.S. phone company who had button-holed him to complain that none of the old-line telco suppliers was doing anything to solve his Web problems.

Roth handed the Baby Bell's CEO his Webtone memo to Nortel's rank and file. "He said he was at least glad we were moving on it," Roth recalled a while later. "But then he said, 'You know, honestly, Nortel isn't known for data networks.'"

Roth also realized he was asking a lot of his company. You could count on the fingers of two hands the major corporations that had successfully reinvented themselves in recent times — 3M, Hewlett-Packard, a few others. The list of failed attempts — Burroughs, Sperry Rand, DEC, Massey-Ferguson, Monsanto — was endless. Without its lifeline from Bell Canada, Nortel itself might have lasted perhaps a decade after emerging from the womb of Western Electric in the early 1960s, when it was reborn as a company that would have to earn a living from products of its own design.

"Nothing says we'll survive this transformation," Roth had to admit in that difficult autumn of 1998 when his stewardship was being openly questioned. But Roth had seen that he had no choice in the matter. "The transition from traditional switch technology to data networks is a revolution we have to win. We win it or we die."

NORTEL OWES ITS existence to an unlikely midwife. Robert Carlton Scrivener, son of a Bell Canada lineman, was a history and philosophy major at the University of Toronto who had paid his way through school by peddling Bibles door to door. He was a Bell man through and through. That owed something to Providence. His first job after graduation, as a Depression-era Bell Canada telephone operator earning $100 a month, was in Brantford, Ont., not far from the spot where Alexander Graham Bell made history at the homestead of his father, Melville. It owed even more to Scrivener's intense pride in making history himself at Bell Canada.

As he worked his way up the ranks, Scrivener had left every switching station in better shape than what he'd first encountered. And it wasn't long after he was put in charge of the massive Montreal traffic department that his superiors were able to report that Scrivener's latest bailiwick was the most efficient switching centre in the entire Bell System, as the North American phone grid was then known.

Scrivener was a generalist. It is a wonder that no business school is named for him; he so perfectly represents the business-school ideal of the multifunctional manager, a species that rarely flourishes off campus.

Scrivener was Bell Canada's first advertising manager, in 1946. The appointment had amused him. He knew nothing, he said, about marketing. Much later, by following Scrivener's dictate that R&D be driven by the imperatives of marketing, Nortel was able to wrestle business away from AT&T's Western Electric division on its home turf in the U.S. When he became Bell Canada's chief financial officer, with responsibility for overseeing the utility's worrisome investment in what was then called Northern Electric, Scrivener declared with some pride that "I don't know the difference between a bond and a debenture." Yet it was Scrivener who in 1973 arranged one of the biggest initial public offerings in Canada to that point, selling off a chunk of Bell Canada's stake in Nortel to give the subsidiary its first taste of semi-autonomy — and, more to the point — self-reliance. "You're talking to a guy who wouldn't know a software if I tripped over it," said the father of Bell-Northern Research (BNR). He had insisted on that fractious 1971 mating in the belief that world-class products would emerge from Nortel only if its engineers, who were trained in designing and manufacturing them, were forced to work with the Bell Canada engineers who had to make them work in the field. With his constant scrutiny of its budgets, and exhortations that it stay a jump ahead of what the market was currently asking for, Scrivener nurtured BNR into the centrepiece of Canada's research community, and one of the most important R&D organizations in the world.

The partnership among Bell Canada, Nortel and BNR, similar to the relationship among AT&T, Western Electric and Bell Laboratories but otherwise unique in the industry, would prove to be a great selling point with buyers of telecom equipment around the globe. Many of them had never heard of Nortel. But they knew about Bell Canada, which from the 1960s onward was recognized as probably the world's best-run telco.

In 1968, Scrivener gave one of those speeches every CEO dreads having to make, and most audiences are loath to hear — a talk about future developments in his industry. The speech was forgotten and now gathers dust at the Bell archives in Montreal.

"There are lots of things that you don't think of doing now," Scrivener told a gathering of the Ad and Sales Club of Windsor, Ontario, "but when they're available, you will want to do them — certainly the kinds of things that are involved in 'home computers,' which will be the appliances of tomorrow." This was 14 years before Steve Jobs and Steve Wozniack would lift the veil on the era of personal, or "home," computers with the Apple II.

"The more stuff you can crowd on the network, the less costly it is per unit of information transmitted," Scrivener continued. He was given in these years to describing himself as the owner of Canada's two largest copper mines, by which he meant the tangle of telephone wires under the streets of those cities. The best way to exploit those assets, Scrivener liked to explain, would be to transmit ever increasing amounts of computer data over upgraded voice networks — "an almost infinite mass of data," he said in Windsor, "at almost infinite speed." The challenge for companies

like Bell Canada and its Nortel affiliate, Scrivener insisted, was "to provide an electronic highway on demand, available for any kind of message anywhere, anytime."

Twenty-one years later, a Tennessee politician with presidential ambitions
would step into the well of the U.S. Senate and beg his colleagues for federal funding to put his country on the map in fibre optics, a technology that was essential
to the construction of something he was dubbing the "information superhighway." But Al Gore was speaking to a near-empty chamber. It would be another six
years before Amazon.com would go on-line in 1995. And for the first 36 months
of that experiment, it was widely expected to fail.

In the early 1970s, Scrivener was anticipating a day when people would shop
by computer and use their phone at the office to turn on the oven at home. Even
then, when his duties were still divided between Bell Canada and Nortel, his conversation was flavoured with terms picked up in the BNR labs. The "wired city"
and "convergence" were among his favourites. Scrivener had no training in applied
research. But he was fascinated by gadgets, and in particular with anything that
might help him ratchet up the profits at Bell.

Scrivener ruled — and that was the only word for it; Bell Canada was more
rigidly hierarchical than the Vatican — from a regal aerie in the old Bell Canada
tower in Montreal. The man who greeted visitors as they stepped off the elevator
at the 19th floor of 1050 Beaver Hall Hill was a trim six-footer with an aristocratic
nose, thick hornrims, a slight moustache and a forcefully confident manner. The
very picture, in other words, of corporate orthodoxy. The giveaway that Scrivener's
enormous, wood-panelled office was the lair of a would-be mad scientist was the
collection of techno-toys he kept there. Amid the clouds of smoke from Scrivener's
ever-present cigarettes and occasional Royal Jamaican cigars was a sort of World's
Fair of futuristic communications devices.

"Here, look at this." Scrivener would stride across what seemed like an acre of thick
green Wilton carpeting to the "Picturephone" beside his immense desk. He'd push a
button on this mini-TV-phone, and his own face appeared on the screen. Scrivener
would adjust his tie, then jab another button and wait for the face of some remote minion to pop up. "I can talk with and see people in our building and quite a few fellows
in other offices in the city," he'd say matter-of-factly, as if the only marvel to the
Picturephone was that it had not yet been installed in every other CEO's office in the
land. "And I can televise anything on my desk — papers, drawings, books."

"And here, look at this." Now he was holding a sketch of a tiny portable
phone that was under development at BNR. It was to be worn like a wristwatch.
By means of radio-phones, traditional touch-tone phones, TV consoles and
devices not yet imagined, people would someday be accessing data in revolutionary ways, Scrivener said. And "all merchandising in stores will be done by
TV, and work will be taken to the people instead of their coming into shops and
offices. Can you imagine what that will do to public transportation?"

Thirty years later, telecommuting would be in full swing, although the Picturephone would be abandoned and the wristwatch device for accessing the Internet would still be in development. Scrivener would have been surprised about that. In the late 1960s, he was convinced that the inventions in his office were destined to become commonplace appliances, and that Nortel would be at the forefront of perfecting them. "There isn't anything any other manufacturer in the world can do better than we can," he would insist.

Yet only a decade earlier, Scrivener's views had been more in tune with the branch-plant mentality that afflicted most of his peers. Canada had emerged from World War II as the fourth-largest industrial power on earth. But its factories that had geared up for war production, and which later fed the Baby Boom demand for consumer goods, were for the most part foreign-owned. Entire sectors of the economy — autos, aerospace, packaged foods and toiletries, electrical products, and computing devices — were almost entirely directed by absentee owners in the U.S. and Europe. The Canadians who worked in these fields used imported capital and machinery to manufacture goods according to imported designs. Only the shop-floor labour and some of the managers were of domestic origin. Nortel had been no different. For the first 66 years of its life both it and Bell Canada had been controlled by AT&T. And until the early 1960s, the product specifications that Nortel worked from were supplied by AT&T's manufacturing and research arms, Western Electric and Bell Laboratories, respectively. Yet Nortel was better equipped to shape its own destiny than is commonly assumed.

In 2000, Nortel was often described as a century-old firm whose history was packed into the last 30 years, dating from its fateful break with AT&T. That was true, but not quite accurate. Long before trustbusters in the U.S. forced AT&T to shed its foreign operations, its Northern Electric affiliate had become one of the most prodigious manufacturers on the continent.

Nortel, nearly as old as telephone itself, began life as a tiny cog in one of the greatest industrial organizations in history. This was the Bell System, conceived in the early 1880s by Theodore J. Vail. The father of what was to become the world's largest corporation had pioneered a system for rapid mail delivery at the Union Pacific Railroad. He was then recruited to fix a troubled National Bell Telephone Co. in Boston. There his goal was to create a vertically integrated monopoly that would bring order to the chaotic early days of telephony, and supplant the telegraph as the new dominant form of communications. What made Vail a genius was his realization that the telephone was a useless toy without a network. Which, of course, was the same story for the first steam locomotives, which sat idle for want of rails to run on; or the balkanized world of personal computing pre-Microsoft, when the incompatibility of rival operating systems kept PC users from joining a global conversation that would gradually evolve into the Internet.

Beginning in 1878, Vail's National Bell, reorganized a few years later as the American Telephone and Telegraph Co., sought to impose uniformity in the fledgling field of telephony. It gobbled up rival phone companies in the U.S. and Canada. And it gained a captive supplier of telephone equipment in 1882, when Vail bought Chicago's Western Electric Co. from the robber baron Jay Gould in order to deprive Vail's chief rival, telegraph giant Western Union, of its most important source of equipment. What soon emerged from Vail's conception was a transcontinental system where the technology, mode of service and the tariffs were all determined by just one company — Ma Bell. For, as Vail had bluntly explained, "There can be no competition."

The actual inventor of the telephone had no interest in exploiting it for financial gain. The speech therapist from Edinburgh who first succeeded in transmitting a voice signal in his Boston lab at age 27 was a beneficiary of convergence — in this case, by manipulating the emerging technologies of the telegraph, microphone and loudspeaker. In Boston in 1875, Alexander Graham Bell had sent a sound message electrically over a wire to his assistant, Thomas A. Watson, in the next room. Fourteen months later, at the Brantford, Ontario, home of his father, Alexander Melville Bell, the young man then perfected long-distance telephony — and thus revealed its commercial possibilities — by placing a call over a telegraph wire to Paris, some 13 kilometres away. But he promptly sold the U.S. rights to his patent to Boston's National Bell, gave the Canadian rights to his father, and moved on to other fields. At his beloved summer home near Baddeck, Nova Scotia, A.G. Bell experimented with mechanical kites, launched Canada's first aircraft manufacturing enterprise, and recruited to his Aerial Experiment Association a local man named J. A. D. McCurdy, who would make the first powered flight in the British Empire in 1909. Bell's father, meanwhile, secured a federal charter from Canada's young parliament for the Bell Telephone Co. of Canada in 1880. But by then he had already sold the Canadian rights to his son's most famous invention to National Bell, having failed to find a buyer in Canada. Melville Bell then turned to such pursuits as helping to direct the affairs of a new scientific organization in Washington, D.C., called the National Geographic Society.

Vail moved swiftly to consolidate the nascent Bell System's hold on telephony. He dispatched to Montreal a dynamic organizer named Charles Fleetford Sise, an insurance company executive, former Confederate soldier and confidant of the Confederate president, Jefferson Davis, who was then languishing in self-imposed exile in Canada. Technology took a decided back seat to monopolistic considerations in Sise's early strivings. In his first year, he spent nine times more money on buying up Canada's four largest telephone companies than he did on stringing phone lines. In contrast to Vail's coast-to-coast empire building south of the border, however, Sise would fail to extend the Bell System's reach beyond

Ontario and Quebec. The undercapitalized Bell Canada lacked sufficient funds to entice phone operators in the Maritimes and B.C. to sell their firms; and the Western provinces of Alberta, Saskatchewan and Manitoba opted to create state-owned utilities as an expression of regional sovereignty. This apparent setback would ultimately prove a blessing to Nortel. It would get an early taste in competitive bidding for the business of the New Brunswick Telephone Co., Alberta Government Telephones and the like, while for the next century Western Electric would luxuriate in its protected status as the exclusive supplier to 85 per cent of the U.S. telephone system.

The creation of Nortel itself arose from an even more fortuitous disappointment for Sise. He would have preferred, naturally, to buy his equipment from the suppliers that Vail was gobbling up in the U.S. But the young parliament in Ottawa had stipulated it would not protect the firm's Canadian patents unless its phones were made in Canada. Sise therefore set up a Mechanical Department for Bell Canada in 1881, which turned out its first products the following year with a payroll numbering 13 employees. Given the small size of Bell Canada's Central Canadian market, the soon-to-be-rechristened Northern Electric and Manufacturing Co. would be obliged not only to seek business among Canada's other telephone companies, but to become adept at turning out an astonishing variety of products that were unrelated to the telephone.

In a patent-exchange arrangement that began in 1913 and was to last for the next 43 years, Nortel made telephone equipment from designs supplied by its Western Electric sibling. But it also made the police- and fire-alarm call boxes found on Canadian street corners, and the first gramophones and vacuum tubes made in Canada. At its new Shearer Street factory in Montreal, destined to become a one-million-square-foot facility and opened in 1914, the year of Robert Scrivener's birth, Nortel launched a radio transmitter in 1923 that broadcast Sunday services and weekday music programs in order to promote its new line of radio sets. Six years later, Nortel installed the British Empire's first "talkie" moving-picture system at the Palace Theatre in Montreal. Inevitably, Nortel was a major arms supplier in both of the century's world wars, turning out 12,000 shrapnel shells a week in the first global conflict, and electronic gear for Lancaster bombers, Russian tanks and Canadian naval destroyers in World War II — plus magnetron tubes for the radar devices that played a conspicuous role in enabling the RAF to prevail in the Battle of Britain.

The unprecedented prosperity triggered by the postwar Baby Boom stoked Nortel's ambitions. Its "Baby Champ" radio sets, at $25 each, became a fixture in hundreds of thousands of Canadian homes, and encouraged Nortel to try its hand with TV sets, Northern-Hammond organs, two-way police radios for patrol cars, and a pioneering traffic-light control system that was one of the first of its kind to automatically change lights in response to traffic volumes. By the 1960s, Nortel was proving its manufacturing proficiency by taking on contracts to supply components for the Anik satellite that beamed signals into Canada's Far North; to build the world's largest video-switching system for the CBS studios in New York; to provide the U.S. Navy with submarine cable for a deep-water testing site in New York State's Finger Lakes district; and to supply Costa Rica with 30,000 telephone sets that had been specially designed to guard against insects and volcanic dust.

That picture of health was somewhat misleading, however. Nortel was still reliant on imported technology. Its police radios were designed in Chicago (by Motorola), the tubes in its TV sets came from New York (RCA), and on the Anik project it had been a humble subcontractor to a firm based in Texas (Hughes). And for all its cultivation of clients in a multitude of fields, Nortel still derived more than 60 per cent of its sales from a single customer, Bell Canada, which it was supplying with a million telephones a year. Those phones and the other equipment that Nortel made for its principal client were, of course, designed by AT&T.

That explained why for 10 years, beginning in the late 1940s, executives at Bell Canada and Nortel had grown increasingly anxious as they monitored a watershed confrontation between AT&T and a U.S. Justice Department that didn't share Theodore Vail's enthusiasm for monopolies. The American trustbusters had just smashed the Hollywood studio system, which was made to relinquish its stranglehold on neighbourhood theatres; and, in a contest of wills that had implications for Canada, they had forced Pittsburgh-based Alcoa to spin off Alcan Aluminum Ltd. There was no stopping the eager federal attorneys in D.C., who soon had GM and IBM in their sights, as well. In 1956, AT&T counted itself lucky in striking a compromise. It could keep its local phone companies along with Western Electric and Bell Labs, provided that it withdraw from all non-U.S. markets. By a quirk of history, bureaucrats in the U.S. capital had just laid the foundation for a Canadian-owned high-tech industry, and, ultimately, for the first serious challenge to Western Electric's dominance of its home market.

All of that was in the unforeseeable future, of course. For the moment, Bell Canada's investment in Nortel, which it had co-owned with Western Electric, appeared to be of a wasting asset. Nortel in the 1950s was a sclerotic, high-cost operation that lacked significant expertise in marketing, export sales and product innovation. It had scarcely any R&D capabilities of its own, and was about to be cut off from one of the greatest research organizations in history. Since its founding in 1925, Bell Laboratories had filed an average of a patent a day. In the 20th century, Bell Labs had nurtured more Nobel Prize winners in scientific disciplines (11) than Canada could boast in all realms of human endeavour. Those researchers had spearheaded some of the most important technological developments of the century. These included the laser, the electronic transistor, the semiconductor, fibre optics, stereo sound, the touch-tone phone, the UNIX computer operating system (the standard for Internet hardware) and the computer language C++ (used in Microsoft's Windows, Netscape Navigator and almost every other piece of commercial software). For some 40 years, Nortel had enjoyed exclusive use of that research in the Canadian market.

To be sure, the break with AT&T would not be abrupt. For a decade after the split up, as AT&T sold off most of its shares in its northern affiliates (it shed its last Bell Canada shares in 1975), Nortel would still have access to blueprints from Western Electric and Bell Labs. But under terms of the consent decree that AT&T signed with the U.S. Government, AT&T was now required to make its technology licences available to all comers. Over time, Nortel would find itself paying steadily more money for steadily less access to AT&T's research treasures.

In 1962, Bell Canada had handed the task of deciding what to do about Nortel to its new vice-president of finance, who was asked to prepare a study on its future prospects. That could have been the death knell for Nortel. Robert Scrivener's recommendations were sure to be acted upon; Bell's directors admired him as a problem-solver. And Scrivener did not admire Nortel, which he regarded as a managerial backwater.

Scrivener had impeccable credentials in the business that Bell Canada cared most about, which at the time was not Nortel, but the phone system. During the crazy postwar years of unprecedented — and wholly unanticipated — demand for basic phone service, Scrivener was the man who had walked into the besieged Toronto traffic department and cleaned up a backlog of more than 20,000 unfilled phone orders in a matter of weeks. His response to Hurricane Hazel in 1954 had been to bring a cot to work on the first day of the crisis and maintain his residence at the central Toronto switching centre for a week until phone service was restored to every last customer. "It burned my behind to find that Bell Canada was not able to beat those Bell System operations" in the U.S., Scrivener would say. "We used to make excuses for why the Canadian system was too different to be able to compete with the U.S. phone companies. It was a kind of psychosis, and I fought it and we eradicated it, finally, until we were on top by any measure — quality of service, reliability, cost control, profitability." Under his direction, Bell Canada's efficiency rose to the point where its rates for phone service were the cheapest in the world. He liked to recall a civil-defence exercise prompted by the Cuban missile crisis in 1962, in which a simulated nuclear attack on southern Ontario and Quebec wiped out 15 major cities. Scrivener's proudest boast was that "we still had 60 per cent survivability in the communications network."

He was also a renegade. Early in his stint at a remote switching facility, Scriviner had told a fellow employee that it was the most poorly laid-out, ass-backward operation he'd ever seen. Scrivener was unaware that he was addressing his new boss, a vice-president, no less, who had personally designed the appalling setup. The station was totally rebuilt, however; Scrivener was promoted, and he maintained a lifelong friendship with the hapless vice-president. Later in his career, Scrivener was a legendary presence at summits of fellow Bell System executives in the U.S., where he would suggest that Vail's monopoly vision was becoming a brake on innovation. This was a decade or so before AT&T was stripped of its local phone companies, when both it and its "Baby Bell" spinoffs were also deprived of the sheltering umbrella of regulated rates and monopolistic barriers to competition. In the aftermath, AT&T and the Baby Bells would indeed prove to be ill-prepared to protect their markets from innovative upstart providers of local and long-distance phone service. In the 1950s and 1960s, Scrivener's doubts about AT&T's competitive prospects did not, however, diminish his respect for the virtues of monopoly dominance. Scrivener was proving his mettle as a consolidator, having negotiated the deals by which Bell Canada gained control of telephone utilities in Atlantic Canada. This phase of Scrivener's career in corporate finance had culminated in the task of repatriating Western Electric's remaining shares in Nortel. In his mind, at least, that inauspicious start to Scrivener's 20-year association with Nortel was not an event worthy of celebration.

If Scrivener did not exactly hate Nortel in the early 1960s, this wasn't clear to anyone within earshot of the man in charge of determining its fate. Even before he was given the unhappy job of sizing up Nortel's prospects, "I had begun to study their financial statements," said Scrivener, who was confounded by Nortel's inability to turn a decent profit. "Each of those statements fed my growing sense of horror. They couldn't get their costs under control."

Bell Canada had pumped about $50 million into Nortel to keep it viable, and was getting no return on its investment. In Scrivener's estimation, Bell Canada had just acquired 100 per cent of a "clunker" in Nortel. "I recall some speeches being made at that time about, 'Hooray, independence has arrived.' Then Northern proceeded to fall flat on its face — the earnings just went right downhill." There was no mystery to that. Everything about Nortel seemed to offend Scrivener's sense of proper management principles. "It simply wasn't an up-to-date, hard-hitting, efficient, well-run manufacturing company. It was a hot-house plant, a company that was run by engineers for one customer." And that customer-owner had run out of patience. "It was clear," said Scrivener, "that we would have to fix Northern or get rid of it."

Ridding itself of Nortel was a tempting proposition. The two firms were barely on speaking terms, relations had become so miserable. Nortel was of dubious value without Western Electric's technology. But "the Japanese, Swedes and Americans, all of them would have been delighted to buy it, and get their foot in the door in Canada," said Scrivener. His frustration had stopped just short of recommending that Bell Canada itself stop buying from Nortel to make it get its costs in line. If Nortel didn't make sense as a stand-alone entity, it might still work as a branch plant for NEC, Ericsson or International Telephone & Telegraph (ITT).

A number of factors worked to spare Nortel of that fate. These were the days before rampant outsourcing. Bell Canada had to think hard about the consequences of rupturing an 80-year association with a captive supplier that had grown up with Bell and had an intimate knowledge of its requirements. There was also the political fall-out to consider at a time of rising economic nationalism in Canada. By the early 1960s, Nortel was one of Canada's largest employers, with a workforce of 13,000 people. And it was beginning to score some modest hits with products of its own design.

Those had resulted from Nortel's first serious R&D effort. Two years after the landmark consent decree, a four-man research shop had been set up in Nortel's Belleville plant. Over the next few years, it migrated to Ottawa, in order to be close to the government-financed National Research Council, and by 1961 Nortel was employing 42 engineering researchers in the nation's capital. Forty years later, Nortel would boast a bigger geographic "footprint" than Lucent, Siemens, Ericsson or any of its other competitors, with remote outposts that sucked up engineering and software talent in places like Vienna, Bombay and Ho Chi Minh City. But in 2000, Ottawa would remain the heart of Nortel's R&D empire, home to the single largest concentration of its researchers — or about 8,000 of the firm's worldwide research staff of 25,000 people.

The pioneers in Ottawa first made their mark with a product that exploited an opportunity created by the break with AT&T. The SA-1 was a community branch exchange that catered to the needs of small towns, a market that Western Electric had ignored. That precedent, established with the first switching system to be designed by Nortel, was to be repeated on a larger scale over the coming years, as Nortel sought to get a step ahead of the market in digital swtiching, fibre optics and other technologies that its former sibling would prove slow to exploit. Another coup resulted from Nortel's decision in 1966 to hire a newly graduated industrial designer named John Tyson as its first full-time designer. Knowing nothing about telephones, Tyson set out to design one that didn't look like its homely, any-colour-you-want-as-long-as-it's-black predecessors. After rejecting names suggested by colleagues (Tinkerbell, Expophone), Tyson, then just 26, settled on Contempra for his stylish invention. Thousands of Canadians, it turned out, were willing to add $1.75 to their monthly phone bill in order to obtain a telephone designed in Canada, the first since the one Alexander Graham Bell had experimented with 92 years earlier, and available in mauve, bright red, deep blue and many other colours. In the dozen or so years following its 1968 launch, the Contempra sold 3.25 million units in 15 countries, and was exhibited at New York's Museum of Modern Art.

Encouraged by those successes, Scrivener, who ascended to the Bell Canada presidency in 1968, committed Bell to fixing Nortel rather than dumping it. And he gave the go-ahead for a much more ambitious Nortel project. With its second switching product, Nortel would be competing against an AT&T switch that was too large and costly for rural service in Canada. Nortel's SP-1 switch, with an affordable selling price of between $1.5 million and $2.5 million, was destined also to be popular with the 1,500 or so small independent phone companies in the U.S. that comprised the 15 per cent of the industry not owned by AT&T, giving Nortel a flagship product for its first significant foray into the world's biggest market. The SP-1 was a hybrid, the first switch to combine traditional electromechanical technology with software design and leading-edge microcircuitry. It took Nortel's researchers several notches up the learning curve. Its semi-computerized control system would enable phone companies to profit from selling their customers such features as speed-calling, call-forwarding, call-waiting and three-way calling. The SP-1 also marked the first stage in the minaturization of telephone branch exchanges. In the 1960s, no small town in Ontario and Quebec was without its discreet Bell building, filled with enormous racks of clacking relays that consumed huge amounts of power. In 1998, Bell Canada announced that it was selling off scores of such buildings. Now that entire switching systems could be fit onto a few silicon chips, Bell Canada could finally get out of the real-estate business.

But again, the revolutionary impact of computerized switching was discernible in the 1960s to just a handful of techno-savants. Few of whom, apparently, toiled in the executive ranks at Nortel. Scrivener would have fits over the SP-1 and its successor, the SL-1 (for stored logic). Not because of its enormous development cost of $91 million — a bet-the-company proposition for a company the size of Nortel, with sales of just $300 million or so. The thing that kept Scrivener in a constant stage of agitation was Nortel's stubborn reluctance to embrace the new technology.

The SP-1 was based on a revolutionary Western Electric design dubbed the "ESS." As the date approached for the expiry of Nortel's patent-exchange arrangement with Western Electric, Scrivener had succeeded only after much effort in pressuring Nortel to select the promising "ESS" switch as its last proprietary licence from Western Electric. The ESS was a technological marvel. It was the world's first switch to use a stored program (SP), or software, to manipulate its mechanical relays, and was Bell Labs' costliest project to date. It was also a big product designed to handle a large amount of traffic, and Scrivener had to badger Nortel some more to re-engineer it into a smaller product to serve a niche market. "We couldn't just have a 'me-too' product to Western, because Western was geared to mass production," Scrivener said. "To make it in the States, to get people to know us, we needed a product that was different, and was superior to the next guy's."

Nortel didn't see it that way at first, and gave the SP-1 low priority. Even after the first one was installed by Bell at the Expo '67 world's fair in Montreal, Nortel's engineers, trained in mechanical design and not the brave new world of software and semi-conductors, were slow to grasp that they had gained a potential head start in the emerging technology of computer-controlled switching. They were also wildly unfocused, still trying to design everything for everyone.

That was no surprise, given Nortel's can-do heritage of turning out everything from sleigh bells to 5,000 different types of wire and cable. But Bell Canada, which was paying the bills, could no longer afford that scattershot approach. "R&D consumes dollars like a child eats toffees in a candy factory," noted Scrivener, who was coming to the conclusion that R&D was too important to be entrusted to Nortel. Its engineers had needed Bell's engineers to explain to them why the ESS had to be modified. Nortel was guilty of "letting long-haired guys in white coats just run around and talk with themselves," Scrivener complained. "I want to say to them, 'What can you *sell?* Design that. What can you sell in five or ten years' time? Design that. Design it from the beginning for low-cost production, using new technology. And start thinking now about how you're going to market it, otherwise you'll end up designing the wrong thing."

Scrivener settled on a radical approach for breaking bad habits in R&D. His solution, in 1971, was to launch Bell-Northern Research as a pooling of Bell's and Nortel's research talent. There were "loud screams" from Bell as he poached some of its best engineers. More screams from Northern, since BNR was to function outside its manufacturing culture. To head this unorthodox outfit, Scrivener repatriated from Bell Labs a Torontonian named Donald Chisholm, an electrical engineer and PhD in physics. The new hire didn't have long hair — he was a bearded bear of a man with a balding pate — but he eschewed the title "Dr." and was very sharp. He struck most people of his acquaintance as the most brilliant man they'd ever met.

This eccentric technological guru had been directing AT&T's contributions to NASA's Apollo manned space program. He brought to Ottawa a touch of the zaniness that was soon to characterize the technology patch in Silicon Valley. In case anyone doubted the mood of creative informality he meant to establish, Chisholm took employees' children on hot-air balloon rides, taught his staffers how to bunny hop, and arranged for the Grenadier Guards to march through the BNR facility to startle the troops. He also set a goal to create a northern version of Bell Labs. To that end, Chisholm promptly set up additional R&D centres at five other Nortel plants in Ontario and Quebec. And he imposed a fiscal discipline by requiring that each product group fund R&D from its own budget. The first-year budget of BNR itself, at $36 million (U.S.), would seem trifling from the perspective of 2000, when Nortel's R&D spending was to hit $2.5 billion (U.S.). But it was big enough to meet the payroll of what was already one of Canada's biggest private research operations, whose 1,800 scientists and engineers included 55 staff members with doctorates. Among the latter, the bearded, sandal-shod Chisholm was a conspicuous rebuke of Bell's conformist tradition. Yet the suits at Bell revered him. He was, said Scrivener's second-in-command at Bell, Walter F. Light, "the man who had the knack for knowing not just where today's technologies are but where tomorrow's technologies are going."

Scrivener was still in need of someone of Chisholm's ability to streamline Nortel's manufacturing side, and turn it into a nimble, low-cost operation. He was sobered by the bureaucratic paralysis at Western Electric, which often kept it from exploiting the most promising technologies in its own grasp. His greatest fear was that Nortel, already a flat-footed organization, would take on still more deadwood as it achieved the heady growth targets he had set for it. "The management problems in the monolithic firm are absolutely horrendous, because you can protect all kinds of dodos," Scrivener said. "We needed someone who didn't share Nortel's paternalistic mindset to clear out a whole lot of people who were really just taking in one another's laundry."

Scrivener's search led him to another outsider. John C. Lobb, who came on board as Nortel's CEO six months after Chisholm cut the ribbon on opening-day at BNR, had been Harold Geneen's takeover strategist during ITT's glory days as a voracious conglomerate, and had then pulled off a dazzling turnaround at a rust-belt manufacturer, Pittsburgh's Crucible Steel Co. At Nortel, Lobb turned each product into a profit centre with bottom-line responsibilities, and soon gained renown for asking plant-floor workers what they were making. Woe betide the hapless factory hand who replied "circuit boards." Lobb would boom: "We make *profits*, not circuit boards." He had a Churchillian resolve and was alleged to possess a sense of humour, but was intensely disliked in many quarters. None more so than the executive suite, where he was estimated to have axed all but two of the factotums who briefly toiled at his side over his six-year reign.

Scrivener had been imploring Nortel to adopt a no-excuses approach to quality and low-cost production, which he expressed as "BIG targets" — for "Best in the Industry Goals." But he had been doing so from the remove of Bell headquarters. Lobb, closer to the action, made failure to adhere to big goals a firing offence. In doing so, he managed to boost productivity by 60 per cent. Sales in his first year almost doubled, to more than $700 million (U.S.), and profits nearly trebled, to $12 million (U.S.). And they were to continue soaring as Lobb used the SP-1 to lead Nortel's charge into the U.S. market, where there were more than 1,500 small independent telephone companies outside the Bell System. The SP-1 was a winner. "It wasn't the first electronic switch in the world," said a top Nortel executive, recalling the dozen or so firms that were suddenly rushing to compete with Nortel in the niche it had identified. "But it was the first damn one that worked."

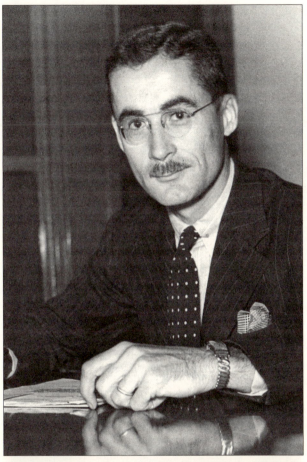

Robert Scrivener (top), father of the modern Nortel Networks, was the veteran telephone utility executive who decided to revive Bell Canada's flagging equipment arm rather than abandon it after its umbilical cord with AT&T was fatefully cut in the 1960s. With his huge investments in R&D and his own credibility as the CEO of one of the world's best-run phone companies, Scrivener was able to persuade other phone utilities around the world to embrace Nortel's new status as a firm that designed its own products. In the late 1960s, a prescient Scrivener committed Nortel "to provide an electronic highway on demand, available for any kind of message, anywhere, anytime." Like Scrivener, John Roth (bottom) sought to reinvent Nortel, this time as a leader in Internet technology. For his pains, the neophyte CEO was initially scorned on Bay Street for venturing into unknown territory in what seemed like a desperate bid to bring Silicon Valley urgency to a firm that was 102 years old when Roth took the helm in 1997.

Nortel's first major factory (above), on Shearer Street in Montreal, was an industrial landmark that turned out everything from sleigh bells to police call-boxes on city street corners. By the 1990s, Nortel's future was tied to signals on slender strands of glass (left) rather than old-fashioned copper wire. Thanks largely to Nortel's enormous R&D presence in Ottawa (below), the city by 2000 was a world capital of the optical-networking technology that Roth was using to build a second-generation Internet that would be more reliable and easier to use than the current version.

CEO Walter Light (below, centre), Nortel's globe-trotting supersalesman in the 1970s and 1980s, helped identify Roth (below, left) as a rising star when the young engineer was running Nortel's R&D operation. With his solid credentials in R&D, Roth was later able to turn Nortel's engineering culture on its head, demanding that research projects be scrapped unless they could be quickly translated into marketable products — and profits. By 2000, Roth was recognized as the most Internet savvy CEO in the telecom world. His peers in computing, from Bill Gates to Carly Fiorina (above), the newly appointed CEO of Silicon Valley icon Hewlett-Packard Co., were making pilgrimages to Roth's office in Brampton, Ont. to strike joint venture partnerships with the Canadian giant in new-age networking.

Lobb wasn't a slash-and-burn artist. His sharp marketing instincts got Nortel's foot in the door south of the border. And his commitment to R&D saw Nortel's reliance on imported designs fall from 80 per cent to 10 per cent between 1960 and 1970. He chewed up managers, but promoted from within, and when he left, three-quarters of Nortel's top managers were folks who had been there before he arrived. Best of all for Scrivener, Nortel under Lobb was at last headed by a kindred spirit. Scrivener was still seething over Nortel's rejection of a set of sales objectives he'd presented to its stone-faced executives. "I was told they were impossible," Scrivener recalled. "Later, I showed them to Lobb. No problem, he said, we'll be there by 1974. We were talking exactly the same language." But to Scrivener's chagrin, Lobb would always be remembered as a tyrant, albeit a necessary one. Not until the mid-1980s would Western Electric get around to conducting a similar shake-up, eliminating several layers of management. And by that time, the future Lucent had lost considerable market share to Nortel on its home ground.

Increasingly, the language spoken by Scrivener and Lobb was of a disruptive new technology called fully digital switching. This was a dagger pointed at Nortel's new product line of hybrid switches. The SP-1 family was destined to reap $900 million in revenues, more than 10 times its development costs. No one knew that in 1970, however, when a joint task force of Bell and Nortel engineers led by Don Chisholm warned Scrivener about rapid advances in software and large-scale integrated circuits (the exotic new field of "molelectronics," or molecular electronics, as it was then called). This revolution on the horizon would make the SP-1 obsolete by 1980, shaving five years off its life expectancy. Or so Chisholm was insisting. AT&T and Nortel's other major competitors thought otherwise. They disputed the practicality of fully computerized switching systems. But Scrivener's engineers thought all-digital was the future because it heralded a vast improvement in performance and a reduction in maintenance costs over the existing technology. Meanwhile, the bet-the-company SP-1 was still a year away from hitting the market. Just the same, Scrivener endorsed his own engineers' assessment. In doing so, he committed Nortel to developing a product line of untested market appeal that was fated to propel the company into the front ranks of the world's telecommunications suppliers.

In a nutshell, digital would make possible the Internet era by getting telephones to speak the same language as computers. It would enable users of the World Wide Web to access information stored in the form of a computer-bank data by means of telephone lines and wireless signals. Electronic switches in widespread use in the 1960s could process only analog voice signals, which took the form of wavelengths. Digital signals, by contrast, are pulses of binary digits, the zeroes and ones that are the universal language of computers. In the process of routing calls, digital switching also computerizes, or "digitizes," the signals it is transmitting, be they voice, data or video. Digital systems held the promise of firing signals at greater speed and volume than analog switches, greatly enhancing the efficiency and profitability of existing phone lines. The advent in the 1960s of semiconductor chips — pinhead-sized microelectronic circuits that could be used as devices for converting analog to digital signals — introduced a quantam leap in reliability. Made from purified sand, or silicon, semiconductors had no moving parts or delicate wire filaments. They were infinitely less prone to breakdown than the relay switches then in widespread use. The truly transformative event was the computer memory chip unveiled in 1967 by inventors Robert Noyce and Gordon Moore, co-founders of Silicon Valley's Intel Corp. These devices enabled computer makers to replace the mazes of wire circuits then used to store and transmit data with tiny chips. That breakthrough opened the door to much smaller and more powerful computers. It was seized upon by Nortel in 1969, which signed a licensing agreement with Intel to gain the ability to design and make its own memory chips and the devices that digitized analog signals. That was to be a key technology in Nortel's whispered project — so secret it was referred to within Nortel simply as the "E-Thing" — to create the world's first line of fully computerized switches.

Any hesitation that Scrivener might have felt about Nortel's next audacious move was erased in the mid-1970s when the company began to lose major bids among U.S. clients for its hybrid SP-1 switches. In May 1976, Nortel shook up the industry by commiting itself to introducing a complete series of all-digital switching systems. Over the next few years, it would roll out products to serve every niche, from private branch exchanges for hotels and small businesses to giant central-office switches for telcos that could handle 350,000 calls per hour. That is, Nortel was *promising* to do so. Apart from questionning the market's desire for such advanced technology, the industry doubted any company's ability to bring such sophisticated products to market against such an unforgiving timetable.

Once again, the risk was enormous — $300 million in development costs to perfect an untested technology. Worse, for the duration of the new-product rollout, Nortel's best clients could be expected to withhold orders for the company's existing products until they saw what the flashy new models were capable of. Determined to make a splash, and put its own employees on notice that the digital initiative could not be allowed to fail, Nortel went ahead with its unveiling of "Digital World." For the occasion, Lobb invited the CEO of every telephone company on the continent for the digital unveiling to Disney World. More unusual than the site (the theme park was a Nortel customer) was the identity of the new Nortel chairman who led the proceedings that day, none other than Robert C. Scrivener.

At France Telecom, Illinois Bell and Nippon Telephone & Telegraph, the talk that spring was about the peculiar Canadian who had abruptly demoted himself from head of one of the world's most respected phone companies to run its much smaller manufacturing arm. The reaction was one of shock at Bell Canada, as well. A. Jean de Grandpre, informed that he was to replace his former boss as head of the utility, had just one question for Scrivener: "You did mean it when you said you are working for me?"

The move was unheard-of, bizarre even. That, of course, had been the point. The erstwhile Nortel critic had been thoroughly won over by its future prospects. To make that point absolutely clear, Scrivener was now bringing his credibility as a telco operator to bear on the task of winning the confidence of other buyers of phone equipment around the world. The technology, he knew, would not sell itself. "Marketing is the whole thing," he said. "Without marketing, the whole thing is dead." Scrivener elected himself Nortel's chief marketer. There was, he insisted "no reason why a company with its origins in Canada shouldn't be the biggest manufacturer of hardware of this type in the U.S.," Scrivener said. "I'll sing the 'Star Spangled Banner' if that's what it takes to get $100 million in U.S. sales," vowed Nortel's new boss as he embarked on a round of sales pitches among potential U.S. clients.

He also braced for the inevitable cannibalization of Nortel's older products. But this was to be Nortel's finest hour to date. Its digital marvels — first, a switch for business users (the Meridian), then a small switch for rural markets, and finally the monster DMS-100 switching system for big telcos — all met their scheduled delivery dates. And they worked. At a crucial moment of transition in its industry in the early 1980s, Nortel was the only company in the world with a complete line of fully computerized switching gear. It enjoyed a two- or three-year lead in next-generation technology just as demand for it was about to explode. A dramatic U.S. court decision in 1982, to take effect two years later, called for AT&T to restrict itself to the long-distance business, and divest its 22 local phone companies. By 1984, Nortel was selling digital equipment to 21 of them. Scrivener's golfing buddies at AT&T had told him he was nuts to modify the ESS. But Nortel's risky 1960s foray into the U.S. with the modified SP-1 had given the Canadian interloper a reputation for reliability, and a reason for U.S. buyers to trust Nortel's new Digital World line. And the AT&T spin-offs were eager to support Nortel as a well-known alternative to their former sole supplier, Western Electric. Between 1975 and 1985, Nortel's sales in the U.S. jumped from $92 million to $2.3 billion.

If there were outer limits to convergence of old and new technologies in communications, Robert Scrivener professed he could not see them. As early as the mid-1970s, he had spoken of a coming world dominated by high-speed networks whose emergence would be triggered by the arrival of uniform operating standards. He discerned "a change in philosophy, away from the sole use of computer communications by relatively few large organizations on private networks, toward common, universal data networks, available to small and large users alike — and, ultimately, to the individual. The network will be for the use of the people, as it should be." Data networks would make every type of information — sports, scientific, medical — readily available to everyone, "and bring the office, classroom and store into the home."

The ubiquity of such networks lay far off in the future, however. Scrivener was to learn this the hard way, with his one big career stumble. In 1974, Nortel had been spurned in a friendly takeover offer for Dictaphone Corp., the big U.S. dictating machine maker. In the twilight of his career, Scrivener moved with undue haste to make his dream of an "office of the future" a reality. With a short burst of acquisitions beginning in 1977, Nortel cobbled together a motley assortment of U.S. firms that turned out computer terminals, word processors, fax machines, high-speed printers and gimmicky devices that were supposed to make them all work together. It only made sense to bring convergence to the office environment, Scrivener reasoned. Between 1960 and 1970, white-collar productivity had inched up by 4 per cent, while blue-collar workers had increased their efficiency by 83 per cent. There was a ready explanation for that. The average North American production worker was supported by $50,000 worth of equipment; his office counterpart was given just $2,000 worth of tools to work with.

Like companies as varied as IBM and Exxon Corp., however, Nortel had allowed itself to be caught up in the prevailing hype about all things electronic. Some of these advertised wonders were poised for obsolescence. Word processors, for instance, became the Edsels of the office with the imminent arrival of desktop computers. Other products, including high-speed printers and fax machines, would have to await further technological refinements before coming into widespread use. It would also need a change in attitudes. "In executive suites, you still find very few terminals," Light conceded in 1981; the market wasn't ready for the idea of the wired office. In 1980, the year of Scrivener's career retirement, Nortel wrote off its "office of the future" investments. That setback, coinciding with a recessionary downturn, led to a net loss on the year of $185 million; Nortel shares dived from $55 to $29.50.

Scrivener was to be accorded a hero's farewell, however. At the outset of the digital campaign, he had predicted that "competition will be bloody. Up to half of the current telecommunications makers of the world will go broke. It's like the makers of automobiles and supersonic jets — there will be room for only a few survivors." He was right. A score of also-rans like Rolm Corp., Plessy PLC and Stromberg-Carlson had disappeared from the phone-equipment market, clearing the field for a half-dozen remaining giants, Nortel being the smallest. In time, even their ranks would be thinned, as ITT and GTE bowed out of the race and Europe's Siemens, Ericsson and Alcatel found themselves largely sidelined by an Internet phenomenon whose entrepreneurial impulses were centred in North

America. For now, Nortel was waving the crest of success, although its survival instincts would be tested again before long.

During Scrivener's four years at the helm, Nortel's U.S. presence had grown exponentially — from five to 25 factories stateside, and from 802 to 13,000 U.S. employees. Its bottom line showed a profit of $113 million for 1979, up from $4 million a decade earlier when Scrivener had dispatched Lobb on his clean-up mission. Nortel's shares soon recovered, as well. In 1982, they were changing hands at a record price of $82. "What Scrivener did was revolutionary," said a Bay Street analyst, "turning a sleepy supplier to Bell Canada into a vigorous, dynamic telecommunications supplier to everyone." Edmund Fitzgerald, future CEO at Nortel, said the nice thing about the company was that all the right decisions had been made in the 1970s. "Though a lot of people gave lip service to digital, "Northern was willing to gamble its wad," Fitzgerald said. "Now the world is chasing Northern to catch up."

The task of building on Lobb's early success in the U.S. was taken up by a tag team of Fitzgerald and Walter Frederick Light. Transplanted from Bell to serve as Nortel's CEO from 1979 to 1984, Light was an engineer born in the Ontario mining town of Cobalt. He was a career telephone man who liked to call telecommunications "as significant to Canada as oil is to Saudi Arabia." He was a gregarious salesman who claimed there wasn't a telco CEO in the world that he couldn't get on the phone. Which was probably true. The Nortel executives assigned to accompany Light on his globe-trotting sales trips were impressed by his easy access to top-drawer clients. In Sweden, where officials at the phone utility Televerket greeted Light as a head of state, a Nortel executive once asked one of his Swedish counterparts why they always fussed over the visiting Canadian. The reply was: "Do you think I ever get to meet the chairman of Ericsson?" For Ericsson, a giant multinational, the local phone company was small potatoes. To Light, however, stealing business from under Ericsson's nose was a tremendous morale booster. "Within the worldwide telecommunications industry," he crowed, "Televerket's choice of Northern Telecom [the firm's new name since 1976] over all comers, including Ericsson, was the equal of Buckingham Palace replacing the Royal Horse Guards with a Swedish regiment."

Edmund Bacon Fitzgerald, who was Light's lieutenant as president and replaced him as CEO from 1984 to 1989, had been recruited for his impeccable credentials as a U.S. corporate statesman. He was a former U.S. Marine and son of a prominent insurance and shipping executive for whom the ill-fated Great Lakes freighter *Edmund Fitzgerald* had been named. Trained in mechanical engineering, Fitzgerald had turned the family firm, a Milwaukee-based maker of construction equipment named Cutler-Hammer Inc., into a leading supplier of defence electronics products to the Pentagon. As a veteran of several Fortune 500 boards, co-founder of baseball's Milwaukee Brewers, and a cultivator of

Republican contacts in Washington, D.C., Fitzgerald was uniquely suited to the challenge of expanding Nortel's beachhead in the U.S. Known to friends as Fitz, he was unfailingly polite, almost shy in contrast with the charismatic Light. But he was no less effective than Light as a peripatetic supersalesman.

When Fitz rolled into a new town, minions accompanying him in the back of his limousine would try to brief him on the low-level contacts at potential client companies. Fitz would glance out the window. "This is, what — St. Louis?" Then he'd rattle out the names of CEOs at local firms — Monsanto, Ralston-Purina, General Dynamics — with whom he rubbed shoulders on the Business Roundtable, various blue-chip corporate boards or the GOP fundraising circuit. He would try to meet all these prospective or existing Nortel clients over the next day or so. And then it was on to Chicago or Beijing.

Nortel's aggressive U.S. campaign in the 1980s was now prompting some American phone-equipment makers to publicly question the Canadian company's suitability as a supplier to government agencies. They might have been still more indignant had Nortel not worked to play down one particular contract that any other supplier would have bragged about. Since 1985, telephone calls at the White House had been handled by a Nortel switching system installed by the Chesapeake & Potomac Telephone Co.

Keeping his own indignation in check, Fitzgerald calmly made the case with protectionists on Capitol Hill that Nortel was an exemplary U.S. corporate citizen, with 19,000 employees at 130 plants, R&D centres and sales offices in 11 states by the mid-1980s. At that same time, questions were being raised in Canada about Nortel's increasingly suspect patriotism. In the late 1990s, John Roth would come under fire over the defection of all but four of Nortel's top 27 executives to the U.S. and other offshore markets. That trend had begun much earlier, though. In a strategy that would later prove vital to companies like Honda Motor Co. Ltd. and Magna International Inc., Nortel had started in the 1970s to signal its commitment to U.S. customers by erecting a bricks-and-mortar presence in their backyard. The firm listed its stock on U.S. and other foreign exchanges, and began to report its financial results in U.S. dollars. These changes went down badly with economic nationalists in Canada, who anticipated that the entire company was about to decamp to the U.S. This would prove to be a time, Fitzgerald later explained, when Nortel would have to do its best to appear American in the U.S. and Canadian in Canada. As it happened, Nortel was ramping up its Canadian spending on plants and R&D even as its U.S. presence grew ever more substantial. Nortel was absorbing about a quarter of all the graduates in electrical engineering and computer science from Canadian universities each year. And it was becoming something of a graduate school itself for high-tech entrepreneurs. Alumni of BNR and Nortel launched scores of companies, including Mitel Corp., Corel Corp., Newbridge Networks Corp. and JDS Fitel Inc. (later JDS Uniphase

Corp., a world leader in fibre-optics networking gear). When it decided to exit the satellite business, Nortel sold its assets in this field to Spar Aerospace Ltd, which later gained renown by developing the "Canadarm" remote manipulator system for NASA's Challenger space shuttle program.

Cracking markets outside North America would prove more difficult than the U.S. campaign. In Europe and Asia, state-owned telephone companies were the norm, and they were often obliged to buy from local suppliers. And in competing with the likes of Ericsson and Siemens, the Canadian firm was up against rivals that had been operating in the global arena since before the turn of the 20th century. Given the limited size of the Swedish market, the telegraph repair shop that Lars M. Ericsson opened in 1876 had long ago achieved the status of a sprawling multinational. Both Ericsson and the telegraph-equipment firm co-founded in 1847 by Werner von Siemens and Johann Halske had also diversified into every field of electronics. Siemens could subsidize a loss-leading contract for telephone equipment with profits from its electrical-wiring contract at Toronto's SkyDome, and trump Nortel in a bidding match for a Dutch university's phone system by throwing in free medical equipment from one of its other divisions.

Like Western Electric, however, these other titans of the telecom-equipment world were in the habit of ignoring niches that could be lucrative for an up-and-comer. When Deutsche Bundespost, the German postal authority, couldn't get the data-communications gear it needed from Siemens, it bought from Nortel. And that high-profile contract led to orders from other prominent clients, such as Barclays Bank in Britain and the U.S. Federal Reserve System.

Nortel also used what it called a Trojan Horse strategy to gain international exposure. It had no funds to spare from the expansion drive in the U.S., and wasn't about to jeopardize its bid for glory in the world's largest market. By 2000, Nortel would have its own network of plants and R&D centres around the world. But in the first tentative stages of its global expansion, in the 1960s, it simply licensed its products in European, Asian and other offshore markets to local suppliers. Decades later, Nortel phones and switching devices would still be on the job in homes, hotels and offices in the remotest parts of the world. But they were stamped with names like Televerket, General Electric Co. (Britain), Olivetti (Italy) and Telerad (Israel), among others. The strategy yielded a decent stream of licensing fees while spreading the word about Nortel's growing technological abilities.

From the moment it first set foot outside Canada, Nortel also exploited its own former status as a colonial outpost. It had long been dictated to by Western Electric, and knew better than to make its own clients and partners feel inferior. If Ericsson, Siemens and Alcatel tended to impose their own solutions on local problems, Nortel would win friends by being acutely responsive to local sensibilities. "People are naturally self-centred in their own communities," Scrivener had said, "so why not adapt to them instead of telling them they are stupid and that their designs are no good?"

Nortel's global ambit would expand to 105 countries by 2000. Activities in each nation were characterized by a philosophy dating from the 1960s that called for local manufacturing; the recruitment and training of local managers; and the transformation of branch plants initially set up to serve local markets into vigorous exporters that generated foreign exchange for their home countries. The role model was Nortel's first overseas factory, in Turkey, opened in 1967. The Istanbul-based operation, called Netas, evolved into a mini-Nortel, and was soon Turkey's biggest exporter of electrical products. In time, Nortel's plants in Britain were exporting to 35 countries, and more than 90 per cent of Nortel's employees in France were engaged in export-related activities.

The same method was applied to R&D. Lacking the resources of Bell Labs, Nortel became a sponge for technological expertise gained from striking R&D partnerships with 130 universities around the world, including the Massachusetts Institute of Technology, Beijing University and Russia's Academy of Sciences. Under more pressure than larger competitors to get the biggest bang for its buck in R&D, Nortel was forced to become adept at seizing upon innovations that emerged in far-flung outposts of its own research network, and applying them as widely as possible. R&D centres in Ottawa and England collaborated on fibre-optics research, and a Nortel science centre in Russia provided much of the algorithmic underpinning of wireless gear that Nortel sold worldwide. In one particularly telling example of integration in R&D and manufacturing, Nortel supplied a specialized video microchip to a client in New Zealand that was initially developed at Nortel's R&D facility in Ireland, modified by engineers in India, fabricated in the U.S., packaged in Malaysia and then field-tested back in Ireland before final shipment to Australasia.

Nortel was not alone in trying to banish the "not-invented-here" syndrome (NIH), but it showed more resolve than some rivals. A wireless R&D project between Nortel and Motorola faltered when Roth, who then headed Nortel's wireless division, could not get his Schaumberg, Illinois, partner to see that its in-house technology was about to be superceded by better ideas coming out of Europe. Motorola was soon eclipsed in the cellphone market by Ericsson and Nokia Corp., a firm so new to the wireless market that in its native Finland it was still mostly known for its earlier status as a leading maker of galoshes. Nortel could not afford a NIH mentality. "Our strategy is that when we see a promising technology we should seize it, because it's essential that we reduce the time spent getting a product to market," said Nortel's president of technology, Gedas A. Sakus. "If we see someone out there who can give us leverage, we do a licence deal, or form a joint venture with them, or just acquire a company outright."

Above all, Nortel was persistent. It began courting customers in China in 1972, but wasn't a factor in that market until Light made Nortel's first big sale there in 1983. Another decade would pass before Nortel began linking Beijing with provincial capitals in China's first national data network. For four years in the 1990s, a Nortel negotiating team had plenty of time to grow accustomed to a diet of rice, worms and barbecued rat in an ultimately successful bid to supply $500-million (U.S.) worth of big central-office switches. The Chinese not only played Nortel against rival bidder AT&T's Western Electric unit, but also changed its own negotiating team three times — an old trick. "That way," an exhausted Nortel negotiator explained, "your concessions are still on the books, but theirs are revoked." Fitz could tell the same story in Japan, where in 1985 Nortel became the first non-Japanese telecom supplier to land a contract with the state phone utility, Nippon Telephone and Telegraph (NTT), which selected it over AT&T. That was the payoff from Light's initial contacts in Japan in the 1970s, and then five years of intense lobbying by Fitzgerald at NTT, the world's second-largest telephone utility. "I gave away tons of Eskimo carvings," he reported. "Some of them were heavy enough to bring certain small ministers to their knees."

What Nortel notably didn't offer was under-the-table payments. Its European competitors, in particular, were often in the news for their alleged role in scandals involving high-level government and business figures. In taking the high road, Nortel was imposing a prohibition on dubious practices that could migrate to other parts of its worldwide operations, and seeking to avoid both unflattering publicity and complicated distractions. Speaking of the barter deals that were proposed by some prospective clients, a Nortel executive allowed that "far too often they want accessibility to arms, and we can't do that, of course."

Nortel was doing well enough on the strength of its products. NTT, for instance, soon had reason to congratulate itself on its deal with Nortel. A few hours after the ribbon-cutting on Nortel's installation of a small switching system in the Tokyo suburb of Shonan, Fitz was awakened from his sleep by an earthquake. The epicentre had been Shonan, and bits of the station's old mechanical cross-bar relay switches had been flying around the building. But the new Nortel system had functioned smoothly throughout the ordeal.

In retirement at his seaside retreat in Vero Beach, Florida, Scrivener had been chuffed on learning of that system's survivability. When Nortel equipment in Baghdad failed a similar test after the city came under fire from U.S. cruise missiles for several weeks in 1991, he was disheartened. But then, Operation Desert Storm had not been a simulated attack like the 1960s experiment in Southern Ontario, and Nortel's microwave radio network — the backbone of the Iraqi national telecommunications system — had been a prime target of the bombing campaign. Scrivener was far more bothered that year by worrisome reports closer to home of upheaval at Nortel's head office.

Scrivener had once offered a tart reply to an interviewer who asked him to account for Nortel's success. "Our customers became a kind of extended family," he said. "We were nice guys to do business with, we didn't try to screw anybody out of anything. We handled ourselves in such a way that they liked to do business with us and if we made a mistake, we fixed it. No arguments, ever." Possibly, he ventured, the company's national origins had played a role in that. "Canadians are well-educated, skillful and honest. We're not fakers. Fake values or phony sophistication haven't hit us yet." But five years before his death in 1996, Scrivener was dismayed to learn that Paul G. Stern, Nortel's latest CEO, did not answer to that description.

Stern, the son of a U.S. diplomat, was born in Czechoslovakia and was raised in Mexico and the U.S. He spoke fluent English, Spanish and German and understood Italian and French. He was a graduate in electronics engineering with a Ph.D. in physics and insisted on being addressed as "Dr. Stern." After what he described as heroic stints at E.I. du Pont, IBM, Braun AG and Rockwell International — which he detailed in his memoir, *Straight to the Top* (1990) — Stern had finessed the 1986 merger of ailing computer makers Burroughs Corp. and Sperry Corp. into the unhappily named and ultimately ill-starred Unisys Corp. The flashy résumé, and Stern's political connections as a fundraiser for George Bush's presidential bid, had inspired Fitzgerald to recruit as his successor a man he estimated to be a passable clone of himself. Stern promptly slighted Fitzgerald's tenure. "I'm sad to say there are still pockets of mediocrity in this company," Stern said upon arriving at Nortel. "And I don't tolerate mediocrity."

During his stormy regime, beginning in 1989, Stern was able to report that Nortel's sales outside North America had increased fivefold, and that profits had tripled to a record $536 million (U.S.). When he was abruptly pushed out of the firm just three years later, with two years left in his employment contract, some U.S. observers would lose no time in depicting him as a victim of Canadian parochialism. "Stern opened a second headquarters near Washington, D.C., created an executive office dominated by Americans with no telecommunications experience, and fostered a demanding, no-excuses culture that seems abrasive by Canadian standards," reported *Business Week*. The U.S. journal feared for Nortel's prospects under Stern's surprise replacement, Jean Monty, given that "the French Canadian's résumé is no match for that of Stern."

Nortel was not eager to clarify the record. It chose instead to help Stern obscure the circumstances of his sudden reappearance on the job market. As his erstwhile employer held its tongue, Stern announced that he had completed his giant work at Nortel and could be persuaded to step into the breach at other firms that had recently fired their CEOs, perhaps at IBM or Westinghouse Electric Co.

He had done some good at Nortel. Using his political and business connections in Mexico, Stern built Nortel's fledgling presence there into a significant operation. A partnership he forged with France's Matra Communications S.A. helped Nortel catch up in wireless technology. And by inking the deal in which Nortel took complete ownership of ITT's former telecom-supply business in Britain, he gave Nortel a front-row seat in the privatization of telecommunications brought about by Margaret Thatcher.

Stern's true obsession, however, had been the rapid maximization of profits. Indeed, he had been hired largely for this purpose: Nortel's profits had dropped 50 per cent in 1988, and a recurrance of bureaucratic sclerosis had been fingered as the reason. Stern's failing was in execution. There had been the little things, like forbidding employees from taking valued clients to ball games, or using company time to hold their own Christmas parties, even as Stern himself deployed company funds for his new jet and a mansion in suburban Washington. More problematic was his arrogance, which had driven about a dozen top executives out of the company and into the management ranks of competing firms, following a botched reorganization that severed Nortel's ties to customers.

And the customers had gone into revolt. They had turned Stern down flat when he asked some of them to "front-load" their future orders to help goose Nortel's current profit. There was real chutzpah in those requests, since Nortel had chosen that same moment to cut back on R&D, which in the Stern era slipped to 11 per cent of sales from the traditional 14 per cent. Nortel's customers were racing to upgrade their digital switches to incorporate a plethora of money-making features. But for the first time, Nortel was doing an inadequate job of testing the ever more sophisticated software that its clients required. And for the first time, Nortel's switches were crashing.

When word of faulty products made its way around the world, the Chinese negotiators mentioned above would find the reports of Nortel's bug-ridden software useful in dragging out negotiations. Long before that, the Baby Bells and Nortel's other big U.S. customers had begun to complain. Stern brushed off the complaints. That was a career-eliminating move, as perhaps only a stranger to the telecommunications industry could fail to see. The Baby Bells realized they could go to a higher court. "They complained to everyone," Roth recalled, "because Nortel refused to listen." Specifically, they complained to BCE Inc., the new holding company set up to control both Bell Canada and Nortel. Stern was summoned to a BCE board meeting at a safe remove from headquarters. In a stormy confrontation with the telco executives from BCE in a London boardroom, Stern was informed that a veteran Bell executive, Jean Monty, had been installed as Nortel's president as a prelude to Stern's anticipated departure, as quietly but quickly as he could manage it. The French Canadian executive soon restored Nortel to robust health, immediately committing hundreds of millions of dollars to fixing the bad computer software code in Nortel's digital switching equipment, and hitting the road to win back the confidence of his peers in the telco world.

In 1993, Nortel took a staggering $1-billion (U.S.) writeoff to pay for the over-due software improvements as well as severance payments for some 5,200 employ-ees that Stern had roughly dispatched. Nortel shares plunged in value. Stern did not resurface at IBM, or elsewhere. Headhunters less credulous than Fitzgerald discovered that Stern's résumé contained assertions somewhat at variance with records on file at certain schools and at least one former employer. These things happen, of course, but Stern's ouster at Gillette's Braun division in Germany after a bungled downsizing effort was not so easily overlooked. There had also been his maladroit closing of a Sperry plant in Bristol, Tennessee, over the objections of a U.S. Senator from that state, which made Stern something of a political liability now that Al Gore was Vice President. Fortunately for Nortel, Gore was still a fan of the Canadian company. It was among the biggest employers in his state. In pre-Stern days, Nortel had taken the trouble to escort the future presidential candidate on tours of its facilities in the Volunteer State, and answer his surprisingly informed queries about the implications of fibre optics. On his goodwill tour of British Telecom, BellSouth Corp., NTT and other angry clients, Monty now rushed to repair Nortel's reputation for good manners.

The world soon forgot Stern, but Nortel did not. Scrivener's debacle with U.S. takeovers had been instructive: Nortel made just one major acquisition, Stern's $3.5-billion (U.S.) deal for the ITT division, since that disaster. The Stern episode was another lesson, this time in the folly of hiring a single-suited cost cutter. His successor, as it happened, also had a somewhat narrow focus. Monty lusted after the CEO post at BCE. He would get his wish by 1997. In the meantime, he lost no time in grooming an inside candidate to replace him. Someone who, like Scrivener, thought the real action was at Nortel. John Roth believed Nortel was poised to mastermind the inevitable convergence of voice, data and video signals. "We're in the right business at the right time," he said in the mid-1990s on becom-ing Monty's heir apparent. "Networks are at the very heart of the information society."

There are times at which it is right *not* to listen to customers, right to invest in developing lower-performance products that promise *lower* margins, and right to aggressively pursue *small*, rather than substantial, markets.
— Clayton M. Christensen, *The Innovator's Dilemma:*
When New Technologies Cause Great Firms to Fail, 1997

MOST OF THE COMPANIES described in this book achieved great-ness by exploiting a trend or technology that was "disruptive." This was the label given by Christensen, a professor at the Harvard Business

School, to forces of change that saw unlikely upstarts wrestling market leadership from entrenched giants in one industry after another.

Long before that phenomenon had a name, Laurent Beaudoin bet his company on the idea that Bombardier's small regional jets might someday challenge Boeing's conventional jetliners for supremacy on domestic routes. Isadore Sharp's concept of intimate inns with amenities that catered to time-pressed executives was a disruption little understood by Hilton, Hyatt and Sheraton, operators of traditional convention hotels. As a champion of an upgraded version of the lowly house brand, Galen Weston had taken control of his industry from grocers wedded to high-volume sales of national brand merchandise.

Scrivener and his successors at Nortel had built the company's fortunes on a disruptive technology. Well into the 1990s, demand for Nortel's digital switches was still booming, thanks to deregulation in the global telecommunications industry, which had unleashed a wave of competition among upstart phone companies that used Nortel's high-performance equipment to vie for business with former monopoly telcos. "Nortel is like an arms merchant," BCE's chairman, Lynton Wilson, said in 1997. "It's supplying the equipment for all these new entrants."

But the prosperity triggered a sense of alarm in Roth. Hadn't Sears Roebuck been at the height of its success in 1962, when it chose to ignore the experiment in discount retailing that Sam Walton launched that year? If IBM hadn't ruled the computer world with its mainframes, would it have ignored the potential of mini-computers? The lead that upstart Digital Equipment Corp. (DEC) achieved in minicomputers blinded it to the threat posed by personal computing. And, Apple Computer Corp., trailblazer of the PC age, had been five years late climbing onto the portable-notebook bandwagon. Each of these firms was an exemplar of the voguish precepts of sticking to your knitting and customer satisfaction. Each had focused on doing just one thing, and finding better ways of doing that one thing. Then the world had suddenly abandoned that thing in favour of a disruptive alternative, one which these former leaders couldn't hope to learn fast enough to dislodge the firms that had pioneered it.

Nortel had humbled Western Electric with its all-digital systems. By the time of Roth's appointment as CEO, the world was still beating a path to Nortel's door, rewarding it for its continual improvement of its disruptive technology. But it seemed to Roth that Nortel, now at the top of its game, might follow the likes of IBM and DEC, and suffocate on the success that its core product had brought it.

"You know why great companies fail?" he said. "Suddenly, one morning, their chief asset becomes their chief liability."

As an engineer, Roth was proud of Nortel's enormous DMS-100 central-office digital switching system as a triumph in design. He had worked on it himself, in the 1970s. "It was 26 million lines of computer code," said Roth, "more than Ronald Reagan's Star Wars scheme. People said it was impossible for any company to build a software product that big. Well, we did it."

Roth paused. He grimaced. The DMS-100, Nortel's great cash cow, was now on the verge of becoming "a huge liability," he said. Nortel was obliged to constantly upgrade it as telcos demanded more functionality to accommodate an ever-increasing number of lucrative features, things like call display and automatic redialling. "Systems that large are fantastically expensive to maintain as a viable asset," Roth said. He seemed to be describing Willy Mays, who could calculate the exact trajectory of a deep fly ball the second it made contact with a slugger's bat. Then, late in a career that lasted about three seasons too long, Mays was losing lazy fly balls in the sun no matter how much more time he spent at practice.

In those days, baseball general managers were patient with legends of the game. And even now, companies like Nortel were sabotaged by clients that clung to products that were nearing obsolescence. "Your customers have a huge investment in the existing technology," Roth said. "They know how to install it, run it, fix it. For the longest time, they'll simply keep asking you to make improvements on the existing technology, because it's easier for them. 'Just keep making a bigger box,' they say."

Then, abruptly, your flagship product is deemed passé. Telegrams surrender to telephony, steel-belted tires to radials, minicomputers to PCs. "Just like that, your customers drop you," Roth said. "They lead you to the edge of the cliff, and then they drop you off it." He shook his head. "The courage in tech is adapting new technologies in spite of your customers. Your customers aren't going to teach you to be best-in-class in a new technology."

Nortel's leadership in its field, Roth felt certain, was about to be undercut by a new disruptive technology. In the summer of 1997, before taking up his CEO duties at Nortel that fall, Roth toured Silicon Valley and some of the world's other high-tech hot spots, talking with young firms that were experimenting with technologies that might unlock the full potential of the Internet. "And I came back thinking, my God, this is the event of the new century, and we're missing it," Roth said. "The good news is everyone else in telecom, except Cisco, is also missing it."

The Internet at that time was still an untamed frontier of incompatible technologies, whose commercial practicality was in doubt. Two of the Internet's biggest and best-run Web site operations, America Online and Yahoo!, had crashed repeatedly in trying to cope with huge increases in traffic. As late as 2000, some five years after the trailblazing Amazon.com had first gone on-line, anonymous high-tech vandals managed to break into a dozen of the most prominent Web businesses. During a tense two weeks, the hackers contaminated the premises of auction house eBay, the stock-trading service E*Trade and the other Internet victims with rogue computer messages and commands. As one on-line vendor after another hung a "denial of service" sign in the door, it was clear that even the Web's most popular vendors could not ensure the security of financial transactions. On-line visitors continued to multiply in number, but a great many of them were sitting on their wallets. Profits continued to elude even the smartest Web-based businesses, which had collectively succeeded in creating a large population of window shoppers.

Whoever fixed the Internet's technological problems was going to make a lot of money. Major telecom players that resisted the challenge were going to be relegated to the sidelines in the new era of telecommunications. "E-Commerce represents a Category 5 hurricane that will only gain in intensity," said Roth. "If you're not prepared for this you're either going to get blown away by it or get buried by the people who are prepared." At about the time of his Jaguar epiphany, Roth framed his big goal for Nortel.

To begin with, Nortel would re-engineer its bigger DMS switches to run on Internet Protocol (IP), one of the working languages of the new medium. That was sure to have the effect of cannibalizing sales of the older, and still highly profitable, DMS products. So be it. "As the saying goes," Roth sighed, "if you're going to be cannibalized, it's best to dine with friends."

Nortel would then scrap each product in its existing portfolio that had no future in the Internet, retool its remaining products into best-of-class pieces of the Internet puzzle and raid Silicon Valley and other tech communities across North America for expertise in every facet of the Internet that it lacked. In the course of that rapid transformation, Nortel's client list was going to expand far beyond the traditional phone companies that had put bread on its table since 1881. Soon, 90 per cent of Roth's sales calls would be to the hordes of Internet service providers (ISPs), to the small and large companies and government agencies that sought to do business with each other and the public in cyberspace, and to the "dot com" entrepreneurs who wanted someone — Nortel, in Roth's design — to build their entire Web network and perhaps even run it for them while they quite sensibly concentrated on the merchandise they proposed to sell on-line.

The commercial and cultural impact of the Internet, Roth had already told his own employees, would be as ground-shaking as the advent of the printing press. As Gutenberg II took hold, an increasing share of the $250 (U.S.) billion spent each year by the telecommunications industry would be on Internet-friendly equipment. Roth wanted Nortel to cut itself in for as big a slice of that action as possible. This would require that Nortel be reinvented.

You don't transform a 117-year-old company overnight. You go at it in stages. Just two months after taking office as CEO, Roth had sent an e-mail message to his 75,000 employees alerting them to the danger ahead. "The market in which we're competing has changed drastically, and so has our competition," Roth had said in his seminal "Webtone" memo of December 1997. "In addition to competing against our traditional competitors, we're going head-to-head with the best in the computing industry, the best in the consumer electronics industry, and the best in the data-networking industry. And those new competitors were born and raised in an environment vastly different from the one we grew up in."

Stage One was startling enough. Roth was asserting that Nortel and its peers were flirting with irrelevance as Cisco and *its* rivals gained the upper hand in designing the communications networks of the future. Nortel already built the fibre-optics pipelines that carried Internet traffic, even if it was admittedly behind the curve in developing the devices that routed the traffic, and in the equipment which patched incompatible networks into each other. It seemed to Roth that his firm should be the general contractor on the estimated $1.5-trillion project to build a second-generation Internet that was faster, more reliable and secure and easier to use than the current model.

Roth couldn't be that blunt about his big goal in that first encyclical. "It was just too audacious at that point to say we were going to reinvent the Internet — our people needed something less incredible to adjust to," Roth said later. And so he had merely committed Nortel to creating "Webtone" networks, a comforting play on dialtone that heralded a new Internet that would be as user-friendly as electricity and as ubiquitous as indoor plumbing. "Webtone wasn't as threatening to Nortel employees as saying, 'We're going to rebuild the Internet.' Nobody would believe that. But that's exactly what I had in mind."

In Stage Two, following hard on the Webtone pronouncement, Roth pushed Nortel's engineers to roll out a string of modest Web-related products to demonstrate the company's growing Internet capabilities. These included futuristic devices that would allow phone companies to offer Internet connections 17 times faster than current modems; a prototype cellphone with a small screen for viewing Web sites; and a browser for downloading software from Internet vendors who specialized in renting it on a per-use basis.

In case Nortel's lab rats hadn't caught his drift about the "culture of speed" he meant to unleash at the firm, Roth spent his early months as CEO drawing up a list of R&D projects that had been underway for too long. "And I started personally cancelling them," Roth recalled. "I didn't have to cancel many before the organization started getting to work on them before I could get to them." Nortel, Roth explained, would no longer carry R&D projects that lasted five years. Given that the norm in Silicon Valley was to push a new product out the door each "Web year" (a fiscal quarter), Nortel would have to understand that "if we can't deliver a product within 18 months, and it really should be 12 or even nine months, we're working on the wrong project." The reason for the urgency, Roth explained, was that "existing products on average are shrinking in value by 1 per cent a week."

Roth took this same message to Nortel's sales force. The company, he said, was going to abandon any line of business that wasn't growing at 20 per cent or more, and dump products that weren't among the top three market-share leaders in their niche. That was to be a wrenching decision, he knew. "Older products tend to be more profitable than new ones — R&D costs are lower, and the sales effort is not as great since customers simply order upgrades," said Roth. "There's always a temptation to want to keep selling such profitable products. But the danger is that you're caught trying to improve the old stuff long after your customers have decided to move on to next-generation products."

Roth's exercise in triage didn't win him a lot of friends at first. But it was a technology culture he was trying to change, and it helped that he was an engineer and not a lawyer or financier. In orchestrating his change, Roth could lean heavily on his reputation within the firm as an executive with indisputable tech smarts.

The grandson of a Lutheran minister who emigrated from Germany to Alberta, Roth was the only child of a radio operator for bush pilots employed by Canadian Pacific Airlines. Growing up in Lethbridge, Red Lake and Winnipeg, he'd watched his father, a ham-radio enthusiast, build large transmitters and receivers. He obtained his own grounding in tech at McGill University in the esoteric field of microwave engineering, and was soon designing satellites for RCA in Montreal. Moving to Nortel's lab in Ottawa in 1969, Roth was disappointed when the company lost a design bid for the Anik satellite to Hughes Aircraft, but was heartened when Hughes adopted a design similar to the innovative one his team had conceived.

A stint as manager of the digital "E-Thing" project convinced Roth that Digital World was going to be a voracious consumer of microchips. He startled colleagues with his success in persuading Nortel to ramp up its chip production to the point where the company became Canada's biggest maker of semiconductors. He also managed "SWAT" teams that dropped into troubled operations in the U.S., sometimes taking over whole divisions and running them until their technology, manufacturing and marketing problems had been solved, and also advising head office on businesses that should be kept or abandoned.

Roth had applied a similar survival-of-the-fittest philosophy after being elevated to the presidency of BNR in 1982. "I found an organization that had everyone trying to do everything and having a license to go after everything," said Roth, confirming Scrivener's belief that the struggle to keep an R&D "skunkworks" focused on practical innovations was never-ending. Annoyed to discover that researchers in Ottawa, Montreal and Mountain View in Silicon Valley were often working at cross-purposes, Roth reorganized BNR into product groups that brought engineers working in different disciplines together to expedite the development of promising technologies. He was unsentimental about the inevitable fallout. "It was painful for a lot of individuals," Roth acknowledged, "because many people didn't want to work in an environment with less autonomy, so we parted company."

Roth's own survival skills came to the fore during the Stern regime, when the new CEO slashed Roth's BNR budget. "We all felt that the organization was as low as it could sink, from a certain point of view, of morale and everything else," Roth would later say of that dismal period. Then again, he hadn't joined the managerial exodus. In buying STC, Stern had handed BNR one of Europe's biggest R&D labs, at Harlow, England, with 13,000 employees and a depth of expertise in fibre optics. And Stern's joint venture with Matra had given Nortel access to wireless technology, the ticket for Roth's ascent to Nortel's CEO suite. In the early 1990s, Roth prevailed over Nortel skeptics who viewed cellular telephony as a fad like CB radios. By the mid-1990s, wireless was Nortel's biggest and fastest-growing division, accounting for 25 per cent of total revenues. At that point, Roth was already a lock as Jean Monty's heir apparent. And by the time that was made official, with Roth's appointment as COO in 1995, Monty had already handed most of Nortel to Roth to refashion to the point where "the company I was going to take over was really my own design."

The company Roth took over had built 220 data networks in 150 countries in recent years for the world's biggest banks and corporate clients such as Microsoft, NTT, American Airlines, Merck, Coca-Cola, Bank of America, Federal Express and the Dallas Cowboys, along with government agencies in North America and Europe. It had just gained a two- or three-year lead in optical networking by being the first to market, in 1996, with a device that transmitted data along fibre-optic cables at the speed of 10 billion bits per second. And before becoming CEO, Roth had also begun to place heavy bets on Internet Protocol, thinking that IP was destined to become the dominant working language of the Web. Lucent thought otherwise. It was backing the rival ATM (asynchronous transfer mode). But Nortel, itself a major supplier of ATM equipment, commited itself to IP because, while it was less reliable than ATM, it had the potential to carry far more data. It was also the favoured language of the tinkerers in Silicon Valley, who regarded ATM as old-world. And, like many disruptions that start out as engineering eyesores, IP showed promise of becoming the VHS to ATM's Betamax as the technology became more refined.

Roth's radical tendencies had also led him to dismantle his own alma mater, Bell-Northern Research. In Scrivener's time, it had been essential to liberate researchers from Nortel's staid manufacturing culture by setting them up in a separate organization. Now the time had come to bring the engineers back inside, tying them to specific product groups within Nortel. "The era of having the R&D operation out in the woods is over," said Roth, who wanted his researchers to work more closely with Nortel's marketing staff and its customers. Nortel understood its big telco clients, but it would soon be dealing with a new crowd of technologically challenged customers. These were the information technology (IT) officers at small and large corporations who had the task of building an in-house data network. Or the entrepreneurs who were competing with the former telco monopolies as alternative suppliers of phone, cable and Internet services. Nortel's new customers, Roth explained, were going to be "marketers, not engineers. They won't know what kind of network they need, except that they need it now, because they want to mail out their sales brochures next week. It's like if you were going to start up a new airline, you wouldn't begin by designing jet engines. You'd go out and buy an airplane from Boeing. Our customers want to buy the aircraft with the engines already humming."

But Roth was by no means certain, on becoming CEO, that his early exhortations alone would succeed in accelerating the pace of internal change sufficiently to give Nortel a critical mass in Internet technology before Cisco gained an insurmountable lead, or traditional foes like Lucent woke up to the business opportunity of the new century. And Nortel got a rude reminder in 1997 that its nascent efforts in data networking were falling short of the mark when MCI rejected it for an anticipated $250-million (U.S.) contract, handing the prize to Newbridge Networks of Kanata, Ontario.

The time for incremental growth in data networking was long past. Nortel needed to gain a big, instant presence in that field. Roth had to move before Lucent got the same idea and subjected Nortel to a series of bidding wars over hot tech acquisitions. Roth's first major target was Bay Networks, which ranked second to Cisco in "routers," the traffic cops of Internet transmission. Bay's flat sales of the previous year made it affordable. Its customer base of banks, airlines, automakers, power utilities and other major corporate users of in-house data networks complemented Nortel's strength in building electronic highways between cities. Most important, Bay was a huge talent pool. In one stroke, Roth would snap up 7,000 engineers with IP expertise. That aspect of the deal, not understood by its early critics, would come into sharp relief months later when Nortel and other major firms were forced to sue companies they accused of poaching their engineers and proprietary research. In plotting the Bay acquisition, Roth met with some internal resistance from Nortel researchers who would have preferred to develop the router technology internally. But Roth, who had already made his decision, told them Nortel's customers weren't asking for Nortel routers and Nortel devices for connecting to the Internet. They didn't care where the Internet gear came from. They just wanted it, they wanted it now, and Nortel risked losing orders for entire networks if it couldn't equip them with Internet components.

Bay turned out to be a bargain. Nortel paid a price equal to three times Bay's revenues, while Lucent would later pay 17 times sales for the smaller Ascend Communications, whose expertise was in ATM devices. The Bay acquisition also went off more smoothly than expected. The technology in Bay's new-product pipeline turned out to be first class, and was quickly integrated into Nortel's wider portfolio for clients of all descriptions. Nortel was now in the same ballpark as Cisco and other rivals in the speed with which it could deliver Internet-based phone systems to corporate clients such as the Safeway grocery chain and Kinko's copy centres, and to institutional customers like the University of Texas at Austin.

Bay also represented a chance to infuse a computing-world sense of urgency into Nortel's slower-moving telecom culture. "Spending $6.9 billion [U.S.] on Bay was a declaration to both the industry and our own employees that we were serious," said Roth, who wanted to overlay the culture of the 7,000 Bay workers onto that of the 70,000 Nortel employees, not the other way around. "The acquisition had a powerful motivating effect inside Nortel, introducing a sense of competition. The $6.9-billion message to the troops was, 'Roth isn't just talking about building Webtone. He's going to do it. We better get with his agenda and start developing this stuff, because if he keeps buying these companies he's not going to need me.'"

Roth kept buying companies, usually paid for with Nortel shares rather than cash. The stunning recovery in Nortel's share price beginning in the fall of 1999 helped stem the usual tide of post-takeover defections at Bay, whose employee shareholders had received Nortel stock. It also gave Roth the "currency" to buy still more firms that filled remaining holes in Nortel's product line-up with a minimum of pain to Nortel's treasury.

Most of the takeover candidates that Roth had been sizing up since his summer swing through Silicon Valley in 1997 were just three or four years old, and were run by thirtysomething geeks who took an odd sort of pride in profit-and-loss statements that would embarrass a loan shark. The technology they were trying to develop had unproven efficacy and market appeal. Some of the outfits that seemed most promising to Roth had yet to field-test their first product, much less sell one to a paying customer. Yet these firms were poised to skyrocket in value in a late 1990s stock-market that was placing astronomical values on any company that had a passing acquaintance with the Internet.

Roth's purchase of Shasta Networks of Sunnyvale, California, in April 1999, obtained for a relatively modest $340 million (U.S.), enabled Nortel to provide its phone company clients with software tools for creating E-commerce systems without adding costly hardware. Clarify Inc. of San Jose, acquired six months later for $2.1 billion (U.S.), gave Nortel the ability to help its corporate clients track their own customers' orders and other needs on-line. The $3.25 billion (U.S.) that Roth laid out for Qtera Corp. of Boca Raton, Florida, in January 2000 gave Nortel expertise in lowering the cost of Internet transmission. Data couldn't be sent more than 500 kilometres over a fibre-optic line before it started to erode, requiring that it be regenerated with the use of expensive equipment. Qtera was working on technology that could shoot a data message some 4,000 kilometres without a recharge. Three months after that deal, Roth swooped down on a tiny outfit named Xros

Corp., also based in Sunnyvale. He lavished $3.2 billion (U.S.) worth of Nortel stock on the firm's employees, all 90 of them. With that kind of money, a deep-pocketed investor could have had his pick of Sunoco, Goodyear Tire & Rubber or the Nordstrom department-store chain, each with more than $5 billion (U.S.) in sales and several thousand employees. But no one was buying "Old Economy" companies in 2000.

Xros typified the Internet exuberance of the early 21st century. The company was three years old. Its founder, a micromachinist named Armand Neukermans, was experimenting with a device, consisting of thousands of silicon mirrors each the size of a baby's fingernail, which, if tilted in a certain way, could send light beams hurtling down fibre-optic pathways at unprecedented distances without the need to regenerate them. For this device, which took up less space on Roth's book-shelf in Brampton than his scale-model Plymouth Prowler, Nortel had paid each of Xros' employees the equivalent of $36 million (U.S.) worth of Nortel shares. The value placed on Xros defied conventional logic. "But look at it this way," said Roth. "I gave up 1.7 per cent of Nortel stock to get Xros. And the next day, Nortel stock went up 5 per cent, because the market thought Xros added great value to us. That's the new math."

Another factor in the equation was Roth's early taste of success with using takeovers to inject urgency into the process of getting new products to market. A year before the Xros deal, Roth had bought the one-year-old Aptis Communications of Chelmsford, Massachusetts for $305 million (U.S.), the largest amount ever paid for a tech company that had yet to ship a product. But Nortel was to gain a head start over rivals when Aptis lived up to its promise. In the summer of 1998, roughly a year ahead of competitors, Aptis was shipping Internet access switches that could handle 1,344 calls simultaneously. There could be no telling how long his luck would hold. But so far, Roth's cards were coming up aces. In the meantime, he was keeping firms like Xros out of the hands of the competition. "Cisco inhales companies," said Francis McInerney of North River Ventures Inc. in New York, who was one of the industry's most respected analysts. "So the right amount of money for Nortel to pay for these companies is whatever keeps them from Cisco or Lucent."

Cisco was the acknowledged leader in Internet technology, a status it achieved by simply buying 55 tech-laden companies in the decade since it had gone public in order to finance a takeover blitz with its own shares. About two-thirds of cor-porate takeovers don't work out, of course; and the failure rate is higher in the tech sector. The 14-year-old Cisco was a rare example of how to build a company from scratch by mastering the art of smoothly integrating acquisitions. In 2000, Cisco had a stock-market value of close to half a trillion dollars. It had surpassed Microsoft in market capitalization and trailed only General Electric among the most valuable companies in the world.

It seemed reasonable to wonder if any company could hope to match that performance. "Cisco definitely has the machinery in place to wring value out of its acquisitions," said Brendan Hannigan, a networking analyst at the U.S.-based Forrester Research. "It remains to be seen whether Nortel can do the same."

The Bay example was encouraging. The firm's sales had slipped only 12 per cent since the takeover, once Nortel pruned Bay of products it didn't need. That dip compared favourably with the 30 per cent to 70 per cent drop in revenues at most data-networking firms in the first year after a takeover. And Nortel had impressed its new Silicon Valley hires with its tactful handling of the change of command. "We went into the deal with a feeling of trepidation that this enormous company would simply dictate how things were going to happen," said Skip McAskill, a senior Bay executive. Instead, Bay management was "surprised by the openness, friendliness and professionalism that Nortel exhibited."

In return for surrendering their independence, start-up tech firms that knew their limitations found in Nortel a company that could put their prized innovations on the global map, and also handle scut work like accounting and marketing. "We don't have all the experience of building the support organization for a major telecom product," Xros president Greg Reznick had said. "We think Nortel does that as well as anybody, if not better."

Roth was proud of the collaboration between Nortel and the newest members of its extended family. Nortel was able to show the acquired firms how to generate a healthy volume of sales for their new products. "One company we acquired told us they expected to do $50 million in revenue in 1999," Roth said. "They ended up doing $200 million — far more than they thought they were capable of." Roth invited the new firms to scout Nortel's ranks for the expertise they needed in marketing, engineering and general management. For its part, Nortel asked a Bay executive, Phyllis S. Brock, to revamp its own on-line sales operation. She soon had Nortel conducting almost $10 billion (U.S.) in sales on the Internet. (Amazon.com, the biggest independent on-line merchant, had sales of $1.6 billion U.S. in 1999.)

Roth didn't let the acquisitions distract him from his non-stop mission to transform Nortel's own culture. He scrapped the decades-old "banding" system for determining employee compensation and perks, a Dilbert-like staple of life at Nortel and other large corporations that arbitrarily determined everything from salary ranges to the size of one's office according to the title a person held in the organization. Employees would now be compensated according to the complexity of their jobs. Which meant that managers and engineers could be enticed to join an exciting new project without fear of taking a pay cut because they'd have fewer people to supervise. Roth also created an "internal IPO" program. Without braving all the risks of entrepreneurial life, employees could launch start-ups within Nortel, betting their bonuses on projects which, if successful, would reward their founders in the form of an internal initial public offering not unlike the IPOs that were minting millionaires by the dozen each day in Silicon Valley. Nortel had already spun off one such firm, an Ottawa-based outfit called Channelware, which had come up with a system for enabling Web users to access sites that made software available for rent or purchase. Some Nortel veterans had worried that the IPO concept might poison the ranks with envy. Yet Roth liked the idea of separating the entrepreneurial wheat from the chaff in his own ranks. "I like to see skin in the game," he said. "The projects have attracted risk-takers. People who are risk-averse need not apply." There were already, Roth liked to boast, "hundreds and hundreds of millionaires in Nortel." Why not more?

Credited though he was with having a gentle manner in one-on-one dealings with people, Roth had been faulted on some occasions for an overly analytic take on personnel issues. He didn't apologize for it. Roth was apt to go off on his own, to Silicon Valley or home to work on the stained-glass lamps and windows he handcrafted in Caledon, and return with a plan for upsetting the old order, which he would then impose without consulting anyone. To be sure, Roth didn't feel the need to exhaustively brief his top lieutenants. In the reorganizations of BNR and Nortel itself, in which he'd admirably simplified the lines of command, Roth had filled all the key executive posts with people who shared his view of the future. And he tended to be unsentimental about the potentially harsh consequences for employees who didn't fall into line with his program. That was a trait he shared with his predecessors as CEO.

Several factors accounted for Nortel's success in exploiting disruptive trends rather than allowing itself to be crushed by them. Being a proverbial underdog was one: Of necessity, Nortel had to work harder and smarter than entrenched rivals in the small fraternity of global telecom suppliers. Another was the company's tradition of tag-team leadership — the pairings of Scrivener and Lobb, Light and Fitzgerald, Monty and Roth. (Stern, notably, had flown solo.) What no one outside the company talked about was its long list of hard-assed bosses. It was not beyond Lobb to humiliate a doomed executive by firing him in a room filled with his colleagues; he wasn't the type of boss who took people aside to identify their shortcomings. Even the genial Light had taken a certain pleasure in keeping his co-workers stressed. "I didn't want to take a contented army to war," said Light. When they complained, he offered to lessen their responsibilities. "Then they worked twice as hard."

Leaders of revolutions tend to regard the people around them as falling into two camps: co-conspirators and potential saboteurs. The latter group acts out of spite, love of tradition or simple fear of the unknown. Asked how he proposed to keep the talent at his acquired companies, typically the biggest challenge in any takeover, Roth was apt to talk instead about the people he wanted to be rid of. "We know who we want to keep," he'd say, describing his approach to the due diligence process that preceded consummation of a takeover transaction. "You've got to structure the deal so that people you need will stay, and those who need to go — and there are always some you need to go — will do so gracefully." Among Nortel's existing workforce, Roth put the same blunt message to employees whom he addressed by e-mail, going over the heads of their managers. "What are you doing for the customer?" Roth would ask in these missives. "How does your job help Nortel serve the customer? If you can't describe it, then maybe you should look for a different job inside Nortel."

Roth was equally unsparing with rivals. "Twenty-five billion dollars later, Lucent still needs to go shopping," Roth said, identifying the holes that remained in the former Western Electric's Internet strategy after its extravagant outlay for Ascend.

The former Western Electric, it must be said, had suffered from an extraordinary combination of bad luck and even worse management. Back in 1973, AT&T's then chairman, John de Butts, had chided his friend Scrivener for his decision that year to give Nortel a taste of autonomy by having Bell Canada issue some of its Nortel shares to the public. (The break was made complete in 2000, when Bell Canada's holding company, BCE Inc., spun off its remaining 37 per cent stake in Nortel to its own shareholders.) In some quarters of the Bell System, Scrivener's decision to push Nortel out of the nest was viewed as a heretical attack on Vail's doctrine of the vertically integrated monopoly. Scrivener was no heretic; he worshipped the Bell System. But he also had an historian's perspective on the fleeting nature of monopolies. No industrial monopoly — judging from the experience of the oil barony of John Rockefeller, the railroad empire of Cornelius Vanderbilt or the suzerainty in computing first by IBM and then Bill Gates — has lasted much more than a decade. After it was forced, finally, to give up its local phone companies in the early 1980s, AT&T had cut the budget of Western Electric's affiliate, Bell Labs. The Fort Knox of telecom R&D had suffered a lack of direction ever since. And not until it had destroyed some $4 billion (U.S.) worth of shareholder value with its spectacularly ill-advised diversification into computers with the purchase of NCR Corp. did AT&T resolve to get out of the manufacturing business, shedding both NCR and Western Electric in the mid-1990s. Western Electric didn't have to start finding its own way in the world until 1996, or 23 years after Nortel had first been subjected to the judgment of the stock market. The new company, christened Lucent, a name meant to suggest luminescence, came out of the gate badly trailing its former Canadian subsidiary in advanced fibre-optics technology and data-networking equipment. Roth had to respect his adversary's heft: Lucent was still twice Nortel's size in annual revenues. But in 1976, when Scrivener had declared the U.S. market to be open season for Nortel and other interlopers, Western Electric had been nine times bigger than Nortel.

In 1998, Lucent misjudged the speed at which its customers were abruptly dropping conventional circuit-switching products in favour of optical networks. Unable to meet the demand, Lucent watched many of its clients defect to Nortel. Its stock lost $64 billion (U.S.) in value in a single day in early 2000 when the company reported lower-than-expected profits. On February 10, 2000, during another of his trips to Silicon Valley, Roth settled down to breakfast in his San Francisco hotel room and read in his *Wall Street Journal* that Nortel had overtaken Lucent in stock-market value. Nortel slipped behind Lucent after a few days; and both firms still trailed Cisco in that department. It was Cisco's John Chambers, not Roth, who was getting under the skin of Lucent CEO Rich McGinn with his evangelizing on the need for telcos to jilt their old-world suppliers and convert to Cisco's Internet-friendly IP devices. "The truth is that IP is not ready for prime time," McGinn protested. "We have avoided the Elmer Gantry excesses and made a conscious effort not to create an image that is greater than the substance."

Roth had already benefited from Lucent's persistent belief into the late 1990s that the transition to a Web-based telecommunications universe would be gradual. But he thought Chambers was fooling himself if he really believed the big telcos were going to trash all of their equipment overnight and back up a truck at Cisco's door for networking gear to replace it. "Network operators have invested about $1 trillion in building circuit-based networks over the last 15 to 20 years," Roth said. "No one is going to write off that investment and then raise another $1 trillion to replace it. Why would they take out all that equipment and put their traffic onto a technology that's not proven and isn't any more efficient?" Roth loved to goad Chambers by reminding the telecom world that routers were the culprits in an estimated 57 per cent of breakdowns on the Web. Cisco held 80 per cent of the router market. But in case it wasn't obvious whom Roth was mocking, the Nortel CEO would add, "I bet I can learn to spell 'IP' faster than Cisco can learn to spell 'reliability.'"

The traditional giants in telecom equipment couldn't hope to catch up with Cisco in routers. Which was fine with Roth. In a strategy that amounted to giving away its own routers, Nortel opted to license Bay's router technology to more than 100 companies. Microsoft would now use it in its software packages; Intel would imbed it in its new "router-on-a-chip" technology; and, quite soon, hundreds of companies would be using it in everything from cellphones to hand-held computers. Nortel itself would make its routers a piece of standard equipment in the networks it built for its telco customers, and for the corporate buyers that were Cisco's core clientele.

Exhibiting a bit of the arrogance the old-line telecom suppliers were known for, Roth had decided to turn Cisco's key product into a mere commodity, like corn or soybeans, where no farmer's crop is distinguishable from the next. It was a brilliant, and highly insulting, gambit. Cisco had been charging exhorbitant prices for its routers, which it regarded as a proprietary technology. That had been the undoing of Apple in the 1980s: it refused to share its personal computing technology, allowing Microsoft to steal the market by licensing its own technology to a host of PC makers, to the point where it became the universal standard for operating systems. Roth, for whom routers were a sideline, was proposing to make them a mere add-on to every manner of networking equipment, and thereby deprive Cisco of its lavish margins on a product that was the keystone of its franchise. He did the unthinkable in launching a price war with Cisco, devaluing not only its products but those of several bystanders. Ericsson's in-house journal *Tellus*, acknowledging that Nortel "has a much stronger image than Ericsson in the IP and datacom market," complained that "All around the world [Roth] is on the offensive, buying market shares through kamikaze-like pricing strategies."

"We have routers, switches, every kind of equipment, some of our own design and some that we get from others," said Roth, who insisted that Nortel should not be mistaken as a mere parts supplier. It had long been a maker of complete telephone networks; now it was going to make complete Internet-friendly voice, data and video networks. And it didn't care where the parts came from — its own R&D labs, the companies it acquired, or purchased off the shelf from other firms. "We have no axe to grind," he said. "We no longer keep score by the profit and loss on individual products. We do it by measuring our customers' satisfaction with an entire network that we custom-build for them, in which we've bundled all of the necessary products, obtained from whatever source is appropriate."

In 2000, Cisco was still the firm to beat. True to form, it was using takeovers to push its way into fibre optics, where it generated $1 billion (U.S.) in sales in its first year after getting optical-networking religion. Nortel, however, had a $10-billion (U.S.) presence in that arena, and a decades-old relationship with the telcos that placed the largest orders for enormous fibre-optics-based networks. "Cisco makes a lot of noise, but the bottom line is Nortel is way ahead of them in delivering fibre-optics products," said John Armstrong, an analyst with Dataquest, based in Cisco's hometown of San Jose. Nortel also had 15,000 service employees in the field, helping clients maintain and upgrade their systems, a complement roughly equal to Cisco's entire workforce. "The days are gone when Silicon Valley saw Nortel as just that weird Canadian telephone company that bought Bay Networks," said *Upside*, a leading U.S. money management publication for tech investors. "Suddenly it's Nortel, not Lucent, that looks like the company that might give mighty Cisco a run for its money."

Roth was dismayed, however, that Nortel's growing stature abroad was not matched, at least in his view, by an appreciation at home of Nortel's increasing difficulty in attracting top engineering and managerial talent. "I meet Canadian high-tech entrepreneurs all the time — in Menlo Park, Boston, Silicon Valley," he said. "I seldom meet them in Canada. We're losing their entrepreneurial magic." The problem, said Roth, who began to wage a public crusade for tax reform beginning in the fall of 1999, was the 25 per cent tax gap between high-income earners in Canada and the U.S. Noting that of Nortel's 400 top executives, only 27 remained in Canada, he warned that the exodus was likely to continue. "I have a Canadian management team, but they're mostly living outside Canada," he reported. "Each one came into my office and said, 'You know, John, I think I should be located in the U.S. because . . .' and they made up a story. The interpretation is, 'I want more take home pay.'"

Roth's observations were well-received by the predominantly conservative mass media of the times, and were typically granted front-page exposure in journals such as *The Globe and Mail* and the *National Post*. These were not especially nuanced observations. Nortel owed its existence to Ottawa's 19th-century insistence on domestic manufacture of telephone equipment. The semiconductor expertise that enabled it to develop its Digital World products had been derived in part from the federally funded Ottawa laboratories of the National Research Council in the 1960s. Ottawa had kicked in $6 million in R&D grants toward the $91-million (U.S.) total cost of developing the first digital products with which Nortel had taken on the U.S. market — not a large sum, Walter Light had said, but "it was important. At that time, every dollar was key." In 2000, Nortel, like Bombardier and Canada's other leading multinationals, was continuing to make liberal use of the federal Export Development Corp. to provide financing to offshore clients who otherwise couldn't afford to buy its products. Tuition and private-sector donations covered just 17 per cent of the cost of running Canada's universities, whose publicly funded output was essential not only to Nortel but firms such as Microsoft, which on a proportionate basis took probably more graduates from Ontario's University of Waterloo each year than from Stanford or M.I.T.

Roth had complained that "what frustrates me is that Canada is such a great country to live in — but we sure have not created an economic climate to keep our top talent in Canada." Roth's patriotism was not in question. He himself had always been based in his home country, highly unusual for the CEO of a multinational, at a time when the CEO of Ford Motor Co. hailed from Lebanon and a native of Australia was running Coca-Cola Co. In his 30-year career at Nortel, Roth himself had rejected several opportunities to be transferred to its U.S. operations. In 2000, 50 per cent of Nortel's worldwide research staff was still located in Canada; and Roth's hiring spree of 5,000 engineers to ramp up Nortel's capabilities in fibre optics was concentrated in Ottawa and Montreal. In case anyone doubted the continued importance of Roth's beloved R&D complex in the nation's capital, which he described as "the future of our corporation," he held his first annual meeting as CEO there, instead of in the usual hotel ballroom.

Many things had changed at Nortel, however. In its third year under Roth, Nortel was already a significantly different firm than the one he was appointed to run. It had largely pulled out of manufacturing, having sold or closed factories employing 11,500 people, even as it hired thousands of Internet-trained engineers and spent more than $600 million to meet the booming demand for its fibre-optics technology. About 80 per cent of its activity was now in software design. And Internet research accounted for most of Nortel's R&D efforts, up from just 5 per cent in 1997.

In 1999, more than 40 per cent of Nortel's revenues of $22 billion (U.S.) came from products it was selling that year for the first time. It was the leading supplier of optical-networking systems to AT&T, MCI, Britain's Cable & Wireless, Australia's Telstra and most of the world's other largest operators of telecommunications networks. And it had built more than half of the dozen or so new Web networks to be constructed in Europe over the previous three years.

Nortel was also a stock-market darling. It accounted for 32 per cent of the Toronto Stock Exchange 300 Composite Index in 2000, up from 3 per cent in 1984. The fourfold increase in its share price since early 1999 had singlehandedly caused the TSE to outperform the New York Stock Exchange during that period. In April 2000, tech stocks finally began to come down to earth. The market, one U.S. fund manager said at the time, had been acting "like a balloon looking for a pin." Nortel's market value had peaked on March 24 at $308 billion (Cdn.). By May 24, the stock had lost $90 billion (Cdn.) in value, a drop of 33 per cent. Even greater damage was done among the scores of tiny "dot com" start-ups with invisible profits. But Nortel's employee-shareholders were no less well-off than holders of stock in other big telecom suppliers, which had also slipped in the market downdraft. Cisco shares were down 40 per cent from their all-time high, also recorded in March 2000. And by that point Roth had already acquired most of the technology he needed, taking advantage of the overheated market to use stock certificates rather than bank debt to widen his company's lead in R&D. Nortel's financial performance had actually continued to improve during the great tech-stock sell-off. And the firm was making impressive gains in the market for so-called third-generation wireless products. In May 2000, British Telecommunications PLC gave Nortel an order to supply it with wireless components worth several hundred million dollars, a contract that had been expected to go to market leader Nokia. On the strength of such orders, Nortel's shares were once again hitting new highs in July, having regained all the lost ground since the panic selling of tech stocks.

Roth had been philosophical in the fall of 1998, when Nortel's shares had been savaged by stock-market investors. Nortel had struggled before. In the 1960s its profits never exceeded $11 million (U.S.) as it struggled to get along without Western Electric. In the 1970s, its new U.S. division went through four presidents in six years as it fought to establish a foothold for its digital switches. Three times, under Scrivener, Stern and Roth, the stock had dived by 50 per cent or more. Nortel was a resilient firm, however, one whose greatest technological achievements were inspired by threats to its own existence and chaotic changes in its industry.

Now it was riding high. George Gilder, the U.S. technology guru, was hailing Roth as his industry's "paradigm leader." At Hewlett-Packard Co., the granddaddy of Silicon Valley firms, and a collaborator with Nortel, Intel and Microsoft in an Internet office-products venture, CEO Lewis E. Platt said Roth deserved "high marks for making Nortel very Net-aware and Net-savvy." Early in 2000, Roth strode into a company conference in a San Antonio convention hall and was greeted by a standing ovation from 4,000 of his salespeople, many of whom had doubted his Webtone strategy two years before. And at a summit in Tucson with his top executives, Lucent's Rich McGinn was taping "Wanted" posters on the walls to identify the company's worst enemies. The deliberations of McGinn's crew were conducted under the gaze of Cisco's Chambers and John A. Roth.

When he heard of it, Chambers was enraged by the stunt. "McGinn made it personal," wailed Chambers, who prided himself on a gentle demeanour that was a key to Cisco's success in assimilating takeover candidates. "It sent a bad message to his employees." Roth was merely amused. "We have to stop making ourselves larger than life," he said. "You want to be caught up in the race, but you don't want to get consumed by it."

Besides, fame was supposed to be fleeting. "Eighteen months ago a lot of people thought I was nuts," Roth said in March 2000. "A year later, I'm a genius, I'm brilliant." Save the accolades, he said, for the obscure academics and computer enthusiasts who pioneered the primitive Internet in the 1960s, and ultimately forced Roth's industry to reinvent itself. "For 100 years, we were still basically working with a technology little changed from what Alexander Graham Bell gave us. The glory for Nortel is that no other firm is better able to manage the transition from Bell's invention to an Internet that truly works than we are, if we don't mess it up."

He glanced over his shoulder at a PC terminal in his office that was tracing the arc of Nortel's share price that day. "Shows you how the stock market creates heroes. But there are *thousands* of stock-market darlings, they come and go. The test will be what this company looks like long after I'm gone."

Then he said, "But I do love it, the respect this company is earning. The skeptics know who we are now. We're getting dangerous."

APPENDIX 1

GEORGE WESTON LTD

The World's Largest Grocers

George Weston Ltd is among the world's 25 largest food retailers in annual sales volume. As measured by profits, the Canadian firm counts among the top 10 grocers. With a payroll of 124,000 people in 2000, it is the eighth-largest employer in the industry worldwide.

		Profits ($ millions)	Revenues ($ billions)	Employees
1.	J. Sainsbury, U.K.	1,526	27.7	178,000
2.	Tesco, U.K.	1,417	28.9	131,000
3.	Carrefour, France	1,071	29.9	144,000
4.	Marks & Spencer, U.K.[1]	921	13.8	72,000
5.	Safeway, U.S.[2]	807	24.5	170,000
6.	Metro AG, Germany[3]	631	51.1	250,000
7.	Royal Ahold, Netherlands	597	28.9	280,000
8.	Albertson's, U.S.	568	16.0	100,000
9.	Safeway, U.K.	576	12.6	76,000
10.	George Weston, Canada	521	10.3	124,000

Figures are U.S. dollars for the 1998 fiscal year.

Source: Company reports

---

[1] Marks & Spencer is a retailer of general merchandise and food.

[2] Safeway, based in Pleasanton, California, owns Canada Safeway Ltd., with 1998 revenues of $3.1 billion (U.S.) and 30,000 employees.

[3] Metro is a diversified retailer — food, electronics and department stores.

APPENDIX 2

WARDAIR LTD

Chronology

During its 36 years of operation, Wardair Ltd grew from a bush-plane operation with a single aircraft based in Yellowknife, N.W.T., into one of the world's most highly regarded full-service carriers. By the late 1980s, however, Wardair succumbed to the debts it had amassed in attempting to transform itself from a charter airline to full-fledged scheduled status, and was sold to Canadian Airlines International.

1946:
Max Ward, age 25, launches his first air operation, Polaris Charter Co., in Yellowknife.

1953:
Ward launches a new firm, Wardair, with one plane, a de Havilland Otter. Ward is the first aviator in Western Canada to put the Otter, a breakthrough aircraft with much larger capacity than its bush-airline predecessor, the Beaver, into commercial use.

1961:
After building up the North's biggest freight-hauling operation, Ward heads south to develop the nascent holiday charter business.

1966:
With his first jet, a Boeing 727, Ward introduces Boeing jetliners to the Canadian market.

1967:
Wardair captain Don Braun delivers supplies to a Canada-U.S. team of researchers 16 miles from the geographic North Pole. His Bristol 170 Freighter is the first wheeled aircraft to land on top of the world.

1970:
Wardair sets a range record for the Boeing 727, flying 3,930 statute miles from Windsor, Ontario to Gatwick.

1972:
Wardair sets a range record for the Boeing 707 with a 7,776-statute-mile non-stop flight from Honolulu to London.

1973:
Wardair takes delivery of its first 747, named for Canadian bush pilot Phil Garratt, just three years after the first edition of the revolutionary plane goes into service with Pan Am.

1978:
Wardair is the first Canadian buyer for the de Havilland Dash 7, a revolutionary STOL (short takeoff and landing) aircraft. Its orders help ensure the success of a plane in which Air Canada and CP Air have no interest. Wardair sets a range record with a 747 flight from Gatwick to Honolulu, the longest-ever westbound flight for the aircraft. A Wardair Dash 7, the *Don Braun*, airlifts Queen Elizabeth II and Prince Philip on a tour of northern Alberta.

1979:
Wardair carries 32,000 of the 50,000 Vietnamese refugees brought to Canada by Canadian airlines.

1986:
After two decades of lobbying, Ward obtains federal approval to become a full-fledged scheduled carrier on domestic routes across Canada. After less than two years of offering scheduled flights abroad, Wardair is named the world's finest scheduled carrier by *Holiday Which?* magazine. It will take top honours again a year later.

1986:
Ward introduces Airbus jetliners to Canada. The plane's commercial viability is untested, and among North American carriers, only Eastern Airlines has taken a chance on it. Other carriers are wary of buying aircraft from the upstart Airbus Industrie, a consortium of European aircraft makers, for fear of alienating key supplier Boeing Co.

1987:
Wardair has the wrong mix of aircraft for its new status as a scheduled carrier. With the proceeds from the sale of long-range 747s and DC-10s, it replaces its entire fleet, buying short-haul aircraft better suited to heavily travelled domestic

routes within Canada. Ward announces plans to spend a staggering $1 billion on 12 brand-new Airbuses, 16 MD-88s and 24 Fokker F100s.

1988-89:

An estimated loss of $100 million, and the desperate need for another $200 million in cash to stay aloft, forces Ward to give up his airline just three years after realizing his lifelong dream of becoming a full-service scheduled carrier. On May 2, 1989, Wardair is sold to Canadian Airlines International for $248 million.

1999:

Facing insolvency, Canadian Airlines International forges a proposed deal in which AMR Corp., parent of American Airlines, and Toronto merchant bank Onex Corp. will buy the airline and merge it with Air Canada. The Onex-AMR bid is withdrawn after a court decision rules the proposed transaction is illegal, citing a federal law that prohibits any party from acquiring more than 10 per cent of Air Canada. Air Canada then succeeds with a $92-million counteroffer to buy Canadian Airlines.

At the point of Wardair's disappearance just a decade earlier, there had been three major airlines. Now there is just one, and Air Canada has achieved the quasi-monopoly status that predecessor TCA enjoyed when it was created in the 1930s.

APPENDIX 3

FOUR SEASONS HOTELS INC.

Selected Four Seasons and Regent Properties in 2000

Isadore Sharp's first property, the Four Seasons Motor Hotel in Toronto's red-light district, opened in 1961. By the late 1990s, Four Seasons Hotels Inc. was the world's leading luxury hotelier, with more than 50 Four Seasons and Regent hotels and resorts in operation, and another 19 properties under development, in 22 countries in North America, Europe, Asia, Australia and the Caribbean.

Accolades—1990s

Beginning in the early 1980s, Sharp decided to focus on luxury, and shed his firm's mid-market properties. Since that time, a distinguishing characteristic of Four Seasons' hotels and resorts was that they commanded the highest room rates in town. The pricing strategy was supported by the success of most properties in achieving preferred status among discriminating patrons. Each hotel at some point, and usually repeatedly, had been cited in reader surveys conducted by leading magazines and newspapers as the best hotel or resort in its city or region.

Zagat Survey 1997
• best hotel chain

Travel & Leisure 1998
• 18 of the top 100 hotels were Four Seasons properties
• best Caribbean resort

Institutional Investor 1998 Readers' Survey
• 16 Four Seasons properties were included among the world's 100 best hotels, with nine placing in the top 25, making Four Seasons the top chain in this prominent survey of international financiers

Conde Nast Traveler 1998 Reader's Survey
- 17 Four Seasons properties were among the top 100 in *Traveler's* worldwide ranking
- 11 of the ranking's 25 top North American hotels were Four Seasons properties
- Four Seasons claimed top spot in the survey's ranking of Pacific Rim hotels and its category for Asian resorts
- The magazine's annual "Gold List" of the world's top hotels and resorts included references to almost every property in the Four Seasons portfolio

AAA Five Diamond Awards 1999
- 15 Four Seasons properties and four restaurants won top honours, making Four Seasons the leader in this venerable survey for the 18th consecutive year

Selected Four Seasons and Regent Properties in 2000

Bali
Four Seasons Resort Bali at Jimbaran Bay
— 147 guest apartments, each with landscaped courtyard and plunge pool, and separate, connecting villas for sleeping, bathing and dining; at the sister Four Seasons Resort Bali at Sayan, 18 suites and 26 villas, each with a private plunge pool, amid rice fields overlooking the Ayung River gorge.

Mae Rim Valley, Thailand
The Regent Resort Chaing Mai at Mae Rim Valley
— 64 Lanna-style pavilions set among rice terraces in northern Thailand, not far from the border with Burma and Laos. One of the few world-class resorts whose local diversions include both golf and elephant trekking.

Maldives
Four Seasons Resort Maldives at Kuda Huraa
— 106 villas at a secluded tropical resort covering an entire coral atoll in the Indian Ocean southwest of Sri Lanka. Rated as one of the world's top 10 destinations for deep-sea diving.

Istanbul
Four Seasons Hotel Istanbul
— 65 rooms framing an open courtyard in a facility remodelled from a century-old neo-classic Turkish prison, near the Blue Mosque, Topkapi Palace and Spice Bazaar.

Milan
Four Seasons Milano
— 98-room facility in a refashioned 15th-century monastery.

Paris

Four Seasons Hotel — George V Paris

— 245 rooms mid-way between the Arc de Triomphe and the Eiffel Tower. Named for King George V of Britain, the opulent Art Deco landmark was a centre of world affairs from the time of its opening in 1928. It was an official branch office of the League of Nations, served as headquarters for Gen. Dwight D. Eisenhower during the liberation of Paris, and Yves St. Laurent, among other designers, presented his new collections in the grand ballroom. Extensively renovated by Four Seasons in the late 1990s.

Carlsbad, California

Four Seasons Resort Aviara

— Golf resort with 331 rooms and a course designed by Arnold Palmer, with adjoining 240-unit time-sharing complex.

Ka'upulehu-Kona, Hawaii

Four Seasons Resort — Hualalai at Historic Ka'upulehu

— 243 bungalow-style rooms on the upscale North Kona Coast, featuring a Jack Nicklaus-designed golf course on the Senior PGA tour.

Las Vegas

Four Seasons Hotel Las Vegas

— 424 rooms in the Mandalay Bay Resort & Casino, a 60-acre development at the south end of the Las Vegas Strip.

Los Angeles

Four Seasons Hotel Los Angeles at Beverly Hills

— 285 rooms in a tropical-gardens setting, a haunt for film-industry executives who like to give their expense accounts a workout in a quiet residential setting.

The Regent Beverly Wilshire

— 395 rooms in a 1920s landmark hotel at the corner of Wilshire Boulevard and Rodeo Drive.

Nevis

Four Seasons Resort Nevis, West Indies

— 196 rooms on 350 oceanfront acres on this sister island to St. Kitts in the Leeward Islands, including a Robert Trent Jones golf course.

New York

Four Seasons Hotel New York

— 370 rooms in Manhattan's tallest hotel, on 57th Street between Park and Madison avenues. The hotel, designed by I.M. Pei, was the costliest hotel-building project in history when construction began in the 1980s.

The Pierre

— Fifth Avenue landmark with 202 rooms, across the street from Central

Park at 61st Street. The historic apartment-hotel was largely occupied by long-term tenants who rubbed shoulders with well-heeled transients under the famed *trompe l'oeil* ceiling in the Rotunda.

Punta Mita, Mexico

Four Seasons Resort Punta Mita

— 100-room oceanfront resort with a Jack Nicklaus golf course, plus coral reef snorkelling and whale watching, northwest of Puerto Vallarta.

Four Seasons Resort Club at Punta Mita

— 90 villas in a time-share facility adjoining the resort.

San Francisco

Four Seasons Hotel San Francisco

— 77-room hotel under development as part of the upscale Yerba Buena Tower complex of retail and office space. Four Seasons launched its first Residences project at this hotel — a collection of corporate apartments on the top floors of the building that could be purchased at prices starting at $1 million (U.S.).

Toronto

Four Seasons Hotel Toronto

— The chain's 380-room Canadian flagship, anchor for the upscale Yorkville shopping district and focal point in September for the annual Toronto International Film Festival.

Washington, D.C.

Four Seasons Hotel Washington

— 56 rooms next to the historic Chesapeake & Ohio Canal and Rock Creek Park. A Georgetown hangout for politicians and lobbyists.

APPENDIX 4

OLYMPIA & YORK DEVELOPMENTS LTD

The Reichmann Empire

At the height of his powers, in the late 1980s, Paul Reichmann was the greatest property developer on earth. His projects were built by Toronto-based firm called Olympia & York Developments Ltd, a private firm owned by brothers Paul, Albert and Ralph Reichmann, their mother, Renée, and their wives.

At its peak, O&Y owned and had under development about 50 million square feet of prime office space in 35 North American cities and London, England — an amount roughly equal to all the office space in downtown Toronto.

Paul and Ralph Reichmann erected their first building, a $70,000 Toronto warehouse for the family's tile-importing business, in 1958. Thirty years later, the Reichmanns had a portfolio of more than 100 office buildings in Canada, the U.S. and Europe. They were the biggest commercial landlords in New York, with more than twice the space of the second-ranking Rockefeller family.

Before the O&Y empire collapsed in 1992 in one of the biggest corporate bankruptcies in history, the Reichmanns were thought to be worth more than $13 billion (U.S.). They were ranked by *Fortune* as the world's fourth-richest family, just behind the Arab sheiks and British royals.

In addition to the assets shown below, the family also owned Toronto-based Olympia Floor & Wall Tile, by far the largest supplier of flooring materials in Canada. This firm was run by Ralph Reichmann and was the Reichmanns' first business in North America after the family emigrated from Tangier in the 1950s.

Olympia Tile survived the early 1990s meltdown in real-estate values, with the Reichmann ownership intact. But the property holdings and the equity stakes in major corporations, for which Paul was the strategic genius and Albert the chief administrator, were lost in the bankruptcy or sold prior to it.

Later in the 1990s, the Reichmann family was able to regain control of a flagship O&Y project, First Canadian Place in Toronto, the tallest office building in Canada. And Paul reclaimed a significant ownership stake in Canary Wharf, the enormous campus of corporate head-office buildings in London's Docklands district that triggered O&Y's collapse.

Worldwide Property Holdings

At various times, O&Y held ownership interests in the following buildings, which were either developed (**D**) or acquired (**A**) by the Reichmanns. Projects are shown in approximate chronological order of development or purchase. These projects were owned directly by the privately held Olympia & York Developments Ltd. Note that the Reichmanns had interests in many other properties through their equity stakes in publicly traded real-estate firms, listed separately.

- *Olympia Square Don Mills, Ont. (D)*: The Reichmanns' first mixed-use project (office and retail space).
- *North American Tower (D) 1964-67:* Commissioned by Mutual of New York; later known as the MONY Life Insurance Co. of Canada Building; 220,000 square feet.
- *Forester House (D):* Worldwide head office for the Independent Order of Foresters insurance company, known as the IOF Tower.
- *Shell Canada Data Centre, Don Mills, Ont. (D) c. 1966:* 165,000 square feet.
- *Global House, University Avenue, Toronto (D) 1967:* Anchor tenant, Global General Insurance Co.; 380,000 square feet.
- *Texaco Canada building, Don Mills, Ont. (D) late 1960s:* Head-office building for the Canadian arm of U.S-based Texaco Inc., with 240,000 square feet.
- *Bell Canada Data Centre, Don Mills, Ont. (D) late 1960s:* 400,000 square feet.
- *Blue Cross Building, Don Mills, Ont. (D)*
- *Nestlé Building, Don Mills, Ont. (D)*
- *Ontario Federation of Labour Building, Don Mills, Ont. (D)*
- *Xerox Building, Don Mills, Ont. (D)*
- *York Centre, York and King Streets, Toronto (D) late 1960s:* The Reichmanns' first office tower in Toronto's financial district, with 900,000 square feet of space (later the Aetna Canada building).
- *Place Bell Canada, Ottawa (D) 1970s:* Designed by Edward Durrell Stone; 1.5 million square feet.
- *C.D. Howe Building, Ottawa (D) 1970s*
- *L'Esplanade Laurier, Ottawa (D) 1970s*

- Ottawa Citizen *building, Ottawa, Ont. (D)*
- *Four Seasons Hotel, Ottawa (D)*
- Toronto Star *building, Toronto (D) 1971:* Landmark waterfront office tower with 900,000 square feet, plus a printing annex.
- *Sunoco Building, University Avenue, Toronto (D)*
- *Government of Ontario building, Toronto (D):* Offices for the provincial ministry of consumer and commercial relations.
- *First Canadian Place, Toronto (D):* Mixed-use project.
  - *First Bank Tower (1975)*: World's tallest bank headquarters when completed, at 72 storeys, and designed by Edward Durrell Stone. New head-office home for Canada's oldest bank, the Bank of Montreal.
  - *Exchange Tower (1982)*: 36-storey office tower with 1.5 million square feet, and a three-storey pavillion for the new home of the Toronto Stock Exchange.
- *The "Uris buildings," Manhattan, 1977*: A package of eight New York office buildings acquired by O&Y in 1977 from National Kinney Corp., an arm of Steve Ross's Warner Communications Inc., for a cash outlay of just $46 million and the assumption of $288 million in mortgages. By the late 1980s, O&Y's Uris buildings, with a total of more than 11 million square feet of space, would be worth an estimated $3.5 billion. The portfolio was originally developed by the venerable New York real-estate family headed by Percy and Harold Uris, sons of a Latvian immigrant ironworker. Their 55 Water Street, at 3.3 million square feet, was the world's largest commercial office building when it opened in 1971.
  - 55 Water Street, Manhattan (A).
  - 1290 Avenue of the Americas, Manhattan (A); then the Sperry Rand Building.
  - 245 Park Avenue, Manhattan (A); then the American Brands Building.
  - 2 Broadway, Manhattan (A).
  - 320 Park Avenue, Manhattan (A); then the ITT Building.
  - 850 Third Avenue, Manhattan (A); then the Western Publishing Building.
  - 10 East 53rd Street, Manhattan (A); then the Harper & Row Building.
  - 60 Broad Street, Manhattan (A).
- *North York Medical Arts building, Toronto (D)*
- *Doulton House, London, Eng. (A) 1979*
- *La Boursidiere, Paris (A) 1979*
- *Market Square, Toronto (D) 1980-82*: Mixed-use project: shopping, theatre and

luxury condos; partnership with Ronto Developments of Toronto, which was the lead developer.

- *Park Avenue Atrium, Manhattan (restoration), early 1980s*: 1.1 million square feet of office space at the former 466 Lexington Avenue.

- *Queen's Quay Terminal, Toronto waterfront (restoration), early 1980s*: Renovation project, designed by Eb Zeidler, that transformed what had been a derelict warehouse, once one of the biggest waterfront terminals on the Great Lakes, into an upscale complex with 850,000 square feet of space for offices, shopping and luxury condos.

- *Esso Plaza, Calgary (D) 1981.*

- *Shell Centre, Calgary (D) 1980s:* 33-storey office tower.

- *Alberta Natural Gas building, Calgary (D) early 1980*: 28-storey tower.

- *Fountain Plaza, Portland, Ore. (D) early 1980s*: 700,000 square feet of office and retail space, plus apartments and cinemas.

- *Arco Tower, Dallas (D) 1982*: 49-storey, 1.3-million-square-foot office building.

- *1 Liberty Square, Boston (restoration), 1981*: 150,000 square feet of office space in a restored, century-old building that was once home to the Boston Stock Exchange.

- *Exchange Place, Boston (D) early 1980s*: 40-storey office tower with 1.1 million square feet of space.

- *Olympia Center, Chicago (D) 1980s*: 63-storey office tower in rose-coloured Swedish granite developed in partnership with Chicago investor Sam Zell.

- *1999 Bryan Street, Dallas (D) 1982*: 36-storey, 760,000-square-foot office tower.

- *400 Hope Street, Los Angeles (D) 1982*: 26-storey building with 710,000 square feet of office space.

- *One Financial Plaza, Springfield, Mass. (D) 1982*: 17-storey building with 380,000 square feet of space.

- *One Corporate Center, Hartford, Conn. (D) 1981*: 16-storey office tower with 425,000 square feet of space.

- *One Commercial Plaza, Hartford, Conn. (D) 1983*: 26-storey, 696,000-square-foot office tower.

- *World Financial Center, Manhattan (D) 1980-87*: The biggest office development in the history of Manhattan, and the largest attempted since ground was broken for the Rockefeller Center in the 1920s. WFC, planning for which began in 1980, was built on a sandbar created by landfill taken from excavation for the foundation of the neighbouring twin towers of the World Trade Center.

The WFC project created 8 million square feet of space in six buildings, representing about 3 per cent of all the commercial office space in Manhattan at the time, at the southern tip of Manhattan adjoining the Wall Street financial district. WFC included four towers designed in the post-modern style by Cesar Pelli, dean of architecture at Yale University, and ranging in height from 33 to 51 storeys. The project included two nine-storey "sentry" buildings at the entrance to the site, plus an immense Winter Garden atrium and a mile-long promenade along the Hudson River. WFC became the head-office home for American Express Co., Merrill Lynch & Co. Inc., Oppenheimer & Co. and Dow Jones & Co. (including the newsroom for *The Wall Street Journal*).

- *59 Maiden Lane, Manhattan (A) early 1980s*: Formerly the head office for City Investing, a conglomerate that owned Home Insurance Co., Motel 6 and other firms, and which sold its head office to O&Y in a deal that was to have City Investing become a high-profile tenant in the new World Financial Center. Ultimately, City Investing opted to wind up its operations before it could move in to WFC.

- *125 Broad Street, Manhattan (A) 1983*: Formerly American Express Plaza, which Amex sold to O&Y in a deal that saw Amex become a key tenant in World Financial Center.

- *One Liberty Plaza, Manhattan (A) early 1980s*: Formerly the Merrill Lynch building, which the huge brokerage sold to O&Y in a deal that saw Merrill Lynch become a major tenant at WFC.

- *Scotia Plaza, Toronto (A)*: Canada's second-tallest office tower, at 68 storeys, and developed by Robert Campeau, from whom O&Y bought its stake.

- *Canary Wharf, London (D)*: Largest office project ever built in Europe, with one million square metres of office space, built on reclaimed land in the Docklands neighbourhood of London's Isle of Dogs district.

  - *One Canada Place* at Canary Wharf: Tallest office building in Britain, at 50 storeys.

Stock-Market Portfolio

- *Block Bros. Industries Ltd, Vancouver (1978-79)*: Canada's fourth-largest real-estate brokerage.

- *English Property Corp. Ltd, London (1979)*: Leading British real-estate developer, with 10 million square feet of leasable space at properties in England, Ireland, Belgium and France. O&Y sold these off within four years of its $140-million purchase, however, finding the British and continental European markets too slow for their liking. O&Y's real interest in English Properties was its

40 per cent indirect control of the Canadian property developer Trizec Corp. Ltd.

- *Trizec Corp. Ltd, Calgary (40 per cent)*: Canada's No. 3 real-estate developer, with 24 million square feet of leasable space in office towers, shopping malls and residential projects, whose flagship properties included the landmark Montreal office complex Place Ville Marie, and the Yorkdale and Scarborough Town Centre shopping malls in Toronto. Trizec traced its history to the 1950s, when a predecessor firm was created by legendary U.S. developer William Zeckendorf. Shortly after O&Y invested in the firm, Trizec bought Ernest W. Hahn Inc., one of the U.S.'s largest mall operators. After the 1990s meltdown in North American real estate, a restructured Trizec, now controlled by Toronto financier Peter Munk, would re-emerge as TrizecHahn Corp.

- *Brinco Ltd (1980)*: A Newfoundland natural resources firm originally developed by the Rothschild family; 50.1 per cent was acquired by Olympia & York in 1980.

- *Cassair Resources Ltd, Vancouver*: Asbestos producer.

- *Abitibi-Price Inc., Toronto (1981)*: World's largest newsprint maker; acquired for $618 million.

- *Trilon Financial Corp. (13 per cent)*: Holding company jointly controlled with Edward and Peter Bronfman's Edper Investments Ltd. Trilon controlled Royal Trustco Ltd, Canada's largest trust company and second-largest real-estate broker; London Life Insurance Co., Canada's No. 4 life insurer; and a merchant banking operation. O&Y gained its stake in Trilon in exchange for its 23 per cent interest in Royal Trustco, acquired in 1981.

- *Noranda Inc., Toronto*: One of the world's leading diversified natural resources firms, with interests in base-metals and precious-metals mining and smelting, aluminum, oil and gas and forest products. Jointly controlled with Peter and Edward Bronfman.

- *MacMillan Bloedel Ltd, Vancouver*: Canada's largest forest-products company.

- *Bow Valley Industries Ltd, Calgary (7 per cent)*: Oil and gas development in Western Canada and the North Sea.

- *Canada Northwest Energy Ltd, Calgary (20 per cent)*: Oil and gas production firm.

- *Cadillac Fairview Corp. Ltd, Toronto (22 per cent) 1984*: O&Y paid $232 million for its stake in North America's second-largest real estate developer, with a burgeoning collection of properties in Canada and leading U.S. cities. CF's trophy properties included the Toronto Eaton Centre, the Toronto-Dominion Centre and Vancouver's Pacific Centre.

- *Landmark Land Co. Inc., Carmel, California*: Property developer.
- *Gulf Canada Ltd, Toronto (1985)*: Leading Canadian oil and gas producer; the firm's gas stations and refineries were promptly sold to Canada's state-owned Petro-Canada and to Ultramar PLC of Britain.
- *Hiram Walker Resources Ltd, Toronto (1986)*: Oil and gas producer, natural gas distributor (Consumers Gas) and Canada's second-largest liquor firm (maker of Canadian Club whisky); the spirits operation, Hiram Walker-Gooderham & Worts Ltd., was immediately dealt off to Britain's Allied-Lyons PLC, maker of Tetley tea and already a distributor of Hiram Walker liquors in overseas markets.
- *Interprovincial Pipe Line Ltd:* Canada's longest oil pipeline, carrying oil from Western Canada to refineries in Eastern Canada and the U.S. Midwest.
- *Home Oil Co. Ltd*: Oil and gas producer in Western Canada.
- *Consumers Gas Co. Ltd:* Canada's largest natural-gas utility (later Enbridge).
- *Santa Fe Southern Pacific Corp. (19.9 per cent) 1987-88*: Leading U.S. railroad with extensive oil and gas assets and nine million square feet of office space. O&Y was thwarted in its effort to obtain board representation at the firm.
- *Campeau Corp., Toronto (29.7 per cent) 1985-88*: Leading Canadian real-estate developer, whose major properties included the 68-storey Scotia Plaza in Toronto, head office of the Bank of Nova Scotia. Campeau Corp. self-destructed soon after becoming the world's biggest department-store operator with Robert Campeau's daring, late-1980s acquisitions of Allied Stores (Brooks Bros, Ann Taylor) and Federated Department Stores (Bloomingdales). When Campeau Corp. collapsed in 1989, O&Y lost most of its $560-million investment in the firm.

APPENDIX 5

MAGNA INTERNATIONAL INC.

Dynamic Growth

Few companies in non-high tech industries can match Magna's growth record over the past 20 years. Frank Stronach's firm has blossomed in tandem with the heightened outsourcing of parts-making by the world's major automakers, the most significant trend in vehicle manufacturing in the last decades of the 20th century.

Note, however, that rapid growth has come at a price: heavy spending on new plants and technologies to win the confidence of automakers has often put a crimp on profits.

The Fastest-Growing Auto-Parts Maker

All of the leading auto-parts makers were beneficiaries of the outsourcing trend by Detroit's Big Three and by automakers in Europe and Japan. But Magna got a head start in persuading automakers to entrust it with specialty parts-making and complete and partial vehicle assembly, and has profited even more substantially.

	Sales ($billions U.S.) 1978	1998	% change	Profits ($millions U.S.) 1978	1998	% change
Magna International[1] Aurora, Ontario, Canada	$0.128	$9.2	+7,091%	$6.6	$506.2	+7,570%
Dana Corp. Toledo, Ohio	$2.3	$12.8	+475%	$134.0	$534.0	+299%
Johnson Controls Milwaukee, Wis.	$0.599	$12.6	+2,004%	$37.2	$338.0	+802%
TRW[2] Cleveland, Ohio	$3.8	$11.9	+213%	$174.0	$447.0	+157%

Source: Company reports

---

[1] Figures for Magna are in Canadian dollars. For all other firms, figures are in U.S. dollars.

[2] TRW has significant non-auto parts operations, including defence contracting and credit verification services.

Magna International Inc. Sales and Profits, 1978-98

	Sales (Cdn $ millions)	% change	Profits (Cdn $millions)	% change	Employees
1978	$128.2	—	$6.6	—	2,500
1979	$166.3	+30%	$8.5	+29%	2,500
1980	$183.5	+10%	$5.6	-34%	2,500
1981	$232.1	+26%	$6.9	+23%	3,000
1982	$226.5	-2%	$3.8	-45%	3,000
1983	$302.5	+35%	$14.7	+287%	4,000
1984	$493.6	+63%	$31.5	+114%	5,500
1985	$690.4	+40%	$43.2	+37%	8,150
1986	$1,027.8	+49%	$47.3	+9%	10,300
1987	$1,152.5	+12%	$40.3	-15%	12,218
1988	$1,458.6	+27%	$19.5	-52%	15,800
1989	$1,923.7	+32%	$33.6	+72%	17,500
1990	$1,927.2	+0.2%	($224.3)	—	16,000
1991	$2,014.5	+5%	$16.5	—	15,800
1992	$2,358.0	+17%	$98.0	+499%	14,500
1993	$2,606.7	+11%	$140.4	+43%	15,500
1994	$3,568.5	+37%	$234.4	+67%	20,000
1995	$4,795.4	+34%	$317.0	+35%	21,900
1996	$5,856.2	+22%	$309.0	-3%	26,800
1997	$7,691.8	+31%	$603.4	+95%	36,000
1998	$9,190.8	+19%	$506.2	-16%	49,000

Source: Company reports

APPENDIX 6

BOMBARDIER INC.

Defending Federalism and Celebrating Roots

Laurent Beaudoin Defends Federalism

In a series of speeches Laurent Beaudoin made in the weeks leading up to Quebec's 1995 referendum on sovereignty, the CEO of Bombardier Inc. stood virtually alone among his corporate peers. In the aftermath of the rejection of the Meech Lake Francophone constitutional accord five years earlier, francophone business leaders who had defended federalism at that time had since gone to ground. To the extent he was effective in winning some Quebeckers to his point of view, Beaudoin's role in the debate was substantial. For in the end, the "No" side ultimately prevailed by only the narrowest margin — less than 1 per cent of the vote.

Five days before the October 30 vote, Beaudoin addressed the chamber of commerce in Ste-Foy, a suburb of Quebec City, where he had begun his career as a management accountant some 44 years earlier:

> Because this is a crucial moment, I would like to go over the reasons why Quebeckers should remain in Canada. I do not intend to set straight the false interpretations of some of my previous statements. However, I must pick up on a certain remark made by the premier of Quebec, who accused me of "spitting on Quebeckers."
>
> I would like to tell Mr. Parizeau that my own personal evolution as chief executive officer of Bombardier over the last 32 years absolutely refutes his unwarranted remark. The whole history of our company is a clear demonstration of my strong attachment to Quebec. At Bombardier, in the last 32 years, we have been taking risks and working relentlessly to build a great enterprise in Quebec and with Quebeckers, an enterprise whose reach now extends across Canada and internationally.
>
> We have always had the interests of Quebeckers at heart whenever we had to make critical choices.

In 1973, when we anticipated problems in the snowmobile market because of the oil crisis, we could have sold our company to foreign interests, as so many others did. In 1974, we could have also closed our Moto-Ski snowmobile plant in La Pocatiére because of a severe decline in sales.

We took a risk in deciding to enter the production of subway cars for the Montreal subway. We converted our La Pocatiére plant and kept our workers. We also hired and trained hundreds more. Since then, we have built some 3,000 subway and commuter train cars, mostly for export markets.

This plant has become the main employer in the region and is now making a significant contribution to its dynamic economy. This is what we have done for Quebeckers in La Pocatiére.

At the same time, we consolidated our snowmobile production in Valcourt, Quebec, saving the majority of jobs in the process. When some financial consultants suggested we sell this part of our company to direct our resources to more promising sectors, we decided to stay the course and to diversify our operations in Valcourt through the launch of various products, with mixed results.

But our efforts and our determination finally paid off. We have reinvested in the development of new snowmobile models and in our production lines in Valcourt. And we developed the personal watercraft, the Sea Doo. Increased sales of watercraft and snowmobiles brought the work force to more than 3,000 employees. This is what we have done with and for Quebeckers in the Eastern Townships.

And what did we do after our acquisition of Canadair in 1986? We won new contracts to produce aircraft components for Boeing, Airbus and other companies; we developed the Regional Jet; and we revamped the Challenger business jet and our fire-fighting amphibious aircraft. Since the acquisition, the number of employees has gone from 4,000 to 8,000 in Dorval and Saint-Laurent. And Canadair has become the spearhead of the Canadian aerospace industry.

This is what we have done with and for Quebeckers in Montreal. Mr. Parizeau, is this what you call "spitting on Quebeckers"?

There are now close to 13,000 employees working for Bombardier across Quebec, and to these we could add the large number of men and women who are employed by our suppliers. We have business relationships with more than 2,150 subcontractors, suppliers and partners across Quebec, in the Bas St-Laurent, Beauce, Mauricie and Bois-Francs regions as well as the Eastern Townships and the large urban areas of Quebec City and Montreal.

Over the past 10 years, our company has invested more than $2.25 billion in Quebec, in its plants, equipment, R&D and in new product development. We have kept control of our company in Quebec, and we have expanded its reach across Canada and the world.

Mr. Parizeau, don't all of our achivements in Quebec prove that we have made a dynamic contribution to the economy of our community? When you say you are proud of our strong economy and when you use it as an argument for the "Yes" side, you keep forgetting to say that our accomplishments have been brought about thanks to the Canadian federation.

Because they are Canadians, Quebeckers have made important breakthroughs everywhere in Canada. I am especially familiar with examples in aerospace and mass transit equipment.

We merged both of Canada's aircraft manufacturers — Canadair in Montreal and de Havilland in Toronto — under the Bombardier umbrella. By acquiring Urban Transportation Development Corp. (UTDC), also based in Ontario, we have done likewise in the mass transit sector and have become the North American leader.

In both sectors, we can now do business in international markets with much stronger entities which are backed by the two government levels, federal and provincial. These are real accomplishments made by Quebeckers based on the fact that Quebec is a part of Canada.

Until now, I have spoken about Bombardier's achievements. But there are many other examples to illustrate how Quebec companies have been successful on a Canadian scale: Canam Manac, Jean Coutu, Videotron, BioChem, Quebecor, Transcontinental and many more.

These major breakthroughs in Canadian as well as in international markets have been achieved with Quebeckers, who are the major beneficiaries. Our employees are not inward-looking, or confined to Quebec, nor is their personal growth constrained by the fact they are French-speaking.

At Bombardier, French-speaking Quebeckers have reached key positions all over the world. A Quebecker is now president of de Havilland, a company with nearly 4,000 employees, in Toronto. Quebeckers hold important positions at Learjet in Kansas and at Shorts in Northern Ireland. The president of UTDC in Kingston, Ont. is also a Quebecker.

Quebeckers are in lead positions in our Concarril subsidiary in Mexico, at our plant in Barre, Vermont, and at the boat producton facilities we just acquired in Benton, Illinois.

French-speaking Quebeckers are now working in Turkey on the Ankara subway, and in Malaysia on a commuter train project for Kuala Lumpur. There are also French-speaking Quebeckers in our personal watercraft marketing and test centre in Melbourne, Florida and in our snowmobile distribution and sales centre in Wausau, Wisconsin.

Bombardier is not unique in this respect. I refer to French-speaking managers working around the world for SNC-Lavalin, le Groupe Roche and other engineering companies, for cable firm Videotron, les pharmacies Jean Coutu, publishing and printing company Quebecor, and steel-joist maker Canam Manac. And let's not forget the French-speaking executives at the head of important Canadian and international companies: Jean Monty at Nortel, Jacques Bougie at Alcan, Yves Landry at Chrysler Canada, Gilles Ouimet at Pratt & Whitney, Charles Sirois at Teleglobe, and many others.

With all this evidence, who can still believe that the French language and French-speaking Quebeckers have not established themselves in the world of business, both in Quebec and Canada?

We control all of the instruments of our economic, cultural and social development. Quebec has never been more in charge of its own destiny than at the present time. And changes in political structure will not help us solve all the problems we face nor to create more jobs. After 300 years of history, why destroy a country that has provided us with the standard of living we enjoy today? It would be easy to destroy our country, but building another would be long and hard.

Messrs. Parizeau and [Lucien] Bouchard [leader of the separatist Bloc Québécois party] are behaving as if they can dictate the rules of economic development.

They are being unrealistic when they tell us about Quebec's future after separation. They choose to ignore the costs of the transition and the costs of the new political structures as well as the consequences of a devalued Quebec currency and the unavoidable rise in interest rates. They even want people to believe that it will be easier to create new jobs in an economy disrupted by such radical changes.

They think they know better about how our fellow Canadians will react to Quebec sovereignty. They would even have us believe they can predict where Americans will stand on the matter.

One day they speak of a common currency, and the next day about a currency they will control. In Hull, they say we will keep our Canadian passport; and in the Beauce, that we will have a Quebec passport.

At noon, they say that they will achieve independence before securing a partnership with Canada; and in the evening they say the offer of a partnership will come first.

One day they tell us they will maintain and even improve social programs. The next day they say the deficit will be reduced to $5 billion, without raising income taxes, which is impossible without making drastic cutbacks in social programs.

Despite its imperfections, Canada's current structure has allowed for a remarkable development of Quebec enterprises in the last 30 years. We must recognize the positive contribution of the Canadian federation to Quebec. If we are to believe those who want a sovereign Quebec, everything that goes wrong is Ottawa's fault and everything that goes well is thanks to Quebec.

In their vision of Quebec, the leaders of the "Yes" do not recognize how far Quebeckers have gone in mastering their own economy and culture. In doing so, despite our internal debates, we have played a major role in transforming Canada's political society and in developing its economy.

We have built a unique and strong society in Quebec through our sense of attachment to both Quebec and Canada. This dual sense of belonging has enabled us to create powerful institutions in both Quebec and in Canada to ensure our economic and cultural security. It has enabled us to demonstrate our cultural talents, our entrepreneurial skills and the capabilities of our work force in Quebec, in Canada and in the world.

We have no reason to stop and question the fact that Quebec belongs in the Canadian federation. The country that some Quebeckers are still looking for has long since been discovered. It is Canada, a rich, diversified and welcoming country with an entrenched sense of sharing.

Late in the evening on October 31, 1995, as it became clear that the sovereignty option had been rejected by voters, Quebec premier Jacques Parizeau did not hide his bitterness. In a televised speech to a hall of Yes supporters, he blamed the outcome on "money and the ethnic vote." The reference was to the heavily financed No campaign, and overwhelming support for the status quo among Quebec's visible minorities. That same night, Bernard Landry, the PQ finance minister, lashed out at a hotel clerk whom he took to be a recent immigrant, accusing her of thwarting the destiny of Quebec's francophone majority.

Landry apologized for his remarks the next day. That same day, too, Parizeau announced his resignation as premier. His outburst the previous night reinforced the impression long held by some in Quebec and elsewhere in Canada that the province's nationalist movement was influenced by racist tendencies. PQ officials hastened to express their horror at Parizeau's remarks, which they insisted were not characteristic of the sovereignty movement. Only fleeting mention was made in media accounts of the fact that a majority of the premier's audience appeared to share his conviction, having applauded a comment that every premier across the country condemned as a racist slur.

298 NO GUTS, NO GLORY

No group in Quebec felt more isolated, arguably, than the Jewish community of Montreal. Doubly cursed as stalwarts of national unity and outsiders to the province's Catholic tradition, many Montreal Jews felt they had been purposefully isolated from the business and social mainstream of the province.

Three weeks after the fateful referendum vote, Beaudoin made the inaugural speech at Montreal's Jewish Chamber of Commerce. Referring to fears of a backlash against minority groups in the province, Beaudoin acknowleged that "for many Quebeckers, the post-referendum period we are now entering is fraught with anxiety." But in words calculated to reassure his audience, he urged it to seize opportunities for a renewed federalism "for the benefit of your community and all Quebeckers.

"The Jewish community of Montreal has played a key role in developing the economy of the Montreal region, of Quebec and of Canada. Its entrepreneurs and professionals have made a remarkable contribution to the prosperity of our country."

Joseph-Armand Bombardier Celebrates his Small-Town Roots

In 1952, the founder of Bombardier Inc. invited his employees at Valcourt, Quebec to a reception that marked the 10th anniversary of the firm. For his speaking notes, he scribbled these words on an old Christmas card:

> I don't remember any precise moment when difficult work seemed new or strange — so I learned to work, to economize, to give. It is with these tools only that I undertook life's task at Valcourt at the age of 19 years.
>
> Often I was guided by the wise advice of my parents. It was in fact here that Papa didn't approve of my closing the garage in 1938 so that I could occupy myself entirely with "Auto-Neige," and it is my mother who two years later advised me to enlarge the factory, because, she said, "If you can help others, my son, it is your duty to do so, and it is what your father and I have tried to do and we have never regretted it."
>
> Maman lit the torch that still burns in me and with the grace of God it will not blow out until my death, or even better I hope to have the happiness of communicating it to others so that it can be carried for a good long time.
>
> This torch, this Flame, is the desire to help my compatriots succeed in life and to prove once again that the French Canadians are better than mere carriers of water. Without hesitation, I put myself to work and four months later we had at Valcourt the inauguration of our first factory in 1940. Twelve years passed . . . work, economizing, the effort maintained, benedictions from heaven and your cooperation, made the enterprise what it is today and the goal envisioned by your humble servant was realized bit by bit.
>
> In Valcourt an atmosphere is realized where there is a good life, away from the turbulence of a big city, for it leaves us more time to think, to pray, to love.
>
> You contribute a lot to propagate here and in the world this ardent flame that I received from my parents, and I want to communicate it — it translates into:
> Love of Work
> Love of your children and the future
> Love of God.

APPENDIX 7

NORTEL NETWORKS CORP.

The Buying Spree and the Current Network

In an unprecedented talent raid by a Canadian company on the U.S. tech community between 1998 and 2000, Nortel CEO John Roth spent about $18 billion (U.S.) to snap up a dozen or so firms whose technology embellished Nortel's existing R&D strengths in fibre optics and so-called end-to-end networks — the service of providing a customer with a complete telephone system, from handsets to refrigerator-sized switching machines and fibre-optic relay devices.

1998:
Roth spends $302 million (U.S.) to buy **Broadband Networks Inc.** of Winnipeg for its expertise in wireless transmission of voice, data and video signals. He pays $305 million (U.S.) for the one-year-old **Aptis Communications Inc.** of Chelmsford, Massachusetts, whose ultra-high-speed routers help telephone companies and Internet service providers meet booming demand for Web access. In its biggest takeover to date, Nortel pays $6.9 billion (U.S.) to acquire **Bay Networks Inc.** of Santa Clara, California, the world's second-largest maker of data-networking gear. And it pays $300 million (U.S.) for **Cambrian Systems Corp.** of Kanata, Ontario, which provides fibre-optic gear for connecting corporate networks to the Internet.

Nortel pays $340 million (U.S.) for **Shasta Networks Inc.**, a Sunnyvale, California, firm whose software enables phone companies to offer their clients virtual private networks and E-commerce capabilities without adding costly equipment. It pays $378 million (U.S.) for **Periphonics Corp.** of Bohemia, New York, which makes software for corporate call centres. And it spends $2.1 billion (U.S.) to buy **Clarify Inc.** of San Jose, California, whose software lets corporations conduct sales, marketing and customer service over the Internet.

2000:

Nortel spends $778 million (U.S.) to purchase four-year-old **Promatory Communications Inc.** of Fremont, California, a company with just $1 million (U.S.) in sales and whose 100 employees design equipment that boosts the transmission capacity of conventional copper wires. Roth pays $3.25 billion (U.S.) for **Qtera Corp.** of Boca Raton, Florida, a two-year-old firm with no revenues, whose 170 employees are developing equipment that greatly extends the distance that signals can be sent over fibre-optic lines before they erode and need to be regenerated, thereby reducing transmission costs. Nortel spends $64.5 million (U.S.) for **Dimension Enterprises Inc.** of Herndon, Virginia, which designs Internet data centres that are not unlike freeway truck stops — on-line clusters of Web sites that also serve as compounds for powerful communications equipment such as servers, routers and data-storage units. It pays $3.2 billion (U.S.) for **Xros Inc.** of Sunnyvale, California, a firm with 90 employees which has developed an optical switch that uses microscopic mirrors to redirect light waves without first converting them into electronic signals. Nortel spends $1.43 billion (U.S.) for **CoreTek Inc.** of Wilmington, Massachusetts, a six-year-old firm with no revenues, whose 120 employers are developing fibre-optics technology that uses lasers to direct bands of light into empty channels, thus avoiding collisions with other traffic. It pays $395-million (U.S.) for **Architel Systems Corp.**, a Toronto-based developer of telecom software that enables Internet and phone networks to manage E-commerce and other services for their customers. In May 2000, Nortel spends $35.5 million to acquire the two thirds of **Photonic Technologies Inc.** of Sydney, Australia, that it didn't already own; Photonics, in which Nortel took a one-third interest in 1998, makes optical network devices that speed the transmission of data on fibre-optic pathways.

Nortel and Its Worldwide Rivals

(All figures in U.S. dollars.)

Company	Rank among world's biggest companies	1998 sales (US$billions)	1998 profits (US$billions)	Employees
1. Siemens (Germany)	22	$66.0	$0.370	416,000
2. Fujitsu (Japan)	51	$41.0	($0.107)	188,000
3. NEC (Japan)	60	$37.2	($1.236)	157,773
4. Lucent Technologies (U.S.)	97	$30.1	$0.970	141,600
5. Motorola (U.S.)	100	$29.4	($0.962)	133,000
6. Bosch (Germany)	105	$28.6	$0.445	189,537
7. Alcatel (France)	145	$23.6	$2.602	118,272
8. L.M. Ericsson (Sweden)	148	$23.2	$1.639	103,667
9. Nortel Networks (Canada)	216	$17.6	($0.537)	58,000
10. Nokia (Finland)	283	$14.5	$1.910	44,543
11. Cisco Systems (U.S.)	—	$8.5	$1.350	15,000
12. 3Com (U.S.)	—	$5.4	$0.030	12,920

Note: Nortel's revenues are generated almost entirely from the sale of telecommunications equipment. Revenue figures for several of the above firms, including Siemens, Fujitsu, NEC, Motorola, Bosch, Ericsson and Nokia, include sales derived from substantial activities outside the field of telecommunications, such as engineering, defense contracting, semiconductors and aviation and automotive electronics. Nortel losses in 1998 arose in large part from goodwill adjustments related to its Bay Networks acquisition. In 1997, Nortel earned a profit of $812 million (U.S.). In 1999, Nortel's operating profit was $1.7 billion (U.S.), up from the previous year's $1.1 billion (U.S.), on sales of $22.2 billion (U.S.), a 26 per cent gain over 1998. After accounting for acquisition-related costs, Nortel's net loss in 1999 was $170 million (U.S.).

Source: Company reports

Nortel's R&D Commitment

In 2000, Nortel employed more engineers and technical workers than any Canadian company — 9,250 people in a worldwide R&D workforce of about 25,000 employees. Its researchers collectively filed an average of three patents each working day.

Nortel's $2.5 billion (U.S.) in R&D spending in 1999 equalled 14.1 per cent of its total sales, a greater commitment than that of chief rivals Lucent Technologies Inc. (11.6 per cent) or Cisco Systems Inc. (13.6 per cent). Nortel's largest R&D centre was in Ottawa, but it operated a total of 42 centres in 17 countries, and had research ties to more than 120 universities worldwide.

Selected Nortel R&D Sites

- *Netas (Istanbul)*: Turkey's biggest private-sector R&D centre; designs equipment for Turkey and markets in Central Asia.
- *Woollongong (Sydney)*: Has the global mandate for Nortel's work on Advanced Intelligent Networks (AIN).
- *BUPT (Beijing)*: R&D joint venture with Beijing University of Posts and Telecommunications; designs wireless and network products for the Chinese market.
- *Harlow (England)*: Nortel's largest European R&D site; conducts research into networks, chip design, fibre optics and other telecommunications products.
- *Moscow*: Headquarters for Nortel's Russian R&D program, which spans 17 sites in five Russian cities where development work is conducted on cellular, PCS, network, laser and other products.
- *Bombay*: Has mandate for new-product development in India and key Asia-Pacific markets such as Japan.
- *Bois d'Arcy (France)*: Develops telecommunications equipment for the French market in partnership with Matra Communication S.A.

- *Friedrichshafen (Germany)*: Joint venture with DaimlerChrysler SA to develop products for Germany and Eastern European markets.
- *Mission Park (Santa Clara, California)*: Global mandate for Meridian 1, the world's best-selling private branch exchange.
- *Richardson (Dallas)*: Nortel's leading lab for wireless technologies.

Source: Nortel Networks Corp.

NOTES

1: Garfield and Galen Weston

Page 12: "The big question then, was should this chain be closed up. . ." quoted in *Business Week*, Sept. 8, 1975.

Page 12: "We've got a pedigree. . ."; quoted in *Business Week*, Sept. 8, 1975.

Page 13: "I deal in bread and dreams"; cited in *The Globe and Mail*, Feb. 13, 1988.

Page 15: "I'm not going to build a costly monument. . ."; cited in *Business Week*, Sept. 8, 1975.

Page 15: "A business that would never know completion. . ."; cited in *Business Week*, Sept. 8, 1975.

Page 15: "It was an awful cropper. . ."; cited in Charles Davies's *Bread Men: How the Westons Built an International Empire*, published in 1987 by Key Porter Books Ltd.

Page 15: "I am the greatest living exponent of enthusiasm. . ."; cited in *Bread Men*.

Page 16: "Forward, yes forward. . ."; cited in *Bread Men*.

Page 17: "In Fort Worth, we saw a sign. . ."; quoted in *Business Week*, Sept. 8, 1975.

Page 17: "One of the first conglomerate operators. . ."; quoted by Peter C. Newman in *The Canadian Establishment*, published by McClelland & Stewart Ltd. in 1975.

Page 17: "Believe me, every black pickaninny. . ." cited in *Bread Men*.

Page 17: "It's the beginning of the end. . ."; cited in *Bread Men*.

Page 17: "Buying companies, then getting someone to run them. . ."; quoted in *Business Week*, Sept. 8, 1975.

Page 18: "The secret of life is to think big. . ."; cited in *Bread Men*.

Page 19: "Since 1928, George Weston Ltd. has probably acquired. . .'" background study by Donald Tigert in 1976 for the Royal Commission on Corporate Concentration.

Page 19: "We say they don't need to go that high. . ."; cited in *Bread Men*.

Page 19: "Profits and sales in our bakery division. . ."; cited in *Bread Men*.

Page 20: "Metcalf believed that as long as sales increased. . ."; quoted in *Business Week*, Sept. 5, 1975.

Page 20: "We just grew like Topsy. . ."; quoted in *Business Week*, Sept. 8, 1975.

Page 22: "It was an organization largely staffed. . ."; quoted in *Canadian Business*, March 1981.

Page 23: "Dozens of young Canadian executives. . ."; *Ibid.*

Page 23: "You didn't have Cadillac Fairviews in Ireland. . ."; quoted in *Canadian Business, Ibid.*

Page 23: "After three years in the department store business. . ."; *Ibid.*

Page 23: "The quick and dirty profit opportunities. . ."; quoted in *Business Week*, Sept. 8, 1975.

Page 23: "I'm part of a family culture. . ."; quoted in *The Globe and Mail*, Feb. 13, 1988.

Page 23: "We had the nucleus of a fine company"; quoted in *Canadian Business*, March 1981.

Page 24: "Just so many obvious. . ."; quoted in *Canadian Business*, March 1981.

Page 24: "Turkeys are very dumb birds. . ."; cited in Anne Kingston's *The Edible Man: Dave Nichol, President's Choice and the Making of Popular Taste,* Macfarlane Walter & Ross, 1994.

Page 26: "The company was in bad shape. . ."; quoted in *Canadian Business*, March 1981.
Page 26: "Did not attract intellectuals. . ."; quoted in *The Globe and Mail*, Feb. 13, 1988.
Page 27: "I don't know what he's afraid of. . ."; quoted in *Canadian Business*, December 1988.
Page 31: "We knew it had to be done. . ."; quoted in *Canadian Business*, March 1981.
Page 32: "Refusal to contemplate anything new"; Conrad Black writing in his 1993 memoir, *Conrad Black: A Life in Progress*, published by Key Porter Books Ltd.
Page 32: Weston was "rubbing his hands excitedly. . ."; from *A Life in Progress*.
Page 32: "The profligate corruption. . ."; from *A Life in Progress*.
Page 36: "Anyone who buys anything from Conrad. . ."; cited in *A Life in Progress*.
Page 37: "Generic packaging is supposed to look terrible. . ."; quoted in *Harper's*, March 1986.
Page 37 "It had never occured to me. . ."; from *A Life in Progress*.
Page 38: "We've got to get into new, unique merchandise. . ."; quoted in *The Globe and Mail*, Feb. 13, 1988.
Page 38: "I am a walking Loblaw logo"; cited in *The Edible Man*, Macfarlane Walter & Ross, 1994.
Page 39: "Was really in the pail"; from Gerry Pencer's memoir, *The Ride of My Life*, Key Porter Books Ltd., 1999.
Page 40: "The irony. . .recognized brands in the country"; Toronto Board of Trade speech, Jan. 24, 2000.
Page 40: "We don't care where people are from. . ."; quoted in *The Edible Man*.
Page 40: "Big-league, cross-border terrorists"; cited in *The Edible Man*.
Page 41: "Innovation hadn't been there. . ."; quoted in *Canadian Business*, August 1994.
Page 43: "The implication of Dave's leaving. . ."; cited in *The Edible Man*.
Page 43: "Dave Nichol has launched more failed products. . ."; cited in *The Edible Man*.
Page 44: "Why would I do that. . ."; from *The Ride of My Life*.
Page 45: "What he was doing was questionning my integrity"; quoted in *The Globe and Mail*, Nov. 25, 1999.
Page 45: "I think that Galen has been afflicted. . ."; quoted in *Vanity Fair*, May 1994.
Page 46: "Everyone knew I'd be in England"; cited in *Bread Men*.
Page 47: "He has recruited some very good executives. . ."" quoted in *Financial Times*, May 14, 1994.
Page 47: "A piece of stupidity. . .I taught myself. . ."; quoted in *Financial Times*, May 14, 1994.
Page 47: "So that we would hear what my father. . ."; quoted in *Vanity Fair*, May 1994.
Page 48: "He was determined. . .he went over the horizon. . ."; quoted in *Vanity Fair*, May 1994.
Page 49: "If successful, Windsor will. . ."; Peter Katz essay in *The New Urbanism: Toward an Architecture of Community*, McGraw-Hill Inc., 1994.
Page 49: "Elite colony. . ."; cited in *Vanity Fair*, May 1994.
Page 50: "Galen keeps tight control. . ."; quoted in *Business Week*, Sept. 8, 1975.
Page 51: "We do our research. . ."; quoted in *The Financial Post Magazine*, Summer 1999.
Page 51: Shoppers "always had the impulse. . ." quoted in *Financial Post*, Apr. 19, 2000.
Page 51: "Maybe the next Pavarotti. . ."; Toronto Board of Trade speech, Jan. 24, 2000.
Page 51: "Imagine what the world will be like. . ."; Institution of Engineers of Ireland lecture, April 14, 1999.
Page 53: "Loblaw is growing faster. . ."; in a Merrill Lynch research report on Loblaw Cos. Inc., May 4, 2000.
Page 53: "A quality-and-value image. . ."; quoted in *Canadian Business*, July 1984.
Page 54: "I asked Galen at the outset. . ."; *Ibid*.
Page 54: "Tis not the gales. . ."; adapted by Garfield Weston from "Winds of Fate," by the late 19th-century American poet Ella Wheeler Wilcox.
Page 54: "I was brought up with an ethic. . ." quoted in *The Globe and Mail*, Feb. 13, 1988.

2: Max Ward

Except as indicated below, quotes by Max Ward are from his memoir, *The Max Ward Story: A Bush Pilot in the Bureaucratic Jungle*, published by McClelland & Stewart Ltd in 1991.

Page 57: "Max Ward is still—will always be—a hero. . ."; interview with the author, September 1999.

Page 61: "With 300,000 of the population. . ."; cited in Shirley Render's *Double Cross: The Inside Story of James A. Richardson and Canadian Airways*, Douglas & McIntyre, 1999.

Page 62: "There will be no stunting. . ."; *Ibid.*

Page 66: "The Americans would play an essential part. . ."; Peter Piggott in his *Flying Colours: A History of Commercial Aviation in Canada*, Douglas & McIntyre, 1997.

Page 66: "Development of two transcontinental routes. . ."; cited in *Double Cross*.

Page 67: "I only saw them from a distance. . ."; interview with the author, December 1999.

Page 73: "High public praise, Ward discovered. . ."; Piggott in his *Wingwalkers: A History of Canadian Airlines International*, published in 1998 by Harbour Publishing.

Page 75: "It was fun. . ."; interview with the author, December 1999.

Page 76: "I like to think that if I'd been at Kitty Hawk. . ."; Warren Buffett essay in *Fortune*, Nov. 29, 1999.

Page 77: "They all wanted someone to start up another airline. . ."; quoted in *The Globe and Mail*, Sept. 7, 1999.

Page 78: "Max Ward changed the standard. . .": speech to the British Travel Interests Seminar, 1980.

Page 78: "Today aviation is driven more by finance. . ."; in *Flying Colours*.

3: Isadore Sharp

Page 79: "I'm in bed with my customers. . ."; interview with the author, May 2000.

Page 79: "Well, it's not the Four Seasons"; cited by Sharp in Baron Investment Conference speech, Oct. 15, 1999.

Page 81: "They're so good here at the Four Seasons"; quoted in *National Post*, June 5, 1999.

Page 81: "Issy taught me how to be classy. . ."; *Connoisseur*, February 1990.

Page 82: "Four Seasons uses the softest toilet paper. . ."; cited in *Lifestyles 5745*, Summer 1985.

Page 82: "When I say quality car. . ."; quoted in *enRoute*, November 1978.

Page 82: "Every Four Seasons determines. . ."; interview with the author, April 1986.

Page 83: "Cheap doesn't sell anymore"; Canadian Club of Toronto speech, Mar. 12, 1984.

Page 83: "We can achieve blue-chip status. . ."; Baron Investment Conference speech, Oct. 15, 1999.

Page 84: "I have made mistakes. . ."; Canadian Club of Toronto speech, Mar. 12, 1984.

Page 88: "Our entire business has changed. . ."; Arthur Hailey, *Hotel*, Doubleday & Co. Inc., Garden City, N.Y., 1965.

Page 89: "My father would build a house. . ."; quoted in *Lifestyles 5745*, Summer 1985.

Page 90: "When everybody looked at it. . ."; quoted in *Achievers Magazine*, Winter 1989.

Page 90: "From the beginning, Issy was the instrument of genius. . ."; interview with the author, April 1986.

Page 91: "All the rooms face in. . ."; quoted in *Executive*, October 1972.

Page 91: "I was just trying to put one deal together. . ."; interview with the author, May 2000.

Page 91: "Years later, Rosalie told me. . ."; Canadian Club of Toronto speech, Mar. 12, 1984.

Page 92: "Some people would come out. . ."; quoted in *Achievers Magazine*, Winter 1989.

Page 93: "They were trapped. . ."; interview with the author, May 2000.

Page 93: "It will be a more personal. . .air conditioning. . ."; interview with the author, May 2000.

Page 93: "And the British. . .my chief asset. . .I knew their family history. . ."; interview with the author, May 2000.

Page 93: "The place prints money. . ."; interview with the author, April 1986.

Page 94: "London's Inn on the Park demanded clairvoyance"; *The Cornell Hotel and Restaurant Administration Quarterly*, May 1979.

Page 94: "Not only gave me insight. . ."; Baron Investment Conference speech, Oct. 15, 1999.

Page 94: "I'm not even sure I liked the hotel business. . .if a hotel was a good real-estate deal. . ."; interview with the author, May 2000.

Page 95: "Four Seasons was like an iceberg. . ."; interview with the author, April 1986.

Page 95: "Suddenly Four Seasons seemed amorphous. . ."; interview with the author, April 1986.

Page 95: "Here was Issy with a public-relations problem. . ."; interview with the author, April 1986.

Page 96: "I kept saying no. . .They worked around the clock. . ."; interview with the author, May 2000.

Page 97: "A company like Marriott. . ."; interview with the author, April 1986.

Page 97: "With our hotel, which is in one of the most historic. . ."; quoted in *Business Life*, November 1982.

Page 98: "I told Issy, 'You've got to be kidding. . ."; quoted in *Business Life*, November 1982.

Page 98: "We're selling a feeling of casual elegance. . ."; quoted in *Canadian Hotel & Restaurant*, October 1983.

Page 99: "I once read a single sentence. . ."; University of Guelph speech, May 20, 1988.

Page 99: "So that a company is eager to pay the extra $50. . ."; interview with the author, April 1986.

Page 102: "Part of what these people pay for. . ."; quoted in *Toronto Life*, May 1986.

Page 102: "It's not a small detail. . ."; quoted in *Foodservice & Hospitality*, December 1989.

Page 102: "Managing a service business. . ."; quoted in *Fortune*, May 31, 1993.

Page 102: "Last night I couldn't even open the curtains. . .we spend so much money making corridors lovely. . ."; *Connoisseur*, February 1990.

Page 103: "At a time in the beginning. . ."; interview with the author, May 2000.

Page 103: "All the great impresarios. . ."; interview with the author, May 2000.

Page 104: "I think being born Jewish. . ."; quoted in *Lifestyles*, Spring 1990.

Page 105: "If you're in a hurry. . ."; quoted in *Canadian Business*, Feburary 1982.

Page 105: "Regent was New York. . ."; interview with the author, May 2000.

Page 105: "Clever financial alchemy"; *The New York Times*, January 1994.

Page 106: "Having taken this thing on a nightmare journey. . ."; cited in *Report on Business Magazine*, May 1995.

Page 106: "We'd love to. . ."; cited in *Report on Business Magazine*, May 1995.

Page 106: "Many of our competitors. . .like dentistry and accounting. . ."; interview with the author, May 2000.

Page 107: "What I wanted was Sharp himself. . ."; quoted in *Business Week*, Oct. 13, 1997.

Page 107: "I was wrong. . ."; cited in *Report on Business Magazine*, May 1995.

Page 107: "Has tended to believe that the elegance. . ."; writing in *The New York Times*, June 27, 1993.

Pages 107-108: "You hear the term 'head-office requirement'. . ."; quoted in *Connoisseur*, February 1990.

Page 108: "I have managers who say. . ."; interview with the author, May 2000.

Page 108: "Managers who weren't helping to build team spirit. . ."; *Journal for Corporate Growth* essay, Vol. 5, No. 3, 1989/90.

Page 108: "I felt I'd grown up with this fellow. . ."; interview with the author, May 2000.

Page 108: "A big part of our culture is storytelling. . ."; interview with the author, May 2000.

Page 108: "Egregious capital structure"; cited in *Masters of Change: Profiles of Canadian Businesses Thriving in Turbulent Times*, edited by Daniel Stoffman, McGraw-Hill Ryerson Ltd., 1997.
Page 108: "There's never been any threat. . ."; interview with the author, May 2000.
Page 109: "It gets people in Toronto more accustomed. . ."; interview with the author, May 2000.
Page 109: "I used to worry that my shadow was too big. . ."; interview with the author, May 2000.
Page 110: "Sharp's personal stamp. . ."; quoted in *Canadian Business*, December 1998.
Page 110: "Has an electrifying effect. . ."; interview with the author, April 1986.
Page 111: "The danger is not that we will suddenly. . ."; British Travel Interests Seminar speech, 1980.
Page 111: "He's already the host to the elite. . ."; interview with the author, April 1986.
Page 111: "We've only just broken the surface. . ."; interview with the author, April 1986.

4: Paul Reichmann

Page 113: "It is gratifying to build a monument"; quoted in *Maclean's*, Feb. 23, 1981.
Page 116: "The health of O&Y. . ."; quoted in *The Economist*, June 1984.
Page 116: "A first-class urban complex. . ."; in Ada Louise Huxtable, "Battery Park City," *Architecture, Anyone?*, University of California Press, 1986.
Page 116: "From the marbled caverns. . ."; in Anthony Bianco, *The Reichmanns: Family, Faith, Fortune, and the Empire of Olympia & York*, Random House Canada, 1997.
Page 116: "We have to thank them. . ."; cited in *The Reichmanns*.
Page 117: "At Olympia & York, I was the guilty party. . ."; quoted in *The Toronto Star*, Mar. 7, 1999.
Page 120: "My observation has always been. . ."; in William Zeckendorf, *Zeckendorf*, Plaza Press, 1987.
Page 120: "Montreal had little wealth. . ."; cited in Michael Bliss, *Northern Enterprise: Five Centuries of Canadian Business*, McClelland & Stewart Ltd., 1987.
Page 123: "Toronto is really a new city. . ."; quoted in *The Economist*, June 1984.
Page 123: "We felt it looked horrible. . ."; cited in *The Reichmanns*.
Page 131: "There's just more money coming. . ."; interview with the author, September 1983.
Page 131: "The first was when the Dutch. . ."; quoted in *New York*, Feb. 24, 1986.
Page 131: "Nothing could have started worse. . ." *Architecture Anyone?*
Page 133: "When they leave the office. . ."; interview with the author, October 1986.
Page 134: "North American drive. . .in New York you couldn't rent. . ."; quoted in *The Economist*, June 1984.
Page 135: "The monstrous Canary Wharf. . ."; in HRH The Prince of Wales, *A Vision of Britain: A Personal View of Architecture*, Doubleday, 1989.
Page 136: "It's every bit as bad. . ."; cited in *The Reichmanns*.
Page 137: "This is not a risky project. . ."; cited in *The Reichmanns*.
Page 137: "What sets O&Y apart. . ."; quoted in *The Wall Street Journal*, Sept. 5, 1989.
Page 137: "They are very strange, reticent people. . ."; quoted in *New York*, Feb. 24, 1986.
Page 137: "The most intense part of my life. . ."; interview with the author, October 1986.
Page 138: "I never want to be subservient. . ."; interview with the author, October 1986.
Page 138: "While it is a pity. . ."; interview with the author, October 1986.
Page 139: "Do something which others. . ."; cited in *The Reichmanns*.
Page 139: "A shrewd player but a true gambler. . ."; *Ibid.*
Page 139: "My religion won't let me go to Las Vegas. . ."; *Ibid.*
Page 140: "I would not be surprised. . ."; in the television documentary *Faith and Fortune: The Reichmann Story*, Alan Handel Productions Inc., 2000.

Page 140: "Against our religion. . ."; *Ibid.*
Page 142: "I am proud our family. . ."; interview with the author, October 1986.
Page 143: "Rarely has extreme commercial ambition. . ."; in *The Reichmanns.*
Page 144: "We don't have to buy. . ."; quoted in *Financial Post*, July 28, 1999.
Page 144: "One of the lessons I have learned. . ." quoted in *Financial Post*, Mar. 8, 1999.
Page 144: "Know Canary Wharf can deliver. . ."; quoted in *The Globe and Mail*, April 22, 2000.
Page 145: "The worry that there had been. . ." quoted in *The New York Times*, Jan. 9, 2000.
Page 145: "Reichmann has certainly been vindicated. . ."; quoted in *Financial Times*, The Globe and Mail, Mar. 2, 1999.
Page 145: "The ultimate value of Canary Wharf will be double. . ."; quoted *Financial Post*, Mar. 8, 1999.
Page 146: "Cities take time. . ."; quoted in *Financial Times*, Feb. 9, 1999.
Page 146: "At the awesome O&Y. . ." in Donald Trump, *Trump: The Art of the Comeback*, Times Books, 1997.
Page 146: "Obvious to a six-year-old child to see. . ."; quoted in *The Economist*, June 1984.
Page 146: "Today if I visit one of my former buildings. . ."; quoted in *Financial Post*, Mar. 8, 1999.
Page 146: "Maimonides preferred that his students. . .I'm probably one of the crazies"; interview with the author, October 1986.

5: Andrew Sarlos

Page 150: "Whether it's building a hydroelectric project. . ."; quoted in *Executive*, November 1982.
Page 153: "You buy his cup of coffee. . ."; quoted in *The Financial Post*, Sept. 19, 1981.
Page 153: "There wasn't one segment. . ."; quoted in *Executive*, November 1982.
Page 153: "They didn't shrink from. . ."; quoted in *The Toronto Star*, Feb. 13, 1984.
Pages 153-154: "He's the only man I know. . ."; quoted in *The Globe and Mail*, June 29, 1996.
Page 154: "One of the things I learned. . ."; quoted in *The Toronto Star*, Feb. 13, 1984.
Page 154: "Hold on another day. . ."; quoted in *The Globe and Mail*, July 6, 1988.
Page 154: "The only question is. . ."; quoted in *The Financial Post*, Sept. 19, 1981.
Page 154: "You go into the casino. . ."; quoted in *The Financial Post*, Sept. 19, 1981.
Page 155: "Failure has a good attribute. . ."; quoted in *Executive*, November 1982.
Page 156: "If he has any problem. . ."; quoted in *The Globe and Mail*, June 29, 1996.
Page 158: "When you've been in prison. . ."; quoted in *The Financial Post Magazine*, September 1983.
Page 158: "It's easier to make money. . .as you would the plague"; from Sarlos's 1993 memoir, *Fireworks: The Investment of a Lifetime*, published by Key Porter Books Ltd.
Page 160: "Twice before, Andy had faced death. . ."; eulogy in *The Globe and Mail*, May 19, 1997.

6: Frank Stronach

Page 162: "From time to time self-destroying. . ."; cited in *Maclean's*, Sept. 30, 1996.
Page 164: "A nation of warehouse operators. . . changing linens and making hamburgers. . ."; cited in *Report on Business Magazine*, April 1990.
Page 164: "The Western world will lose a lot of industrial jobs"; quoted in *Maclean's*, Mar. 29, 1999.
Page 164: "Twenty years after he and Magna. . ."; *Maclean's*, Mar. 29, 1999.
Page 168: "I was restless. . ."; cited in *Canadian Business*, May 1988.
Page 169: "For her bone structure. . ."; quoted in *Maclean's*, Mar. 29, 1999.
Page 173: "When Magna nearly bought the farm. . ."; interview with the author, February 1998.

Page 176: "Magna is a virtual car company. . ."; quoted in *Maclean's*, Sept. 30, 1996.

Page 176: "Whatever Frank wants. . ."; quoted in *Canadian Business*, May 1988.

Page 176: "The thing about Magna. . ."; cited, *Ibid.*

Page 177: "We want to be part of your child's formative years. . ."; cited, *Ibid.*

Page 178: "There are only three economic models. . .we still believe in entrepreneurship. . ."; cited, *Ibid.*

Page 181: "If he wants to go ahead with this crazy stunt. . ."; interview with the author, February 1998.

Page 181: "And they would shit their pants"; cited in *Financial Post*, May 26, 1999.

Page 181: "Being sole supplier. . ."; quoted in *Canadian Business*, Nov. 26, 1999.

Page 181: "Magna is the best auto-parts company. . ."; interview with the author, February 1998.

Page 182: "This is what Frank is like. . ."; quoted in *Maclean's*, Mar. 29, 1999.

Page 182: "Perhaps the most important. . ."; cited in *Canadian Business*, May 1988.

Page 182: "I constantly have 100 projects. . ."; cited in *The Globe and Mail*, Feb. 10, 1998.

Page 182: "The mountains will stay"; quoted in *Maclean's*, Mar. 29, 1999.

7: Laurent Beaudoin

Page 183: "With any new product, I'm excited. . ."; quoted in *Forbes*, Apr. 19, 1999.

Page 184: "Our planes are already there. . ."; quoted in *The Globe and Mail*, May 29, 1999.

Page 185: "The promise of European-style high-speed service. . ."; cited in *The Toronto Star*, Aug. 9, 1999.

Page 186: "Everyone would prefer. . ."; quoted in *Report on Business Magazine*, April 1999.

Page 187: "My main goal at Bombardier. . ."; quoted in Matthew Fraser, *Quebec Inc.*, Key Porter Books Ltd., 1987.

Page 188: "Car mon pays, c'est hiver"; cited in *Quebec Inc.*

Page 190: "I don't think well when I am wet"; cited in Stephen Franklin, *The Heroes: A Saga of Canadian Inspiration*, McClelland & Stewart Ltd., 1967.

Page 190: "Had a typical president's office. . ."; quoted in *The Heroes*.

Page 194: "Bombardier was not part of my career plans. . ."; quoted in *Quebec Inc.*

Page 195: "I'm not a religious man. . ."; quoted in Alexander Ross, *The Risk Takers*, Maclean-Hunter Ltd., 1975.

Page 196: "The old man dropped everything. . ."; *Ibid.*

Page 196: "Mr. Bombardier was a very strong character. . ."; *Ibid.*

Page 196: "Laurent used to come to me. . ."; *Ibid.*

Page 198: "Some economists have referred to snowmobiles. . ."; *Ibid.*

Page 198: "They used to call me a hero. . ."; *Ibid.*

Page 199: "You had this $8-million company. . ."; *Ibid.*

Page 200: "Management, labour relations, equipment. . ."; quoted in *Quebec Inc.*

Page 203: "It keeps me in shape"; quoted in *Quebec Inc.*

Page 207: "Corporate executives don't want to sit in a prenatal position. . ."; cited in David Donald, general editor, *The Encyclopedia of Civil Aircraft*, Prospero Books, Etobicoke, Ont., 1999.

Page 210: "Bombardier would not buy Shorts. . ."; cited in *The Globe and Mail*, Oct. 4, 1999.

Pages 210-211: "Who scarcely a moment ago. . .Without the support of the federal government's export financing. . ."; Montreal Board of Trade speech, Oct. 3, 1995.

Page 212: "Finding enough for the barbecue tonight?"; quoted in *The New York Times*, July 29, 1999.

Page 213: "The PQ had such a negative image. . ."; quoted in *Quebec Inc.*

Page 215: "As Bombardier has achieved critical mass. . ."; quoted in *Report on Business Magazine*, April 1995.

Page 215: "If the stampede starts. . ."; quoted in *Financial Post*, May 24, 1999.

Page 216: "I hope it could happen one day. . ."; quoted in *Forbes*, Apr. 19, 1999.

8: Robert Scrivener and John Roth

Page 217: "There isn't anything any other manufacturer. . ." quoted in *The Toronto Star*, July 23, 1976.

Page 217: "You know why great companies fail?"; interview with the author, April 2000.

Page 218: "The promise of the Internet. . ."; Canadian Advanced Technology Assn. speech, December 1999.

Page 219: "We didn't handle that meeting right"; interview with the author, October 1998.

Page 219: "At 10:06 a.m. of that meeting. . .what Nortel is known for." Interview with the author, April 2000.

Page 219: "They were telling me. . ."; interview with the author, April 2000.

Page 220: "I'd give Nortel an 'F'. . ."; quoted in *Business Week*, Nov. 8, 1999.

Page 220: "Bay is a handyman's special. . ."; interview with the author, October 1998.

Page 220: "I almost think all tech. . ."; interview with the author, August 1998.

Page 221: "Telco suppliers like Nortel. . ."; interview with the author, August 1998.

Page 223: "It's very therapeutic. . ."; quoted in *National Post Business*, November 1999.

Page 225: "I sat there afterward, thinking, 'This is powerful'. . ."; cited in *The Right-Angle Turn Into the Heart of the Internet*, Nortel internal document, 2000.

Page 229: "I have a lot of respect for John Roth. . ."; quoted in *Maclean's*, Aug. 2, 1999.

Page 231: "We intend to lead the networking revolution. . ."; quoted in *Business Week*, Feb. 8, 1999.

Page 232: "He said he was at least glad. . ."; interview with the author, October 1998.

Page 232: "Nothing says we'll survive. . ."; interview with the author, October 1998.

Page 233: "You're talking to a guy who wouldn't know a software. . ."; internal Nortel interview, 1983, Nortel Networks Corp. archives.

Page 233: "There are lots of things you don't think of doing now. . ."; Windsor Ad and Sales Club speech, March 1968.

Page 234: "I can talk with and see. . .all merchandising in stores. . ."; quoted in the Montreal *Gazette*, Apr. 21, 1971.

Page 239: "It burned my behind. . ."; internal Nortel interview, 1983.

Page 239: "We used to make excuses. . ."; quoted in *The Montreal Star*, Apr. 17, 1976.

Page 240: "I had begun to study their financial statements. . .it was clear that we would have to fix Northern. . ."; internal Nortel interview, 1983.

Page 242: "We couldn't just have a 'me-too' product. . ."; internal Nortel interview, 1976.

Page 243: "Letting long-haired guys in white coats. . ." ; internal Nortel interview, 1983.

Page 243: "I want to say to them, 'What can you *sell*. . ."; internal Nortel interview, 1976.

Page 244: "The management problems in the monolithic firm. . ."; internal Nortel interview, 1983.

Page 244: "It wasn't the first electronic switch. . ."; quoted in David Thomas, *Knights of the New Technology: The Inside Story of Canada's Corporate Elite*, Key Porter Books Ltd., 1983.

Page 248: "I was told they were impossible. . ."; internal Nortel interview, 1976.

Page 250: "You did mean it when you said. . ."; cited in *Ma Bell: A Jean de Grandpre and the Meteoric Rise of Bell Canada Enterprises*, Random House, 1992.

Page 250: "Marketing is the whole thing. . ."; internal Nortel interview, 1976.

Page 250: "No reason. . . I'll sing the 'Star Spangled Banner'. . ."; quoted in the Montreal *Gazette*, Mar. 25, 1976.

Pages 250-251: "A change in philosophy. . ."; International Conference on Computers and Communications speech, Aug. 5, 1976.

Page 251: "In executive suites. . ."; quoted in the Montreal *Gazette*, Mar. 14, 1981.

Page 251: "Competition will be bloody. . ."; internal Nortel interview, 1976.

Page 252: "What Scrivener did was revolutionary. . ."; quoted in *The Financial Times of Canada*, Feb. 25, 1980.

Page 252: "Though a lot of people gave lip service. . ."; quote in *The Financial Times of Canada*, Mar. 16, 1981.

Page 252: "As significant to Canada as oil is to Saudi Arabia. . ." quoted in *Knights of the New Technology*.

Page 252: "Do you think I ever get to meet. . ."; cited in Peter C. Newman, *Nortel: Past, Present and Future*, Northern Telecom Ltd., 1995.

Page 252: "Televerket's choice of Northern Telecom. . ."; Bell-Northern Research seminar, June 1, 1977.

Page 254: "People are naturally self-centred. . ."; internal Nortel interview, 1983.

Page 255: "Our strategy is that when we see a promising technology. . ."; interview with the author, April 2000.

Page 256: "That way your concessions. . ."; quoted in *Report on Business Magazine*, August 1995.

Page 256: "I gave away tons of Eskimo carvings. . ."; quoted in *Report on Business Magazine*, August 1989.

Page 256: "Far too often they want accessibility to arms. . ."; *Ibid.*

Page 257: "Our customers became a kind of extended family. . ."; quoted in *Nortel: Past, Present and Future*.

Page 257: "Canadians are well-educated, skillful and honest. . ."; quoted in the Montreal *Gazette*, Apr. 21, 1971.

Page 257: "I'm sad to say there are still pockets of mediocrity. . ."; quoted in *Report on Business Magazine*, August 1989.

Page 257: "Stern opened a second headquarters. . .the French Canadian's résumé. . ."; *Business Week*, Feb. 15, 1993.

Page 258: "They complained to everyone. . ."; interview with the author, April 2000.

Page 260: "Nortel is like an arms merchant. . ."; quoted in *Report on Business Magazine*, July 1997.

Page 261: "It was 26 million lines of computer code. . .Systems that large. . ."; interview with the author, April 2000.

Page 261: "Your customers have a huge investment. . .your customers aren't going to teach you. . ."; interview with the author, April 2000.

Page 261: "And I came back thinking. . ."; interview with the author, April 2000.

Page 262: "E-commerce represents a Category 5 hurricane. . ." CATCH SOURCE

Page 262: ". . . if you're going to be cannibalized. . ." CATCH SOURCE

Page 263: "It was just too audacious. . ."; interview with the author, April 2000.

Page 263: "And I started personally cancelling them. . .if we can't deliver a product. . ."; cited in *Right-Angle Turn Into the Heart of the Internet*.

Page 264: "Older products tend to be more profitable. . ." CATCH SOURCE

Page 264: "I found an organization. . ."; internal Nortel interview, 1983.

Page 264: "It was painful for a lot of individuals. . ."; internal Nortel interview, 1983.

Page 265: "We all felt that the organization was as low as it could sink. . .;" quoted in *The New York Times*, Oct. 6, 1997.

Page 265: "The company I was going to take over. . ." quoted in *Report on Business Magazine*, April 2000.

Page 266: "Marketers, not engineers. . ."; quoted in *A World of Networks*, internal Nortel journal, 1995.

Page 267: "Spending $6.9 billion on Bay. . ."; cited in *Right-Angle Turn Into the Heart of the Internet*.

Page 268: "But look at it this way. . ."; interview with the author, April 2000.

Page 269: "We don't have all the experience. . ."; quoted in *The Globe and Mail*, Mar. 20, 2000.

Page 269: "One company we acquired. . ."; interview with the author, April 2000.

Page 270: "I like to see skin in the game. . ."; cited in *Right-Angle Turn Into the Heart of the Internet*.

Page 270: "I didn't want to take a contented army to war. . ."; quoted in *Nortel: Past, Present and Future*.

Page 270: "We know who we want to keep. . . You've got to structure the deal. . ."; interview with the author, April 2000.

Page 271: "What are you doing for the customer?. . ."; cited in *Right-Angle Turn Into the Heart of the Internet*.

Page 271: "Twenty-five billion dollars later. . ."; quoted in *Business Week*, Feb. 8, 1999.

Page 272: "The truth is that IP is not ready for prime time. . ."; quoted in *Forbes*, Feb. 7, 2000.

Page 272: "Network operators have invested. . ."; cited in *Right-Angle Turn Into the Heart of the Internet*.

Page 272: "I bet I can learn to spell 'IP'. . ."; cited in *The Globe and Mail*, Nov. 10, 1999.

Page 273: "Has a much stronger image. . ."; cited in *Maclean's*, Aug. 2, 1999.

Page 273: "Cisco makes a lot of noise. . ."; quoted in *Financial Post*, Mar. 10, 2000.

Page 273: "The days are gone when Silicon Valley. . ."; *Upside*, April 2000.

Page 273-274: "I meet Canadian high-tech entrepreneurs. . .I have a Canadian management team. . ."; *Ibid.*

Page 274: "It was important. At that time. . ."; essay in *Chimo*, February/March 1983.

Page 274: "What frustrates me. . ."; quoted in *Ivey Business Journal*, November/December 1999.

Page 276: "McGinn made it personal. . ."; quoted in *Business Week*, Feb. 8, 1999.

Page 276: "We have to stop making ourselves larger than life. . .Eighteen months ago a lot of people thought I was nuts. . ."; interview with the author, April 2000.

Page 276: "Shows you how the stock market creates heroes. . ."; interview with the author, April 2000.

SELECTED BIBLIOGRAPHY

This book is based on the author's reporting over the past 15 years on the companies and individuals profiled in these pages. My first interviews with Andrew Sarlos, Isadore Sharp and Paul Reichmann date from the mid-1980s. In the case of Max Ward, however, it was this project that provided the first opportunity to interview the aviation pioneer. And interviews with John Roth took place over a two-year span as he transformed Nortel Networks with an $18-billion buying spree of Internet-related companies between 1998 and 2000.

As to the style of writing in this book, I have tried to give equal consideration to tangible corporate strategies and the more elusive peculiarities of character. That effort has been influenced by two authors who raised business journalism to an art.

Peter C. Newman's *Canadian Establishment* series may be unrivalled for its depiction of the men and women who shaped Canada's business evolution in the 20th century. But the book with which Newman pioneered the narrative style of financial journalism, at age 29, is *Flame of Power: Intimate Portraits of Canada's Greatest Businessmen* (Longmans, Green & Co., Toronto, 1959). This seminal book remains an inspiring chronicle.

There is no volume to compare with historian Michael Bliss's *Northern Enterprise: Five Centuries of Canadian Business* for its epic sweep and deft blending of social, political and business history. It is a remarkably detailed presentation of entrepreneurial achievement, an engaging account that is rich in provocative insights.

Introduction

Collins, Jim. "Built to Flip," *Fast Company*, March 2000.

Ross, Alexander. "How Peter Munk Was Sunk By Euphoria of Success," *The Financial Post*, Nov. 1, 1969.

Roth, John. "Creating a New Era of Networking," The Institution of Engineers of Ireland, Dublin, 1999.

Chapter 1: Garfield and Galen Weston

Black, Conrad. *Conrad Black: A Life In Progress*, Toronto: Key Porter Books Ltd., 1993.

Brunt, Stephen. "Public Fortune, Private Life [profile of Galen Weston]," *The Globe and Mail*, Feb. 3, 1988.

Davies, Charles. *Bread Men: How the Westons Built an International Empire*, Toronto: Key Porter Books Ltd., 1987.

D'Souza, Patricia, and Sean Silcoff. "On Special This Week: Supermarkets," *Canadian Business*, Dec. 24, 1998/Jan. 8, 1999.

Engel, Naomi. "The Art of Being a Weston," *Country Estate*, Autumn 1991.

Fetherling, Douglas. "Northern Telecom at the Crossroads," *Canadian Business*, July 1978.

Filler, Martin. "Weston Civilization," *Vanity Fair*, May 1994.

Hampson, Sarah. "Return Dave's Calls — Please," *The Globe and Mail*, Nov. 25, 1999.

Hitt, Jack. "The Theory of Supermarkets," *The New York Times Magazine*, March 10, 1996.

Katz, Peter. *The New Urbanism: Toward an Architecture of Community*, New York: McGraw-Hill Inc., 1994.

Kingston, Anne. *The Edible Man: Dave Nichol, President's Choice and the Making of Popular Taste*, Toronto: Macfarlane Walter & Ross, 1994.

Nadeau, Jean Benoit, and Julie Barlow. "Shopping for Wow!" *Report on Business Magazine*, October 1995.

Newman, Peter C. *The Canadian Establishment*, Toronto: McClelland & Stewart Ltd., 1975.

Olijnyk, Zena. "Supermarket chic: Architect Leslie Rebanks has transformed what used to be big boxes that sold groceries into cultural phenomena"; *Financial Post*, Apr. 19, 2000.

Pencer, Gerry. *The Ride of My Life*, Toronto: Key Porter Books Ltd., 1999.

Ross, Alexander. "Galen Weston's Great Turnaround," *Canadian Business*, March 1981.

Stevenson, Mark. "The Hired Hand Waves Goodbye," *Canadian Business*, August 1994.

Urry, Maggie. "The brothers Weston cross swords," *Financial Times*, May 14, 1994.

Whiteson, Leon. "Corporate Architecture: Its Causes and Cure," *Canadian Business*, July 1984.

Chapter 2: Max Ward

Donald, David, general editor. *The Encyclopedia of Civil Aircraft*, Etobicoke, Ont.: Prospero Books, 1999.

Piggott, Peter. *Flying Colours: The History of Commercial Aviation in Canada*, Vancouver: Douglas & McIntyre, 1997.

Piggott, Peter. *Wingwalkers: The History of Canadian Airlines*, Vancouver: Harbour Publishing, 1998.

Render, Shirley. *Double Cross: The Inside Story of James A. Richardson and Canadian Airways*, Vancouver/Toronto: Douglas & McIntyre, 1999.

Ward, Max. *The Max Ward Story: A Bush Pilot in the Bureaucratic Jungle*, Toronto: McClelland & Stewart Ltd., 1991.

Chapter 3: Isadore Sharp

Byrne, Harlan S. "Four Seasons Hotels: The secret — service," *Barron's*, May 11, 1998.

Goldberger, Paul. "A grand hotel, but not what you'd call homey," *The New York Times*, June 27, 1993.

Harris, Marjorie. "Issy Sharp's finest season," *Canadian Business*, February 1982.

Hawkins, Chuck. "Four Seasons heads for the beach," *Business Week*, April 24, 1989.

King, Paul. "Building a team the Sharp way: At Four Seasons, excellence means treating guests as royalty and staff as somebody," *Canadian Business*, November 1990.

Kingston, Anne. "Too Good to Be True? How Four Seasons weathered the storm to become the largest operator of luxury hotels in the world," *Report on Business Magazine*, May 1995.

Kummer, Corby. "A man for Four Seasons," *Connoisseur*, February 1990.

Martin, Douglas A. "Four Seasons tries to pamper its way to profits," *The New York Times*, July 7, 1985.

Symonds, William C. "Is Four Seasons throwing caution to the wind?" *Business Week*, August 3, 1992.

Timson, Judith. "Golden eggs from the Golden Rule: Four Seasons' Issy Sharp's rich — and nice," *Toronto Life*, May 1986.

Weber, Joseph. "The whirlwind at Four Seasons," *Business Week*, Oct. 13, 1997.

Chapter 4: Paul Reichmann

Barsky, Neil. "Paul Reichmann scales real estate's heights, including Sears Tower," *The Wall Street Journal*, Sept. 5, 1989.

———— . "Olympia & York finds that it isn't immune to real-estate crunch," *The Wall Street Journal*, Oct. 25, 1991.

Bennett, Neil. "Paul Reichmann's fall and rise," *National Post*, March 8, 1999.

Bianco, Anthony. *The Reichmanns: Family, Faith, Fortune and The Empire of Olympia & York*, Toronto: Random House Canada, 1997.

Charles, HRH The Prince of Wales. *A Vision of Britain: A Personal View of Architecture*, London: Doubleday, 1989.

Francis, Diane. "How Canadian Developers are Remaking U.S. Cities," *Canadian Business*, August 1980.

Foster, Peter. *The Master Builders: How the Reichmanns Reached for an Empire*, Toronto: Key Porter Books Ltd., 1986.

Goldenberg, Susan. *Men of Property: The Canadian Developers Who Are Buying America*, Toronto: Personal Library, 1981.

Greenspon, Edward. "Canary Wharf depends as much on new attitudes as new buildings," *The Globe and Mail*, April 13, 1990.

Klein, Joe. "They'll take Manhattan: The brash new builders," *New York*, Feb. 24, 1986.

Lenzner, Robert. "Try, try again: How did defeated developer Paul Reichmann stage that remarkable comeback at Canary Wharf?" *Forbes*, June 14, 1999.

Lynn, Matthew. "Will Canary Wharf fly?" *The Toronto Star*, London, March 7, 1999.

Milner, Brian. "Paul Reichmann's ship comes in at Canary Wharf," *The Globe and Mail*, Mar. 2, 1999.

Newman, Peter C. *The Acquisitors: The Canadian Establishment, Volume Two*, Toronto: McClelland & Stewart Ltd., 1981.

Peagram, Norman. "The Reichmanns never gamble," *Euromoney*, June 1984.

Weber, Joseph. "Reichmanns redux," *Business Week*, Nov. 15, 1999.

Chapter 5: Andrew Sarlos

Best, Patricia. "The Shuttle Diplomacy in the Polysar-Nova Struggle," *Financial Times of Canada*, June 13, 1998.

Lutsky, Irv. "Unlikely trio the brains behind investment firm with big ideas," *The Toronto Star*, Nov. 19, 1979.

McFarland, Janet. "Sarlos Goes Home," *The Globe and Mail*, June 29, 1996.

Porter, Anna. "Lives Lived: Andrew Sarlos," *The Globe and Mail*, May 19, 1997.

Robinson, Allan. "HCI Moneymen Talk About Deals, Risks, Plans, and The Bear Market," *The Financial Post*, Sept. 19, 1981.

Rose, Barbara Wade. "Hungarian at The Gate," *The Financial Post Magazine*, September 1993.

Ross, Alexander. *The Traders: Inside Canada's Stock Markets*, Toronto: Collins, 1984.

Sarlos, Andrew. *Fireworks: The Investment of a Lifetime*, Toronto: Key Porter Books Ltd., 1993.

Smith, Vivien. "Dean of Arbitrage Has The Midas Touch for Wealthy Investors," *The Globe and Mail*, July 6, 1988.

Walker, Dean. "The Ecstasy and Agony of Going On Your Own," *Executive*, November 1982.

Chapter 6: Frank Stronach

Berman, David. "Which Part Doesn't Fit?" *Canadian Business*, Feb. 26, 1999.

Dolphin, Ric. "His Race, His Rules," *Canadian Business*, May 1988.

Freeman, Alan. "Stronach returns to his homeland a hero," *The Globe and Mail*, Feb. 2, 1998.

Hart, Matthew: "Frank as he'll ever be," *Financial Post Magazine*, May 1986.

Kalawsky, Keith. "No Hands: Magna Has Created the World's Most Advanced Automotive Parts Plant," *Canadian Business*, Nov. 26, 1999.

Kidd, Kenneth. "Magna's Next Hurrah," *Report on Business Magazine, The Globe and Mail*, June 1992.

Noble, Kimberley. "Frank Stronach: Empire Builder," *Maclean's*, March 29, 1999.

Sloan Jr., Alfred J. *My Years With General Motors*, New York: Doubleday, 1990.

Stackhouse, John. "Magn-etic: He's Personally His Own Politician," *The Globe and Mail*, Feb. 12, 2000.

Stoffman, Daniel. "Stalled," *Report on Business Magazine, The Globe and Mail*, April 1990.

Upbin, Bruce. "Magna inside?" *Forbes*, Sept. 21, 1998.

Wells, Jennifer. "Magna in Overdrive," *Maclean's*, Sept. 30, 1996.

Chapter 7: Laurent Beaudoin

Allard, Christian. "The Fast Track: Bombardier is now a world power in mass transit," *Canadian Business*, January 1990.

Carpenter, Thomas: *Inventors: Profiles in Canadian Genius*, Willowdale, Ont.: Firefly Books (Camden House), 1990.

Franklin, Stephen. *The Heroes: A Saga of Canadian Inspiration*, Toronto: McClelland & Stewart Ltd., 1967.

Fraser, Matthew. *Quebec Inc: French-Canadian Entrepreneurs and the New Business Elite*, Toronto: Key Porter Books Ltd., 1987.

Holloway, Nigel. "Bombardier's master builder," *Forbes*, April 19, 1999.

Innes, Eva, Jim Lyon and Jim Harris. *The Financial Post 100 Best Companies to Work For in Canada*, Toronto: Harper Collins Publishers Ltd., 1990.

Kidd, Kenneth. "Cleared for Takeoff: de Havilland's wings are being trimmed by new owner Bombardier," *Report on Business Magazine, The Globe and Mail,* November 1992.

Kidd, Kenneth. "The Bombardier Express: With the Launch of its Global Express Executive Jet, Bombardier is Positively Soaring," *Report on Business Magazine, The Globe and Mail,* April 1996.

Precious, Carole. *J. Armand Bombardier,* Markham, Ont.: Fitzhenry & Whiteside Ltd., 1984.

Ross, Alexander. *The Risk Takers: The Dreamers who Build a Business From An Idea,* Toronto: Maclean Hunter Ltd., 1975.

Walmsley, Ann. "Meet the New Boss: Bombadier's Robert Brown Has a Tough Act to Follow," *Report on Business Magazine, The Globe and Mail,* April 1999.

Chapter 8: Robert Scrivener and John Roth

Biersdorfer, J. D. "In the Beginning: The Origins of the Internet," *The New York Times Book Review,* Jan. 27, 2000.

Brown, Heidi. "Northern Light: Nortel's John Roth is an Unlikely Radical," *Forbes,* May 17, 1999.

Christensen, Clayton M. *The Innovator's Dilemma: When New Technologies Cause Great Firms to Fail,* Boston: Harvard Business School Press, 1997.

Elstom, Peter. "Lucent's Ascent," *Business Week,* Feb. 8, 1999.

Fetherling, Doug. "Northern Telecom at the Crossroads," *Canadian Business,* July 1978.

Greenfeld, Karl Taro. "Do You Know Cisco?", *Time,* Jan. 17, 2000.

Hafner, Katie. "Putting the W's in www," *The New York Times Book Review,* Oct. 24, 1999.

Keller, John J., with Edith Terry. "How Northern Telecom is Riding out the Storm," *Business Week,* Jan. 26, 1987.

Laver, Ross. "Nortel's Driving Force," *Maclean's,* Aug. 2, 1999.

Lieber, Ron. "Startups: The 'Inside' Stories — Follow the Lead of a Team from Nortel Networks," *Fast Company,* March 2000.

McNish, Jacquie. "Citizen Roth," *The Globe and Mail,* Nov. 27, 1999.

Nee, Eric. "The Upstarts are Rocking Telecom," *Fortune,* Jan. 24. 2000.

Newman, Peter C. *Northern Telecom: Past, Present, Future,* Brampton, Ont.: Northern Telecom Ltd., 1995.

Pearce, Ed. "Networking the World," *Ivey Business Journal,* November/December 1999.

Salter, Michael. "Shoot the Moon: Northern Telecom, the Pride of Canadian Industry, is Facing its Toughest Test," *Report on Business Magazine,* August 1989.

Spears, John. "Firmly Rooted Here: Nortel Goes Global, Won't Quit Country," *The Toronto Star*, Jan. 27, 2000.

Surtees, Lawrence. *Pa Bell: A. Jean de Grandpré and the Meteoric Rise of Bell Canada Enterprises*, Toronto: Random House, 1992.

———— . "Northern Telecom: The morning after," *The Globe and Mail*, May 5, 1993.

Symonds, William C. "High-Tech Star: Northern Telecom is Challenging Even AT&T," *Business Week*, July 27, 1992.

———— . "He Came, He Saw, He Cleaned Up . . . He Left: Northern Telecom's Paul Stern is Outta There," *Business Week*, Feb. 15, 1993.

Takach, George. "Is Northern Telecom Heading South?", *Saturday Night*, February 1985.

Walmsley, Ann. "The Deal That Almost Got Away," *Report on Business Magazine*, August 1995.

Weber, Joseph. "Racing Ahead at Nortel," *Business Week*, Nov. 8, 1999.

Weinberg, Neil, and Nikhil Hutheesing. "Wired and Restless: The Empire that Richard McGinn Built at Lucent Is Being Shaken to Its Foundations," *Forbes*, Feb. 7, 2000.

INDEX

DATE DUE